RUSSIAN TV SERIES IN THE ERA OF TRANSITION

RUSSIAN TV SERIES IN THE ERA OF TRANSITION

GENRES, TECHNOLOGIES, IDENTITIES

Edited by Alexander Prokhorov,
Elena Prokhorova, and Rimgaila Salys

BOSTON
2021

Library of Congress Cataloging-in-Publication Data

Names: Prokhorov, Alexander, 1965- editor. | Prokhorova, Elena, editor. | Salys, Rimgaila, editor.
Title: Russian TV series in the era of transition : genres, technologies, identities / edited by Alexander Prokhorov, Elena Prokhorova, and Rimgaila Salys.
Description: Boston : Academic Studies Press, 2021. | Series: Film and media studies | Includes bibliographic references.
Identifiers: LCCN 2021035865 (print) | LCCN 2021035866 (ebook) | ISBN 9781644696439 (hardback) | ISBN 9781644696446 (paperback) | ISBN 9781644696453 (adobe pdf) | ISBN 9781644696460 (epub)
Subjects: LCSH: Television series—Russia (Federation)—History and criticism. | Television broadcasting—Russia (Federation)—History.
Classification: LCC PN1992.3.R8 R87 2021 (print) | LCC PN1992.3.R8 (ebook) | DDC 791.450947—dc23
LC record available at https://lccn.loc.gov/2021035865
LC ebook record available at https://lccn.loc.gov/2021035866

ISBN 9781644696439 (hardback)
ISBN 9781644696446 (paperback)
ISBN 9781644696453 (adobe pdf)
ISBN 9781644696460 (epub)

Book design by Tatiana Vernikov
Cover design by Ivan Grave
On the cover: still from the series *Ol'ga* (see pp. 190-213 of this volume)

Published by Academic Studies Press
1577 Beacon Street
Brookline, MA 02446, USA
press@academicstudiespress.com
www.academicstudiespress.com

CONTENTS

NOTE ON TRANSLITERATION

Transliteration follows the simplified Library of Congress system, except for some spellings conventionally accepted in English, such as "Petersburg." Final Cyrillic "-ий" in personal names, surnames, and place names is transliterated as "y": Todorovsky, Tarkovsky, Nizhny Novgorod. Transliteration may vary slightly because of different systems used in published material and individuals' preferred spelling of their names.

INTRODUCTION

In the introduction to her book *Between Truth and Time: A History of Soviet Central Television*, Christine Evans argues that television is the essential part of Putin-era popular culture and that in many ways it is "the culmination of a long Soviet—now Russian—era of television."[1] For his part, Konstantin Ernst, the CEO of Channel One, Russia, notes that the 1999–2000 season shaped the system of genres still dominating domestic television today. He also adds that this system is about to change.[2] In this collection we examine both the continuities and the radical transformations of that inherited system during the past two decades.

The most significant change is the transition from broadcast to post-broadcast television that triggered increased demand for new content and infrastructure. First, the scale of domestic TV series production has been growing by leaps and bounds. For example, in 2017 only 5% of all TV series were foreign adaptations. In 2016, 478 TV series and films were put into production, compared to only 304 in 2015.[3] Second, as Vlad Strukov and Vera Zvereva point out, in the 2010s Russia finally—and somewhat belatedly—transitioned to digital post-broadcast television, which redefined the media environment in which new Russian TV series are produced, distributed, and consumed.[4] Third, streaming is quickly becoming the primary delivery mode for serialized content—the main mechanism for broadening and fragmenting audiences. In addition to traditional broadcast channels, which multiplied beyond the three majors (Channel One, Channel Russia-1, and NTV), Subscription Video on Demand (SVoD) services, such as Start, Amediateka, ivi.ru, KION, Okko, TNT Premier, Kinopoisk, Yandex.Efir, and more.tv emerged as major content delivery platforms, challenging broadcast television

1 Christine Evans, *Between Truth and Time: A History of Soviet Central Television* (New Haven: Yale University Press, 2016), 2.

2 *Koroli serialov: Ernst, Akopov, Todorovskii, Murugov, Slepakov i drugie, Redaktsiia*, YouTube video, October 17, 2019, https://www.youtube.com/watch?v=j3MwMP_syjk&t=2174s.

3 See Irina Efimova, "Russian Television Series: Recent Trends," *Kinokultura* 66 (2019), http://www.kinokultura.com/2019/66-efimova.shtml.

4 See Vlad Strukov and Vera Zvereva, *Ot tsentral'nogo k tsifrovomu: Televidenie v Rossii* (Voronezh: Izdatel'stvo Voronezhskogo gosudarstvennogo pedagogicheskogo universiteta, 2014), xi–xvii.

and traditional cable providers that emerged after 1991. Many of these streaming services are backed by major financial institutions. Sberbank, for example, finances Okko. Strukov and Zvereva conclude that this technological shift signifies a major change in actors and a redistribution of political and economic power.[5]

The producers who run SVoDs also often operate their own production companies. For example, Alexander Akopov runs Amediateka streaming service and owns the COSMOS Studio to produce television series. Amediateka also delivers HBO content on the territory of the Russian Federation. Producers consider broadcast and cable delivery as targeting primarily more senior audiences, while streaming services are designed for younger viewers, offering controversial content to more "tolerant" viewers. Ernst notes, for instance, that Channel One deliberately produces three types of TV series. Those that air on Channel One try to tread lightly in order not to offend more senior and conservative audiences. The content for streaming services includes more violence and sexually explicit content. The third type of TV series is for dual use: it can appear at a later hour on cable channels and at the same time go directly to streaming services.[6]

What also differentiates the present moment from the origins of new domestic serialized productions twenty years ago is the availability of Russian language TV series for transnational audiences. In the past five years, many of these have become available on Netflix and Amazon Prime: *To the Lake* (*Epidemiia*, 2019), *Better than Us* (*Luchshe, chem liudi*, 2018), *Sparta* (2018), *Sleepers* (*Spiashchie*, 2017), *Trotsky* (2017), *The Method* (*Metod*, 2015), *Fartsa* (2015), *Locust (Sarancha*, 2015), *Catherine* (*Ekaterina*, 2014), *Silver Spoon* (*Mazhor*, 2014), among others. For viewers across the globe, especially the Russophone users who do not need subtitles, content became available not only through streaming services but also through the online services of legacy channels. As a result, the viewership has become truly global. This is a remarkable change from the 2000s when Russian television was filled with licensed adaptations of original Western, most notably American, TV shows, such as *My Fair Nanny* (*Moia prekrasnaia niania*, 2004—a remake of *The Nanny), Happy Together* (*Schastlivy vmeste*, 2006—a remake of *Married with Children*), *The Voronins* (*Voroniny*, 2009—a remake of *Everybody Loves Raymond*), and others. In contrast, Russian companies now produce original content that is distributed globally.

5 Ibid., xvi–xvii.

6 *Koroli serialov.*

Notably, in 2018 domestic TV series producers established their own TV series festival, titled *Pilot*, which opened in the city of Ivanovo. In August 2018, a festival of web series, *Realist Web Fest*, opened in Nizhny Novgorod. Series from fourteen countries, including Russia, Turkey, Uruguay, and the US, among others, competed in the main program. In 2019 this festival featured TV series from twenty-four nations. By now there are studios, such as Zebra Hero, that specialize in what they claim to be "edgier web series."[7] Festivals for television series are a major international trend as well: for example, the Cannes International Series Festival, *Canneseries*, was launched in France in 2018. At the Thirtieth Kinotavr Film Festival in 2019, art film director Boris Khlebnikov presented a pilot episode of his TV series *Storm* (2019), produced by Start streaming service. The script was written by an acclaimed screenwriter and film director, Nataliia Meshchaninova.[8] In 2020 events involving online platforms occupied a prominent place at the Thirty-First Kinotavr Film Festival. For the first time, the program included pitching of ideas for future TV series. Scriptwriters proposed their TV series to streamers such as Premier, more.tv, Okko, Start, and MTS Media, rather than traditional television channels. Akopov summarizes the trend by noting that the TV series format is "the future of motion picture production."[9] It remains to be seen how the TV series boom will affect the film industry in coming years.

Quality Drama between the Broadcast and Post-Broadcast Television Years

In the 2010s Russian television entered the era of what Kristin Thompson calls "quality television"—drama with values similar to those of art cinema, which seeks to enlighten as well as entertain. Specifically, Thompson claims that these new productions adhere closely

7 "My pridumyvaem i snimaem derzkie veb-serialy . . . nasha sila komediinye formaty, kotorye khorosho zakhodiat v internet." See "Web-serialy i korotkometrazhki," Zebra Hero, https://www.zebrahero.com/web-series.

8 In January–February 2020, Kinotavr Festival, in cooperation with the streaming platform Okko, launched a new format: "Kinotavr International Festival Special Edition," a series of premiere and exclusive screenings of foreign films that have not yet been released to Russian film distribution. This type of partnership between a major national film festival and a leading streaming service testifies to the increased cultural status of post-broadcast delivery venues. See "Kinotavr Special Edition," Kinotavr.ru, https://www.kinotavr.ru/en/special.

9 Susanna Al'perina, "Festival' teleserialov Pilot otkrylsia v Ivanovo," *Rossiiskaia gazeta*, September 13, 2018, https://rg.ru/2018/09/13/reg-cfo/festival-teleserialov-pilot-otkrylsia-v-ivanovo.html.

to what David Bordwell describes as the features of art cinema: "a loosening of causality, a greater emphasis on psychological or anecdotal realism, violations of classical clarity of space and time, explicit authorial comment, and ambiguity."[10] In media studies, quality television is a period designation for film-like American cable drama of the 1980s–90s, such as *Hill Street Blues* (1989), *Twin Peaks* (1990), and *The Sopranos* (1999)—shows quite diverse in genre, theme, and ideology. In the case of Russian television, such heterogeneity is especially striking when one compares recent television series, some of which are discussed in this collection, with those that formerly dominated Russian television in the 1990s. In her discussion of domestic TV series, Irina Efimova lists three main features of what she calls socially engaged TV drama, which is, in our view, an equivalent of quality television: (1) topical themes that raise painful social issues, (2) a complex and often deeply flawed protagonist, and (3) genre hybridity.[11] In this collection, *The Affairs* (*Izmeny*, 2015), *Ol'ga* (2016), and *The Method* sit squarely in this category. At the same time, just as *Game of Thrones* (2011) is undoubtedly considered quality television production, so are *Orlova and Aleksandrov* (2015), *The Thaw* (*Ottepel'*, 2013), and *Catherine*: not only do they showcase high production values and cinematic quality picture, but the historical settings and conflicts they fantasize are not reducible to soap opera narrative turns. For instance, they deal with such complex matters as the legitimacy of political power and cultural memory. Not surprisingly, many of these series are sold globally and are recognized as counterparts of quality TV drama in the West.

Famous directors and actors used to avoid television productions, fearing damage to their artistic reputation, whereas now film and theater stars such as Konstantin Khabensky, Anna Mikhalkova, Aleksei Serebriakov, Paulina Andreeva, and Sergei Bezrukov willingly appear in TV series. Moreover, major filmmakers and producers, such as Valery Todorovsky, take on television projects and have even switched almost completely to quality television productions. The demand for these series has become a way for directors, scriptwriters, and actors to earn a steady income, while also allowing creative space to fully develop character and plot. Todorovsky's *The Thaw* became a major cultural event of the year, if not of the decade, overshadowing many cinematic oeuvres and setting a high bar for quality television in future

10 Cited in Kristin Thompson, *Storytelling in Film and Television* (Cambridge, MA: Harvard University Press, 2003), 110.

11 Efimova, "Russian Television Series Recent Trends."

years. Avdot'ia Smirnova and Nataliia Meshchaninova combine their careers as prominent filmmakers and scriptwriters with producing TV series, such as the 2008 *Fathers and Children* (*Ottsy i deti*) and *An Ordinary Woman* (*Obychnaia zhenshchina*, 2018, 2020) respectively. Iana Troianova exemplifies a major theater and film actress who alternates between cinematic collaborations with Vasily Sigarev and Smirnova and TV series, such as the dramedy *Ol'ga* and other television projects. The new profession of showrunner has emerged in the production of domestic series in Russia. Producers Aleksandr Akopov, Ilya Kulikov, Valery Todorovsky, Aleksandr Tsekalo, Irina Sosnovaya, and Semen Slepakov combine management, creative authority, and business clout to supervise big-budget and, at times, more daring serialized productions.

In the absence of domestic streaming platforms during the early 2000s, television producers experimented with quality drama content in the late-night time slot. In 2008 Channel One offered its viewers a program they titled *City Slickers* (*Gorodskie pizhony*), which targeted an audience that was more familiar with Western television shows and craved more complex, edgier series. Ernst described *City Slickers'* audience as high-earning intellectuals who watch traditional broadcast television only sporadically and expect a better quality picture and sophisticated storytelling.[12] Not surprisingly, Channel One offered *City Slickers* to those high-end customers in HD and in its first year the program included such hits as *The Office* (2005) and *Californication* (2007). While most TV series broadcast within the framework of *City Slickers* were American, Channel One also included British and French productions. Notably, many series produced by and for streaming services, such as Netflix's *House of Cards* (2013), appeared the same year on *City Slickers*.[13] The program ceased to exist in 2016; by that time Channel One TV productions were being sold for streaming globally and Russian late-night TV viewers migrated to streaming platforms, first Western and later increasingly domestic.

12 Vera Tsvetkova, "Gorodskie pizhony—vydaiushchiisia produkt," *Nezavisimaia gazeta*, July 25, 2018, https://www.ng.ru/tv/2008-07-25/13_opros.html.

13 Channel One advertised the release of *House of Cards* on *City Slickers* as both a breakthrough in quality of image resolution and the storytelling itself: "Watch *House of Cards* under the *City Slickers* rubric. It is broadcast in HD. Trust us, in this case high definition refers not only to the quality of the image but also to the story." See "'Pervyi kanal' nachal pokaz 'Kartochnogo domika' v formate HD," *TV Mag*, February 18, 2013, https://tricolortvmag.ru/article/serials/dom-kotoryy-postroil-kevin-speysi/. Even Vladimir Putin became a fan of *House of Cards* and advised his Minister of Defense to watch it in order understand US politics (See Mikhail Zygar'. *Vsia kremlevskaia rat'*. Al'pina Didzhital 2016, 186).

With the appearance of quality television drama in after hours on Channel One, the process of "legitimating television," as Michael Z. Newman and Elana Levine put it, is underway in Russia as well. In their study of US television in media convergence era, Levine and Newman contend that the rise of quality television redrew the lines and the hierarchies within the industry itself as well as in the broader cultural sphere.[14] Productions released on domestic and international SVoD platforms acquired higher cultural status, which, many might argue, is similar to art cinema. Levine and Newman suggest that these quality productions target more selective media audiences, that is, more educated and socially mobile viewers. Film critics pay considerable attention to these new TV series, in stark contrast to a general dismissal of broadcast television in the 1990s. Meanwhile, in her recent article Larisa Maliukova, cinema reviewer for *Novaia Gazeta* and a leading film journalist, notes that quality television productions are by now frequently superior to current Russian cinema, not least because of censorship through financial control both on the big screen and on broadcast television channels.[15] While this fragmentation of both the types of available content and of consuming audiences has national peculiarities, Russia follows the global trend of legitimating (some) television.

Methodology

Despite the obvious political and cultural clampdown, especially after 2012 with Putin's return to presidency for a third term and the annexation of Crimea two years later, Russian television has become more diverse and open to global trends than ever before. We chose a genre approach to examine such formats as quality television drama, low- budget web television mini-series, as well as Channel Culture (Kul'tura) documentary productions aspiring to high culture status. The articles in this collection share several thematic considerations. First, analysis of gender and agency is central to all articles in the collection. Second, many articles tackle the issues of cultural memory, be it World War II, the Soviet past in general, the 1990s as an era of reforms and social transformation, or Russia's imperial heritage. Even the articles that deal with the

14 Michael Z. Newman and Elana Levine, *Legitimating Television: Media Convergence and Cultural Status* (New York: Routledge, 2012), 7.

15 Larisa Maliukova, "Serialy—kino 5:0. Pochemu nash polnyi metr proigryvaet otechestvennym zhe serialam s razgromnym schetom," *Novaia gazeta*, February 7, 2021, https://novayagazeta.ru/articles/2021/02/07/89109-serialy-kino-5-0?fbclid=IwAR23xF0lnNdzg8iki5Oq6znjDlGp_iCp7Ih8gClptjQVYmeFGxTUPvzaEtM.

present, such as *Ol'ga* or *The Method*, evoke memories of Russia's recent past that continue to haunt the characters. Third, the collection covers an entire gamut of formats that appear in traditional legacy television and on new internet-based platforms. Fourth, the collection examines global narrative trends such as neo-noir, historical costume drama, celebrity biopic, and dramedy. Many of these global genres are broader than traditional broadcast TV genres such as the sitcom or soap opera. The contributors to this collection contend that genre fusion is one of the primary features of contemporary television drama. They also examine the shifts in political and economic power which, in mediated form, manifest themselves through these new hybrid structures.

Many recent monographs about Eastern European and Russian television problematize the tendency to "exoticize" national television cultures, especially in their socialist or post-socialist instantiations. For example, in her 2016 book *TV Socialism*, Aniko Imre analyzes Eastern Bloc television as the field of experimentation and successful implementation of many ideals of the ethos of transnational public broadcasting. In a similar spirit, our collection acknowledges certain particularities of recent Russian serialized productions, while at the same time examining them as inseparable from the global flow of ideas, genres, and formats.

One important way of categorizing TV series is the foregrounding of contemporary versus historical setting. As recently as five or six years ago Russian television was flooded with historical series about the glorious security services or biopics about Soviet-era generals and film stars. The number of historical series has declined because scriptwriters and directors face pressure to produce a monolithic, nationalist interpretation of the past that limits creativity and is apparently less interesting to audiences. Currently, and especially on streaming services, there is a variety of high quality productions about contemporary Russia. These series deal with social problems and identity issues, and often use contemporary language to speak about them.[16] The latter point is especially important in view of the 2014 law banning the use of profanity in arts and media. While this law has been observed on the federal television channels, streaming platforms are much more lax about enforcing the law. Contemporary dramas and

16 For example, *Call DiCaprio!* (*Zvonite DiKaprio*, 2018) deals with stigma surrounding AIDS, *House Arrest* (*Domashny arest*, 2018) depicts systemic corruption, *Gold Diggers* (*Soderzhanki*, 2019) examines the issues of class and sexuality in present-day Russia.

comedies avoid politically sensitive topics while freely engaging a broad spectrum of issues and situations that are personally relevant to viewers.

The series about present-day Russia take viewers away from the affluent central Moscow to the nation's heartland which, as far as we are concerned, begins one mile outside of the capital downtown, and includes both the so-called provinces and working-class neighborhoods of big cities, such as Chertanovo in Moscow (the setting of *Ol'ga*). Among other notable recent examples are *Chicks* (*Chiki*, 2020), *The Affairs* (*Izmeny*, 2015), and *Bitches* (*Stervochki*, 2011). Many of these heartland series feature women as protagonists who are not afraid to challenge social power. A striking example of this unconventional trend is *An Ordinary Woman*, a crime dramedy in its second season. The protagonist—a mother of two with a third child on the way—owns a flower shop, which serves as a front for her sexual services business. The hybrid genre of this series allows female agency to be at the center of both dramatic and dark comedic sequences. According to Meshchaninova, this is what "an ordinary woman" does: she takes charge in impossible situations and does not shirk responsibility when all social institutions fail her.[17]

What is also striking about these series set in present-day Russia is the generational, ethnic, and class diversity of characters. These series depict a cross-section of Russian society and explore it as a complex and heterogeneous community. Usually such projects are available on streaming services and offer a counterpoint to the federal channels' news and propaganda talk shows, where present-day Russia looks like a throwback to Brezhnev-era programming with its lack of ethnic and gender diversity, and dearth of meaningful social commentary. It is also worth noting that there are some important limitations to television's ability and willingness to engage with certain genres. For example, courtroom drama is extremely rare on Russian television and avoids contemporary settings, an understandable gesture of self-protection in the current political climate. Dmitry Kott's 2020 courtroom drama *Defenders* (*Zastupniki*, 2020), produced by Channel One, is a good, albeit rare, example. The series is set during the late Thaw and describes the transition from a liberal to a more oppressive environment.

In contrast, many historical television dramas offer a more idealized, fantasy-prone representation of the Russian and Soviet imperial past. With some exceptions, there are three

17 Anna Fedina, "Nataliia Meshchaninova—o vtorom sezone 'Obychnoi zhenshchiny,' podrostkakh, stendape, i konkurentsii s Netflix," *Vogue*, December 21, 2020, https://www.vogue.ru/lifestyle/nataliya-meshaninova-o-vtorom-sezone-obychnoj-zhenshiny-podrostkah-stendape-i-konkurencii-s-netflix.

main centers/settings: Soviet Moscow, imperial St. Petersburg, and the battlefield (usually and obviously from World War II). Each of these settings presents a certain set of values, conflicts, and characters. *Penal Battalion* (*Shtrafbat*, 2004), as Stephen Norris demonstrates, explores the previously taboo topic of Gulag prisoners at the frontline. *The Thaw* and *Orlova and Alexandrov*, as Lilya Kaganovsky and Rimgaila Salys show, are self-reflexive texts, laying bare their lack of historical authenticity by drawing on celebrity and backstage ethos and paradigms, and both are acutely aware of the global conventions of period drama. Similarly, *Catherine* and *The Great* (*Velikaia*, 2015) are savvy examples of global royal drama conventions. However the latter series engage in fantasies of historical authenticity reinforced by palace/museum settings and carefully reconstructed costumes.

Structure of the Collection

We open our collection with an article that examines a very different, and distinctively Russian idea of televisual quality. Alyssa DeBlasio discusses the ethos of the Kul'tura channel and argues that it was the "first thematic channel" on post-Soviet Russian television. Its claim to quality looks back to the Soviet-style promise of enlightenment and "culturedness."[18] The author traces the evolution of Kul'tura in the broadcast and post-broadcast era from a public channel to what is essentially a specialized venue for a niche audience. The idea of targeting a niche audience in this respect is not different from Channel One's strategy of airing *The Method* close to midnight because it featured violence and graphic sexuality and thus attracted younger viewers.

Stephen Norris examines the TV series *Penal Battalion*, which set important benchmarks for the recent memory wars, most importantly the clashes surrounding the Great Patriotic War. The series deals with the previously taboo topic of penal battalions—the Gulag in the frontlines. While the topic is controversial, Norris contends that the series played a major role in articulating a new Russian Orthodoxy-infused patriotism.[19]

18 See also Catriona Kelly, *Refining Russia: Advice Literature, Polite Culture, and Gender from Catherine to Yeltsin* (Oxford: Oxford University Press, 2001).

19 By now these patriotic serialized fantasies have inspired theme parks with an ideological agenda, such as the recently opened Patriot Park (2016) in the suburbs of Moscow. The official name of the park is Military-Patriotic Park of Culture and Leisure of the Armed Forces of the Russian Federation. It is an uncanny pairing of two

The next two essays engage with the genre of television biopics. Rimgaila Salys examines the celebrity biopic *Orlova and Aleksandrov*, which focuses on the film star couple of the Stalin era. She situates the series in the biopic culture of recent Russian television, which often whitewashes the Soviet, and especially Stalinist, past. Salys argues that the series encodes Putin-era values pertaining to gender, sexuality, class, and religion as a Stalin era cultural legacy. Alexander and Elena Prokhorovs' article on the recent series about Catherine the Great examines another variation of the celebrity biopic—the subgenre of royal drama. While the series follow the global trend by showcasing big budgets, spectacular mise-en-scène, and quality drama narrative, they also project political and ideological concerns of Putin-era Russia onto the eighteenth-century imperial past.

While Valery Todorovsky's *The Thaw* is not a biopic proper, it is something of a TV series *à clef*, alluding to major filmmakers, cinematographers, and cultural administrators of the 1950s and 60s. In her article about Todorovsky's series, Lilya Kaganovsky contends that the director engages in a self-reflexive treatment of the late Soviet past. She argues that *The Thaw* tries to play a double game: on the one hand it does not overtly aspire to historical authenticity; on the other it is aware of its power to manipulate and evoke nostalgia. In other words, *The Thaw* examines the tension between revealing and hiding at the heart of this backstage melodrama; hence the article's title, "Between Pornography and Nostalgia."

The second part of the volume deals with series set in the present, the topic that in the words of Anton Dolin, the editor-in-chief of *Art of Cinema* magazine, Russian filmmakers fear to touch.[20] Perhaps for this reason TV series choosing to deal with contemporaneity often violate conventional societal norms. Many of them, especially those chosen by the contributors to this volume, depict women as central characters, often flawed and complex, who serve as narrative focalizers. Tatiana Mikhailova's article about TNT Channel's series *The Affairs* focuses on a female protagonist who transgresses social conventions, asserts her agency, and explores her sexuality. The article also examines the heteronormative family as a social institution in deep crisis. The authors of the next article analyze Iury Bykov's TV series *The Method* and *Sleepers*,

ideological dominants: on the one hand a vast display of military hardware, on the other an imposing Russian Orthodox Cathedral with kenotic St. Boris and Gleb at its gate.

20 Cited in Viktoriia Stoliarova, "Mneniia razdelilis': reaktsiia obshchestvennosti i kritikov na serial *Chiki*," TVK, July 30, 2020, https://tvk6.ru/publications/news/51768/.

arguing that the filmmaker uses neo-noir as a lens to explore present-day Russia, including the emergence of repressed trauma from the late Soviet era.[21]

Vlad Strukov explores the TV representation of family in the context of the neoliberal economy and global media regime. On the basis of STS channel's dramedy *Ol'ga* (2016–2020), the author examines the rise of "friemily" and other non-traditional forms of community in Putin-era Russia. Finally, Saara Ratilainen takes readers beyond legacy television to web series culture. Using as a case study one of the most successful amateur-produced web series *Bitches* (2011), she discusses the series' treatment of women's agency as criminals, the proliferation of new forms of authorship, amateur web video production, and associated social network fan culture.

We conclude our volume with several interviews that give voice to those who produce content, both for broadcast and post-broadcast television. Alexander Dulerain is the creative producer of TNT TV Channel and chief content officer of Storyworld Entertainment, a global arm of the TNT Broadcasting Network. Dulerain produced such hit comedy series as *Our Russia (Nasha Rasha*, 2006–2011*)*, *Interns* (*Interny*, 2010–2016), and *House Arrest* (*Domashny arest*, 2018). He also produced *Ol'ga* and *Affairs* discussed in this volume. Sergei Fiks is a renowned scriptwriter and producer. For many years he worked as programming director for TV channel NTV and as producer and senior executive for VGTRK media company and Channel Russia-1. Fiks is a member of the Russian Television Academy. Denis Gorelov is a film and culture critic who worked with Leonid Parfenov on the cult documentary TV series *Namedni* (*The Other Day*, 1997–2003). Nataliia Meshchaninova is an award-winning TV and film director and scriptwriter. She co-wrote scripts for Aleksei Fedorchenko's *Anna's War* (*Voina Anny*, 2018), Boris Khlebnikov's *Arrhythmia* (*Aritmiia*, 2017) and TV series *Storm* (2019), among others. In 2020 she directed season two of *Ordinary Woman.* Maksim Stishov, the author of the hit series *Bal'zakovskii vozrast, ili Vse muzhiki svo . . .* (*Balzac Age, or All Men are Bast . . .*, 2004–2007), is a screenwriter, producer, director, and one of the first showrunners on Russian television. Their interviews provide snapshots of the state of the industry in Russia.

[21] Russian television neo-noir is a protean generic mode, which plays with contemporaneity, historicity, and pure fantasy. While *The Method* and Konstantin Bogomolov's 2020 series *A Good Person* (*Khoroshii chelovek*) are set primarily in the present, *To the Lake* engages with a dystopian near-future, and the Major Cherkasov crime dramas—*Mosgaz* (2012), *Executioner* (*Palach*, 2014), *Jackal* (*Shakal*, 2016), and others—explore the Soviet 1960s and '70s.

We thank the College of Arts and Sciences at William & Mary, which partially funded this publication. We would also like to thank the Reves Center for International Studies (in particular Steve Hanson), the Department of Modern Languages and Literatures (in particular Silvia Tandeciarz), the Russian and Post-Soviet Studies Program (in particular Frederick Corney), as well as colleagues at Film & Media Studies Program (in particular Arthur Knight, Elizabeth Losh, and Rich Lowry) for their continuous support. We are especially grateful to the organizers of the Pittsburgh Russian Film Symposium, Nancy Condee and Vladimir Padunov, for creating an atmosphere of productive dialogue and introducing Elena and Alexander to leading film and media critics in Russia today. Inspiring conversations, in person and on Zoom, with our colleagues, Helena Goscilo, Marina Balina, Viktoria Belopolskaia, Birgit Beumers, Eliot Borenstein, Anton Dolin, Ilya Kukulin, Mark Lipovetsky, Masha Mayofis, Viktor Matizen, Serguei Oushakine, Alena Solntseva, Elena Stishova, Alexei Yurchak, and many others greatly assisted our research. We thank Dasha Prokhorova for translating the interviews and her genuine interest in Russian media. We appreciate our anonymous reviewers' helpful suggestions. Finally, we would like to thank again our wonderful and patient contributors.

—Alexander Prokhorov, Elena Prokhorova, Rimgaila Salys

Bibliography

Al'perina, Susanna. "Festival' teleserialov Pilot otkrylsia v Ivanovo." *Rossiiskaia gazeta*, September 13, 2018. https://rg.ru/2018/09/13/reg-cfo/festival-teleserialov-pilot-otkrylsia-v-ivanovo.html.

Efimova, Irina. "Russian Television Series: Recent Trends." *Kinokultura* 66 (2019). http://www.kinokultura.com/2019/66-efimova.shtml.

Ernst, Konstantin. "Mnenie." YouTube video, April 2, 2015. https://www.youtube.com/watch?v=YKpLHMFn7yc.

Evans, Christine. *Between Truth and Time: A History of Soviet Central Television*. New Haven: Yale University Press, 2016.

Fedina, Anna. "Nataliia Meshchaninova—o vtorom sezone 'Obychnoi zhenshchiny,' podrostkakh, stendape, i konkurentsii s Netflix." *Vogue*, December 21, 2020. https://www.vogue.ru/lifestyle/nataliya-meshaninova-o-vtorom-sezone-obychnoj-zhenshiny-podrostkah-stendape-i-konkurencii-s-netflix.

Imre, Aniko. *TV Socialism.* Durham: Duke University Press, 2016.

Kelly, Catriona. *Refining Russia: Advice Literature, Polite Culture, and Gender from Catherine to Yeltsin.* Oxford: Oxford University Press, 2001.

Koroli serialov: Ernst, Akopov, Todorovskii, Murugov, Slepakov i drugie. Redaktsiia. YouTube video, October 17, 2019. https://www.youtube.com/watch?v=j3MwMP_syjk&t=2174s.

Maliukova, Larisa. "Serialy—kino 5:0. Pochemu nash polnyi metr proigryvaet otechestvennym zhe serialam s razgromnym schetom." *Novaia gazeta,* February 7, 2021. https://novayagazeta.ru/articles/2021/02/07/89109-serialy-kino-5-0?fbclid=IwAR23xF0lnNdzg8iki5Oq6znjDlGp_iCp7Ih8gClptjQVYmeFGxTUPvzaEtM.

Newman, Michael Z., and Elana Levine. *Legitimating Television: Media Convergence and Cultural Status.* New York: Routledge, 2012.

"'Pervyi kanal' nachal pokaz 'Kartochnogo domika' v formate HD." *TV Mag,* February 18, 2013. https://tricolortvmag.ru/article/serials/dom-kotoryy-postroil-kevin-speysi/.

Stoliarova, Viktoriia. "Mneniia razdelilis': reaktsiia obshchestvennosti i kritikov na serial *Chiki.*" TVK, July 30, 2020. https://tvk6.ru/publications/news/51768/.

Strukov, Vlad, and Vera Zvereva. *Ot tsentral'nogo k tsifrovomu: Televidenie v Rossii.* Voronezh: Izdatel'stvo Voronezhskogo gosudarstvennogo pedagogicheskogo universiteta, 2014.

Thompson, Kristin. *Storytelling in Film and Television.* Cambridge, MA: Harvard University Press, 2003.

Tsvetkova, Vera. "Gorodskie pizhony—vydaiushchiisia produkt." *Nezavisimaia gazeta,* July 25, 2018. https://www.ng.ru/tv/2008-07-25/13_opros.html.

"Web-serialy i korotkometrazhki." Zebra Hero. https://www.zebrahero.com/web-series.

Zygar', Mikhail. *Vsia kremlevskaia rat'.* Moscow: Al'pina didzhital, 2016.

The Cultural Euphemism of Kul'tura: Soviet Nostalgia on the Russia-K Channel

Alyssa DeBlasio

On August 25, 1997, Boris Yeltsin signed the decree that would create the first thematic channel in Russian television broadcasting history. The new venture would bear the name of the virtue to which it was dedicated: the pursuit of culture, or *kul'tura* in Russian, which carries with it the specific meaning of "high culture." Over the past twenty years, and through two rebranding campaigns, the Russia-K/Kul'tura channel has become a staple of television viewing and, more broadly, of cultural consciousness in Russia.[1] As the only non-commercial channel in Russia today, the Kul'tura channel's status and viewership has remained stable in large part due to the historical attitude toward television in Russia, where an overwhelming majority of the population report watching several hours of television on a daily basis.[2] At the same time, the Kul'tura brand is predicated on a notion of intellectual and cultural exclusivity, one that is conceptually, aesthetically, and structurally rooted in nostalgia for the Soviet past. The broader cultural mission of the Kul'tura channel capitalizes on viewer nostalgia for the Soviet conception of "culturedness" (*kul'turnost'*) to create "an elevated and insulated space from the rest of television," to quote Avi Santo.[3] Now in its third decade, its third decade, the Kul'tura

1 The channel was initially called RTR-2. On January 1, 1998, it was renamed Kul'tura, and was finally rebranded as Russia-K on January 1, 2010. For the sake of consistency, I will refer to the channel at all historical periods as Kul'tura, both because this is the name it carried for fourteen years and because the channel is colloquially known in Russia as Kul'tura.

2 Elena Vartanova, "The Russian Media Model in the Context of Post-Soviet Dynamics," in *Comparing Media Systems beyond the Western World*, ed. Daniel C. Hallin and Paolo Mancini (Cambridge: Cambridge University Press, 2012), 125.

3 Here Santo is describing the coalition audience of HBO, although as we will see, the unlikely pairing of a popular, for-profit channel and the state-owned Kul'tura channel in fact share an important similarity in their relationship to their respective audiences. See Avi Santo, "Para-Television and Discourses of Distinction: The Culture of Production at HBO," in *It's not TV. Watching HBO in the Post-Television Era*, ed. Marc Leverette, Brian L. Ott, and Cara Louise Buckley (Abington: Routledge, 2008), 37.

channel is catering primarily to a shrinking demographic of viewers over sixty-five years of age who were well into adulthood when the channel was founded, rather than competing for younger viewers in today's hybrid media market.

The Culture of Kul'tura

The debate between "high" and "low" culture has seen a revival in Western scholarship in recent years, alongside the twenty-first century renaissance of HBO, Netflix, and other providers of what is now often called "quality television." Here the idea of "quality," which we will look at in more detail later in this chapter, refers to programming that distinguishes itself, through its high level of production, acting, and writing, from the supposed low forms of network television. In the Russian context, not only has the debate between "high" and "low" always been a relevant lens for cultural criticism, but the construct of "high culture" is critical for understanding the cultural aspirations of Russian television. This is especially true in the case of the Kul'tura channel, which, as a whole, posits both an upward-leaning and backward-looking vision for Russian cultural values.

In their 2009 book *Television and Culture in Putin's Russia*, Stephen Hutchings and Natalia Rulyova argue that although there is a stark distinction between "high" and "low" culture on the Russian television screen, the "low" tends to lean upwards, often aspiring towards the signs and symbols of "high" cultural forms. The authors show how in the STS sitcom *My Fair Nanny* (*Moia prekrasnaia niania*, 2004–2009), it is the tension between "high" and "low" that drives the narrative: while the central character's Ukrainian dialect and "excessive vulgarity provides the essence of the show's comic effect," she is at the same time always viewed in relation to high cultural norms and symbols (such as Pushkin).[4] Hutchings and Rulyova also comment on the makers' decision to change the title from the original *The Nanny* (*Niania)* to the hybrid invoking the reference to a higher culture text, *My Fair Lady*. Hutchings and Rulyova's discussion of fan reactions to the show, on message boards and other forums, confirms that it is not unusual for

4 Stephen Hutchings and Natalia Rulyova, *Television and Culture in Putin's Russia: Remote Control* (New York: Routledge, 2009), 152, 155. Anikó Imre also talks about the "low" versus "high" division in her 2016 study *TV Socialism* (Durham: Duke University Press, 2016), 4–5.

the Russian viewing public to measure a sitcom "against the standards of a classic adaptation," or the presence of what the authors call "the (mis)application of high cultural metalanguage.[5]

The pull towards "high" culture is at the heart of the Kul'tura channel's narrative about its own origins. The idea for a public channel dedicated specifically to high culture was proposed to Boris Yeltsin in the late 1990s by a group of scholars—musician Mstislav Rostropovich, filmmaker Savva Kulish, and most notably, linguist and literary historian Dmitry Likhachev. According to Mikhail Shvydkoi, the Kul'tura channel's first director, at this particular historical moment there were several media oligarchs and financial groups contending for control of Channel Five.[6] Not wanting to hand over more valuable media space to Vladimir Gusinsky or Boris Berezovsky and thereby strengthen the media empires of either, Yeltsin decided to "lend Channel 5 to culture for a period of time," as Shvydkoi explains.[7] While Shvydkoi's political explanation for Kul'tura's founding is compelling, it does not make it any less remarkable that at the apex of the media bubble of the 1990s the last channel on network television was given away to the least profitable pursuit—high culture.

In the 1990s, Likhachev was among the country's leading spokespersons on behalf of high culture. A television channel devoted to cultural values, as he saw it, could serve as a tool for counteracting the damage done by the media content of the post-Soviet free market, which had turned Russia into a country of "loafers."[8] Nobel laureate Zhores Alferov shared these sentiments, stating that "with the exception of Kul'tura, it is impossible for normal people to watch [Russian] television."[9] Lev Karakhan, in turn, praised the channel for signaling a "return to the undefiled reception of cultural and aesthetic values."[10] Vera Tsvetskova from *Nezavisimaia gazeta* went so far as to describe Kul'tura as being "as necessary [to Russia] as

5 Ibid., 152.

6 At the time, the Channel Five slot was occupied by the failing Petersburg TV station.

7 Mikhail Shvydkoi, "Na nas smotreli kak na pridurkov," *Moskovskii komsomolets*, November 1, 2007, http://www.mk.ru/editions/daily/article/2007/11/01/72195-mihail-shvyidkoy-na-nas-smotreli-kak-na-pridurkov.html.

8 Dmitrii Likhachev, *Russkaia kul'tura* (Moscow: Iskusstvo, 2000), 291.

9 "Na podderzhku propravitel'stvennykh SMI iz biudzheta vydelili pochti 61 mlrd rublei," Krasnaia liniia, August 3, 2016, http://www.rline.tv/news/2016-08-03-na-podderzhku-smi-iz-byudzheta-vydelili-pochti-61-mlrd-rubley-/.

10 "Telekanal 'Kul'tura' i kul'tura," *Iskusstvo kino* 1 (January 1999), http://kinoart.ru/archive/1999/01/n1-article1.

inoculating against rabies,"[11] where the perception of being "uncultured" was not articulated simply as a vice, but as a disease that threatens the social fabric of Russia. These and other descriptions about the function and mission of the Kul'tura channel position it as a necessary remedy against *poshlost'* (banality), *tupost'* (ignorance), *bezdel'nichanie* (loafing), and other vices of capitalism—most importantly, *nekul'turnost'* (boorishness).

Indeed, in its early days the Kul'tura channel positioned itself in opposition to the vices of Western capitalism and its influence on post-Soviet Russian values. According to Mikhail Poltoranin, who served as the minister of print and mass media (1990–1992) during the passing of the 1991 Russian Law on Mass Media, Russian network television in the 1990s was losing viewers due to its broadcasting of luxuries and the general "spiritual emptiness" of television programming.[12] Television in the late 1980s and early 1990s undeniably made the growing Western influence on Russian culture more obvious, as it provided "isolated, estranged images," to use Raymond Williams's description, that, through their consumption, could visualize abstract fears of capitalist degradation through the broadcasting of recognizable brands, logos, and products.[13] The infiltration of Soviet TV by the norms and images of capitalism happened against the backdrop of strong, Soviet-based expectations about what quality TV *should be*. In Hutchings and Rulyova's words, "Soviet TV emphasized high literary values as a means of demarcating native television culture from decadent western consumerist 'trash.'"[14] The centralized system of Soviet broadcasting and its emphasis on cultural content established "high" culture expectations against which post-Soviet television necessarily had to compete.

There were two major European meetings on public service broadcasting within three years of Kul'tura's founding, both of which resulted in the passing of resolutions that identified public broadcasting, journalistic freedom, and media pluralism as "essential for democracy."[15]

11 Vera Tsvetkova, "Intelligent, tvorets, nachal'nik," *Nezavisimaia gazeta*, October 19, 2007, http://www.ng.ru/tv/2007-10-19/18_bederov.html.

12 Mikhail Poltoranin, "Poltoranin's Dreams and Hopes," *Post-Soviet Media Law & Newsletter* 11 (October 15, 1994, http://www.vii.org/monroe/issue11/dreams.html.

13 Raymond Williams, "When Was Modernism?," *New Left Review* 1, no. 175 (May–June 1989), https://newleftreview.org/I/175/raymond-williams-when-was-modernism.

14 Hutchings and Rulyova, *Television and Culture in Putin's Russia*, 6.

15 Report from the Fourth European Ministerial Conference on Mass Media Policy (Prague, December 7–8, 1994), 28, https://rm.coe.int/16806461fb.

Russian delegates participated in the 1994 meeting in Prague and that same year Poltoranin argued for a vision of broadcasting in Russia that would "develop and deepen democracy" and "broaden freedom of speech."[16] While the Kul'tura channel was born in the era of such debates, the channel never adopted any such pluralistic or democratic goals. And although Frances Foster and Monroe Price have described how the discussions surrounding the development of new television laws and codes in Russia in the mid-1990s in fact bore significant similarities to American debates in the 1960s over the role of public television,[17] the Kul'tura channel did not share PBS's "utopian impulse"[18] to build civil society in every home, from the living room up. On the contrary, Kul'tura was founded specifically to develop a third—and especially "Russian"—component of Poltoranin's vision: *to provide a spiritual service.*[19] If Kul'tura had a "utopian impulse," it was to create a "pure" space for Russian cultural values, apart from the capitalist and civil discourse of Western media models.[20] As Anikó Imre argues, TV under Soviet socialism "drew on the values of cultural nationalism and a top-down intention to educate and enlighten all social classes."[21]

16 Poltoranin, "Poltoranin's Dreams and Hopes."

17 Monroe Price and Frances H. Foster, "*Izvestiia* as a Mirror of Russian Legal Reform: Press, Law, and Crisis in the Post-Soviet Era," *Vanderbilt Journal of Translational Law* 26, no. 4 (November 1993): 675–738. I have chosen the American channel PBS for comparison, mainly because neither the Kul'tura channel nor PBS collect taxpayer money, unlike the BBC in the United Kingdom and Deutsche Welle in Germany.

18 Eric E. Peterson, "Introduction," in *Public Broadcasting and the Public Interest*, ed. Michael P. McCauley, Eric E. Peterson, B. Lee Artz, and DeeDee Halleck (Armonk, NY: ME Sharpe, 2003), 71–76.

19 Poltoranin, "Poltoranin's Dreams and Hopes."

20 In their work on contemporary Russian television, both Elena Vartanova and Hedwig de Smaele have argued that Russian media models do not lend themselves to one-to-one comparisons with so-called western media models, or "traditional models of media culture, economics, and influence," in Vartanova's words. De Smaele, in particular, has discussed how "the very notion of public service television remains alien" in Russia. See Vartanova, "The Russian Media Model," 122 and Hedwig de Smaele, "The Applicability of Western Media Models on the Russian Media System," *European Journal of Communication* 14, no. 2 (1999): 179. By way of contrast, Imre's *TV Socialism* offers a compelling argument for a "hybrid aesthetic and economic" model of understanding television under socialism, whereby we find "frequent exchanges and collaborations within the region and with Western media institutions," including "a programming flow across borders" and "borrowing from European public service broadcasting." See Imre, *TV Socialism*, 6–7.

21 Imre, *TV Socialism*, 28.

There is nothing unusual about Kul'tura's spiritual mission in the context of the immediate post-Soviet decade, which was permeated by the messianic rhetoric of the "Russian idea." First formulated by Fedor Dostoevsky in 1861, the "Russian idea" was taken up with zeal by Russian intellectuals, artists, and politicians in the 1990s; it postulated a spiritual quality that was uniquely Russian and which, for better or for worse, distinguished Russians from both their European and Asian neighbors. In a 2016 media forecast compiled by Elena Vartanova and Andrei Vyrkovsky, the authors argued that the Russian media industry is influenced by the "national peculiarities of its socio-political development."[22] If the "uniqueness" of the Russian people demanded separate intellectual categories, then why should the Russian people also not demand a different kind of TV? Just as Likhachev was a "spiritual teacher for many [Russians]" in the 1990s,[23] so was the Kul'tura channel viewed as a spiritual font for its viewing public.

One way that the Kul'tura channel has historically reinforced a traditional notion of Russian culture is through programming that explicitly defends and propagates Russian *kul'turnost'*, or "(high)-culturedness." One such show is *Russian Lessons: Readings* (*Uroki russkogo. Chteniia*), which features prominent Russian actors and cultural icons reading and commenting on classic literary texts (such as Pushkin, Chekhov, Gogol, and Kharms). "Classics are classics," reads the shows tagline. "They should never go away."[24] This same vision of culture, one rooted in an appreciation of canonical and national literature, is apparent in the 1997 title sequence to the Kul'tura show *The Place of Things* (*Polozhenie veshchei*). Here, an image of Leo Tolstoy reading one of his own books is inserted into scenes from everyday Russian life (Fig. 1).[25] The mistrustful look on Tolstoy's face (and not on the face of the unsuspecting park-goer, next to whom he has magically appeared) implies that it is modern life that is unwelcome, and not the posthumous appearance of Russia's bard to his people.

22 Elena Vartanova et al., "The Russian Media Industry in Ten Years: Industrial Forecasts," *Westminster Papers in Communication and Culture* 11, no. 1 (December 2016): 66.

23 "Ispolniaetsia 110 let so dnia rozhdeniia akademika Dmitriia Likhacheva," Tvkul'tura.ru, November 28, 2016, http://tvkultura.ru/article/show/article_id/159745/.

24 "O proekte," Tvkul'tura.ru, http://tvkultura.ru/brand/show/brand_id/31697/.

25 "Zastavka programmy 'Polozhenie veshchei,'" Staryi televizor, September 29, 2016, http://staroetv.su/video/vip/27281/kultura/zastavka_programmy_polozhenie_veshhej_kultura_1997_2000.

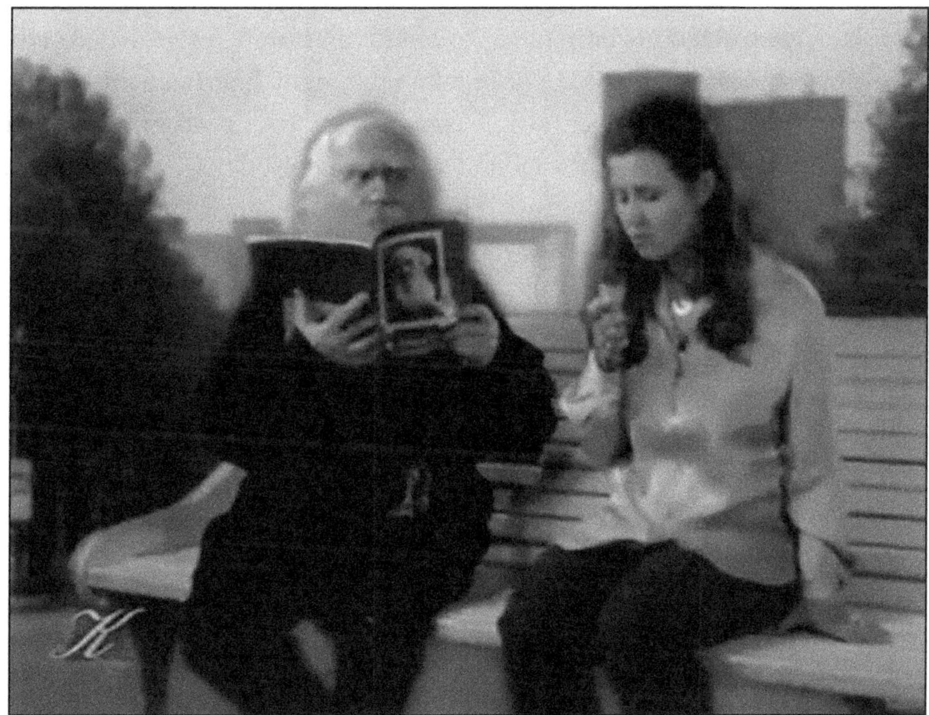

Fig. 1. On the Kul'tura channel, the image of Tolstoy is inserted into scenes of everyday life.

A main goal of the Kul'tura channel has been to promote proper language use among Kul'tura viewers, specifically through exposure to Russian classics.[26] The loss of the Russian language was a personal concern of Likhachev's,[27] and Yeltsin himself described the channel as "a declaration of war for the Russian language," where Kul'tura's founding was just one step in bringing "the present-day Russian language close to that of Pushkin, at the very least purifying it."[28] A news report from 1997 states that in preparation for developing content for

26 See, for instance, Andrei Zolotov Jr., "New Culture TV Channel Ready for Weekend Debut," *The Moscow Times*, October 29, 1997, http://old.themoscowtimes.com/sitemap/free/1997/10/article/new-culture-tv-channel-ready-for-weekend-debut/298341.html.

27 "Ispolniaetsia 110 let."

28 Artyon Protasenko, "B. Yeltsin 'Declares War for the Russian Tongue,' Seeks National Culture Channel," *Post-Soviet Media Law & Policy Newsletter* 38 (July 15, 1997), http://www.vii.org/monroe/issue38/fsu.html#5.

Kul'tura, Shvydkoi "instructed his employees to read Ivan Bunin, a renowned stylist, and not to read Leo Tolstoy, who is considered to have taken too many liberties with the language."[29]

In the second decade of the twenty-first century, Kul'tura's programming retained its emphasis on the preservation of the Russian language. Each episode of the show *The Living Word* (*Zhivoe slovo*), which advertised itself as an "intellectual reality show," investigates a different aspect of the Russian language, including grammar, syntax, and orthography.[30] In the opening episode from 2015, host Vladimir Annushkin concludes with the following monologue:

> My dear friends! You see, feel, and understand how difficult and splendid the Russian language is, how interesting the Russian language is, and how interesting and important—and simply necessary—it is for you and those dear to you to use living Russian speech. Long live the great Russian word![31]

Annushkin ends with the exclamation "*Da zdravstvuet*," which in the original Russian brings immediate associations with the many patriotic slogans of the Soviet period, like "Long live the Communist Party!," or "All hail Marxism-Leninism!" The closing monologue is not just an apology for "high" Russian culture or even a plea to the public; it is an appeal to one of the most recognizable forms of communication by the Soviet state—an appeal to the forms and sources of Soviet authority, albeit in a post-Soviet context.

The casting of *The Living Word* recreates the multilingual and multiethnic character of the Soviet past, as each episode includes native speakers, non-citizens learning Russian as a foreign language, and citizens of post-Soviet space who speak Russian along another national language. But while the visual concept of community in *The Living Word* is wider than just the Russian Federation or even post-Soviet space, the concept of culture is not. *The Living Word* is one example of the ideological education happening in Kul'tura's programming, in which viewers are educated into the broader practices of "culturedness" (*kul'turnost'*)—that is, the cultural norms of reading the canon of classical Russian literature as foundational to a specifically Russian identity, even among "non-Russians" from Russian-speaking countries. The show highlights *proper* pronunciation in order to tamp down accents, dialects, and stylistic

29 Zolotov Jr., "New Culture TV Channel."

30 "O proekte. Zhivoe slovo," Tvkul'tura.ru, http://tvkultura.ru/brand/show/brand_id/59465/.

31 "Zhivoe slovo. Urok 1," Tvkul'tura.ru, http://tvkultura.ru/video/show/brand_id/59465/episode_id/1201412/.

and grammatical infelicities. In episode one, for instance, audience members hone their pronunciation and intonation by reciting Mikhail Bulgakov's chapter on "Pontius Pilate" from *Master and Margarita*. The language lessons in *The Living Word* are often rooted in the study of Russian literary texts, thereby reinforcing the status of the traditional canon and the "truths" it contains.

Not only do programs like *The Living Word* emphasize the importance of high culture and the literary canon, but they also highlight the relationship of text to cultural identity—of reading texts, of faithfulness to texts, of the tactility of books, of the preservation of handwriting and orthographic style, and of the visualization of text on-screen. The show *Russian Lessons: Readings* is one example of the direct, textually based approach of the Kul'tura channel aesthetics, where minimal mediation between the printed word and the audience continuously points back to the text. In *Russian Lessons: Readings*, classic Russian literary texts are read by cultural authorities who, through their act of reading and the visualization of their enjoyment, further the authority of the literary cannon. These texts are often read in their entirety, without pause. The viewer experience is enlivened through collage sequences, as the literary readings continue non-diegetically, without verbal interruption.

Iury Norshtein is one of Russia's most beloved animators, and for his episode of *Russian Lessons: Readings* he selected a chapter from Soviet poet and writer Aleksandr Tvardovsky's lyric novel *Vasily Terkin*. Norshtein sits at a desk that is covered in books, with *Vasily Terkin* open in front of him. He reads the Tvardovsky chapter straight through, nearly by heart, glancing at the book every few lines to find his bearings. In the episode of *Russian Lessons: Readings* featuring filmmaker Nikolai Lebedev, Lebedev too recites his chosen text—Pushkin's short story "The Squire's Daughter" ("Baryshnia-krest'ianka")—as if by heart. Although in Lebedev's case, it is clear that he is reading from a teleprompter (his fixed gaze on a certain spot ahead of him and the fact that he does not turn the pages), he nonetheless holds the book open in his hands all the while, as if the physical text is necessary for the act of reading to occur at all. The editing, graphics, and the very act of reading in *Russian Lessons: Readings* all participate in an aesthetic and conceptual momentum that always points back to the text, highlighting the status of text on screen (Fig. 2).

Moreover, in *Russian Lessons: Readings*, the personal stories and annotations that each guest host includes along with his or her reading reinforce the status of the literary canon. It is only "with time that you understand how extraordinary Pushkin really was," Lebedev explains in

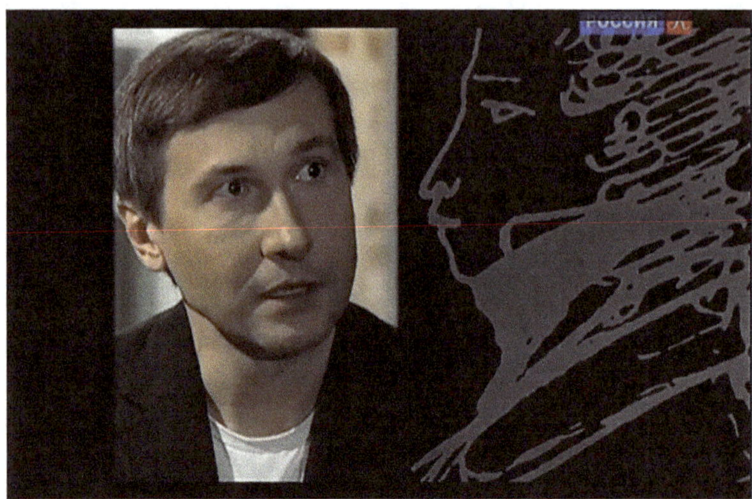

Fig. 2. Mutual reinforcement in Nikolai Lebedev's appearance on *Russian Lessons: Readings.*

his opening monologue (Fig. 2). "We still think in the language of Pushkin, we speak in his language, and we express our sense of self thanks to Pushkin's language," Lebedev continues. "He truly is 'our everything'"[32] The literary readings offered in *Russian Lessons: Readings* are not adaptive or generative, but reinforcing, as we see in Lebedev's repetition of platitudes about Pushkin's influence on Russian culture.

The Living Word also emphasizes the tactile experience of text. In the first episode, participants are asked to copy down a passage from *Master and Margarita* and then their handwriting is displayed on a screen at the front of the room. Next, they are given ink and pens and are asked to write out the same passage in calligraphy, without lifting their hands from the paper. "You must love every little letter," exclaims the host, as he walks the room and comments on the intricacies of each participant's handwriting. This fetishization of the printed word—of its production and its image—in contemporary Russian culture also extends to the domain of cinema: for instance, in "Energy Crisis," the final part of Mikhail Segal's almanac film *Short Stories* (*Rasskazy*, 2012), a clairvoyant librarian harnesses the supernatural power of Pushkin's collected works in order to locate missing children for the local police force.

In the 2016 one-time event *Dedicated to Osip Mandelstam* (*Osipu Mandel'shtamu posviashchaetsia*), actors Iuliia Rutberg, Anatoly Belyi, and Ol'ga Lerman read Mandelstam's

32 "Uroki russkogo. Chteniia. Nikolai Lebedev. A. S. Pushkin, 'Baryshnia-krest'ianka,'" Tvkul'tura.ru, http://tvkultura.ru/video/show/brand_id/31697/episode_id/1430290/video_id/1543226/viewtype/picture/.

poetry and commentary by his contemporaries for an uninterrupted eighty minutes, in honor of the 125th anniversary of the poet's birth.[33] The event was financed by the Federal Agency for Printing and Mass Communication and filmed at the Moscow International House of Music in front of a live audience. Programmatically, *Dedicated to Osip Mandelstam* is in line with the many Kul'tura specials devoted to cultural anniversaries and important historical events. Aesthetically, the anniversary event further illustrates the importance of text and canon to Kul'tura programming, both historically and at present. This and similar programming are also reminiscent of the Soviet genre of literary readings, such as the lengthy scene in Marlen Khutsiev's *I am Twenty* (*Mne dvadtsat' let*, 1964).

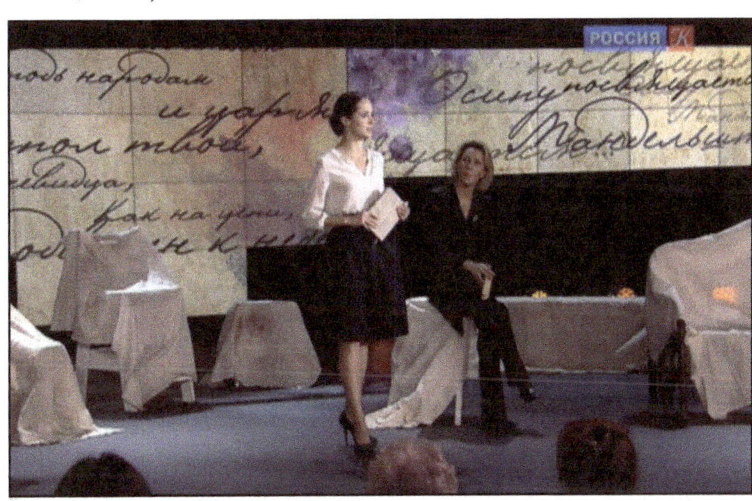

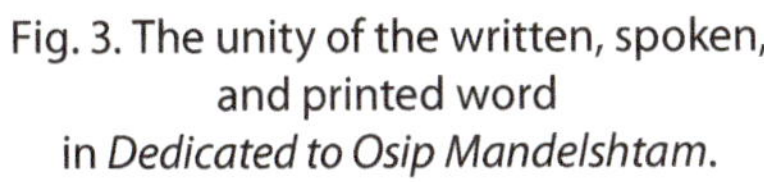
Fig. 3. The unity of the written, spoken, and printed word in *Dedicated to Osip Mandelshtam*.

The readings of *Dedicated to Osip Mandelstam* take place against the background of a long asymmetrical panel of screens, onto which are projected handwritten images of Mandelstam's writings. As the readings change, so do the images of texts; the audience is invited to make a direct connection between the reading of literature and its visualization, where the presence of one confirms the authority of the other (Fig. 3). The authority of culture, in Kul'tura's

33 Although the ubiquitous presence of books and textual visualization harkens back to a nostalgic vision of traditional literary culture, in 2016 a Russian media professional predicted that in the next ten years "the majority of media will become complex audiovisual and text-oriented—with a very different degree of text presence." Perhaps the text-heavy aesthetic and conceptual drive of Kul'tura programming may in fact be bringing the channel more in line with media trends of the future. See Vartanova et al., "The Russian Media Industry in Ten Years," 79.

formulation, comes not necessarily from the image of the author, but from the literary word: the spoken, the read, and the printed word, repeated and reaffirmed in multiple instantiations of its canonical, written form.

We find an obvious early example of the status of word in relation to author in the title sequence to *The Place of Things* (Fig. 1), where even the unmistakable image of Tolstoy is not authoritative enough. Tolstoy must also hold his own book open in front of him, a book that also has his own photograph on the cover, doubly reinforcing the viewer's convictions that Tolstoy the reader and Tolstoy the author are one and the same. Similarly, in a May 1998 broadcast of *And the House Lives* (*I dom zhivet*), Soviet poet Bella Akhmadulina reads her own poetry; and although she reads from memory, in her hands she holds a hardcover copy of her own book. At the level of aesthetics, we might be inclined to write off the presence of the book here and elsewhere as a mere prop, as a functionally superfluous design choice. Yet, in every instance—in the image of Tolstoy, the readings in *Dedicated to Mandelstam*, and Akhmadulina's recitation in *And the House Lives*—it is precisely that superfluity that makes the book's presence symbolically significant. The book does not need to be present to recognize Tolstoy, for Mandelstam's texts to be read, or for Akhmadulina to recite her own work, and yet the book is nonetheless always present, signifying the act of reading in all three instances and offering an additional layer of authority to the authors' own reading of her work.

In these and other programs, the Kul'tura channel counteracts spiritual degradation by offering a virtual space just for Russians, a space that combines the trusted cultural medium of the present with the beloved literary canon of the past. In the next section, we will see how the emphasis on written texts in the aesthetics and content of Kul'tura programming goes beyond the "high" versus "low" cultural debate, indicating not only the upward movement of the channel as it strives towards high cultural forms but also a backwards movement, where the "high" is located firmly in the Soviet past.

In Search of Soviet Quality

In the twenty-first century, debates over American television have shifted away from a "low" versus "high" culture distinction to discussions over the idea of "quality." With HBO as the example, Avi Santo argues that "quality" typically refers to the high quality of the production, acting, writing, and creative innovation of a show. The term "quality," in other words, has been used as a term of exclusivity to set HBO apart from network television, where HBO brands itself *in opposition to* the rest of television, as Santo explains. This marketing strategy is clearly articulated in the network's tagline, "It's not TV. It's HBO."[34] This argument, which Santo made in 2008, could easily be extended to more recent television producers like Netflix and Amazon Studios. And although Kul'tura and HBO are qualitatively different in nearly every way, the audience models of both channels hinge on fostering exclusivity among audiences who perceive themselves to be rising above the banality of TV by, ironically, watching *a different kind of* TV.

What is especially useful for the case of Kul'tura in Santo's discussion of "quality" is not what it conveys about the content itself (for instance, HBO and Netflix viewers pay for content, while Kul'tura viewers do not), but what it says about *how* the content is supposed to be viewed. According to Santo:

> HBO has absorbed the cultural values it believes subscribers are seeking into its own culture of production, even to the detriment of its supposed economic bottom line. In this sense, cultural values inform economic decisions as much as they are shaped by them, complicating traditional political economy arguments that reduce culture down to its means of production and see economics determining such processes in every instance.[35]

This is particularly relevant in the context of Kul'tura if we replace the idea of *production quality* with *cultural quality*: as exclusive content for a "highly cultured" audience.

The concept of "para-televisuality" adds a further dimension to understanding the kind of viewership the Kul'tura channel is building. Santo writes that para-television "purposefully relies on mimicking and tweaking existing and recognizable TV forms," and that "whereas television seeks to attract a mass audience, para-television is designed to build coalition audiences," or audiences that identify with one particular channel, genre, or product.[36] What these two very different channels might have in common, thus, is their commitment to fostering galvanizing identities around their audiences that are purposefully defined and cultivated as

34 Santo, "Para-Television and Discourses of Distinction," 20.

35 Ibid.

36 Ibid., 19 and 30.

"elite," and always in relationship to "low" culture (popular culture, or network television). Public television too has benefited from myths about elitism among its audiences. Studies from the 1980s have shown how PBS viewers see themselves "as TV's aesthetic elite,"[37] are generally more critical of television programming without any educational purpose, and often report feeling "guilt and resentment toward commercial television's alluring lowest-common-denominator entertainment paradigm."[38]

If in the case of HBO, the idea of "quality" hinges on para-televisuality, or the channel's distinguishing itself *from* network programming, then Kul'tura's attempt to build coalition audiences is more a kind of hyper-televisuality. Kul'tura does not mimic and tweak existing television forms to separate itself from the "low culture" of network television; on the contrary, it emphasizes its own televisuality in relationship to its past. This televisuality comes in the form of highlighting the channel's roots in the Soviet television system, as a way to distinguish itself from the "low culture" of post-Soviet network television in Russia. The channel fosters exclusivity precisely by being more and more like TV—or, at least, a specific kind of TV, a form of television that Russians, those who grew up in the Soviet period, have always known television to be.

In the case of Kul'tura, the desire to build coalition audiences around nostalgia for the past takes the form of returning both Soviet and Russian classics to the television screen. According to literary critic Igor' Zolotussky, for instance, Kul'tura "returned Soviet classic television to [Russians]."[39] In the words of Viktor Erofeev, host of the Kul'tura show *Apocrypha* (*Apokrif*), the Kul'tura Channel returned "a side of Russian history and Russian mentality that [Russians] have lost."[40] In an interview from 2007, Shvydkoi described how the backward-looking aspirations of Kul'tura, both in content and aesthetics, were essential to the channel's image:

37 Richard J. Schaefer, "Public Television Constituencies: A Study in Media Aesthetics and Intentions," *Journal of Film and Video* 43, nos. 1–2 (Spring and Summer 1991): 53.

38 Richard J. Schaefer, "The Forces and Constituencies of Public Television: A Study in Media Aesthetics and Intentions," paper presented at the Annual Meeting of the Western Speech Communication Association, Spokane, WA (February 17–21, 1989), 5–6, http://files.eric.ed.gov/fulltext/ED304726.pdf.

39 "Telekanal 'Kul'tura' i kul'tura."

40 Shvydkoi, "Na nas smotreli kak na pridurkov."

> You could glamorize [Kul'tura], and the channel would become more accessible and more people would watch it, but is this the right thing to do? I'm not so sure. Because in that case, the 5-7% of viewers who cannot live without culture would leave.[41]

In Shvydkoi's comments the cultural mission of the channel is mutually exclusive with modern aesthetics and high viewership. To put it another way, in the twenty-first century the vision of the channel is at odds with the industry of television itself.

One way that Kul'tura resurrects the Soviet tradition of television is in its broadcasting format. Not only does the Kul'tura channel still go off the air for several hours each night, but most weeknights the Kul'tura channel still shows the popular children's program *Good Night, Little Ones!* (*Spokoinoi nochi, malyshi*, 1964–present),[42] in the tradition of the Soviet Ostankino broadcast schedule. Rather than create its own children's content, as many other similar channels have been doing successfully for decades, Kul'tura reaches young audiences only through this Soviet-era classic, which also happens to be one of the most highly subsidized shows on Russian television today. The cultural weight of *Good Night, Little Ones!* both appeals to nostalgia and reinforces the conception of Soviet television as "quality TV." Like PBS's *Sesame Street* and other long-running children's programs (although not to the same extent), *Good Night, Little Ones!* has introduced new hosts, a new character, more contemporary animation, spin-off programs, and online components as a way to modernize its content. However, the show's legitimacy is derived not from its contemporary relevance, but from the authority of the nostalgia it evokes—what the show's official website accurately describes as its "massive capital of viewer affection, consistent positive image, and stable high ratings."[43]

Kul'tura also pays homage to its Soviet roots with its regular screening of films. In the early days of Kul'tura broadcasting, special attention was paid to screening cinematic versions of Russian literary classics, with a particular emphasis on adaptations of Tolstoy's *War and Peace*.[44] The cherished Soviet tradition of literary adaptation found a new patron in the television

41 Ibid.

42 *Good Night, Little Ones!* has been on Channel Kul'tura from 2014 to the present with another short run in 2001–2002.

43 "V efire bolee 50 let!," Spokoinoi nochi, malyshi!, http://www.spokoinoinochi.ru/about.

44 Zolotov Jr., "New Culture TV Channel."

industry not only during the heyday of television in the 1970s, when it was not unusual for blockbuster films to premiere on TV, but especially in the 2000s, when made-for-television literary adaptations became some of the most anticipated media events of post-Soviet history. In a 2017 study, seventy-seven percent of Russian television viewers reported watching feature films and/or documentary films among the top three reasons they turn on their TV sets.[45] On Saturday April 22, 2017, to take one day of Kul'tura programming as an example, thirteen films were screened: five feature films (four Soviet and one American) and eight documentaries (from Russia, Austria, Ukraine, and France).[46]

Today, there is also a significant focus in Kul'tura programming on cinema, cultural celebrities, and the cultural history of film. We have seen the prominent role of film directors in programming that has no explicit film connection—for instance, Norshtein's and Lebedev's respective episodes of *Russian Lessons: Readings*. Of the programs that either focus exclusively on cinema or include cinematic culture as a foundational component, we might look at *Cult Film*, *Lines of Life* (*Liniia zhizni*), *Cultural News* (*Novosti kul'tury*), *Islands* (*Ostrova*), *Masterpieces of Classic Cinema* (*Shedevry starogo kino*), *White Studio* (*Belaiia studiia*), *Spectators* (*Nabliudateli*), and *Laugh-Nostalgia* (*Smekhonostalgiia*, 2000–present), the last of which makes available "the highest forms of Russian [*otechestvennyi*] humor" to the viewing public.[47] Though the Kul'tura channel certainly includes foreign films in its programming schedule, Russian cinema—the history of domestic film, the lives and work of Russo-Soviet directors, and screenings of the films themselves—is an essential component of the Kul'tura channel's vision of cultural enlightenment.[48]

With its aesthetic and conceptual focus on both text and nostalgia, the Kul'tura channel crafts a particular ontology of television. By ontology of television I have in mind the interpretation of the television medium itself—not only what it is, essentially, but the experience of television viewing it crafts for its audiences.[49] First, the channel's faithfulness to recognizable tropes and

45 "Zachem liudi smotriat televizor?," FOM, http://fom.ru/SMI-i-internet/13216.

46 "Teleprogramma," Tvkul'tura.ru, April 22, 2017, http://tvkultura.ru/tvp/index/date/22-04-2017.

47 "Smekhonostal'giia," Tvkul'tura.ru, http://tvkultura.ru/brand/show/brand_id/20884/.

48 These shows on cinema culture go hand in hand with another main focus of Kul'tura programming: important cultural figures, with a particular emphasis on Soviet icons and the role of *lichnost'* (personality).

49 As is the case with film, any ontology of television must keep in mind that the idea of television itself is

touchstones of Soviet culture constructs a specifically Soviet viewing experience, tapping into a desire for period nostalgia that Rimgaila Salys also discusses in her chapter for this volume. It is not even necessarily that the nostalgia Kul'tura sells bears direct relation to the Soviet past. As Valery Todorovsky exclaimed after the release of his 2013 series *The Thaw* (*Ottepel'*), the project was "a myth, not a documentary. But this myth looks a lot like the truth. . . . *The Thaw* is not a realistic reflection of the 60s, but a feeling of that epoch and our understanding of the legend."[50]

Second, in its commitment to broadcasting musical and theatre performances, films, "evenings with . . . ," and recordings of other one-time occasions and special events, the Kul'tura channel also positions itself not as a producer of original content, but as the provider of culture—as *the medium by which culture is brought to the public*. In his work on television in the 1970s, Raymond Williams described how, in early radio and television broadcasts, "the means of communication preceded their content."[51] Though he never used the word "ontology," he was referring to early sound broadcasting and television, when radio and television were used for communicating unmediated information and state messages (for instance, during times of war): in other words, when the function of television hinged on its role as an effective way to "transmit something that was in any case happening or had happened."[52] In the case of Kul'tura, in 2015 alone the channel broadcasted dozens of cultural ceremonies and performances, including the Vienna Philharmonic, the Chicago Symphony, and the International Orchestra for Freedom, as well as the International Youth "Nutcracker" Competition and the opening and closing ceremonies of the Year of Literature event. There are also series like *The Usual Concert with Eduard Efirov* (*Obyknovennyi kontsert c Eduardom Efirovym*), which screens historical footage of notable performances from the archives of the National Film Foundation of the Russian Federation (Gosfil'mofond Rossii). By removing some of the layers (including aesthetic,

a metaphor for a range of processes and experiences, ranging from the act of watching to the transmission of data to the creation and production of content. It is thus impossible to achieve any comprehensive ontology of television, as television is a signifier that refers simultaneously to everything about the industry and to nothing in particular.

50 Sergei Efimov, "Segodnia 'Ottepel',' a zavtra—kholoda . . . ," *Komsomol'skaia pravda*, December 4, 2013, http://www.kp.ru/daily/26167.2/3054154/.

51 Raymond Williams, *Television: Technology and Cultural Form* (New York: Schocken Books, 1975), 25.

52 Ibid., 30.

production, or commercial) between the source of culture and its viewers, Kul'tura's ontology of television thereby appears to close the gap between medium and source, so that the name Kul'tura might indeed become synonymous with high culture itself.

When in 1999 journalist Dmitry Ukhov criticized the channel for "not making use of the ontological substance of live broadcast at all," I understand him to have been asking that Kul'tura close the gap between culture and medium even further.[53] Ukhov criticized Kul'tura for not producing culture live: why broadcast orchestra performances, when the channel could have its own orchestra?[54] Ukhov's vision for Kul'tura appears to be on the former end of a spectrum of media philosophy that ranges from the immediacy that Williams assigned to early television (as mere provider of content) to the complex web of creation and mediation that we assign to television production today. We have already seen how, indeed, the aesthetics of the Kul'tura channel often point to the immutable text, emphasizing textuality and tactility in a way that claims to be prior to production. Thus, where ontology is concerned, Kul'tura programming often denies its televisuality: it does not place the highest value on surpassing or improving on the visual text through the creative potential of television art, but returns time and time again to the text in its most canonical, traditional, and static form—the printed volume, the ink-penned letter, or the transmission of a theatre or orchestra performance.

Nostalgia and Euphemism on the Russian Screen

Aleksandr Arkhangel'sky's eight-episode series *The Department* (*Otdel*) premiered on the Kul'tura channel on September 6, 2010. The series is loosely based around the members of the Moscow Logic Circle, a group of philosophers who came of intellectual age in Moscow in the 1950s and whose work would later (after the group disbanded) define the philosophical climate of the 1960s. This group includes philosophers Merab Mamardashvili, Georgy Shchedrovitsky, Boris Grushin, and logician and novelist Aleksandr Zinov'ev; by extension, the miniseries also discusses the lives and work of Iury Levada, Aleksandr Piatigorsky, and others. These philosophers were united not only by their common affiliation with the Institute of Philosophy in Moscow, but by an important shared belief: the idea that the Soviet system could still be

53 "Telekanal 'Kul'tura' i kul'tura."

54 Ibid.

reformed from within and, specifically, from within the discipline of philosophy, or what Arkhangel'sky calls their "romantic passion for cognition."[55] The work of this important group of thinkers is widely accepted as a last socialist renaissance in Soviet philosophy—a generation whose intellectual coming of age happened to coincide, for the purposes of this volume, with the formation of a television system in the Soviet Union.

The series was written and produced by Arkhangel'sky, a journalist and producer best known to Kul'tura viewers as the face of the talk show *Meanwhile* (*Tem vremenem*), which he has hosted since 2002.[56] *The Department* opens with the founding of the new Institute of the International Workers Movement in 1966 in Moscow. The series purports to track the founding and development of the Institute's Department of Social Consciousness, and the scholars and students affiliated with it. Most of the footage in the series, however, comes from the Golitsyn Palace on Volkhonka Street, which housed the Institute of Philosophy of the Russian Academy of Sciences from 1929 to 2015. The series also includes footage from different universities throughout Moscow, thereby contributing to a conflation of space in which "the department" refers not to one particular place, but is a stand-in for intellectual space in general in the late Stalinist and immediate post-Stalin period. The (former) building of the Institute of Philosophy, in which most of the series' footage was shot, exists in a metonymic relationship to what Arkhangel'sky broadly calls "free thought"—those intellectual traditions and voices that were able to survive and even thrive *within* the system, in spite of the hostile academic environment of the Soviet period.

The philosopher Merab Mamardashvili, in particular, has come to serve as the exemplar of freedom within the philosophical generation of the 1950s and the 1960s. Here the concept of freedom extends not only to the wide range of topics on which he wrote and lectured (the history of bourgeois philosophy, film, European literature, and ancient philosophy), but to his very presence among the Moscow intelligentsia of the era. In their memoirs, his friends and colleagues regularly mention his refined sense of fashion and taste, which bore the marks of sojourns to the unreachable oases of the bourgeois world, like Italy and France. One account

55 Aleksandr Arkhangel'skii, *Otdel* (2010), 8 series, Russia K, Episode 2, 9:28.

56 For a brief period in the late 1980s, Arkhangel'sky worked with the editorial board of the most prestigious philosophy journal in Russia, *Problems of Philosophy* (*Voprosy filosofii*), and so his interest in philosophy is not entirely unprecedented, even if he does not consider himself a philosopher in any formal sense of the word.

recalls how Mamardashvili was reported to the Moscow authorities in the 1970s for the cultural dissonance of his bourgeois sartorialism: corduroy jeans, beautiful sweaters purchased abroad, European outerwear, and a tobacco pipe.[57] In her description of her first meeting with Mamardashvili, screenwriter Nataliia Riazantseva described how "he really did look like a guest from abroad."[58]

The representation of Soviet philosophy in *The Department*, like the legacy of Mamardashvili, is guided by the aesthetics of nostalgia. The series is not about philosophical ideas (indeed, no philosophical ideas are raised), but about a nostalgia for the intelligentsia of a bygone era. Mamardashvili, Shchedrovitsky, and others are remembered in the series not for their lasting philosophical contributions, but for their personalities, their role in the secret kitchen meetings of the Soviet intelligentsia, and their cavalier attitudes in the face of Soviet censorship. Most of the content of *The Department* is made up of interviews with people who knew these men personally (their widows, colleagues, family members), and they tell personal stories and offer intimate reflections on this great generation, from their first-person points of view—in other words, from memory. In *The Department*, thus, this extraordinary age in Soviet philosophy is presented not as a generation that lives on in philosophical discourse today, but as one that remains alive in the hearts and memories of those who knew them best. *The Department* speaks more to a mentality about the Thaw than the actual ideas of that era; it is not a series about Soviet philosophy, but about a perception of philosophy that peaked in the 1960s, with Mamardashvili and others, and that has since been lost.

The aesthetics of this nostalgia for a lost intellectual heritage are expressed in *The Department* through repeated takes of empty corridors and lecture halls at the Institute of Philosophy, as well as takes of the opening and closing of the doors to the building's only elevator, with no passengers in sight. Empty hallways and elevators not only highlight our historical distance from that intellectual moment and the impossibility of its return; these ominous takes are also a euphemism for the persecution that these philosophers experienced, each to a different degree. Among the philosophers featured in *The Department*, Shchedrovitsky was excluded from the Party in 1968; Piatigorsky and Zinov'ev fled the Soviet Union altogether in 1974 and

57 Uldis Tirons, "I Come to You from My Solitude," *Eurozine* (June 2006), http://www.eurozine.com/i-come-to-you-from-my-solitude/.

58 Nataliia Riazantseva, "Adresa i daty," *Znamia* 11 (2011), http://magazines.russ.ru/znamia/2011/11/ra4.html.

1978, respectively; Eval'd Il'enkov committed suicide in 1979; and Mamardashvili was banned from travelling outside the Soviet Union for two decades (after an unsanctioned trip to France in 1967) and in 1980 was finally given the choice either to return to Georgia or leave the Soviet Union altogether.

While Arkhangel'sky's *The Department* does not ignore the political challenges that intellectuals faced during the late Socialist period, a broader critique of the Kul'tura channel has been that its programming eschews political dialogue and exists in a "cultural vacuum," to quote Zolotussky.[59] In 1999, when the channel had been on air for just over two years, Karakhan lumped Kul'tura together with the alienated media of the Russian constitutional crisis of 1993, when tanks fired upon the Russian White House against Yeltsin's political opponents. As Karakhan recounts, "There were tanks on the street, but on television they were showing Petr Chaikovsky and Marius Petipa's wonderful ballet *Swan Lake*. Unfortunately, it seems that the new [Kul'tura] channel is also a sort of academic euphemism instead of a substantive conversation about actual events occurring in culture."[60] Criticisms about the Kul'tura channel's apolitical approach to culture continue to the present, and take their most apparent form in Vladimir Putin's identification of Kul'tura as his favorite channel.[61] The Kul'tura channel, in other words, must be apolitical to the extent that the president of the country can watch and remain unoffended.

Here Karakhan's concept of euphemism is important, because the cultural space of the Kul'tura channel does not avoid politics *altogether*, but often avoids politics *explicitly*, relying instead on euphemism as an artistic device. We can see euphemism at work in Arkhangel'sky's next series for the Kul'tura channel, *Heat* (*Zhara*, 2011), which positions the 1972 Moscow fires as a breaking point in late-Soviet consciousness. The devastating fires of that summer ignited, as Arkhangel'sky puts it, a fire that had long been dormant in the minds of Soviet citizens: the fires broke out at the same time that the country had fallen into deep economic stagnation under Brezhnev, once many of the liberal reforms of Khrushchev had been revoked. *Heat* pays special attention to the role of religion, religious thinkers, and philosophers in the decade of

59 "Telekanal 'Kul'tura' i kul'tura."

60 Ibid.

61 Qtd. from Hutchings and Rulyova, *Television and Culture in Putin's Russia*, 10.

the 1970s, where the metaphor of inextinguishable fire refers to the inability of Soviet power to stifle the religious convictions of its people.

What *Heat* does not mention, however, is that the Russian capital had just recently experienced another devastating heatwave, during which peat fires broke out in the Moscow region of Russia in late July 2010. Thick, dangerous smoke blanketed much of central European Russia, stretching from St. Petersburg to Ryazan. An estimated 56,000 people died from excessive heat, smoke inhalation, or the fires themselves.[62] The 2010 fires are generally recognized as the beginning of a new social movement in Russia: more specifically, as the end of the apathetic "noughties" (the first decade of the 2000s) and the beginning of social activism in Russia, which can be seen in rising rates of volunteerism and protests, and culminated in the protests surrounding the national elections of 2011 and 2012.[63]

Neither *The Department* nor *Heat* draw any direct comparisons to political unrest on the eve of Putin's third term, but this does not mean viewers are not invited to make these comparisons on their own. Twice in the eighth episode of *The Department* we see clips (once in historical footage, and then again in quotation) of philosopher Iury Kariakin's speech on the day of the 1993 State Duma elections: "Russia, come to your senses! You've lost your mind."[64] It is difficult to imagine viewers watching *Heat* on the Kul'tura channel in October of 2011, only a few months after the fires in Moscow and the same month as the first white ribbon protests without at least considering a connection between screen and life.

For another example of political euphemism on the Kul'tura channel, we might turn to its treatment of Russia's annexing of Crimea in 2014. Viewership data from 2015 supports the fact that nationalism was running high and that the issue of Crimea was at the center of these feelings. In 2015, for instance, the shows with the top three highest ratings were, in this order: (1) the military parade in honor of the seventeenth anniversary of victory in World War II; (2) the documentary film *Crimea: The Way Home* (*Krym. Put' na rodinu*); and (3) the documentary film

62 These statistics come from the Munich Reinsurance group, the Geneva Association, and the Swiss Reinsurance group. For the Geneva Association's informational bulletin on the Russian wildfires of 2010, see Brian Woodrow, "A Cautionary Note of Comparative World Fire Statistics, and Specifically the Case of the Russian Wildfires of 2010," *World Fire Statistics* 27, 2011, http://genevaassociation.org/PDF/WFSC/GA2011-WFS27-Woodrow3.pdf.

63 I discuss *Heat* and the 2011 peat fires in more detail in *The End of Russian Philosophy. Tradition and Transition at the Turn of the 21st Century* (London: Palgrave Macmillan, 2014), 87–89.

64 Aleksandr Arkhangel'skii, *Zhara* (2011), Russia K, 8th episode, 22:30.

President (*Prezident*), about the first fifteen years of Vladimir Putin's presidency.[65] In 2015 there were also several documentaries about Crimea screened on the Kul'tura channel. One such documentary was *Crimea: Enigmas of Civilization* (*Krym: Zagadki tsivilizatsii*, 2015), a popular-science series in four episodes that investigates the castles, caves, and other archeological and anthropological riches of the Crimean Peninsula, and which fits into the substantial amount of programming on Kul'tura dedicated to ethnography.[66] None of the documentaries that Kul'tura screened that year are political in nature, but they premiered on the channel at a historical moment when airing documentaries about Crimea could not be apolitical. What is more, *Crimea: Enigmas of Civilization* avoids explicit discussion of contemporary politics to a degree that is farcical, and the language of the documentary refers to Crimea in Russian imperial rhetoric. The voiceover of the first series opens by announcing how Empress Catherine the Second called Crimea "the most precious pearl of her crown," thereby extending the history of Russian imperial mandate in Crimea from the eighteenth century to the present.[67]

The euphemistic approach to political content on the Kul'tura channel is also apparent in *Dedicated to Osip Mandelstam*, where the political realities of Mandelstam's life and death too remain at the level of subtext. As the actors read their texts, they move about on a stage lined with furniture; the furniture is covered with white cloths, as servants might have done in an aristocratic house when the master has gone away. Most Kul'tura viewers will know where Mandelstam has gone: he spent the last five years of his life in the GULAG, dying in a transit camp in 1938 on his way to a second sentence in Siberia. The white sheets in the set design thus serve as a euphemism for his absence, standing in for the unspoken political explication. The hosts read Mandelstam's "Kremlin Highlander," the epigram on Stalin for which the poet was first arrested and sent to the camps, but the poem is referred to only as "Highlander" ("Gorets") in the closing credits, with the offending adjective removed from the title. In *Dedicated to Osip Mandelstam*, the overt political narrative is again left to the sphere of metaphor and suggestion.

65 "Samye populiarnye telekanaly i programmy Rossii," *The Village*, September 26, 2016, http://www.the-village.ru/village/business/news/246173-tv-rating.

66 For instance, *Russia, My Love* (*Rossiia, liubov' moia*) and *Letters from the Provinces* (*Pis'ma iz provintsii*).

67 "Krym. Zagadki tsivilizatsii," Tvkul'tura.ru, 2:57, http://tvkultura.ru/video/show/brand_id/59336/episode_id/1190534/video_id/1169331/viewtype/picture/.

Conclusion

Having celebrated its twenty-year anniversary in 2017, the Kul'tura channel—Russian television's "island of good taste"[68]—is on the threshold of selling Soviet nostalgia to a generation of viewers born after the dissolution of the Soviet Union. Today, the average Kul'tura viewer is a sixty-two-year-old woman,[69] and the average Russian television viewer is not inclined to watch Kul'tura at all. Though Russian viewers on the whole rank Kul'tura their eleventh favorite channel among twenty-three choices,[70] comparable data shows that actual viewership statistics place the channel at the sixteenth position for most watched in Russia.[71] In other words, there is a disparity between the way that viewers *feel* about Kul'tura and their *actual viewing practices*; Russians are more inclined to think highly of the channel than they are to watch it. Indeed, already in 1999, critic Kirill Razlogov called Kul'tura "a channel of the old generation. It is the culture of the generation of the 1960s, maybe even the 1950s."[72]

We have seen how the Kul'tura channel works to build coalition audiences from a distinctive position on Russian television: it is the longest running thematic channel in a market in which thematic channels are gaining popularity[73]; it is the only non-commercial channel left in an increasingly commercializing market; it is the only channel on Russian television dedicated to "high" cultural values; and, in a media model that is still highly influenced by state authority, the channel is, in the words of contentious politician Vladimir Zhirinovsky, a "state channel in the fullest sense of the word, because it fulfills the most important function of government—to foster patriots of Russia!"[74] We have also seen how the Kul'tura channel distinguishes itself from

68 Hutchings and Rulyova, *Television and Culture in Putin's Russia*, 10.

69 "Doklad o finansovo-khoziaistvennoi deiatel'nosti federal'nogo gosudarstvennogo unitarnogo predpriiatiia 'Vserossiiskaia gosudarstvennaia televizionnaia i radioveshchatel'naia kompaniia' po itogam raboty za 2016 god," VGTRK, 7, https://cdn-st1.rtr-vesti.ru/mh_files/001/795/Doklad_2015.pdf.

70 Ekaterina Dobrynina, "Rossiiane ne mogut zhit' bez televizora," *Rossiiskaia gazeta*, February 21, 2013, https://rg.ru/2013/02/20/televidenie-site.html.

71 "Samye populiarnye telekanaly."

72 "Telekanal 'Kul'tura' i kul'tura."

73 "Doklad," 7.

74 Shvydkoi, "Na nas smotreli kak na pridurkov."

the "low" status of post-Soviet network television by leaning upwards, toward "high" culture, and backwards, toward the Soviet past. Just as the discipline of philosophy in Arkhangel'sky's *The Department* is, to use Karakhan's term, an "academic euphemism" for nostalgia for a lost generation of intellectuals, so are the aesthetics of nostalgia at work on the Kul'tura channel. The channel crafts "an elevated and insulated space from the rest of television" around a reverence for values of a bygone era: classic Russian literature, high forms of culture, television in a pre-capitalist era, the Russian language as Pushkin spoke it, and deference to text in its most canonical, immutable form.[75]

Bibliography

Aleksandr Arkhangel'skii. *Otdel*. Russia K. 2010.

———. *Zhara*. Russia K. 2011.

De Smaele, Hedwig. "The Applicability of Western Media Models on the Russian Media System," *European Journal of Communication* 14, no. 2 (1999): 77–97.

DeBlasio, Alyssa. *The End of Russian Philosophy. Tradition and Transition at the Turn of the 21st Century*. London: Palgrave Macmillan, 2014.

Dobrynina, Ekaterina. "Rossiiane ne mogut zhit' bez televizora." *Rossiiskaia gazeta*, February 21, 2013. https://rg.ru/2013/02/20/televidenie-site.html.

"Doklad o finansovo-khoziaistvennoi deiatel'nosti federal'nogo gosudarstvennogo unitarnogo predpriiatiia 'Vserossiiskaia gosudarstvennaia televizionnaia i radioveshchatel'naia kompaniia' po itogam raboty za 2016 god." VGTRK. https://cdn-st1.rtr-vesti.ru/mh_files/001/795/Doklad_2015.pdf.

Hutchings, Stephen and Natalia Rulyova. *Television and Culture in Putin's Russia: Remote Control*. Abingdon: Routledge, 2009.

Imre, Anikó. *TV Socialism*. Durham, NC: Duke University Press, 2016.

"Ispolniaetsia 110 let so dnia rozhdeniia akademika Dmitriia Likhacheva." Tvkul'tura.ru, November 28, 2016. http://tvkultura.ru/article/show/article_id/159745/.

"Krym. Zagadki tsivilizatsii." Tvkul'tura.ru. http://tvkultura.ru/video/show/brand_id/59336/episode_id/1190534/video_id/1169331/viewtype/picture/.

Likhachev, Dmitrii. *Russkaia kul'tura*. Moscow: Iskusstvo, 2000.

[75] Ibid; Santo, "Para-Television and Discourses of Distinction," 37.

"Na podderzhku propravitel'stvennykh SMI iz biudzheta vydelili pochti 61 mlrd rublei." Krasnaia liniia, August 3, 2016. http://www.rline.tv/news/2016-08-03-na-podderzhku-smi-iz-byudzheta-vydelili-pochti-61-mlrd-rubley-/.

"O proekte." Tvkul'tura.ru. http://tvkultura.ru/brand/show/brand_id/31697/.

"O proekte. Zhivoe slovo." Tvkul'tura.ru. http://tvkultura.ru/brand/show/brand_id/59465/.

Peterson, Eric E. "Introduction." In *Public Broadcasting and the Public Interest*, edited by Michael P. McCauley, Eric E. Peterson, B. Lee Artz, and DeeDee Halleck, 71–76. Armonk, NY: ME Sharpe, 2003.

Poltoranin, Mikhail. "Poltoranin's Dreams and Hopes." *Post-Soviet Media Law & Newsletter* 11 (October 15, 1994). http://www.vii.org/monroe/issue11/dreams.html.

Price, Monrie, and Frances H. Foster. "*Izvestiia* as a Mirror of Russian Legal Reform: Press, Law, and Crisis in the Post-Soviet Era." *Vanderbilt Journal of Translational Law* 26, no. 4 (November 1993): 675–738.

Protasenko, Artyon. "B. Yeltsin 'Declares War for the Russian Tongue,' Seeks National Culture Channel." *Post-Soviet Media Law & Policy Newsletter* 38 (July 15, 1997). http://www.vii.org/monroe/issue38/fsu.html#5.

Report from the Fourth European Ministerial Conference on Mass Media Policy (Prague, December 7-8, 1994). https://wcd.coe.int/com.instranet.InstraServlet?command=com.instranet.CmdBlobGet&InstranetImage=411463&SecMode=1&DocId=517420&Usage=2.

Riazantseva, Nataliia. "Adresa i daty." *Znamia* 11 (2011). http://magazines.russ.ru/znamia/2011/11/ra4.html.

"Samye populiarnye telekanaly i programmy Rossii." *The Village*, September 26, 2016. http://www.the-village.ru/village/business/news/246173-tv-rating.

Santo, Avi. "Para-Television and Discourses of Distinction: The Culture of Production at HBO." In *It's not TV. Watching HBO in the Post-Television Era*, edited by Marc Leverette, Brian L. Ott, and Cara Louise Buckley, 19–45. Abington: Routledge, 2008.

Schaefer, Richard J. "Public Television Constituencies: A Study in Media Aesthetics and Intentions." *Journal of Film and Video* 43, nos. 1–2 (Spring and Summer 1991): 46–68.

———. "The Forces and Constituencies of Public Television: A Study in Media Aesthetics and Intentions." Annual Meeting of the Western Speech Communication Association (Spokane, WA, February 17–21, 1989). http://files.eric.ed.gov/fulltext/ED304726.pdf

Shvydkoi, Mikhail. "Na nas smotreli kak na pridurkov." *Moskovskii komsomolets*, November 1, 2007. Interview. http://www.mk.ru/editions/daily/article/2007/11/01/72195-mihail-shvyidkoy-na-nas-smotreli-kak-na-pridurkov.html.

"Smekhonostal'giia." Tvkul'tura.ru. http://tvkultura.ru/brand/show/brand_id/20884/.

"Telekanal 'Kul'tura' i kul'tura." *Iskusstvo kino* 1 (January 1999). http://kinoart.ru/archive/1999/01/n1-article1.

"Teleprogramma." Tvkul'tura.ru, April 22, 2017. http://tvkultura.ru/tvp/index/date/22-04-2017.

Tirons, Uldis. "I Come to You from My Solitude." *Eurozine* (June 2006). http://www.eurozine.com/i-come-to-you-from-my-solitude/.

Tsvetkova, Vera. "Intelligent, tvorets, nachal'nik." *Nezavisimaia gazeta*, October 19, 2007. http://www.ng.ru/tv/2007-10-19/18_bederov.html.

"Urok russkogo. Chteniia. Nikolai Lebedev. A.S. Pushkin, 'Baryshnia-krest'ianka.'" Tvkul'tura.ru. http://tvkultura.ru/video/show/brand_id/31697/episode_id/1430290/video_id/1543226/viewtype/picture/.

"V efire bolee 50 let!" Spokoinoi nochi, malyshi! http://www.spokoinoinochi.ru/about.

Vartanova, Elena. "The Russian Media Model in the Context of Post-Soviet Dynamics." In *Comparing Media Systems Beyond the Western World*, edited by Daniel C. Hallin and Paolo Mancini, 119–142. Cambridge: Cambridge University Press, 2012.

Vartanova, Elena, et al. "The Russian Media Industry in Ten Years: Industrial Forecasts." *Westminster Papers in Communication and Culture* 11, no. 1 (2016): 65–84.

Williams, Raymond. *Television: Technology and Cultural Form*. NYC: Schocken Books, 1975.

———. "When Was Modernism?" *New Left Review* 1, no. 175 (May–June 1989). https://newleftreview.org/I/175/raymond-williams-when-was-modernism.

Woodrow, Brian. "A Cautionary Note of Comparative World Fire Statistics, and Specifically the Case of the Russian Wildfires of 2010." *World Fire Statistics* 27. http://genevaassociation.org/PDF/WFSC/GA2011-WFS27-Woodrow3.pdf.

"Zachem liudi smotriat televizor?" FOM. http://fom.ru/SMI-i-internet/13216.

"Zastavka programmy 'Polozhenie veshchei.'" Staryi televizor, September 29, 2016. http://staroetv.su/video/vip/27281/kultura/zastavka_programmy_polozhenie_veshhej_kultura_1997_2000.

"Zhivoe slovo. Urok 1." Tvkul'tura.ru. http://tvkultura.ru/video/show/brand_id/59465/episode_id/1201412/.

Zolotov Jr., Andrei. "New Culture TV Channel Ready for Weekend Debut." *The Moscow Times*, October 29, 1997. http://old.themoscowtimes.com/sitemap/free/1997/10/article/new-culture-tv-channel-ready-for-weekend-debut/298341.html.

The Great Patriotic Serial: *Penal Battalion* (*Shtrafbat*), Historical Taboos, and the Beginnings of the New National Idea

Stephen M. Norris

On March 29, 2005, the organizing committee for planning Russia's annual Victory Day celebrations met in Orel. With just over a month to go before the holiday, the committee wanted to take stock. This was no ordinary committee and no ordinary holiday: Victory Day, as numerous scholars and journalists have written, continues to occupy a sacred space in Russian culture. On that day, Russian President Vladimir Putin chaired the committee, which bore the name Pobeda ("Victory"), and began by stating they had to take care of "some urgent tasks" in order to "set the tone that will correspond to the roles played by our country, our army, and our people [*narod*] in the Victory during World War II."[1]

After two mundane reports from the Secretary of Defense and Deputy Prime Minister, the meeting exploded. Aleksandr Sokolov, the Minister of Culture and Mass Communication, reported on the numerous events that fell under his purview. When time came for questions, the first was from Valentin Varennikov, a veteran of Stalingrad who became a career army officer, eventually earning the rank of general. (Varennikov had also led the war in Afghanistan and had sided with coup leaders against Mikhail Gorbachev in 1991.) At the time, he was a member of the Duma and in charge of its committee on veterans' affairs. He got right to the point:

> Who among us controls television? What else will it give us after they recently gave us *Penal Battalion* [*Shtrafbat*], *Soldiers* [*Soldaty*], *Cadets* [*Kursanty*], *Moscow Saga* [*Moskovskaia saga*], and

The subject of this chapter—the television series *Penal Battalion*—was also one I explored in chapter six of my 2012 book, *Blockbuster History in the New Russia: Movies, Memory, Patriotism*. In order to say something new in this volume, I deliberately chose not to re-read my previous work on the subject and to rely on materials I had not used in 2012. My thanks to the editors of this volume for inviting me to return to the penal battalions and for their patience.

1 "Stenograficheskii otchet o zasedanii Rossiiskogo organizatsionnogo komiteta 'Pobeda,'" March 29, 2005, http://kremlin.ru/events/president/transcripts/22888.

> *Children of the Arbat* [*Deti Arbata*]? It's a lie! It's a lie, all this stuff they throw into the minds of our citizens—it's worse than international terrorism. It distorts peoples' minds; it separates the youth from the Motherland. We categorically protest and ask for control. Now, in what time remains before the holiday, what else will television give us? Please.

Sokolov responded by reminding Varennikov that the Ministry of Culture no longer censored films. He did note, however, that he and his office could express their opinions. In the case of the upcoming holiday, these opinions came in the form of officially approved films that would run in the various festivals, including Mikhail Kalatozov's *The Cranes are Flying* (*Letiat zhuravli*, 1957), Mikhail Romm's *Ordinary Fascism* (*Obyknovennyi fashizm*, 1965), and Andrei Smirnov's *Belorussian Station* (*Belorusskii vokzal*, 1971) (the three he cited).

Later, General Makhmut Gareev, another decorated veteran of the Great Patriotic War and President of the Academy of Military Sciences, also gave a report to the committee. He too groused about the recent war films:

> On the one hand, we address the veterans with goodwill about their Victory, but on the other hand, there are these *shtrafbaty* [penal battalions]. . . . Why should such lousy films be presented by the government to the population? How can you simultaneously congratulate war veterans on the approaching Victory and show on state channels films that offend the people who fought?

What were the television programs that so angered Varennikov and Gareev, "these *shtrafbaty* [penal battalions]"? The two generals-turned-political officials were responding to one of the most-watched and most-talked-about programs of the previous year: Nikolai Dostal"s *Penal Battalion*, an eleven-episode series that premiered on the Russia channel on September 20, 2004. It was the second most-watched serial of 2004, after another World War II series, Andrei Maliukov's *The Saboteur* (*Diversant*, 2004), and the tenth most-watched program that year.[2] The series garnered critical acclaim. It was a finalist for the Golden Eagle for best TV series (along with Andrei Eshpai's *Children of the Arbat* [*Deti Arbata*, 2004]—both lost to Igor' Talpa's *Sarmat*; *The Saboteur* was a finalist for best miniseries). More importantly, *Penal Battalion* won the TEFI,

2 See Arina Borodina, "2004–2014: Chto pomenialos' na rossiiskom televidenii?," Politkom, February 6, 2015, https://politcom.org.ua/2004-2014-chto-pomenjalos-na-rossijskom-tele/.

Russia's equivalent of the Emmy, for best serial of 2004. When the series appeared on DVD, the entire first production of 30,000 sets sold within a month.

The two generals were responding to this commercial and critical success, singling *Penal Battalion* out among the others because of its popularity and explosive content. The fact that this TV series made it into the committee meeting itself speaks volumes about the social and cultural impact of television in the mid-2000s and the role recent serials have played in delving into controversial histories. The anger, however, focused on one of the interpretations of World War II made in *Penal Battalion*; namely, that the Soviet state and its military leadership used criminals and political prisoners as cannon fodder. The Victory of 1945, in other words, did not come about from the "roles played by our country, our army, and our people" as much as the state's willingness to sacrifice its own people.

Penal Battalion therefore helps us understand the ways that history, memory, and politics collided in the 2000s. In its attempt to provide an interpretation of the role penal battalions played, the series was also an early example of both the later fixation on "historical falsification" and the redemptive patriotism that has increasingly dominated Russian culture since the series aired. This form of patriotic culture focuses on Russian Orthodoxy's historic mission and is one in which Russians allegedly found their "spiritual sight" during the war. *Penal Battalion* is therefore a series that initiated and shaped debates about the recent past in post-Soviet Russia and that tapped into a religious-patriotic current that would continue to swell in the years after it aired.

Penal Battalions and the Great Patriotic War

On July 28, 1942, as the Soviet Union waged war against Nazi Germany and German troops occupied most of European Russia, Joseph Stalin issued an order. Order 227 aimed to turn the tide of the war by restoring severe discipline within the Red Army and by punishing anyone deemed cowardly. Known at the time and ever since as the "Not One Step Back!" order because of Stalin's language in it, the statement opened by giving a stark, honest assessment of just how far the enemy had penetrated into the USSR.[3] Stalin cited cowardice as the primary reason for the Wehrmacht's gains, noting that some units gave up "without serious resistance and without

3 The order is translated into English on the website 17 Moments in Soviet History: http://soviethistory.msu.

order from Moscow, thus covering their banners with shame." The result: "The people of our country, who treat the Red Army with love and respect, are now starting to be disappointed with it, lose faith in the Red Army, and many of them curse the Army for its fleeing to the east and leaving the population under German yoke."

Stalin was clear about what needed to be done: "The conclusion is that it is time to stop the retreat. Not a single step back [*ni shagu nazad*]! This should be our slogan from now on." And it was. Soviet media outlets did not publish the entire text of the order, but officers read it to every soldier in the Red Army. Stalin's slogan, however, was broadcast on radio, published on postage stamps, and reported in the press. "Not One Step Back!" became one of the rallying cries associated with the subsequent victory, its harsh measures seemingly justified by the language of the order itself: "We need to protect every strongpoint, every meter of Soviet soil stubbornly, till the last droplet of blood, grab every piece of our soil and defend it as long as it is possible." As one historian has written, the effect among the soldiers was mixed, but "the balance of the reports suggest that it was generally supported by those serving at the front lines, helping to boost morale at a crucial moment of the war." One soldier recalled that "not the letter, but the spirit and content of the order made possible the moral, psychological, and spiritual breakthrough in the hearts and minds of those to whom it was read."[4]

Stalin's pithy slogan survived the war, becoming part of the popular memory associated with the Victory (as it too became Victory with a capital V, or, as Svetlana Alexievich has explained it, how "the history of the war had been replaced by the history of the victory").[5] The content of the order itself, however, did not. The language that followed Stalin's declaration was indeed harsh, calling for "the iron law of discipline" and stating that any retreat meant being declared "traitors of the Motherland" and being "treated as traitors of the Motherland." "Panic-mongers and cowards," Stalin thundered, "are to be exterminated at the site." Because of its harsh language and because of the provisions spelled out in it, the Soviet state suppressed

edu/1943-2/the-nazi-tide-stops/no-one-steps-back/. The original Russian version can be found here: https://ru.wikisource.org/wiki/Приказ_НКО_СССР_от_28.07.1942_№_227.

4 Charters Wynn, "Order No. 227: Stalinist Methods and Victory on the Eastern Front," Not Even Past, http://notevenpast.org/order-no-227-stalinist-methods-and-victory-eastern-front/.

5 Svetlana Alexievich, *The Unwomanly Face of War: An Oral History of Women in World War II*, trans. Richard Pevear and Larissa Volokhonsky (New York: Random House, 2017), xxviii.

Order 227, for it "did not fit with the post-war narrative of unquestionable Soviet heroism and self-sacrifice."[6] The full text appeared in the Soviet press only in 1988, at the height of Mikhail Gorbachev's *glasnost'* campaign.

Perhaps the most controversial aspect of Order 227 was the creation of so-called penal units (*shtrafbaty*). In the order, Stalin noted (correctly) that the Germans had formed penal companies composed of soldiers who had demonstrated cowardice, but claimed (incorrectly) that these units had been deployed "at the most dangerous sections of the front." Stalin proposed doing the same, ordering the creation of penal battalions within the Red Army, where so-called cowards could have "an opportunity to redeem their crimes against the Motherland with blood." The Soviet dictator upped the ante by also ordering the creation of "blocking units [*zagradotriady*]" that would enforce discipline against the new penal battalions and elsewhere, stating that they had the authority to "execute panic-mongers and cowards at site in case of panic and chaotic retreat." The *shtrafbaty* and *zagradotriady* became taboo subjects after the war ended in victory, particularly as the Soviet state established a dominant narrative about the war that stressed the heroism of the Soviet people.[7]

As a result, the memory of these units mostly slipped into hidden channels. They were whispered about over dinner tables, read about only in *samizdat* literature such as Vasilii Grossman's novel *Life and Fate* (*Zhizn' i sud'ba*, 1960), or referenced in songs such as Vladimir Vysotsky's 1964 "Penal Battalions" ("Shtrafnye batal'ony")," by far the most popular source for keeping the memory of the penal battalions alive. Between 1945 and 1984, the word *shtrafbat* appeared only once in *Pravda*, in a 1958 poem by Aleksandr Tvardovsky.[8] As Soviet society began to investigate the dark corners of the past more, the word appeared only four times between 1984 and 1991, twice in articles by former members of the army. During the 1990s, as the new Russia experienced economic and political turmoil, and as *Pravda* lost its significance,

6 Wynn, "Order No. 227."

7 The works of Amir Weiner are particularly important in exploring this process. See his *Making Sense of War: The Second World War and the Fate of the Bolshevik Revolution* (Princeton: Princeton University Press, 2002) and his article "When Memory Counts: War, Genocide, and Postwar Soviet Jewry," in *Landscaping the Human Garden: Twentieth-Century Population Management in a Comparative Framework*, ed. Amir Weiner (Stanford: Stanford University Press, 2002), 167–188.

8 A. Tvardovskii, "Front i tyl," *Pravda*, February 23, 1958, 4. I performed a key word search in Eastview's *Pravda* digital archive database.

shtrafbat appeared only twice more in that publication. Between 2005 and 2009, however, the former paper of the Communist Party contained fifty-five mentions of the penal units. The reason for this explosion of coverage and memory recovery: Nikolai Dostal"s television series *Penal Battalion.*

The serial also led to an intense scholarly debate and rush to find archival sources about the units. One significant result of the series and its popularity is that we now know a lot more about the penal battalions than we did before 2004. After the series aired, major publishers printed memoirs of surviving penal battalion members.[9] Historians put out edited volumes and document collections about these units, many carrying titles such as *The Truth about Penal Battalions* or *The Whole Truth about Penal Battalions.*[10] Aleksandr Pyl'tsyn, an officer who commanded a penal battalion whose memoir appeared with little fanfare in 2003 had his account republished several times and appeared frequently in Russian media to comment on the veracity of the series.[11] Lurid novels about *shtrafniki* filled the shelves of bookstores, capitalizing on the sudden interest in the subject.[12]

In the most extensive study of the penal battalions that draws extensively on these memoirs and documents (and one that acknowledges the role the series played), the historian Alex Statiev

9 See, for example, M. Suknev, *Zapiski komandira shtrafbata* (Moscow: Tsentrpoligraf, 2006).

10 I. Pykhalov, ed., *Shtrafbaty po obe storony fronta* (Moscow: Iauza-Eksmo, 2007); Iu. Rubtsov, *Shtrafniki Velikoi Otechestvennoi: V zhizni i na ekrane* (Moscow: Veche, 2007); V. Daines, *Shtrafbaty i zagradotriady Krasnoi Armii* (Moscow: Iauza-Eksmo, 2008); V. Daines and V. Abaturov, eds., *Pravda o shtrafbatakh—2* (Moscow: Eksmo, 2008); I. Pykhalov, V. Daines and V. Abaturov, eds., *Vsia pravda o shtrafbatakh* (Moscow: Eksmo, 2010), and V. Telitsyn, ed., *Mify o shtrafbatakh* (Moscow: Eksmo, 2010). Many of these volumes contained the same articles and historical documents. This is also not a comprehensive list, for books have continued to appear on the subject, a remarkable testament to the power of the original television series.

11 The book originally appeared as A. V. Pyl'tsyn, *Shtrafnoi udar, ili Kak ofitserskii shtrafbat doshel do Berlina* (St. Petersburg: Znanie, 2003). After the popularity of the series, Znanie reissued the book in 2005. Pyl'tsyn's memoir was also published by Eksmo under the title *Pravda o shtrafbatakh: Kak ofitserskii shtrafbat doshel do Berlina* in 2007. Helion put out an English-language translation by Artem Drabkin in 2006 under the title *Penalty Strike: The Memoirs of a Red Army Penal Company Commander, 1943–1945.*

12 The first novel to appear was Aleksandr Belov, *Shtrafbat: Krov' Serogo* (Moscow: OLMA-PRESS, 2005). Eksmo, a major publishing house in Moscow, put out five *shtrafbat* novels in 2009 alone: Vladimir Pershanin, *Tankist, shtrafnik, smertnik* (Moscow: Eksmo, 2009); Roman Kozhukharov, *"Iskupit' krov'iu!": Novyi roman o shtrafbatakh* (Moscow: Eksmo, 2009); Viacheslav Denisov, *Iz lageria na peredovuiu* (Moscow: Eksmo, 2009); Nikolai Bakhroshin, *Zvezdnyi shtrafbat* (Moscow: Eksmo, 2009); Evgenii Shishkin, *Dobrovol'tsem v shtrafbat* (Moscow: Eksmo, 2009).

compared the Soviet *shtrafbaty* to their German counterparts, thus testing Stalin's rationale for establishing them.[13] Statiev notes that penal battalions have a long history, but that the Soviet state used them more extensively as front-line units, a tradition established by Leon Trotsky during the Civil War. The Nazis also employed penal units, but only to perform hard labor, not to fight. After Order 227, the Red Army established more penal units than ever before, organizing 65 battalions and 1,048 independent penal companies. As Statiev notes, however, "many of these units operated for only several months before they were renamed, disbanded, or destroyed and never restored."[14] Regarding the composition of these units, Statiev concludes that many—"deserters, draft dodgers, thieves and various violators of discipline—deserved to be there." Many other soldiers did not, reflecting the arbitrariness of Stalinist justice.[15]

After Order 227, *shtrafbaty* received more soldiers from former POWs who were deemed to have acted cowardly solely by surrendering. The units also received over one million criminals from the camps, most drafted before the order but sent into the battalions after Stalin's announcement. While *shtrafniki* could be sent back to the regular army after their terms or after heroic service, the processes to do so remained slow, meaning that many died during the waiting period.[16] Casualties ran high in the units: one study claims that the average monthly casualties of penal units in the offensive operations of 1944 were between three and six times as high as those of the regular army in the same operations, but as Statiev concludes, "no reliable statistics on the casualties suffered by penal soldiers exist. According to the testimonies of those who served in Soviet penal units, some of these units were almost entirely eliminated during a single mission."[17] Statiev's study clarifies crucial details of the units: they always fought on the frontlines, performing difficult, deadly missions that meant casualties would be high.[18]

The *shtrafbaty* perfectly reflected the system that employed them, the Stalinist state at war. Some commanders—Konstantin Rokossovsky and Aleksandr Gorbatov, both victimized by

13 Alex Statiev, "Penal Units in the Red Army," *Europe-Asia Studies* 62, no. 5 (2010): 721–747.

14 Ibid., 728.

15 Ibid.

16 Ibid., 730-–732, 737.

17 Ibid., 740.

18 Ibid., 739–740.

the Stalinist purges—were lenient to the units. Others deliberately assigned them to the most dangerous missions, including walking across mine fields, used them as cannon fodder, or took the idea that they needed to atone for their sins with blood literally.[19] Ivan Gorin, a former *shtrafnik*, lamented, "We thought it would be better than a prison camp. We didn't realize at the time it was just a death sentence."[20]

The series exposed a part of wartime history that had not been well studied, leading to serious research about the penal battalions. To understand the significance of the series requires understanding the history lesson sketched out above: revelations about the penal units, memoirs written by former *shtrafniki*, and historical documents about these battalions appeared only *after* the series had aired. *Penal Battalion* the series thus became the first serious attempt to fill in details about these units and to provide meaning to the provisions of Order 227.

Tverdokhlebov's Torment, Glymov's Patriotism: Dostal''s Penal Battalion through the Lens of History

In a November 2004 interview with the *Art of Cinema* (*Iskusstvo kino*), just after his series had aired and already caused a sensation, Nikolai Dostal' talked about why he made it.[21] Dostal' claimed he was not usually interested in war films, but that Eduard Volodarsky's script spoke to him personally because his father had been imprisoned during the war. While he did not serve in a penal unit, "the very fact of his imprisonment negatively affected his professional activities after the war."[22] Dostal' knew the series contained some historical inaccuracies, particularly in the casting of a former POW as the battalion's officer, but these minor issues could be overlooked in light of the larger "artistic truth [*khudozhestvennaia pravda*]" the series tried to convey.[23] As to the larger "truth," Dostal' pulled no punches. The series aimed to reveal

19 Ibid., 738–741. Alexander Hill reached similar conclusions to Statiev's in his history of the Red Army at war. See his *The Red Army and the Second World War* (Cambridge: Cambridge University Press, 2016), esp. 354–358.

20 Quoted in Catherine Merridale, *Ivan's War: Life and Death in the Red Army, 1939–1945* (New York: Picador, 2006), 157.

21 Evgenii Gusiatinskii, "Nikolai Dostal': 'Ikh prigovorili k podvigu,'" *Iskusstvo kino* 11 (November 2004): 20–29.

22 Ibid., 20.

23 Ibid., 22.

how Victory had been won because of the flesh sacrificed, because of the people and not the leadership, including the high command. The show also focused on how Order 227 "destroyed not only the *shtrafniki*, but also their relatives, the relatives of those who were captured, and hundreds of thousands of our Red Army soldiers."[24] "The war," he concluded, "was won in spite of everything and despite the many mistakes our generals made."[25] The series, in the end, "focused on how terrible Stalinism was."[26]

Penal Battalion became an important television milestone because, as Dostal' highlighted, it presented an important historical narrative about the implications of Stalin's infamous order. Dostal', the director, and Volodarsky, the screenwriter, provided the first meaningful historical interpretation in any media form of the penal battalions created by the order. In doing so, they did not just attempt to construct an "accurate" rendering of the battalions: they also wanted to use their series to offer a window into the Stalinist state and Stalinist society writ large. Critics, particularly nationalists and military specialists, zeroed in on specific inaccuracies in order to discredit the series as a whole. Other critics, including the two generals at the 2005 committee meeting recounted above, focused less on the nitty-gritty details and more on the supposed harm the series would do by revealing problematic aspects of the war. *Penal Battalion* provoked a number of responses and arguments, making it a significant vehicle in the revision of cultural memory.

The series, while nuanced and explosive in many ways, has a clear narrative arc. It tells the story of one penal unit, its commander, Vasily Tverdokhlebov and the soldiers he is tasked with leading. Across the eleven episodes, the series presents backstories of many of the *shtrafniki*, recounts the unit's participation in battles and missions, and provides glimpses into other taboo subjects such as life under German occupation. In the end, after a particularly brutal and senseless battle, only Tverdokhlebov survives among the original members of the unit. One other member, an Orthodox priest, survives, the meaning of which will be explored in the next section.

Penal Battalion's significance as a work of history is best understood through the journeys of two of its protagonists: the battalion commander, Tverdokhlebov, and his battalion officer,

24 Ibid., 24.

25 Ibid.

26 Ibid., 26.

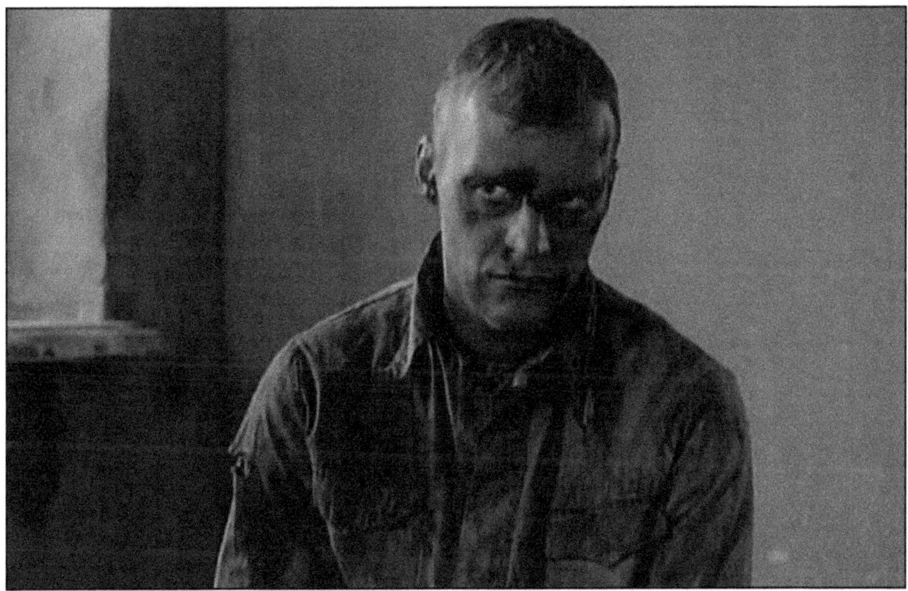

Fig. 1. Tverdokhlebov, back from the dead, is told he has violated Order 227. "In his face there is clarity, stiffness, ineradicable Russianness, or something—the features necessary for the image of Tverdokhlebov." (Gusiatinskii, "Nikolai Dostal'," 27.)

Antip Glymov. The former's journey is one of disillusionment with the communist system he had once served, while the latter's is that of a kulak-turned-criminal who finds something worth fighting for. Over the course of the eleven-part series, and through the words and facial expressions of these two men, we come to understand the nature of this war and of the Stalinist system. Dostal' and Volodarsky humanize the effects of Order 227, a point the director made in an interview, when he argued that the show was a success in part because the actors "managed to play real people," conveying real feelings that spectators responded to.[27] The human focus also allowed the filmmakers to explore a host of topics related to the Soviet Union at war, including the nature of Stalinist society, the nature of fear in the Stalinist era, the Gulag's significance, the role of violence in the USSR, and notions of patriotism and belonging. Every episode features scenes, dialogue, and imagery that would not have been permitted during the Soviet era.

27 Ibid., 21.

Penal Battalion begins dramatically: we find ourselves inside a POW camp controlled by Nazis. Vasily Tverdokhlebov (played by Aleksei Serebriakov, in an incredible performance), a Soviet POW, is held captive along with a number of other Red Army soldiers. They are offered the chance to fight in Vlasov's Liberation Army not for the Nazis, but for "Russia" and against the Bolsheviks. Two, Sazonov and Evseev, agree, because, as they state, "the communists are Christ-killers." Tverdokhlebov declines and is sentenced to death. The two Soviet recruits join their new Nazi comrades in a firing squad. Miraculously, Tverdokhlebov survives his execution and subsequent burial. He rises from the grave (literally) and finds his way back to the Soviet frontlines. There, his story proves too fantastical for an NKVD interrogator to believe: he could be a spy, as the security officer tells him. What is clear is that he has violated Stalin's Order 227. Because he allowed himself to be captured, he has betrayed the motherland. Tverdokhlebov is told he can redeem his sin by commanding a penal battalion. He agrees (Fig. 1).

Our next glimpse of Soviet society comes in the form of a lineup inside a Gulag camp. The prisoners are asked to volunteer for a penal battalion. Only the so-called "politicals," convicted under the notorious Article 58 of the Stalinist Constitution, initially step forward, grateful they can once again prove their communist credentials. Then Antip Glymov (played by Iury Stepanov), the head of a Gulag gang, steps forward. His fellow criminals follow. The unit is formed. As they travel by train to meet Tverdokhlebov, we see how fractured this slice of Soviet society is. Like their comrades who joined Vlasov's army, some of the criminals express their hatred for the Soviet state and its leaders. The new battalion members fight among themselves, with the criminals and the politicals on opposite sides: this camp society is more divided than united. One prisoner is stabbed and killed, and the two groups reach a rough agreement: the criminals agree to give up their knives and the politicals agree not to turn in the instigators. Tverdokhlebov has to try to bring these groups together to turn them into a cohesive fighting unit. He initially appeals to a general sense of patriotism, telling his new unit that others are shedding blood and defending the motherland, so they should too.

The next episode begins by exploring the concepts of patriotism, of belonging, of "us" raised in the first episode. It opens with the men in a trench debating whether they are soldiers or even men because they are *shtrafniki*. In their view, the Soviet state considers them to be neither. After witnessing Glymov's authority over his fellow thieves, Tverdokhlebov appoints him one of the unit's officers. Glymov vacillates, and Tverdokhlebov tells him about the blocking units that will enforce all battles. Glymov agrees to serve as an officer in the battalion, but sardonically responds, "Ah, that's Soviet power, how it loves its people, even those fighting for it in war." When pressed to explain why he volunteered, Glymov declares that even though he is a thief, he still possesses a sense of honor and a patriotic spirit. His village is occupied, he reveals, and he wants the foreign invaders removed. Glymov ends by noting that he has enemies at the front and in the rear, establishing an important theme that will resonate in future episodes: the *shtrafniki* are victimized as much by the state they ostensibly serve as by the Nazis they fight.

Glymov's pessimism is borne out by Tverdokhlebov's first visit to regimental headquarters. There, his three commanding officers reveal their distrust for the new unit, warning Tverdokhlebov not to run out in front of his new battalion because his new men will no doubt shoot him. The officers also tell Vasily his first mission: the *shtrafbat* will walk through a minefield to clear it for the "real" soldiers. This first mission again fills in the work of history the series engages in: the penal battalion can die by stepping on German-laid mines, by being shot by Wehrmacht soldiers, or by being shot by blocking units. When told of the order, Glymov even suggests that they attack the blocking units because they will be fewer in number than the mines or the Germans. Tverdokhlebov persuades the men to go through with the assignment, stating he will lead the charge against the primary enemy, the Germans, because "our land must remain ours!" He leads them over the top, shouting "For the Motherland!" The men follow. Mines kill many of them, German machine guns many more. A few *shtrafniki* retreat and are shot by blocking units. Others reach the German lines, engage in hand-to-hand combat, and take a trench. They have completed their task, but half the battalion has died. Back at HQ, when the most sympathetic general asks whether it was worth it and whether the retreating men were wounded, an NKVD officer tells him they were just criminals and politicals and that the officers have "operated in full compliance with Order 227." The final scene of the episode answers the question posed at the beginning: they are not men or soldiers, but cannon fodder. This is a position the three commanding officers, including an NKVD officer, will never relinquish over the course of the series. Again and again, they are willing to send the *shtrafbat* into dangerous missions, and at times even fruitless missions, to gain intel or to distract the Germans from more extensive offensives. Again and again, they describe the *shtrafniki* as shit, political filth, inhuman. The higher-ups, as the men in the penal battalion understand, are enemies too: the *shtrafniki* only debate whether they are slightly better or just as bad as the Nazi enemies.

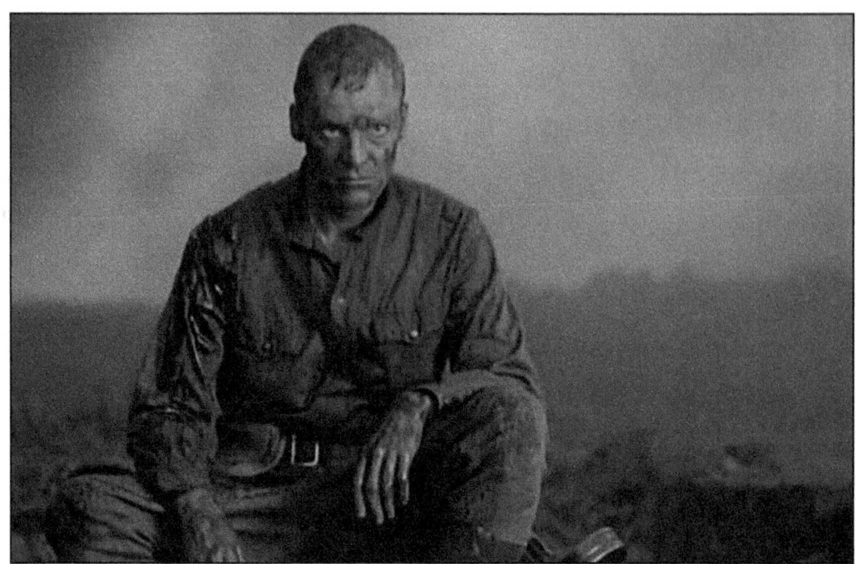

Fig. 2. Tverdokhlebov at the series end. In a sense, he has come full circle, his facial expression at the end nearly the same as the first glimpse we have of him. (*See Fig. 1*). His horror at the outset is over the violence meted out by his enemies, the Nazis. At the end, it is from his realization that his own side engages in similar violence.

The next several episodes build on the historical interpretations provided in the first two. We sympathize more with the *shtrafniki* than with Red Army officers. The men bond, telling jokes, swapping stories, laughing, playing cards. The main villain of the series becomes increasingly clear by episode three: the NKVD major, Kharchenko (Roman Madianov). These episodes reveal that the *shtrafniki* will never truly be rehabilitated for heroism in battle, for the NKVD has final say over this issue.

In the course of the series we learn the life stories of Tverdokhlebov and Glymov from flashbacks and conversations. The former has undergone a journey of disillusionment, from being a good family man and believer in the Stalinist system to a witness of the system's violence. His ideals shattered, Tverdokhlebov finds a different sort of patriotism among the *shtrafniki*. Glymov is a lifelong thief and murderer. He is also the son of a kulak taken during collectivization. As Glymov tells a fellow *shtrafnik* who was once a part of the dekulakization campaign, his mother killed his brother to feed to her other children, including Glymov. After that event, Glymov became a professional thief. When the unit is billeted near a village, Glymov has a brief relationship with a woman, Katia, whose husband has been killed at the front and whose son was hanged by the Nazis. There Glymov has a flashback in which he remembers his arrest and how he saw the multiethnic makeup of the Stalinist penal system. Later, he will recall how he murdered a fellow thief for ratting on his gang. At the front, Glymov will also shoot a fellow *shtrafnik* trying to retreat, thereby enforcing Order 227 on his own. He tells the other penal battalion comrade who witnessed it that he did so because if the NKVD or blocking units enforced the order, they would have reported the dead soldier as a traitor and his family would not receive a pension.

Tverdokhlebov's story allows us to grasp how certain members of Stalinist society could rationalize state violence; Glymov's story shows us just how violent that society could be. By the end, however, Glymov too has come to believe in his new unit and its leader. Starting from different points, Tverdokhlebov and Glymov arrive at the same place: they fight for their motherland, not for Stalin or his system (Fig. 2).

This is an interpretation Dostal' also stressed. The director, when asked about the division between "motherland" (*Rodina*) and "state" (*gosudarstvo*), responded that the two must be viewed as distinct. He expanded:

> After all, even Antip Glymov, a skeptic, a fatalist and a hardened realist, says that in addition to Soviet power, there is also a native land [*zemlia rodnaia*]. Tverdokhlebov also comes to this understanding, although at first the authorities [*vlast'*] and the people [*narod*], the state and the homeland seem to him a single whole. Then he realizes that whoever is in power, the land will still remain the motherland. I believe that these concepts must be divided. Because the authorities are not always adequate to our ideas about government. The motherland always remains unchanged, it does not betray, regardless of who was in power yesterday, today and who will be tomorrow.[28]

In addition to these stories, the series consistently explored topics that Soviet officials deemed taboo. The most important episode in this regard was the seventh, which deals above all with gender violence perpetrated by Soviet soldiers against local women. As the episode begins, the battalion—which has received new members who are mostly hardened criminals—liberates a town. One *shtrafnik*, Stepan Bulyga (Oleg Mazurov), finds a woman, Zoia, hiding in a barn and rapes her. A second *shtrafnik* comes upon them, smiles, and jokingly says "*Hände hoch* [Hands up]." Bulyga, afraid that it is a real German soldier, shoots him, and

28 Ibid., 25.

then enlists a fellow *shtrafnik* who witnessed the shooting to help cover it up. As these events transpire, we get to see a town that was under Nazi occupation wrestle with the ramifications of that experience. The reestablishment of Soviet power, as one elder declares, means the reintroduction of denunciations and state violence. The residents have mostly tried to survive while under occupation, and rightly fear what the Stalinist state will do to them when Soviet power is reestablished. Zoia's grandfather, who tells the village elder and Tverdokhlebov that her father fought for the USSR, reports Zoia's rape and that "our own" soldiers have raped her. Enraged, Tverdokhlebov orders the unit to line up and for Zoia to identify her rapist. Afraid, she runs away. Later, a still-angry grandfather yells at Zoia that she has shamed him and the entire town. No one, she is told, will take on a "spoiled" woman now. Zoia hangs herself. In its depiction of one town's wartime experiences, episode seven explores formerly taboo subjects such as occupation, the similarities between the Nazi and Soviet systems, and the violence committed by Soviet soldiers.

Meanwhile, the town detained Vlasovites, one of whom, Sazonov, is seriously wounded and captured by the battalion. He was one of the soldiers at the very beginning of the series who agreed to join the Germans and who subsequently shot Tverdokhlebov. Rather than treat him as evil, Tverdokhlebov, now disillusioned with the Soviet state he once happily served, engages in a conversation with Sazonov, who states that he too fought for his motherland, just one without the communists. Sazonov points out the irony that for his loyalty to the Soviets, "they" stripped Tverdokhlebov of his rank and sent him to a *shtrafbat*. After their conversation, rather than turn his former executioner in to the NKVD, Tverdokhlebov gives Sazonov a pistol with one bullet, tells him to use it before the morning. As Tverdokhlebov leaves the room, a shot rings out.

The final layer to this episode comes when NKVD Major Kharchenko arrives in the town. He is apoplectic about the supposed marauding the *shtrafniki* have engaged in, about the rape, and about Sazonov's death. Kharchenko immediately gets to the truth of the rape, after speaking first to the *shtrafnik* that covered for Bulyga and then to the rapist himself. Rather than turn Bulyga in, however, he offers him a deal: remain in the unit in return for information on Tverdokhlebov. Bulyga is to be Kharchenko's "eyes and ears inside the battalion." Later, Bulyga will report on Tverdokhlebov's perceived anti-Soviet tendencies, which lands the *shtrafbat* commander back in jail, where he is severely beaten.

The episode features wartime rapes by Red Army soldiers, extensive coverage of Vlasovites, occupation, penal battalions, indifferent Red Army leaders, and venal NKVD officers, almost a laundry list of once-forbidden topics. Kharchenko and Bulyga eventually get their due: the former dies in a raid on a German storehouse, while Glymov shoots the latter in the last episode for cowardice. With these sorts of narratives consistently offered, it is no wonder that *Penal Battalion* generated many responses. One of the most critical, and widely reprinted, came from G. L. Plotkin and S. V. Prishchepa. The two compiled a list of inaccuracies in the series and their account appeared in many of the publications published in the wake of the series. Characterizing the series as "an absurd children's anecdote,"[29] Plotkin and Prishchepa criticized the casting of a convicted officer as the unit's commander, the onscreen uniforms of the penal units, their weapons, the over-the-top villain, the communications used by the divisional commanders, the depiction of one soldier's self-inflicted wound, and the number of tanks used onscreen in a single battle (to name just a few). The overall tone is nitpicky, one that finds the misshapen trees while not examining the meanings of the forest.

Yet Dostal' and Volodarsky attempted to do more than just adhere to strict historical accuracy; they attempted to offer a panorama of Stalinism itself. This is a depiction of a society traumatized by the state's violence. It is a society whose members distrust one another, including national groups and internal enemies; as a result, Soviet citizens tend to wear masks in order to hide their real feelings. Its citizens whisper about purges, violence, and the Soviet leadership for fear of being found out. Self-survival, particularly under occupation, is more important to them than patriotism and sacrifice, in part because they have lived within a system where violence is endemic, boundless, and normalized. Still, residual patriotism and a willingness to defend the motherland against foreign enemies persists even though their own government victimizes the ordinary citizen. This is a quicksand society, one full of anguish and anger, one that is also afraid, yet one that has a sense of nationhood.[30]

29 G. Plotkin and S. Prishchepa, "Serial 'Shtrafbat,'" in *Vsia pravda o shtrafbatakh*, ed. I. Pykhalov, V. Daines and V. Abaturov, 454. In an even more scathing review contained in the same volume, B. Lebedev calls the serial "filthy [*griaznyi*]" and "deceitful [*lzhivyi*]." See "Pravda i lozh' o shtrafnikakh," ibid., 298–300. The Plotkin and Prishchepa article has earlier appeared in Daines and Abaturov, *Pravda o shtrafbatakh*, 2.

30 Here I am drawing on historical works by Jörg Baberowski, Moshe Lewin, Sheila Fitzpatrick, Laurie Cohen, Karel Berkhoff, David Brandenberger, and Oleg Khlevniuk.

In its depictions of this Stalinist society, *Penal Battalion* captured trends present in other serials and feature films from the 2000s. Aleksandr Rogozhkin's *The Cuckoo* (*Kukushka*, 2002) and Aleksandr Atanesian's 2006 film *Bastards* (*Svolochi*) both focused on Soviet citizens deemed "anti-Soviet" and expendable (in the case of *Bastards*, child criminals were used as cannon fodder). Petr Todorovsky's *Under the Sign of Taurus* (*V sozvedii Byka*, 2003) and Dmitrii Meskhiev's *Our Own* (*Svoi*, 2005) examine the experiences of occupation in the war. Aleksei Muradov's series *A Man of War* (*Chelovek voiny*, 2005), like Dostal"s, featured an army full of spies and incompetent leaders while the NKVD victimized ordinary soldiers. Even Soviet spies working abroad to provide valuable intelligence could fall victim to Soviet security forces, the subject of Aleksandr Aravin's 2004 serial, *Red Chapel* (*Krasnaia kapella*). Finally, Andrei Kavun's *Cadets* (*Kursanty*, 2005), based on Petr Todorovsky's experiences, examines the training of young recruits and life behind the front lines of the war, revealing a Soviet society full of "fear, hope, theft, interrogations, heroism, political machinations, black markets, prostitution, and death."[31] The list could go on and on: movies and serials in the 2000s reexamined the war, covered taboo subjects, and offered interpretations similar to *Penal Battalion*'s.[32] As Birgit Beumers argues, these films and serials depicted the war as one that no longer encouraged heroic feats. Their heroes also became victims of war, subject to meaningless violence, a shift that applies to the perception of enemies. "The barrier between 'them' and 'us,'" Beumers writes, "is washed away, and there are no longer winners and losers."[33] In the case of *Penal Battalion*, "there are no saints: there are acts of theft, robbery, gambling, drinking, fights, rape, anti-Semitism, and breaches of military discipline in the battalion." The individual *shtrafnik* is not a hero and is "turned instead into an iconic image of a man with moral qualities, a victim of his own regime and of the enemy."[34]

31 Words I used to describe the series: Stephen M. Norris, "Review of *Cadets*," *KinoKultura* 14 (October 2006), http://www.kinokultura.com/2006/14r-cadets.shtml.

32 See my article, "Guiding Stars: The Comet-Like Rise of the War Film in Putin's Russia: Recent World War II Films and Historical Memories," *Studies in Russian and Soviet Cinema* 2, no. 1 (February 2007): 163–189.

33 Birgit Beumers, "The Serialization of the War," *KinoKultura* 12 (April 2006), http://www.kinokultura.com/2006/12-beumers.shtml.

34 Ibid.

Father Mikhail and Savely Tsukerman: Orthodox Patriotism in Dostal″s *Penal Battalions*

On May 6, 2010, just three days before Russia celebrated the sixty-fifth anniversary of Victory Day, Patriarch Kirill delivered a sermon at St. George's Chapel in Moscow's Victory Park. In it, he mentioned that he had finished a new liturgy specifically for the holiday and that it built on Filaret's famous canonization of the Russian victory over Napoleon. Kirill stated that "the Great Patriotic War was a punishment for our sins" and that the Victory was one ordained by God, who had "delivered a miracle by rescuing our country and all of Europe."[35] The dates of the war's end and of this speech, the Patriarch noted, was "no coincidence," for they fell on the feast day of St. George. In his new liturgy offered three days later at the Cathedral of Christ the Savior, Kirill expanded on this basic message. The Victory meant that Russia's "spiritual sight" had returned, which the Patriarch defined as "the ability to see and to understand errors you have made, to learn important lessons from the experience of the past" so that you could "avoid errors in the future." The Great Patriotic War witnessed this awakening of spiritual sight, he concluded, for "God revealed a truth about ourselves to us"; namely, the absence of faith after 1917. With punishment in the form of Nazi invasion, "He also appeared to us and gave us His glory and strength to our people," making this a "redemptive value of the Great Patriotic War."[36]

Patriarch Kirill's new interpretation of the war's ultimate meaning came more than five years after Dostal″s and Volodarsky's *shtrafniki* had found their spiritual sight. While Tverdokhlebov's journey evokes that of a martyr, the religious interpretation of the series becomes much more overt beginning at the end of the seventh episode, when an Orthodox priest joins the battalion. The redemptive aspect of *Shtrafbat* also comes in the form of a Jewish battalion member, Savely Tsukerman, who joins Tverdokhlebov's unit after the first minesweeping mission. In his first taste of action, Tsukerman finds himself in a shell hole with a dead German soldier. He shoots himself, hoping this wound will get him out of the *shtrafbat*. At a frontline hospital, a surgeon realizes what Tsukerman has done, but decides not to report him. Instead, the soldier is sent back to his penal battalion. As we watch this story, and watch Tsukerman fall in love with a nurse

35 The text appears on the Patriarch's website: http://www.patriarchia.ru/db/text/1154861.html .

36 The liturgy appears on the Patriarch's website: http://www.patriarchia.ru/db/text/1157282.html. See also my review of Nikita Mikhalkov's *Burnt by the Sun 2* cited below.

named Sveta ("Light"), we also learn he was sent to the *shtrafbat* for punching his commanding officer, Bredunov, for his antisemitic slurs. Both Tsukerman and Bredunov wind up wounded and in the same hospital room; they make an uneasy peace. Later, on the battlefield, Bredunov will receive a mortal wound and ask for Tsukerman's forgiveness.

Tsukerman himself finds redemption. The Jewish soldier's initial cowardice in battle is compounded by his unwillingness to turn in Bulyga after he raped the village girl. After this

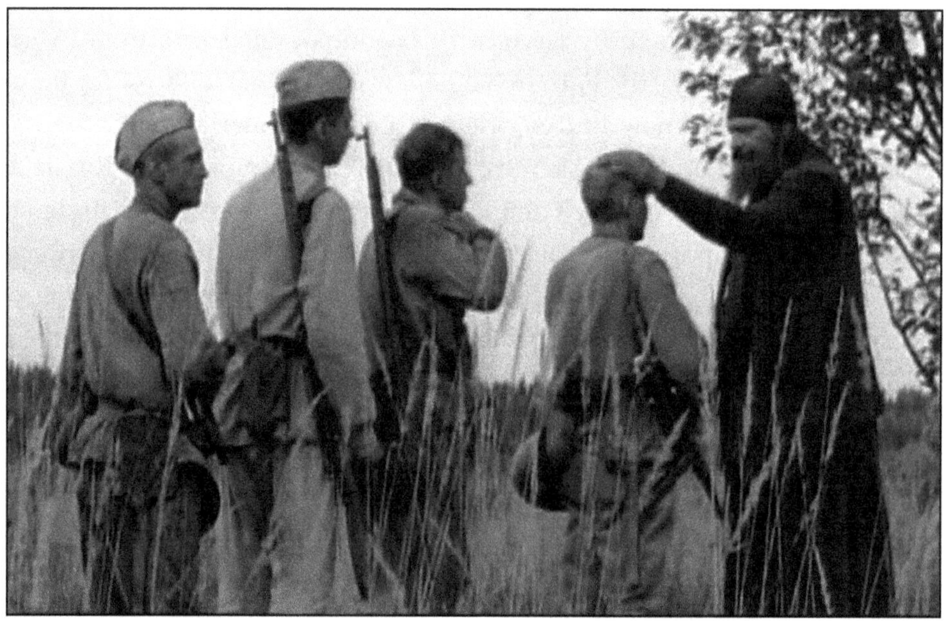

Fig. 3. Father Mikhail blesses the shtrafniki before their final battle. Tsukerman is the second from the left.

episode, the local priest, Father Mikhail, asks to join the unit. Over the course of the last four episodes, Mikhail plays an increasingly important role, offering one of the most significant interpretations of the carnage we watch in the series. He preaches the Beatitudes to the unit, leading one original *shtrafnik*, Stira (Aleksandr Bashirov), to refer to him as "our Soviet priest [*nash sovetskii sviashchennik*]." He tells the unit about St. Sergius, who advocated defense of the motherland, and about Optina Pustyn' monastery, which was founded by a thief who redeemed himself to become a holy man. He tells them about his own participation in the Civil War, when the Bolsheviks "shot priests like they were dogs" and hanged his father, also a priest, from the belfry. He promises to help *shtrafniki* find their faith. He pronounces judgment on Kharchenko after the NKVD major's death, calling him "worse than your sworn enemy" and "a demon." He sings and plays a guitar. In addition, he blesses the unit's members before their final battle, including Tsukerman and Tverdokhlebov (Fig. 3).

Father Mikhail also fights. He uses a rifle in one battle, his hands in another, and a Maxim gun in the final one. During this last fight, one in which once again the generals have decided the *shtrafniki* can be used as a diversion, the entire unit perishes except for two: Tverdokhlebov

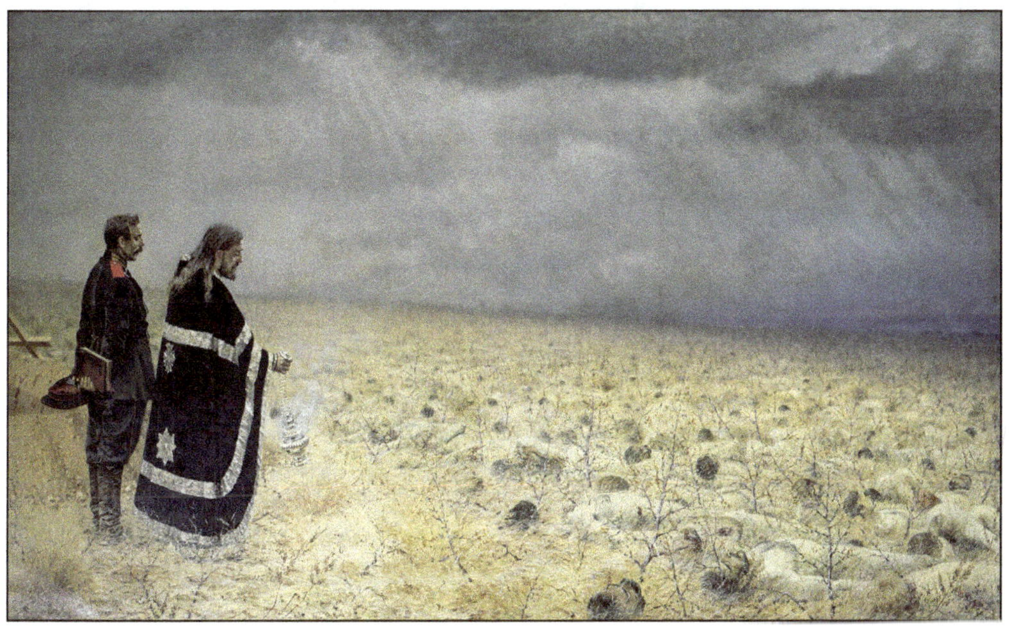

Fig. 4. Vasily Vereshchagin, Defeated: Requiem for the Dead. 1877–1878. Source: Wikipedia Commons.

and Father Mikhail. As he wields his Maxim gun, the priest gazes at the sky and sees a vision of the Holy Mother. Enraptured, he stops fighting. The end sequence reads like an extended cinematic rendition of Vasily Vereshchagin's 1877–1878 painting *Defeated: Requiem for the Dead* (Fig. 4). In it, a Russian officer and Russian Orthodox priest stand and pray over the corpses of dead soldiers. The artist chose not to focus on the heroic aspects of war, but its costs, as the field of dead covers the canvas. Viewers of the painting are therefore forced to come to terms with a basic question: was the human cost worth whatever was gained? *Penal Battalion*'s final sequence recaptures this canvas, but with a twist: while Father Mikhail asks for the heavenly father to "accept these warriors who defended the Russian land" (Fig. 5), words delivered as a

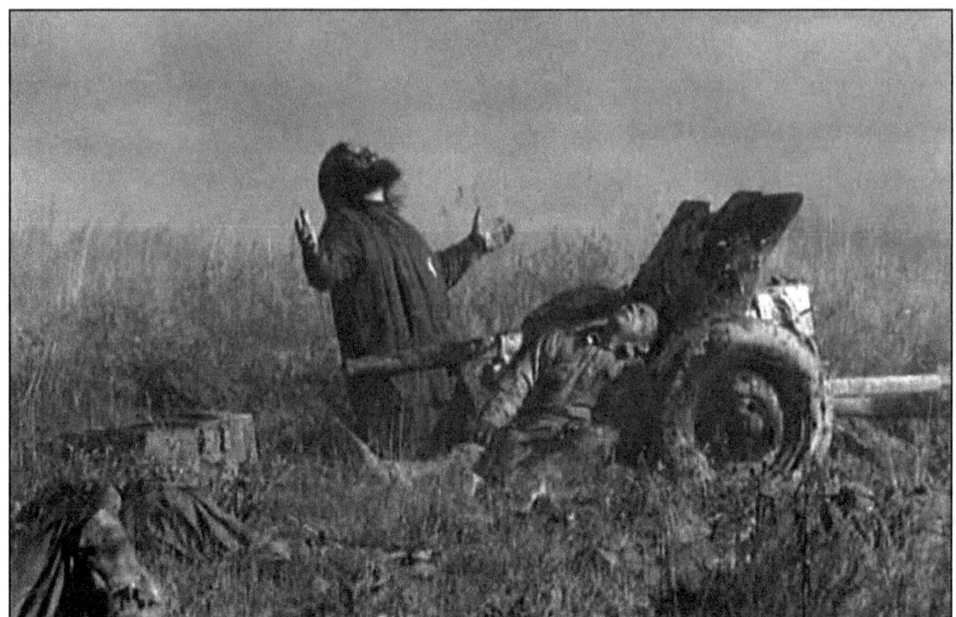

Figs. 5. Father Mikhail blesses the dead.

requiem plays, Tverdokhlebov sits apart, silent, his face revealing that he knows his men were sacrificed by the state for nothing. In this invocation, Tverdokhlebov's gaze suggests the costs were not worth it, regardless of Father Mikhail's blessings.

Dostal', in his 2004 interview with *Art of Cinema*, offered his own take on Father Mikhail's significance: "The appearance of the Virgin is a symbol of faith, a symbol of the church, which also inspired the army to win. When I read the script, for me this image was also unexpected. But, having begun to think about it, I realized that she is quite appropriate in our film."[37] The two survivors also offer an important symbolic conclusion: "Father Mikhail is a symbol of Russia's faith; Tverdokhlebov is a symbol of the Russian soldier, a monument to a soldier."[38] The war certainly did inspire a spiritual reawakening among some: a few documented cases exist of soldiers who entered the priesthood after the war.[39] A few priests, as other recent

37 Gusiatinskii, "Nikolai Dostal'," 26.

38 Ibid., 28.

39 "Sviashchenniki i monakhi—veterany Velikoi Otechestvennoi voiny," *Pravmir*, May 9, 2017, http://www.pravmir.ru/veterany-svyashhenniki-i-monaxini/.

Russian newspaper accounts have reported, did fight during the war after being released from camps.[40]

On the Orthodox website *Pravoslavie.ru*, Deacon Vladimir Vasilik interviewed Aleksandr Pyl'tsyn, the former *shtrafbat* commander who had become a well-known commentator on the units after the TV series aired. The occasion was the publication of Pyl'tsyn's latest book about penal battalions, which appeared in 2016.[41] Entitled "Crime and Punishment in War; Or the Truth about Penal Battalions," the interview gave Pyl'tsyn another chance to rail against the "contemporary myth of Volodarsky's type," a mythology that included too many battalions and too many instances of blocking units. (Pyl'tsyn, in the interview and his memoir, claims he never saw a blocking unit enforce Order 227.)[42] The former commander acknowledged that penal battalions suffered on average six times more casualties than regular units because of the dangerous missions they were sent on. When asked about the moral questions his new book raised about wartime, Pyl'tsyn responded that you "cannot judge the era of the Great Patriotic War by a peacetime yardstick," for "the laws of war are harsh, sometimes cruel, but have to be adequate for war," citing Order 227 as an example. Of course, given the forum, Vasilik asked whether Pyl'tsyn witnessed any "manifestations of religiosity" among the *shtrafniki*. Pyl'tsyn himself stated that "many, perhaps even a majority, possessed a sort of spiritual support, a belief in God that helped them to fight, to hope, and to survive."[43] More than a decade after the series aired, in other words, the most famous living *shtrafnik* embraced the idea of the series that Russia found its faith again at war. In doing so, and despite his criticisms of the series, Pyl'tsyn thus accepted the major interpretation *Penal Battalion* posited.

Just as the series' depiction of the Stalinist system at war was mirrored in other films and serials, so too did this religious element find expression in other films. Vladimir Khotinenko's *The Priest* (*Pop*, 2010) explored the so-called Pskov Orthodox Mission that took place during the

40 See, for example, Valeriia Verkhorubova, "Kak voevali sviashchenniki vo vremia Vtoroi mirovoi voiny," *Komsomol'skaia pravda*, February 3, 2014, https://www.vologda.kp.ru/daily/26189.5/3077545/.

41 Aleksandr Pyl'tsyn, *Shtrafbat: nakazanie, iskuplenie* (Moscow: Aleteiia, 2016).

42 By contrast, Al'bina Gantimurova, a veteran Svetlana Alexievich interviewed, did see blocking units in action, remembering how "our own shot at our own." See *The Unwomanly Face of War*, 37.

43 Diakon Vladimir Vasilik, "Prestuplenie i nakazanie na voine, ili Pravda o shtrafbatakh," Pravoslavie.ru, May 9, 2017, http://www.pravoslavie.ru/103283.html.

war, a mission in which a number of priests were sent to occupied territories. Viewed during the Soviet era as a case of the church's collaboration, Khotinenko instead suggests the priests helped Russians living under occupation to maintain their faith while also helping Soviet POWs and partisans alike. In a roundtable discussion held at Moscow State University about the film, one scholar called it "a new page in our cinematographic history of the Orthodox Church" because it represented "the first serious attempt to show the life of the priesthood during the war." Several Orthodox clergymen commented on the film during the roundtable, disagreeing about its overall quality, but all agreed that it was an important one, for it showed a priest serving, preaching, and performing his patriotic duty even under German occupation.[44]

This examination of how Russians regained their spiritual sight was not entirely off the mark historically, however much it dovetailed with the Russian Orthodox Church's contemporary patriotic mission. Johannes Due Enstad's study of the Pskov Mission revealed that the priests involved "soon learned that popular religiosity was alive and well despite Bolshevik efforts to replace traditional religion with Communism."[45] "Years later," Enstad wrote, "one priest would describe what took place as 'the second christening of Rus′'," identifying in the process the deep reservoirs of patriotic-religious sentiments among the Soviet populace.[46] In general, Enstad concludes, "despite the Soviet government's efforts to the contrary, Russian Orthodoxy still remained a paramount feature of what it meant to be Russian, especially (but not exclusively) among the peasantry."[47]

The most-talked-about film that also offers this basic interpretation of the war was Nikita Mikhalkov's 2010 bloated blockbuster flop, *Burnt by the Sun 2: Exodus* (*Utomlennye solntsem 2: Predstoianie*).[48] It too suggests Russians found their religious faith during the war. It too features a *shtrafnik*. The film unfolds like a three-hour version of the Patriarch's sermon, which was delivered just after the film debuted. *Exodus* opens by attempting to answer the question of

44 "Tserkov' po obe storony fronta," Tat'ianin den', March 24, 2010, http://www.taday.ru/text/357936.html.

45 Johannes Due Enstad, "Prayers and Patriotism in Nazi-Occupied Russia: The Pskov Orthodox Mission and Religious Revival, 1941–1944," *The Slavonic and East European Review* 94, no. 3 (2016): 468.

46 Ibid., 468–469.

47 Ibid., 491.

48 This paragraph draws on my review of the film: Stephen M. Norris, "Review of *Burnt by the Sun 2: Exodus*" *KinoKultura* 30 (2010), http://www.kinokultura.com/2010/30r-bbts2.shtml.

how all the protagonists from 1994's *Burnt by the Sun* (*Utomlennye solntsem*) survived their scripted deaths. The former Red Army colonel, Sergei Kotov (Mikhalkov) was not shot in the purges after all. Instead, he was sent to the special camps for political prisoners under Article 58. Nazi planes strafe the camp. Kotov escapes. He joins a penal battalion in order to fight for his motherland. When he sees fellow *shtrafniki* praying, Kotov asks the penal battalion commander: "People pray here?" The latter responds: "They do whatever they can to defend our Motherland." The comment begins a sequence—spread across this film and the sequel that followed it—of first Kotov and then his fellow comrades recovering their spiritual sight.

Valery Kichin, the prominent Russian film critic, dismissed Mikhalkov's conclusion that "World War II returned God to Russia," arguing that this is "the main historical distortion" of the film.[49] "Anyone who remembers Russia in the middle of the twentieth century," Kichin wrote, "will remember that it was a deeply atheistic country . . . that worshipped another religion: Stalin's cult." "Victory itself," he scolded his readers, "was proclaimed as proof of his genius. Now it is fashionable to explain a new tendency, to explain that the great victory was by the grace of God. This film specifically expresses this tendency."[50] The fashionable tendency Kichin referenced was, of course, introduced by *Penal Battalion*.

Penal Battalion and the New National Idea

Over the course of 2015 and 2016, as he attempted to deal with signs of internal dissent, President Vladimir Putin made repeated announcements that patriotism should serve as Russia's foundation. "Patriotism," he declared in June 2015, is "so deep and strong that no one has ever been or will be able to re-encode Russia."[51] In other statements, Putin declared patriotism a "sacred duty" and love of the motherland a "moral guideline" before finally announcing in 2016 that patriotism itself is Russia's only national idea.[52] One aspect of this national patriotism was the notion of "spiritual braces" (*dukhovnye skrepy*), a notion Putin referenced back in 2012,

49 Valerii Kichin, "Voina i mif," *Rossiiskaia gazeta*, April 27, 2010, https://rg.ru/2010/04/27/predstoyanie.html.

50 Ibid.

51 "Ideas of Patriotism in Russia Strong—Putin," TASS, June 12, 2015, http://tass.com/russia/800452.

52 "Putin Declares Patriotism Russia's Only National Idea," *The Moscow Times*, February 4, 2016, https://themoscowtimes.com/news/putin-declares-patriotism-russias-only-national-idea-51705.

a year after protests broke out in Moscow after Duma elections.[53] Russians needed these braces, he stated, in order to build a strong society, just as he stated later that Russians needed to be patriotic. The lessons of patriotism, Putin told schoolchildren in September 2015, are "passed from generation to generation" and explain "our enormous spiritual power."[54] Maintaining a strong, spiritual, patriotic sensibility allows Russians to "repulse any powerful and treacherous enemy."[55]

Putin's pronouncements reflect the ongoing work of the official Russian Orthodox Church in defining belief as an essential component of Russianness. As Zoe Knox has written, the Church engaged in a widespread "new war for souls" after 1991 because of the idea that Russia had a "spiritual vacuum" needing to be filled.[56] While this project took many forms and involved debates between the church hierarchy and laity, the official church increasingly took on a more prominent political role, offering Orthodoxy as an essential part of new Russian patriotic culture. One aspect of this project came in a renewed relationship with Russian armed forces: the Church even created a synodal department devoted to it. Patriarch Kirill himself stated: "When the time comes for people to perform their duty by rising to the defense of the motherland, this becomes the most important and primary matter of their lives." The church's duty, he noted, was to stress spiritual and moral duties of this kind.[57]

Penal Battalion, in retrospect, captured these trends and offered them to a massive television audience. In a 2006 review of the series, Alexander Prokhorov argued that it redefined Russia's last Soviet myth, that of the Great Patriotic War, by never questioning the "war's mythological status in Russians' popular consciousness." The update came, according to Prokhorov, in how

53 "Putin ob"iavil patriotizm natsional'noi ideei," Lenta.ru, February 3, 2016, https://lenta.ru/news/2016/02/03/putin/.

54 "Putin rasskazal shkol'nikam pro uroki smut i verolomstvo vraga," Meduza, September 1, 2015, https://meduza.io/news/2015/09/01/putin-rasskazal-shkolnikam-pro-uroki-smut-i-verolomstvo-vraga.

55 Ibid.

56 Zoe Knox, *Russian Society and the Orthodox Church: Religion in Russia after Communism* (New York: Routledge, 2004), 84-99.

57 Ibid., 123-24.

Dostal' and Volodarsky answered the question of why soldiers fought and died in the conflict: "Russians fought and suffered for the Russian Orthodox spiritual community."[58]

The series built spiritual braces that chafed some, but they proved to be durable. By delving into taboo histories and offering an interpretation of Order 227's importance, *Penal Battalion* unleashed a vociferous debate about the victory in World War II. It is the rare television series, in other words, that shaped historical memory rather than reflecting it. Dostal''s and Volodarsky's use of Father Mikhail also provided an early snapshot of an emerging trend in post-Soviet Russia: that of a society recovering its spiritual sight through Orthodox patriotism and by doing so, earning redemption. One of the major historical interpretations the series offered, in other words, has become firmly ingrained in narratives about Russian and Soviet culture. Meanwhile, since *Penal Battalion*'s release, the taboo topics the series explored—gender violence, state terror, nuanced discussions about collaboration and accommodation during war—have all but disappeared from the small screen.

Bibliography

Alexievich, Svetlana. *The Unwomanly Face of War: An Oral History of Women in World War II*, translated by Richard Pevear and Larissa Volokhonsky. NY: Random House, 2017.

Baberowski, Jörg. *Scorched Earth: Stalin's Reign of Terror*. New Haven: Yale University Press, 2016.

Bakhroshin, Nikolai. *Zvezdnyi shtrafbat*. Moscow: Eksmo, 2009.

Belov, Aleksandr. *Shtrafbat: Krov' Serogo*. Moscow: OLMA-Press, 2005.

Berkhoff, Karel. *Motherland in Danger: Soviet Propaganda during World War II*. Cambridge, MA: Harvard University Press, 2012.

Beumers, Birgit. "The Serialization of the War." *KinoKultura* 12 (April 2006). http://www.kinokultura.com/2006/12-beumers.shtml.

Borodina, Arina. "2004–2014: Chto pomenialos' na rossiiskom televidenii." Politkom, February 6, 2015. https://politcom.org.ua/2004-2014-chto-pomenjalos-na-rossijskom-tele/.

Brandenberger, David. *National Bolshevism: Stalinist Mass Culture and the Formation of Modern Russian National Identity, 1931–1956*. Cambridge, MA: Harvard University Press, 2003.

58 Alexander Prokhorov, "The *Shtrafbat* Archipelago on Russia's Small Screen," *KinoKultura* 13 (July 2006), http://www.kinokultura.com/2006/13r-strafbat.shtml.

Cohen, Laurie. *Smolensk under the Nazis: Everyday Life in Occupied Russia*. Rochester: University of Rochester Press, 2013.

Daines, V. *Shtrafbaty i zagradotriady Krasnoi Armii*. Moscow: Iauza-Eksmo, 2008.

Daines, V., and V. Abaturov, eds. *Pravda o shtrafbatakh—2*. Moscow: Eksmo, 2008.

Denisov, Viacheslav. *Iz lageria na peredovuiu*. Moscow: Eksmo, 2009.

Enstad, Johannes Due. "Prayers and Patriotism in Nazi-Occupied Russia: The Pskov Orthodox Mission and Religious Revival, 1941–1944." *The Slavonic and East European Review* 94, no. 3 (2016): 468–496.

Fitzpatrick, Sheila. *Everyday Stalinism: Ordinary Life in Extraordinary Times: Soviet Russia in the 1930s*. New York: Oxford University Press, 1999.

———. *Tear Off the Masks! Identity and Imposture in Twentieth-Century Russia*. Princeton: Princeton University Press, 2005.

Gusiatinskii, Evgenii. "Nikolai Dostal': 'Ikh prigovorili k podvigu'." *Iskusstvo kino* 11 (November 2004): 20–29.

Hill, Alexander. *The Red Army and the Second World War*. Cambridge: Cambridge University Press, 2016.

"Ideas of Patriotism in Russia Strong—Putin." TASS, June 12, 2015. http://tass.com/russia/800452.

Khlevniuk, Oleg. *Master of the House: Stalin and His Inner Circle*. New Haven: Yale University Press, 2008.

Kichin, Valerii. "Voina i mif." *Rossiiskaia gazeta*, April 27, 2010. https://rg.ru/2010/04/27/predstoyanie.html.

Kirill, Patriarch of Moscow and All Rus'. "Slovo Sviateishego Patriarkha Kirilla posle Bozhestvennoi liturgii v Sviato-Georgievskom khrame na Poklonnoi gore." Patriarchia.ru, May 6, 2010. http://www.patriarchia.ru/db/text/1154861.html.

———. "Velikaia Otechestvennaia voina iavila nam Bozhiiu pravdu o nas samikh." Patriarchia.ru, May 9, 2010. http://www.patriarchia.ru/db/text/1157282.html.

Knox, Zoe. *Russian Society and the Orthodox Church: Religion in Russia after Communism*. New York: Routledge, 2004.

Kozhukharov, Roman. *"Iskupit' krov'iu!": Novyi roman o shtrafbatakh*. Moscow: Eksmo, 2009.

Lewin, Moshe. *The Soviet Century*. London: Verso, 2016.

Merridale, Catherine. *Ivan's War: Life and Death in the Red Army, 1939–1945*. New York: Picador, 2006.

Norris, Stephen, M. "Guiding Stars: The Comet-Like Rise of the War Film in Putin's Russia: Recent World War II Films and Historical Memories." *Studies in Russian and Soviet Cinema* 2, no. 1 (February 2007): 163–189.

———. "Review of *Burnt by the Sun 2: Exodus*." *KinoKultura* 30 (2010). http://www.kinokultura.com/2010/30r-bbts2.shtml.

———. "Review of *Cadets*." *KinoKultura* 14 (October 2006). http://www.kinokultura.com/2006/14r-cadets.shtml.

Pershanin, Vladimir. *Tankist, shtrafnik, smertnik*. Moscow: Eksmo, 2009.

Plotkin, G., and S. Prishchepa. "Serial 'Shtrafbat.'" In *Vsia pravda o shtrafbatakh*, edited by I. Pykhalov, V. Daines, and V. Abaturov, 453–461. Moscow: Eksmo, 2010.

Prokhorov, Alexander. "The *Shtrafbat* Archipelago on Russia's Small Screen." *KinoKultura* 13 (July 2006). http://www.kinokultura.com/2006/13r-strafbat.shtml .

"Putin Declares Patriotism Russia's Only National Idea." *The Moscow Times*, February 4, 2016. https://themoscowtimes.com/news/putin-declares-patriotism-russias-only-national-idea-51705. Russian text: https://lenta.ru/news/2016/02/03/putin/.

"Putin rasskazal shkol'nikam pro uroki smut i verolomstvo vraga." Meduza, September 1, 2015. https://meduza.io/news/2015/09/01/putin-rasskazal-shkolnikam-pro-uroki-smut-i-verolomstvo-vraga.

Pykhalov, I., ed. *Shtrafbaty po obe storony fronta*. Moscow: Iauza-Eksmo, 2007.

Pykhalov, I., V. Daines, and V. Abaturov, eds. *Vsia pravda o shtrafbatakh*. Moscow: Eksmo, 2010.

Pyl'tsyn, Aleksandr Vasil'evich. *Shtrafbat: Nakazanie, iskuplenie.* Moscow: Aleteiia, 2016.

———. *Shtrafnoii udar, ili Kak ofitserskii shtrafbat doshel do Berlina*. St. Petersburg: Znanie, 2003.

Rubtsov, Iurii. *Shtrafniki Velikoi Otechestvennoi: V zhizni i na ekrane*. Moscow: Veche, 2007.

Shishkin, Evgenii. *Dobrovol'tsem v shtrafbat*. Moscow: Eksmo, 2009.

Stalin, Iosif. "Not One Step Back." Order 227. July 28, 1942. 17 Moments in Soviet History. http://soviethistory.msu.edu/1943-2/the-nazi-tide-stops/no-one-steps-back/. Russian text: https://ru.wikisource.org/wiki/Приказ_НКО_СССР_от_28.07.1942_№_227.

Statiev, Alex. "Penal Units in the Red Army." *Europe-Asia Studies* 62, no. 5 (2010): 721–747.

"Stenograficheskii otchet o zasedanii Rossiiskogo organizatsionnogo komiteta 'Pobeda.'" March 29, 2005. http://kremlin.ru/events/president/transcripts/22888.

Suknev, M. *Zapiski komandira shtrafbata*. Moscow: Tsentrpoligraf, 2006.

"Sviashchenniki i monakhi—veterany Velikoi Otechestvennoi voiny." Pravoslavie i mir, May 9, 2017. http://www.pravmir.ru/veterany-svyashhenniki-i-monaxini/.

"Tserkov' po obe storony fronta." Tat'ianin den', March 24, 2010. http://www.taday.ru/text/357936.html.

Tvardovskii, A. "Front i tyl." *Pravda*, February 23, 1958, 4.

Vasilik, Diakon Vladimir. "Prestuplenie i nakazanie na voine, ili Pravda o shtrafbatakh." Pravoslavie.ru, May 9, 2017. http://www.pravoslavie.ru/103283.html.

Verkhorubova, Valeriia. "Kak voevali sviashchenniki vo vremia Vtoroi mirovoi voiny." *Komsomol'skaia pravda*, February 3, 2014. https://www.vologda.kp.ru/daily/26189.5/3077545/.

Weiner, Amir. *Making Sense of War: The Second World War and the Fate of the Bolshevik Revolution*. Princeton: Princeton University Press, 2002.

———. "When Memory Counts: War, Genocide, and Postwar Soviet Jewry." In *Landscaping the Human Garden: Twentieth-Century Population Management in a Comparative Framework*, edited by Amir Weiner, 167–188. Stanford: Stanford University Press, 2002.

Wynn, Charters. "Order No. 227: Stalinist Methods and Victory on the Eastern Front." Not Even Past. http://notevenpast.org/order-no-227-stalinist-methods-and-victory-eastern-front/.

Orlova and Aleksandrov Redux: The TV Series

Rimgaila Salys

The sixteen-part TV series *Orlova and Aleksandrov,* directed by Vitaly Moskalenko and starring Olesia Sudzilovskaia and Anatoly Belyi, premiered March 16, 2015 on Channel One. Moskalenko's biography is fairly typical for well-educated arts people of the late Soviet era who transitioned from an uneasy coexistence with the Soviet establishment to a successful mid-level career in post-Soviet commercial television. Trained at GITIS (now the Russian Institute of Theatre Arts), he worked as an actor at the Moscow Drama Theatre on Malaia Bronnaia from 1977 to 1988. During the same period, he began publishing short stories, some of which inspired his later cinematic work. In 1989 he completed the Higher Courses for Scriptwriters and Directors, where he studied with the well-known scriptwriter and actor Pavel Finn. In subsequent years Moskalenko co-wrote the script for Vladimir Men'shov's comedy-farce *What a Mess* (*Shirli-myrli,* 1995) and directed several popular films, including *The Chinese Dinner Service* (*Kitaisky serviz,* 1999) and *One Life* (*Zhizn' odna,* 2001). He was involved with Russian TV series from their inception, writing for one of the first programs, *Goriachev and Others* (*Goriachev i drugie,* 1992–1994). Since the early 2000s he has written a number of successful series, such as *Moscow, Central District* (*Moskva, tsentral'nyi okrug,* 2003), *On the Hook* (*Na kriuchke,* 2010), *Zhukov* (2011), *Stanitsa* (2013), and *The Tiger's Yellow Eye* (*Zheltyi glaz tigra,* 2018). Most of his writing for television can be categorized as contemporary melodrama and crime drama (both often with a humorous twist), so that *Orlova and Aleksandrov* represented an opportunity to direct a major TV series based on the lives of the most famous cinematic couple of the Stalin era, unlike his previous work. This was prime time programming guaranteed to attract a large audience, and the lavish production was spiced up with eccentric entertainment, historical anecdotes, tales of tragic lives, a fascination with sex and power, and elegant period mise-en-scènes.

Middle-aged and older audiences, familiar with Orlova and Aleksandrov's classic films, awaited the series with high expectations; uninformed younger viewers—with curiosity. Viewer reactions to *Orlova and Aleksandrov* were predictable, focusing on lack of physical resemblance and expecting imitators to surpass or at least equal the original performers: Sudzilovskaia looks nothing like Liubov' Orlova and besides, she can't sing; Lavrenty Beria, Mikhail Kalinin, and the other luminaries are cartoon characters, as usual; this is a slander on the Soviet era; why does Joseph Stalin clasp his hands below the waist just like Adolf Hitler, and so on.[1] However, the narrative paradigm of the TV series as an entertainment biopic, along with the devices used to construct these lives, are of greater interest than arguments over physical resemblance.

Orlova and Aleksandrov is modeled structurally on the celebratory entertainer biopic of the American studio era (1920s–1960s), still the urtext for American TV biopics of the famous and a model for Russian TV biopics, but the series also works to mythologize the Soviet past and inscribe post-Soviet establishment values through fictional interpolations.[2] Liubov' Orlova was the most popular female film star of High Stalinism and her husband, Grigory Aleksandrov, was the premiere director of musical comedies starring his wife. Aleksandrov's musical comedy films convey the energy and optimism of the young Soviet state; everything else, such as arrests or food and housing shortages, is invisible. The TV series deals with life behind the camera, making the invisible visible, attempting to recover the reputation of the notorious couple from attacks that began with de-Stalinization and continued through perestroika era revelations. Using the conventions of the biopic, *Orlova and Aleksandrov* reframes their lives for next-generation audiences by propagating compensatory family, gender, and religious beliefs that reflect post-Soviet establishment values. Concurrently (and self-reflexively) the series seeks to reclaim figures in the Soviet film industry of the 1930s.

1 See "Orlova i Aleksandrov (2015) obsuzhdenie," Kinoteatr.ru, http://www.kino-teatr.ru/kino/movie/ros/107171/forum/. For information on the making of the TV series, see "Orlova i Aleksandrov smenili 40 parikov na dvoikh," Vokrug.tv, http://www.vokrug.tv/product/show/orlova_i_aleksandrov/, and Alina Babina, "'Orlova i Aleksandrov': Kak snimali serial," Vokrug.tv, http://www.vokrug.tv/article/show/Orlova_i_Aleksandrov_kak_snimali_serial_47118.

2 The biopic has always been a popular film genre in the United States, especially the category of lives of entertainers and creative artists. In the United States between 1927 and 1960 they were the subjects of thirty-six percent of all biopics; between 1951 and 1960 the figure rose to forty-two percent (George F. Custen, *Bio/Pics. How Hollywood Constructed Public History* [New Brunswick: Rutgers University Press, 1992], 206). While film biopics of the studio era were concerned with celebrities, about forty percent of American TV biopics, beginning in the 1970s, developed a second line focusing on ordinary people who had experienced something extraordinary. (An example is *The Brook Ellison Story* (2004), about an eleven-year-old paraplegic who succeeds against all odds.) In these TV biopics a life need not be meritorious or instructive; it has only to be known (Custen, *Bio/Pics*, 220, 222). The American biopic has since evolved into naturalistic, auteurist, parodic, and neoclassical (blended) forms. (Dennis Bingham, *Whose Lives Are They Anyway? The Biopic as Contemporary Film Genre* [New Brunswick and London: Rutgers University Press, 2010], 17). However, entertainer TV biopics and miniseries have always remained popular in the United States, and many of these still follow the conventions of the studio-era film biopic.

In the strict definition of cinematic biopic, a director makes the conscious choice to tell the story of a known person using her or his real name, and audiences therefore have previous knowledge or expectation of what they are likely to see.[3] Biopics that do not use the real names of recognizable individuals are then supposedly less bound by the truth. In theory, the biopic is limited by the premise of reality, the obligation to present actual events from the life of the subject. Few studio-era directors, however, were constrained by the truth and the same mind-set pervades *Orlova and Aleksandrov*. For example, in 1952 Orlova fell ill from a poisoned thorn in a bouquet of black and white roses handed to her after a concert in Lviv, where anti-Russian sentiment was strong. The perpetrator of the crime was never identified.[4] The TV series transforms this actual event into a plot by the jealous Beria to get rid of Stalin's favorite movie star.

2005 witnessed a substantial increase in the production of Russian TV series, which fell into the usual categories of melodrama, crime/detective drama, and comedy, but which was also notable for a surge in military/spy dramas, in accord with the rhetoric of the Putin regime. Biopics comprise a relatively small part of the corpus, averaging approximately two to four series annually, and reaching a high of seven in 2006, 2011, and 2015.[5] The preponderance of biographical series deals with figures from Russian pre-revolutionary and—to a lesser degree—Soviet history. Examples include: *Brezhnev* (2005), *Ivan the Terrible* (*Ivan Groznyi*, 2009), *Rasputin* (2011), *Furtseva* (2011, about Ekaterina Furtseva, minister of culture from 1960 to 1974), *Ekaterina* and its sequels (2014–2016, about Catherine the Great), *Trotsky* (2017), and *Svetlana* (2018, about Stalin's daughter, Svetlana Allilueva). Biographies of arts figures comprise the second most popular subcategory, for example: *Esenin* (2005), *From Flame and Light* (*Iz plamia i sveta,* 2006, about the poet Mikhail Lermontov), *Dostoevsky* (2010), and *Zoia,* (2010, about the actress Zoia Fedorova). However, fully half of biopics on arts figures have singer-entertainers as their subjects, as producers realized the value of preexisting audience recognition of stars, the visual-aural dramatic and nostalgic appeal of music in singers' biopics, and the melodramatic potential of entertainers' lives. These include: *Utesov. A Lifelong Song* (*Utesov. Pesnia dlinoiu*

3 Ellen Chesire, *Bio-Pics. A Life in Pictures* (London and New York: Wallflower Press, 2015), 6.

4 Nonna Golikova, *Liubov' Orlova* (Moscow: Molodaia gvardiia, 2014), 74, http://e-libra.ru/read/364617-lyubov-orlova.html.

5 My source is *Kinoteatr.ru,* but I avoid attempting to calculate exact figures because I am unsure of the completeness of listings.

v zhizn', 2006, about the famous band-leader, singer, and comic actor), *She Couldn't Any Other Way* (*Ona ne mogla inache*, 2012, about the singer Valentina Tolkunova), *Legends about Krug* (*Legendy o Kruge*, 2012, about the bard Mikhail Krug), *Anna German. Secret of the White Angel* (*Anna German. Taina belogo angela*, 2012, about the Polish singer), *Liudmila* (2013, about beloved folk singer Liudmila Zykina), *Petr Leshchenko* (2013, about the Russian-Romanian singer of European renown who died in a Soviet prison hospital), *Liudmila Gurchenko* (2015, about the popular actress, singer, and entertainer), *These Eyes Opposite* (*Eti glaza naprotiv*, 2016, about the singer Valery Obodzinsky), and *Chaliapin. First People's Artist* (*Shaliapin. Pervyi narodnyi*, 2016).[6]

Isaak Dunaevsky's music and Nikolai Dobrynin's dubbed performances of Leonid Utesov songs noticeably enhance *Orlova and Aleksandrov*. However, the series reproduces only one production number, Aniuta and Kostia on the stage of the Bol'shoi Theatre at the end of *Jolly Fellows* (*Veselye rebiata*, 1934), probably because Sudzilovskaia was unable to match Orlova's singing and gestural expressiveness. Singing is much more prominent in other entertainer TV series, such as *She Couldn't Any Other Way*, *Legends about Krug*, and *Petr Leshchenko*. In recent Russian TV series, the entertainers' "feelings" (primarily love, sex, jealousy, and betrayal) are highlighted, assimilating the elements central to fictional TV melodramas.[7] *Orlova and Aleksandrov* is thus an attractive vehicle which combines both emotion and performance.

Borrowing from the Cinematic Biopic

Both Soviet and post-Soviet scriptwriters and directors were familiar with American studio-era classics, first screened in closed sessions for professionals, then released selectively as trophy films, and finally freely available to the public after perestroika. Like the cinematic biopic, *Orlova and Aleksandrov* uses mediating sources (memoirs, TV specials) rather than first-hand material to construct its narrative. Aleksandrov published two, not fully reliable, memoirs and after 1997 there was a flood of biographies and memoirs about Orlova and Aleksandrov,

6 The title of the Chaliapin series appropriates Russian pre-revolutionary culture for the post-Soviet present, producing attractive traditional material for contemporary performers. *Vysotskii. Four Hours of Real Life* (*Vysotsky. Chetyre chasa nastoiashchei zhizni*, 2012) was originally released as a feature film, *Vysotsky. Thank you for Being Alive* (*Vysotsky. Spasibo, chto zhivoi*, 2011).

7 On emotions in non-entertainer TV series, see Vladimir Ruvinskii, "Fabrika eskapistskikh mifov. Real'nost': versiia serialov," *Iskusstvo kino* 10 (October 2016), http://www.kinoart.ru/archive/2016/10.

separately or together, many of them repeating sensational stories about the couple that provided grist for the TV series mill.[8] Scriptwriters Tat'iana and Vladimir Sotnikov and Anna Berseneva studied these and other period materials assiduously. For example, Chairman of the Committee for Cinema Affairs Semen Dukel'sky's obsession with using twenty-four-hour (train) time and his scolding Aleksandrov for not using it, is borrowed from Mikhail Romm's memoirs, and it was Romm, not Aleksandrov, who experienced Dukel'sky's wrath.[9] At times

8 G. V. Aleksandrov, *Gody poiskov i truda* (Moscow: Soiuz kinematografistov SSSR, 1975), idem, *Epokha i kino* (Moscow: Izdatel'stvo politicheskoi literatury, 1976). Selected biographical publications on the couple: I. D. Frolov, *Grigorii Aleksandrov* (Moscow: Iskusstvo, 1976), A. V. Romanov, *Liubov' Orlova v iskusstve i v zhizni* (Moscow: Iskusstvo, 1987), D. A. Shcheglov, *Liubov' i maska* (Moscow: Olimp, 1997), I. D. Frolov, *Liubov' Orlova v grime i bez grima* (Moscow: Panorama, 1997), Mark Kushnirov, *Svetlyi put', ili Charli i Spenser* (Moscow: Terra-Knizhnyi klub, 1998), Iu. Saakov, *Liubov' Orlova. 100 bylei i nebylits* (Moscow: Algoritm, 2002), D. A. Shcheglov, *Liubov' Orlova: Zhizn' i tvorchestvo* (Moscow: Eksmo, 2002), Iu. Saakov, *Liubov' Orlova i Grigorii Aleksandrov* (Moscow: Algoritm, 2005), Nonna Golikova, *Aktrisa i rezhisser: svetlyi put' Liubovi Orlovoi i Grigoriia Aleksandrova* (Moscow: Vagrius, 2005), Iu. Saakov, *Liubov' Orlova. Superzvezda na fone epokhi* (Moscow: Algoritm, 2007), A. N. Khort, *Liubov'* Orlova (Moscow: Molodaia gvardiia, 2007), L. V. Aleksandrova, *Pod sozvezdiem liubvi: Grigorii Aleksandrov—Liubov' Orlova* (Rzhev: Rzhevskaia tipografiia, 2008), Nikolai Nadezhdin, *Grigorii Aleksandrov i Liubov' Orlova: Liubov' na dvoikh* (Moscow: Maior, 2010), Iu. Saakov, *Neizvestnaia Orlova. 100 anekdotov pro zvezdu, ee muzha i S. Eizenshteina* (Moscow: Algoritm, 2011), A. N. Khort, *Liubov' Orlova. Simvol epokhi sotsializma* (Moscow: Veche, 2013), G. V. Aleksandrov, *Moia zhena Liubov' Orlova. Perepiska na lezvii nozha*, comp. Iu. Saakov (Moscow: Algoritm, 2014), Mark Kushnirov, *Liubov' Orlovoi i Aleksandrova. Zhizn' kak kino* (Moscow: Eksmo, 2015), Liubov' Orlova, *O Staline s liubov'iu* (Moscow: Iauza-Press, 2015).

Some examples of anachronisms in the TV series: Orlova worked as an accompanist to silent films in the early 1920s, but in the series she accompanies Chaplin's *Gold Rush* (1925); Kirov was assassinated on December 1, 1934, but the series shows summer outside the window; Stalin approves *Potemkin*, however he was not yet all-powerful in 1925; Beria makes advances to Orlova in 1934–1935, but he was not in Moscow until 1938; German bombers appear in the sky over Riga in 1941 at a daytime Baltflot concert, signaling the beginning of the war, however the planes actually appeared at 4 a.m.; Erdman writes the minister of cinematography removing his name from the *Jolly Fellows* titles, but the ministry was created only during the summer of 1946.

9 After the arrest of Boris Shumiatsky in January 1938, NKVD officer Dukel'sky (1892–1960) was appointed to administer Soviet cinema. Romm recalled: "[Dukel'sky] looks at me, 'Who are you?' I answer: 'I'm Romm, the film director. You sent for me.'

—When?

—For two o'clock.

—And what is it now?

—Two o'clock.

—Fourteen! Fourteen! Two o'clock is at night, during the day it's fourteen. You should learn this, just in case, Comrade Director. You arts workers aren't accustomed to order, but there will be order. Fourteen o'clock during the day; two o'clock at night."

(Mikhail Romm, *Ustnye rasskazy* [Moscow: Kinotsentr, 1991], http://royallib.com/read/romm_mihail/ustnie_rasskazi.html#0).

the scenario seems to be written for the cognoscenti, not millennial viewers. For example, the "Orlova syndrome," a pathological imitation of the star's appearance recognized by 1930s medicine (her bleached blonde hair, short hairstyle, and clothing preferences) is shown in the film, but without explanation. In another segment Orlova is having a suit fitted for a Kremlin reception by one Nadezhda Petrovna, without naming her as Lamanova, the most fashionable pre-revolutionary and Soviet women's clothing designer.

The biopic is an impure genre because it may overlap with other forms, such as the western or gangster film and often uses the conventions of a genre or mode for its structure. In its sixteen parts *Orlova and Aleksandrov* includes historical drama (purges in the film industry), slapstick comedy (the filming of *Jolly Fellows* with its drunken piglet, Fig. 1), absurdist comedy (Faina Ranevskaia's crazy lady act to avoid being recruited as an NKVD informer and Aleksandrov's excuse of urinary incontinence at meetings to avoid Dukel'sky's pressure to join the Party), the detective story (finding the perpetrator of the black rose poisoning),

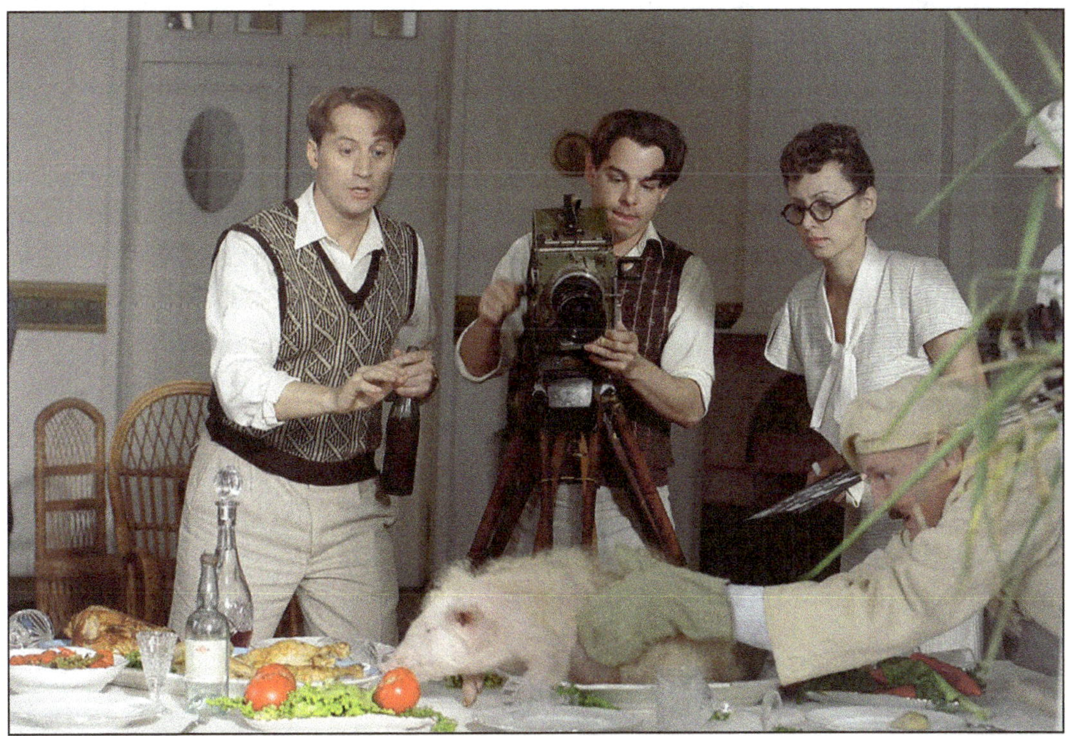

Fig. 1. Animal antics in *Jolly Fellows*.

and romantic melodrama front and center (the Orlova-Aleksandrov love story). Nevertheless, the TV series mainly follows the celebratory biopic paradigm concerned with climbing the ladder of success. American studio-era biopics all contained some variation on three moves: the big break (an opportunity to display talent or simply a lucky opportunity), resistance, and the struggle between innovation and tradition.[10] Orlova's big break is the lead in Vladimir Nemirovich-Danchenko's production of *Pericola,* a Jacques Offenbach operetta, after spending seven years in the corps de ballet. Aleksandrov's musical talent amuses Stalin and leads Boris Shumiatsky, the head of the film industry, to select him to make a musical comedy. Musicians from RAPM (the Russian Association of Proletarian Musicians) and Old Bolsheviks, such as Andrei Bubnov, the head of Narkompros (The People's Commissariat of Enlightenment), all resist what they consider to be frivolous, bourgeois fare in *Jolly Fellows.* The struggle between innovation and tradition has to do with the acceptance of comedy into the Stalinist film canon, along with the introduction of jazz in popular music and film.

Entertainment biopics have a limited menu of accompanying discourses, namely romance, the role of family and friends, and the idea of fame as a community judgment.[11] In biopics Great Work is accompanied by Great Love, which makes a life fully cinematic. The prominent *Orlova and Aleksandrov* love story here is more than an accompanying discourse but is just as important as the ladder of success, which corresponds to the recent TV series emphasis on the star's personal life and emotions as the most engaging angle of entertainer biopics. In studio-era entertainer biopics the family is overwhelmingly a force of resistance to the hero or heroine's aspirations. In *Orlova and Aleksandrov* her mother and especially sister Nonna support Orlova's theatrical success enthusiastically, until she becomes a famous film star. Then the sister moves out and the mother wants to leave because Liuba has become too "categorical" (read domineering), and both soon disappear from the narrative, although in real life Orlova remained close to them for the rest of their lives. In the film biopic, friends of the star either explain his or her greatness or convey uncomfortable truths.[12] Nikolai Erdman, who worked on both *Jolly Fellows* and *Volga-Volga* (1938), explains the success of the former: "There is something in this animal humor. Grisha senses the time—loutish, disgustingly vile, two-

10 Custen, *Bio/Pics*, 206.

11 Ibid., 148–149.

12 Ibid., 153.

faced, deceitful." Eisenstein predicts with his usual directness: "A bad film, awful, but it'll be successful." Aleksandrov's cameraman Vladimir Nil'sen grudgingly acknowledges: "The most terrible thing is that this will become the leading style." Friends and colleagues thus explain Aleksandrov's "greatness," although they do not approve. Erdman also serves as truthteller after Aleksandrov persuades him to remove his name from the credits for *Jolly Fellows*: "Do you remember Koz'ma Prutkov's seventy-fourth aphorism? Having lied once, who will believe you?" Commenting on *The Radiant Path* (*Svetlyi put'*, 1940), Erdman scolds Aleksandrov: "You simpleton. Someday you'll be ashamed that you filmed this rubbish." Community judgment in the TV series is shown via the crowds at Orlova's concerts, but here the gatekeeper to fame is obviously Stalin, who vetted every film.

Orlova and Aleksandrov also employs the formal devices biopics used to fit biography into cinematic conventions. Two separate events may be combined for greater dramatic effect and temporal economy: in the TV series the story of Orlova's first failed screentest because of a small mole on her face is combined with a fictional audition for Aleksandrov and his assistant, with performance help from Utesov. Documentary footage from Kirov's funeral, scenes from *Potemkin* and from Aleksandrov's films add to the appearance of verisimilitude in the narrative, a frequent device in the biopic which, in this instance, furthers the mythmaking of *Orlova and Aleksandrov*.

The biopic typically begins in medias res when the hero/heroine is past the age to be heavily influenced by family. In place of family as model of causality Hollywood biopics inserted self-invention, which is the most common American form of personality construction.[13] A star is allowed to invent his or her own future which evolves into the cult of the individual acting ethically in a free environment.[14] *Orlova and Aleksandrov* begins with the couple as young adults. Aleksandrov has no past when he and Pyr'ev arrive in Moscow and impress Eisenstein in audition through self-invention (talent and spontaneity) as the latter exclaims, "Kakoi zhivotnyi magnetism, zveri. Iz nikh zhizn' pret, b'et kliuchom!" ("What animal magnetism, wild animals. Life is bursting out of them, they're so alive!"). The remainder of the series, mostly set during High Stalinism, has little to do with the individual acting ethically in a free environment—in fact, quite the opposite. In the early years of their careers, fellow director Ivan

13 Ibid., 148–149.

14 Ibid., 150–151.

Pyr'ev defines Aleksandrov's life ethic with prophetic perspicacity: "The circus performer—he's been balancing his entire life!"[15]

Flashbacks were popular in studio-era biopics.[16] Daryl Zanuck, who oversaw many of these films, insisted that each give a clear explanation for the greatness achieved by the entertainer.[17] In *Orlova and Aleksandrov* the flashback reveals the reason, the impetus to fame: as a little girl, Orlova sang with Chaliapin and she keeps a photograph of the performance among her most treasured possessions (Fig. 2). In the TV series flashback Chaliapin murmurs: "She does sing well. A marvelous little girl." On the back of the photo he writes: "May the Lord keep angel Liubochka. May you have an enormous future."[18] His words, the childhood signifier of future greatness, sustain and motivate Orlova in difficult moments—during the family's poverty of the early 1920s and after her marriage to the unloved but well-placed Commissar Andrei Berzin.

Since the success of the love story in *Orlova and Aleksandrov* is parallel and equal in importance to the star's climbing the ladder of professional success, it too must derive from a single source, like Chaliapin's prophecy of Liubochka's future. As in a typical fairytale, love is predestined. In the early 1920s, while bringing milk to sell in Moscow, Orlova is attacked by a knife-wielding thief demanding her (non-existent) profits. Aleksandrov and Pyr'ev, newly arrived from Siberia, come upon the struggling victim, chase off the thief, and try to calm the hysterical girl who now attacks them, pulling a metal button off Aleksandrov's Red Army coat, which she keeps with the treasured Chaliapin photo. Soon afterward fate arranges another intersection of destinies: Aleksandrov's two future wives (Ol'ga Ivanova and Orlova) happen to be present at Aleksandrov and Pyr'ev's acrobatic auditions for Eisenstein's Proletkul't theatre.[19] True love as destiny is hammered home via a folkloric cliché: Orlova calls up the face of her

15 In his youth Aleksandrov worked for a brief time in a circus as a tightrope walker and acrobat. His skills came in handy when acting in Eisenstein's *Wise Man* (*Mudrets*, 1923).

16 Custen, *Bio/Pics*, 149.

17 Ibid., 18.

18 According to Nonna Golikova, Orlova's grand-niece, after the performance of a children's play *Mushroom Hullabaloo* (*Gribnoi perepolokh*), Chaliapin actually exclaimed, "This little girl will be a fa-a-a-mous actress!" (Golikova, *Liubov' Orlova*, 34).

19 Both women also audition for Eisenstein and both are rejected.

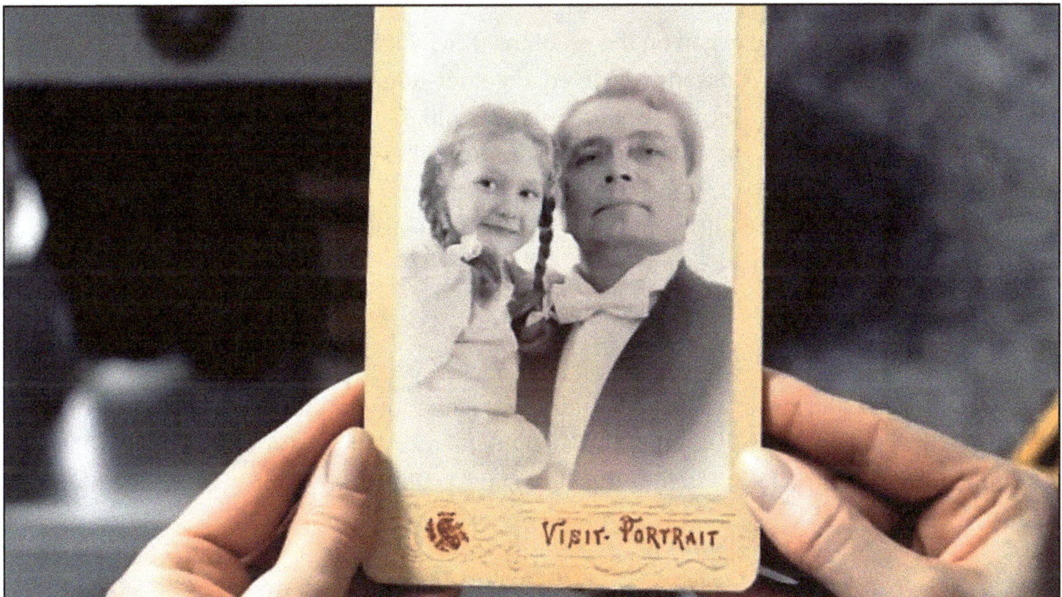

Fig. 2. The treasured photograph of Orlova with Chaliapin.

future intended through a girls' divination game using his coat button in a glass of water, as she chants "My intended, masked one, come to dine with me. Tell me my destiny" ("Suzhenyi, riazhenyi, priidi ko mne uzhinat'. Rasskazhi mne sud'bu moiu"). When Aleksandrov finally becomes acquainted with Orlova after a performance of *Pericola*, she takes him back to the place where he saved her from the bandit, telling him: "I've waited ten years for you." All of this is fiction working to cement the love narrative through well-worn artistic tropes.

Almost every studio-era biopic opened with title cards or voiceover narration (borrowed from documentaries of the period) that set up one of the genre's distinctive aspects, a claim to truth.[20] The old fashioned voice-of-God voiceover (here not God, but Oleg Basilashvili) at the beginning and toward the end of the TV series imparts the "truth" to viewers in pathos-laden and sentimental language (not uncommon in the studio era), and at times with an oddly apologetic tone regarding the series' superficial treatment of other major directors. At the beginning:

20 Custen, *Bio*/Pics, 51.

> The story of this great love began on the set of the film *Jolly Fellows.* Liubov' Petrovna Orlova and Grigory Vasil'evich Aleksandrov lived together almost fifty years. There are many love stories in the world, but this one is unique, unlike any other. A man and a woman, a director and an actress. He—the generator of ideas, she—feminine and delicate, its most subtle embodiment. The starling and the lyre—and that will be the name of their last work.[21]... Two unique creative personalities, two superstars, two tender and faithful hearts. This story will be about them. About a great love.

After Eisenstein's death:

> May movie lovers forgive us for touching upon the memory of the great master in perhaps an overly fragmented way at times. And also the memory of Ivan Aleksandrovich Pyr'ev, a fantastically talented individual and just as paradoxical. May their memory be blessed. Forgive us.

Following cinematic conventions, the sixteenth and last part of the TV series very obviously wraps up all plot lines. Eisenstein dies after a confessional conversation with Aleksandrov; Orlova and Utesov make up a fictional quarrel during a joint performance at Stalingrad. During the making of *Spring* (*Vesna,* 1947), Aleksandrov and Orlova dance in symbolic harmony to a final, edifyingly exaggerated voiceover:

> The time will come and Aleksandrov's films will be deciphered by all the world's comedy writers. Only a few know how to laugh as he did and how to make people laugh like Orlova. Now everyone knows. The innovative *Spring* foretold Fellini's great film *8 ½*, Antonioni and Wenders's films. Chaplin would say, "Aleksandrov revealed a new Russia to the world." Grigory Aleksandrov and Liubov' Orlova lived another thirty years and worshipped each other. They loved like no one else on earth. The director and the actress, the husband and wife. They were true to each other both on the set and in life. Let us go down on one knee in memory of them.

As is typical for the celebratory biopic, the TV series ends at the peak of the star's success—*Spring,* their last musical comedy and final truly successful film, and the marital harmony of

21 *Skvorets i lira* (1974), a completely undistinguished spy film, was never released.

the couple, eliding the aftermath: their subsequent failed films, Orlova's morbid obsession with her appearance, and Aleksandrov's slide into senile dementia.[22]

The Fraught Recovery of Orlova, Aleksandrov, and Friends

For some time the Putin regime has been engaged in whitewashing the Stalin era, while Channel One especially has been engaged in historical mythmaking. New Stalin monuments are going up all over the country.[23] On October 14, 2016 the first monument to Ivan Groznyi, seen as a Stalin surrogate, was dedicated in Orel. Recently Denis Karagodin's publication of the names of his great-grandfather's executioners during the purges has provoked a strong reaction in pro-Kremlin media because the document contravenes the anonymity of state terror, thereby imposing a silence that facilitates the mythologization of the Stalin era.[24] The *Orlova and Aleksandrov* series is not only part of this tendency to whitewash Stalinism, but also works to inscribe establishment values into post-Soviet cultural space.

Biopics of the American studio era entered the famous into the pantheon of cultural mythology and showed why they belonged there.[25] *Orlova and Aleksandrov* acknowledges Erdman, Eisenstein, Meierkhol'd, and Mandel'shtam as heroes of the Stalin era. Aleksandrov

22 In an interview Moskalenko explained that he had shot scenes dealing with the failed film *Starling and Lyre*, but that these were cut by his superiors. ("Fil'my-biografii: nuzhna li vsia pravda o chastnoi zhizni?," Larisa Maliukova, Vitalii Moskalenko, Iurii Kara, interview by Kseniia Larina, January 10, 2015, Radio Ekho Moskvy, https://www.google.com/#q=echo.msk.ru/program/kulshok/1469638-echo/). The stock biopic ending, which worked to mythologize the couple, thus remained operative.

Studio-era biopics frequently employed dissolves to condense the passage of time, as well as montage sequences (series of posters, theatre marquees, newspaper headlines) to document the ladder of success over time (Custen, *Bio/Pics*, 177–178). TV series of eight to sixteen parts do not need these devices. The persona of the star was also important in shaping a filmic biopic life, but the actors of Russian TV series are not invariably first-rank film stars.

23 "V Iakutii ustanovlen sed'moi pamiatnik Stalinu," Sakhalife.ru, October 30, 2019, https://sakhalife.ru/v-yakutii-ustanovlen-sedmoj-pamyatnik-stalinu/; "Meriia Novosibirska razreshila otprazdnovat' den' rozhdeniia Stalina v tsentral'nom skvere goroda," *Takie Dela*, June 6, 2019, https://takiedela.ru/news/2019/06/06/bitva-didzheev-v-chest-stalina/.

24 Sergei Medvedev, "Effekt Karagodina. Pochemu vlast' boitsia tomskogo filosofa?," Republic.ru, November 29, 2016, https://republic.ru/posts/76777.

25 Dennis Bingham, *Whose Lives*, 8–9.

even recites Osia's (as he calls him) "We Live without Feeling the Country beneath Us" ("My zhivem, pod soboiu ne chuia strany") with great pathos—a very unlikely occurrence. But the TV series also works to inscribe Orlova and Aleksandrov into the same cultural pantheon, to recover them and others from post-Stalin accusations of ideological conformism and servility, and to erase the resonance from Aleksandrov and Orlova's two incompetent sunset films, *Russian Souvenir* (*Russky suvenir*, 1960) and the unreleased *Starling and Lyre*. Orlova is framed as close to sainthood, while Aleksandrov is flawed, but well-intentioned, counts on his reputation to help those arrested, but always fails.

The director of *Orlova and Aleksandrov* has commented on his goal for the series:

> The action unfolds in a very dramatic time for the country, and we are trying to show, through the prism of the stories of iconic figures in cinema, how in such a difficult, horrible and terrifying time, very interesting works of literature, painting, music, and film were being created. Without knowing one's own history, it's impossible to move forward and develop, and in making this film, we remember remarkable people and try to reveal that time in order to understand what is happening now.[26]

Moskalenko is referring here to current government pressures on the film industry and television networks, as well as self-censorship among filmmakers, using Aleksandrov as an earlier, analogous case study. The problem is that Moskalenko and company have chosen to recover and mythologize someone who continued doing what he did under Stalin even in the mid-1950s and afterward, when such conformism was no longer necessary. Aleksandrov essentially became a Party functionary for the arts, teaching in the Central Committee's Academy of Social

26 Babina, "'Orlova i Aleksandrov': Kak snimali serial."
Tat'iana Sotnikova, co-author of the screenplay, elaborates: "You know, we probably understood everything about that era. We certainly understood the most important things. Here's what we didn't understand, even three years ago, when we began working on the screenplay: how easily everything may return. Now, when the film has come out, we understand how easily everything comes back, how in a single second, legions of people arise who know only how to be ferociously envious, to annihilate and destroy what has been done by others. They only know how to harass, and organize life so that they're on top, and every person who is capable of thinking up something, of creating, is forced to crawl on his knees before them and beg to be allowed to do something. See how easily all of this is restored, in an instant, with a snap of the fingers. This is what's astonishing and was hard to imagine." (Tat'iana Sotnikova, "Orlova i Aleksandrov. Posleslovie k serialu," interview by Iuliia Muchnik, March 27, 2015, TV-2 Tomsk, http://tv2.today/TV2Old/Orlova-i-aleksandrov-posleslovie-k-serialu).

Sciences beginning in 1955, serving on international friendship committees, and cooperating with the secret police as an agent of influence (*agent vliianiia*), travelling abroad with Orlova to advocate for the Soviet Union and serving the same function at home with visiting western dignitaries. Orlova simply followed his lead.

The TV series also devotes particular attention to recovering Boris Shumiatsky, an old Bolshevik whom Stalin put in charge of Sovkino in 1930 and purged in 1938. Shumiatsky did work to develop the film industry and sent Eisenstein, Tisse, Aleksandrov, and Nil'sen to the United States to learn the latest methods of filmmaking. He was the initiator behind *Jolly Fellows* and contributed to *Circus*, but also contributed significantly to Eisenstein's heart disease by closing down *Bezhin Meadow* (*Bezhin lug*), rejecting all of the director's film proposals, and recommending to Stalin that Eisenstein remain permanently unemployed.[27] According to Mikhail Romm, Shumiatsky was sufficiently despotic and choleric that his arrest precipitated widespread celebration among directors.[28] In *Orlova and Aleksandrov* he is simply a refined gentleman with a portrait of Lenin, not Stalin, in his office, who comforts Ol'ga Ivanova, Aleksandrov's abandoned first wife, looks after Nil'sen and Aleksandrov like a father, has no conflicts with Eisenstein, and stoically awaits his fate.

The TV series frames Stalin as a quiet sadist who makes Aleksandrov do somersaults both literally and metaphorically, but is a slyly cheerful fellow, and most of all—"on tozhe chelovek" (he's human too) because he falls hard for Orlova and pursues her clumsily through two episodes in completely fictional situations (Fig. 3).[29] He even tears up watching *Circus* but, strangely, what moves him is Orlova's Digi-digi-du dance on the cannon. In the end, Stalin

27 "Dokladnaia zapiska B. Z. Shumiatskogo I. V. Stalinu o dal'neishei rabote S.M. Eizenshteina, 19 aprelia 1937 g.," in *Kremlevskii kinoteatr 1928–1953. Dokumenty*, comp. K. M. Anderson, L. V. Maksimenkov, et al. (Moscow: ROSSPEN, 2005), 419.

28 Romm, *Ustnye rasskazy*.

29 Nonna Golikova states that the actress only met Stalin once, at the Kremlin reception for the celebration of the fifteenth anniversary of Soviet cinema. ("Nonna Golikova, rodstvennitsa Liubovi Orlovoi: Serial—lozh'! Mne zvonit vsia strana v iarosti!," Radio Komsomol'skaia pravda, March 26, 2015, https://www.youtube.com/watch?v=IUkRnjJrwQc. According to Golikova, Aleksandrov went to Kremlin receptions without Orlova ("Liubov' Orlova: o chem molchali dnevniki liubimitsy Stalina," TV program, January 20, 2015, https://www.youtube.com/watch?v=kLR3CHuLDVw.

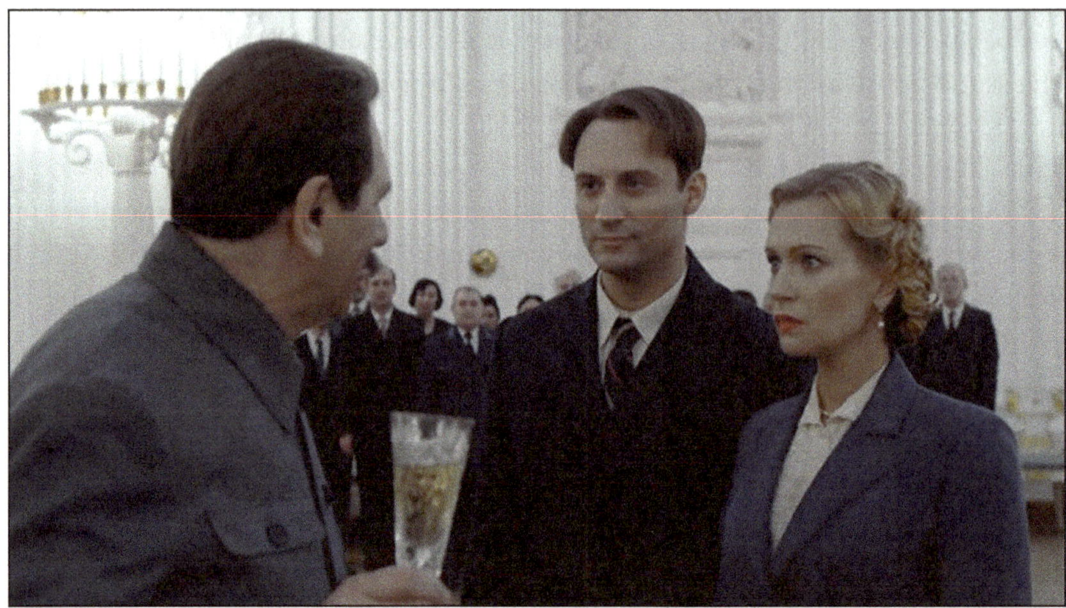

Fig. 3. A Kremlin reception.

most humanely lets Orlova go because she truly loves Aleksandrov, who waits outside the Kuntsevo dacha in the frozen night.[30]

Like other recent TV series, such as *Catherine* and *The Affairs* (*Izmeny*, 2015), *Orlova and Aleksandrov* exploits the sex-power-violence nexus as it bears on the famous couple. During their three-day love fest at the Metropole Hotel, Aleksandrov declares his affection to Orlova and then smears her red lipstick onto her cheek by dragging his finger heavily along her lips and face. Both of them are excited by his display of implicit aggression and make love, piquantly conscious of ever-present state power, represented by eavesdropping OGPU agents. Later Stalin pursues Orlova at Kremlin receptions, sings with her over the phone, compares her favorably to his dead wife, Nadezhda Allilueva, and watches her dance on the cannon in *Circus* with tears of ecstasy. Beria corners Orlova in his office, clearly planning rape, which is only avoided by a warning phone call from Stalin. Aleksandrov's reaction is framed between

30 According to Linda Williams's definition of melodrama, this is the moment of highest pathos as the victim (Orlova) is saved at the last minute and is vindicated before Aleksandrov because she has not betrayed him. Linda Williams, "Melodrama Revised," in *Refiguring American Film Genres*, ed. Nick Browne (Berkeley: University of California Press, 1998), 42–88.

Beria's advances and Stalin's ecstasy. He questions Orlova jealously about the men's behavior, concluding: "Stalin has his eye on you. That's what is happening." In spite of her protests to the contrary and demands for an apology, Aleksandrov pushes her down on the bed with an ironic: "I want to apologize. I never wanted you as much as I do now." The sex-power-violence paradigm enacted by representatives of the state only increases his desire, accompanied by performative violence expressing his power over Orlova.

Orlova and Aleksandrov also works to inscribe establishment post-Soviet values pertaining to gender, sexuality, class, and religion, mostly accomplished through fictional narratives. Orlova is depicted in patriarchal terms as a self-sacrificing near-saint, almost a Turgenev heroine, a strong woman devoted to a weak man.[31] Abandoning her classical music education, she earns money for the family as an accompanist to silent films. During the 1920s she reluctantly marries Andrei Berzin, deputy minister of agriculture, purely to save her mother and sister from starvation.[32] She is knocked unconscious and lands in the hospital when, to help Aleksandrov, she volunteers to ride a bull during the filming of *Jolly Fellows*, a trick Utesov refuses to perform.

Legal abortion was abolished in Russia in 1936. Orlova gives an anti-abortion radio speech, but shortly thereafter has an abortion herself—again the TV series would have us believe—for *altruistic* reasons. In the TV series Olia Rodimtseva, Orlova's 1920s classmate from the Studio for Rhythmic Dance (Studiia plasticheskogo tantsa), appears at her door the day of the radio speech. She has been released from the camps because of ill health as camp authorities make room for coming arrests and explains that her small children and husband were all murdered by the OGPU. The abortion is then justified by Orlova's self-sacrifice: she is determined to protect her long-awaited unborn child from the same fate. In order to preserve the trope of self-sacrifice, the TV series cuts off Orlova's actual anti-abortion speech *before* she talks about the need for exceptions to the new law when a woman "is completing a colossal project or

31 The TV series *Utesov. A Song the Length of Life* follows the same paradigm. Utesov's wife gives up a flourishing career as an operetta singer for her philandering husband, whose infatuations she tolerates during their entire married life.

32 According to Nonna Golikova, the entire family liked Berzin and was happy to see him when he was released from the camps, dying of cancer. She implies that Orlova's marriage was not one of convenience ("Rodstvennitsa Liubovi Orlovoi nedovol'na serialom ob aktrise," Hronika.info, http://hronika.info/kultura/52305-rodstvennica-lyubovi-orlovoy-nedovolna-serialom-ob-aktrise.html).

is preparing for a heroic flight or is completing work on a big acting role on which she has spent several years of her life"[33] It is well known that Orlova did not want children because of her career, but in the TV series her abortion is again attributed to rather improbable self-sacrifice.

In the TV series Aleksandrov is a charming and talented lightweight who can't keep his trousers zipped, even after marrying Orlova. Out of ambition he betrays his friend Pyr'ev in their early days at Proletkul't, and plays a willing Petrushka to Stalin's puppet-master. After cameraman Nil'sen's arrest and his own confession at Mosfil'm of harboring enemies of the people in his film crew in 1938, Aleksandrov goes on an extended alcoholic binge, but is saved by the "love of a good woman," as they used to say in Hollywood westerns. Orlova, though recovering from the black rose poisoning, is again his rock of strength, comforting him with, "I am protecting you" ("Ia Vas okhraniaiu").

In the TV series Orlova has to put up with two fictional infidelities, both of which she forgives, attributing them to the pressure of the purges and subjection to Stalin's whims. Aleksandrov's first love on the side made too good an anecdote for the scriptwriters to omit. Orlova is angry, and jealous of Broshkina, his young girlfriend, an assistant on *Volga-Volga*, and teaches them both a lesson by upholstering the Vnukovo bedroom in the same red fabric worn by the girlfriend to the *Volga-Volga* premiere party and then unmasking their deception by facing them with the red dress in the red bedroom. She forgives Aleksandrov only because "I know what kind of blood the film [*Volga-Volga*] cost," probably the scriptwriters' unintended opposition of the frivolous to the tragic. When Aleksandrov picks up Kurochkina, a second girl with crude country manners working as a dancer in *The Radiant Path*, Orlova is again ready to sacrifice herself when he returns home drunk and in despair over Stalin's rejection of the film: "Am I a burden to you? I'm getting older, I know. . . . But do it so that I don't know. Don't disgrace yourself. It's disgusting." At the start of World War II, because she is constantly away giving concerts for the troops, she is even ready to sacrifice her hard-won career and suggests he work with another actress, like Tselikovskaia or Serova. All these incidents are the stuff of legend but make good melodrama.

33 Qtd. in Kushnirov, *Svetlyi put'*,155. The fictional Rodimtseva appears to be modelled on Nonna Golikova's memory of a woman with a broken back who returned from the camps (Golikova, *Liubov' Orlova*, 95).

In the TV series Orlova heroically takes risks that others avoid. She is invariably friendly to Eisenstein and Pyr'ev, with both of whom Aleksandrov conflicted at various times, and courageously supports Eisenstein (whom she supposedly disliked) by congratulating him publicly at the tense studio screening of *Alexander Nevsky*. She hires Lida, a former Mosfil'm makeup artist who, along with Nil'sen, had been arrested in 1938 and exiled, when no one at the studio will give her a job. She persuades Aleksandrov to write in a role for Ranevskaia in *Spring*, so that she can meet her brother in Czechoslovakia where the film was mostly shot.[34]

In accord with post-Soviet values, Orlova's gentry background and its appurtenances are enlarged upon in the TV series through a mix of truth and fiction. Orlova tells Il'f and Petrov that, as a relative on her mother's side (the Sukhotins), she received an inscribed copy of *Prisoner of the Caucasus* (*Kavkazsky plennik*) and sat on Tolstoi's lap as a child (true). In 1921 she recited from *Eugene Onegin* to Eisenstein in an informal audition (false). Orlova's family had their clothes made by Lamanova before 1917 (very unlikely for an impoverished gentry family). The TV series hypes Orlova's anti-Bolshevik stance during the early twenties (she rails at Berzin: "Swindler! Expropriator!") and underscores her pre-revolutionary era good manners. She tells Aleksandrov: "In my family everyone used 'Vy' [polite second person address] and used that with the servants." And, like Pushkin's Tat'iana Larina, young Orlova believes in traditional girls' divination games.

It also turns out in the TV series that both Aleksandrov and Orlova are religious, another fashionable post-Soviet marker. When Aleksandrov's young son tells him there is no God (according to his teacher), he responds, "She never tried to count the stars in the sky." Orlova's faith is both more pronounced and more practical. After a three-day "day of love" at the Metropole away from the rest of the family, she asks a favor of Aleksandrov, "I want to be married in church. . . . With God we won't be lost. He sees everything. God is for all time" (Fig. 4). Orlova also links the religious ceremony to regulating male sexuality: "Men like you need to be kept in a female cage their entire life." After the church marriage she declares superstitiously, "Now nothing will happen to us." Before the marriage Orlova was not troubled

34 Another self-sacrificing woman is Ol'ga Ivanova, Aleksandrov's unloved first wife who hates "madam," as she calls Orlova, and constantly berates Aleksandrov, but given the opportunity, refuses to betray him to the OGPU, agrees to a divorce, and dies young, still loving Aleksandrov. Again, a fiction that reinforces a regressive stereotype.

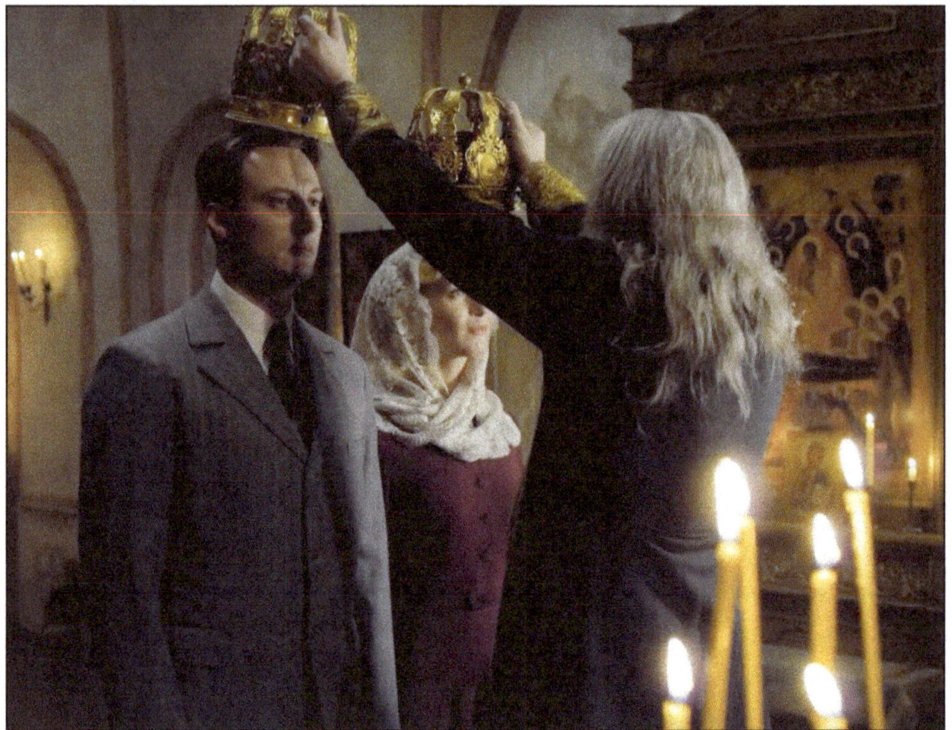

Fig. 4. A church marriage.

in the least by Orthodoxy's views on sexual morality versus her own self-serving affair with the German engineer, Franz, so that religion here seems to be largely decorative.

Like American studio-era biopics such as *Night and Day* (1946, about Cole Porter), *Orlova and Aleksandrov* naturalizes heterosexual marriage as the norm by eliminating other possible forms of relationship in the life of the artist. The TV series deals with Eisenstein's homosexuality and his possible relationship with Aleksandrov by raising the issue obliquely and then having Eisenstein himself give the "correct" answer. The charge of homosexuality is displaced onto Ivanova, Aleksandrov's estranged first wife, who first brings up Eisenstein and Aleksandrov's "abnormal friendship" ("nenormal'naia druzhba"), which she says led Eisenstein to refuse her any work on the set.[35] Shumiatsky, however, counters with an enumeration of creative

[35] Ivanova did work as an editor on *Potemkin* and *October* (Aleksandrov, *Moia zhena Liubov' Orlova*, 40, note 1).

male partnerships and friendships that were never considered abnormal: Pushkin and Del'vig, Stanislavsky and Nemirovich, Il'f and Petrov, Erdman and Mass.

At the end of the TV series Moskalenko places Eisenstein in a fictional squalid room of a communal apartment to increase the pathos of his situation. Aleksandrov visits the dying man, who asks him about the subject of his new film script: "—About love, what else can I do." Eisenstein responds: "You know more than I do about love for a woman"—a red flag. The scriptwriters were obviously concerned about how to handle the issue because at the beginning of the series they inserted Chekhov's 1886 letter to his brother Nikolai outlining ten points for correct living, which Eisenstein makes his Proletkul't actors memorize so that the scriptwriters could have Eisenstein bring up the letter once again at the end as a way to settle the question:

> I made you [memorize it], but I didn't fulfill Anton Pavlovich's cardinal rule: "Well-brought up people must embellish and ennoble their sexual instinct. They don't need bed and horse sweat from a woman, they need cleanliness, elegance, and humanity. Grisha, Grish, you kept to this rule. You devised a family of some sort for yourself. I haven't. You can't treat a woman inhumanely, you can't. I allowed . . . Grisha, one can't cope alone.

Earlier in the conversation Eisenstein mentions that his official wife, Pera Atasheva, ran away from him when he returned to Moscow, or maybe he escaped from her, he cannot remember, so that in the end everything is simplified to Eisenstein's bad treatment of Atasheva. Nevertheless the phrase "I allowed" ("Ia pozvolial") and whatever it implies is left unfinished for those who might notice.[36]

Evgenii Grishkovets has written recently about Russian restorative nostalgia:

36 In an interview two months before the premiere of *Orlova and Aleksandrov*, Moskalenko denied the possibility of any sexual relationship between Aleksandrov and Eisenstein, but talked about his treatment of Eisenstein's homosexuality: "I'm convinced that there were no relations with Aleksandrov. . . . If you consider 'Orlova-Aleksandrov,' then he came to Orlova after he had an entire life history with Eisenstein. . . . I encoded everything that relates to Eisenstein's personal life. I told everything. As Zhukov once said, 'A fool won't understand, an intelligent person will smile.'" ("Fil'my-biografii: nuzhna li vsia pravda o chastnoi zhizni?"). On the gossip in the 1920s and the early 30s about the Aleksandrov-Eisenstein relationship, see Aleksandrov, *Moia zhena Liubov' Orlova*, 113, note 1; 115, 117, note 1. Aleksandr Dobrovinsky, the present owner of the Aleksandrov-Orlova Vnukovo archive, states that he has documentary evidence of Aleksandrov's homosexual relationships. (Irina Mishina, "Nereal'naia liubov'," *Nasha versiia* 44 [November 14, 2016], https://versia.ru/v-filme-orlova-i-aleksandrov-pokazannom-na-pervom-kanale-net-prakticheski-nichego-ot-podlinnoj-istorii-otnoshenij-velikoj-aktrisy.)

> Five years ago it still seemed to me that the topic of Russian and Soviet myths would soon be exhausted, and Russian mainstream cinema would take up something else. It seemed to me that we'd had enough of mythologizing *bogatyri* of the past from among actors, singers, sportsmen, circus performers, military men, scientists and so on . . . No, it turned out not to be enough. The myths about female battalions and tank soldiers began . . . Now the topic of cosmonauts and Soviet writers and poets is being exploited.[37]

Orlova and Aleksandrov is part and parcel of this phenomenon. Using the classic devices of the cinematic biopic, the TV series attempts to recover Grigory Aleksandrov and Liubov' Orlova from accusations of ideological servility through mythologization of the Soviet past and by attributing popular post-Soviet establishment values to the famous couple.

[37] Evgenii Grishkovets, "Opiat' dzhinsy ot fabriki 'Taiga,'" *Rossiiskaia gazeta* 7111 (October 26, 2016), accessed December 3, 2016, https://rg.ru/2016/10/26/grishkovec-ia-ne-ponimaiu-chto-proishodit-s-otechestvennym-kinematografom.html. For example, the TV series *Secret Passion* (*Tainstvennaia strast'*) about Thaw era arts figures premiered on October 31, 2016. On restorative nostalgia, see Svetlana Boym, *The Future of Nostalgia* (New York: Basic Books, 2001).

Bibliography

Aleksandrov, G. *Moia zhena Liubov' Orlova. Perepiska na lezvii nozha.* Comp. Iu. Saakov. Moscow: Algoritm, 2014.

Babina, Alina. "'Orlova i Aleksandrov': Kak snimali serial." Vokrug.tv, March 16, 2015. http://www.vokrug.tv/article/show/Orlova_i_Aleksandrov_kak_snimali_serial_47118.

Bingham, Dennis. *Whose Lives Are They Anyway? The Biopic as Contemporary Film Genre.* New Brunswick and London: Rutgers University Press, 2010.

Cheshire, Ellen. *Bio-Pics. A Life in Pictures.* London and New York: Wallflower Press, 2015.

Custen, George F. *Bio/Pics. How Hollywood Constructed Public History.* New Brunswick: Rutgers University Press, 1992.

"Dokladnaia zapiska B. Z. Shumiatskogo I. V. Stalinu o dal'neishei rabote S. M. Eizenshteina, 19 aprelia 1937 g." In *Kremlevskii kinoteatr 1928–1953. Dokumenty,* compiled by K. M. Anderson, L. V. Maksimenkov, et al., 419. Moscow: ROSSPEN, 2005.

Golikova, Nonna. *Liubov' Orlova.* Moscow: Molodaia gvardiia, 2014.Grishkovets, Evgenii. "Opiat' dzhinsy ot fabriki 'Taiga.'" *Rossiiskaia gazeta* 7111 (October 26, 2016). https://rg.ru/2016/10/26/grishkovec-ia-ne-ponimaiu-chto-proishodit-s-otechestvennym-kinematografom.html.

Kushnirov, Mark. *Svetlyi put', ili Charli i Spenser.* Moscow: Terra-Knizhnyi klub, 1998.

Medvedev, Sergei. "Effekt Karagodina. Pochemu vlast' boitsia tomskogo filosofa?" Republic.ru, November 29, 2016. https://republic.ru/posts/76777.

Orlova i Aleksandrov, directed by Vitalii Moskalenko. Moscow: Favorit Fil'm, 2015. DVD.

Romm, Mikhail. *Ustnye rasskazy.* Moscow: Kinotsentr, 1991. http://royallib.com/read/romm_mihail/ustnie_rasskazi.html#0.

Semenova, N., and V. Poliakov, eds. *Vnukovskii arkhiv. Grigorii Aleksandrov, Liubov' Orlova. Put' naverkh: pis'ma, dnevniki, fotografii i dokumenty zvezd sovetskogo kino iz sobraniia Aleksandra Dobrovinskogo.* Vol. 1. Moscow: SkanRus, 2017.

———. *Vnukovskii arkhiv. Grigorii Aleksandrov, Liubov' Orlova. Evropeiskii dnevnik: pis'ma, dnevniki, fotografii i dokumenty zvezd sovetskogo kino iz sobraniia Aleksandra Dobrovinskogo.* Vol. 2. Moscow: SkanRus, 2018.

Putin-Era Television Productions about Catherine the Great: Active Measures as Period Drama

Elena Prokhorova and Alexander Prokhorov

On November 4, 2014 Channel Russia broadcast the first season of the television series about Catherine the Great's rise to power, produced by Aleksandr Akopov and titled *Catherine* (*Ekaterina*).[1] On November 4 of the following year Channel One responded with the first season of its own television biopic *The Great* (*Velikaia*, produced by Ruben Dishdishian),[2] about the rise to power of the German princess Sophia who later converts to Orthodoxy and becomes Russian Empress Catherine the Great.[3] Channel One limited itself to one season, while Channel Russia has already released three seasons, with the fourth currently in production. It is easy to construe these two texts as the embodiment of Putin-era patriotic rewritings of Russian imperial history. It is, likewise, easy to establish an intertextual link between these new productions and a long tradition of Soviet-era films and television series dedicated to progressive royal empire-builders, such as Ivan the Terrible and Peter the Great.[4] This includes, for example, the late Soviet-East German mini-series *The Youth of Peter the Great* (*Iunost' Petra*, dir. Sergei Gerasimov, 1980). While the fascination with Russia's imperial past and charismatic state builders is shared by post-Soviet television series and their Soviet predecessors, we claim that both Channel One's *The Great* and Channel Russia's *Catherine* take an innovative approach to the depiction

1 On Amazon Prime, *Ekaterina* is titled *Ekaterina: The Rise to Power.*

2 On Amazon Prime, *Velikaia* is titled *Catherine the Great.*

3 Since 2005, November 4 has been celebrated as a new Russian holiday, Nation's Unity Day. Thus, *Catherine* premiered on the holiday in 2014 and *The Great* on the same day in 2015. In this respect, these TV series follow the Soviet tradition of anniversary productions. See for example, Sergei Eisenstein's *October* (*Oktiabr'*, 1928), produced for the tenth anniversary of the October Revolution, or Mikhail Romm's *Lenin in October* (*Lenin v Oktiabre*), released for the twentieth anniversary of the October Revolution in 1937.

4 Among the most important films are Vladimir Petrov's *Peter the First* (*Petr Pervyi*, part 1, 1937; part 2, 1938) and Sergei Eisenstein's trilogy about Ivan the Terrible (part 1, 1944; part 2, 1946, banned and released in 1958; part 3 never completed).

of this famous period in Russia's imperial history.[5] First, they embrace the global trends of big-budget costume dramas: the focus on Catherine's lovers and lots of sex and intrigue. Second, Putin-era television series about the Empress carry a distinct ideological flavor, namely a focus on conspiratorial politics with a primary emphasis—topical if anachronistic—on the role of the security services and "active measures" administered by them.[6]

Catherine was never the subject of a biopic during the Soviet period because the great tsars were in essence stand-ins for Stalin and other Soviet leaders. (In the case of Gerasimov's production, the youthful Peter was a stand-in for the not-so-youthful Brezhnev.) A woman ruler, however, would be a queer gesture for a cinema trying to elevate its patriarchal rulers.[7] In the West, by contrast, there exists a long tradition of films and television series about the famous Russian Empress. For example, Elizabeth Ford and Deborah Mitchell examine the four most notable twentieth-century productions—two American and two British—and the evolving conventions of representing Russia and Catherine.[8] The past few years have witnessed a renewed interest in Catherine and the Russian imperial myth. See, for instance, Helen Mirren's *Catherine the Great* (2019) by HBO and the 2020 dramedy *The Great* produced by Hulu. In this respect, the recent Russian series fit squarely into global fantasies about royalty with their high production values, transnational, streaming-oriented distribution patterns, and their marketing of history as fantasy.[9] In effect, they successfully combine geopolitical wishful

5 Scholars of Russian cinema have examined aspects of Putin-era appropriations of the Russian imperial past. Nancy Condee, for example, argues that post-Soviet productions about imperial history carry vestiges of a vanished past (Nancy Condee, *The Imperial Trace* [Cambridge, UK: Cambridge University Press, 2009], 39–46). Stephen Norris, on the other hand, contends that such productions generate "discussions about patriotism and belonging in the new Russia" (Stephen Norris, *Blockbuster History in the New Russia: Movies, Memory, and Patriotism* [Bloomington: Indiana University Press, 2012], 16).

6 Active measures (*aktivnye meropriiatiia*) is a KGB term for clandestine operations conducted by the security services. For further discussion see, for example, Thomas Rid, *Active Measures: The Secret History of Disinformation and Political Warfare* (New York: Farrar, Straus, and Giroux, 2020).

7 Even in the films set during Catherine's rule, such as Mikhail Romm's *Admiral Ushakov* (1953), the focus is on the male leaders (Ushakov and Potemkin), with Catherine relegated to episodic appearances.

8 Elizabeth A. Ford and Deborah C. Marshall, *Royal Portraits in Hollywood: Filming the Lives of the Queens* (Lexington: University Press of Kentucky, 2009).

9 For further discussion of history as fantasy, see Marita Sturken, "Reenactment, Fantasy, and the Paranoia of History: Oliver Stone's Docudramas," *History and Theory* 36, no. 4 (December 1997): 65.

thinking about robust imperial expansion for domestic distribution with sex, violence, and intrigue in gold-plated, exotic settings for the global consumer.

History as Active Measures

Soviet-era representations of Catherine's rule followed a recognizable pattern: little screen space for the woman in power, and a major focus on epic military operations that had parallels with current events. Stalin-era cinema produced several biopics about Catherine's military leaders and their exploits, such as the imperial triumphs of Fieldmarshal Alexander Suvorov (*Suvorov*, dir. Vsevolod Pudovkin and Mikhail Doller, 1940) or Admiral Fedor Ushakov (*Admiral Ushakov*, dir. Mikhail Romm, 1953). In *Suvorov*, for example, the film opens with a lengthy sequence of victorious Russian troops resting at the gate of Warsaw, having just captured the eastern part of Poland. The historical film creates an epic frame for the recent (1939) annexation of Eastern Poland by the Red Army in the wake of the Molotov-Ribbentrop Pact. These films established the canonical image of Catherine's era as the golden age of Russian imperial expansion.

Putin-era series are equally revealing of the culture in which they are produced and consumed. The major forces for making history here are not the military. There are practically no battle scenes in the film; in fact, most battles are represented by computer-generated maps. Even such a famous Russian general as Suvorov is primarily a person serving at the Empress's court and secondary to Catherine's special agents and diplomats. Instead of the military, Channel Russia's Catherine (played by Marina Aleksandrova) leads a team of favorites and two prominent courtiers—her head of Secret Police (Secret Chancery) Stepan Sheshkovsky (Mikhail Gorevoi) and her chief diplomat Nikita Panin (Sergei Koltakov). According to the series, special operations comprise the major content of her foreign policy. In season three, subtitled "Pretenders," Catherine's rule is challenged on two fronts: from the east by Emel'ian Pugachev's rebel army and from the west by Princess Elizaveta Tarakanova. Suvorov fails to defeat Pugachev in battle but succeeds in bribing his minions who then deliver Pugachev to the imperial army. As for Tarakanova, who is supported by the Poles and funded by the French and the Turks, Catherine assigns her favorite, Aleksei Orlov, and the Russian envoy, Andrei Razumovsky, to capture Tarakanova and bring her to Russia. To this end, Catherine deploys the Russian navy to Italy where Tarakanova conspired with Russia's enemies to claim the Russian throne. However, naval power, as well as naval and diplomatic ranks, only serve as decoys in this operation because the primary forces, according to the TV series, are the Empress's agents on a secret mission—that is, male honeytraps, not battleships or canons. Orlov seduces Tarakanova and stages a fake wedding, all in order to lure her onto a battleship, bring her to St. Petersburg, and imprison her in the Peter and Paul Fortress. Secret agents and active measures thus save the Russian empire by protecting the true autocrat.

Royal Drama and the Nature of Authority

The nature of authority is a central theme in royal dramas, whether they depict fictional clans or are based on real dynasties. In her discussion of the nature of authority in *Game of Thrones* (2011–2019), Judith May Fathallah invokes Max Weber's famous typology of legitimate rule: traditional, rational-legal, and charismatic. Charismatic authority is based on the extraordinary qualities of individuals, often presented as power coming directly from a higher authority. Fathallah notes: "Arguably, *Game of Thrones* constructs charismatic authority as better and more effective than other types."[10] One obvious reason why charismatic authority is so important in fantasy narratives is the filmmaker's desire to satisfy viewers' appetite for spectacle.

When one deals with historically based narratives about royals, the nature of authority becomes a more loaded theme, in part because of the inevitable projection of the past onto the present. A recent drama *The Crown* (2016) offers a useful benchmark for handling this tricky issue. The Netflix series examines traditional authority and its evolution under the pressures of modern power institutions based on rational-legal legitimacy. The show combines an interest in and sympathy toward the British royal family's struggles with the pressures of modernity. In fact, the dramatic interest of most episodes centers on the clash between the modern rational and the traditional. For example, should the queen go to the Welsh village of Aberfan to mourn the loss of over a hundred children who perished in the coal-mining disaster? This question seems to be somewhat anachronistic: *now* we are sure she must go. The way the series represents this question as posed in 1966, however, constitutes the drama. The queen's initial refusal is based on the tradition—the queen visits only hospitals, Elizabeth responds—and is reversed by the episode's end. The last intertitle of the episode tells us that her delay in visiting is one of the greatest regrets of her life.

10 Judith May Fathallah, *Fanfiction and the Author* (Amsterdam: Amsterdam University Press, 2017), 102.

Of the three options for political legitimacy, Russian series about Catherine depict power as relying primarily on the ruler's charisma. When Princess Sophia arrives in Russia as the bride-to-be of Peter the Third, traditional/patriarchal authority is in deep crisis. First, the ruler of the empire, Empress Elizabeth, is a woman who is unable to produce a male heir. Second, Sophia's future husband and the future emperor of Russia lacks two key desires: to perform his responsibilities as a husband and to learn how to rule his empire. With this traditional legitimacy virtually non-existent and no rational-legal justification for Princess Sophia to take over, the only way she can become the empress is via a miracle, giving up part of her humanity, along with her foreign identity, in order to become the Russian autocrat, omnipotent and omniscient. The nature of her power is quite incomprehensible to an earthly television viewer.

The series presents Catherine as an unlikely empress who is chosen by a force beyond human comprehension, and Catherine feels this calling. Despite her mother's disparaging remarks about barbaric Russian mores, she makes efforts to learn Russian, converts to Russian Orthodoxy, and takes a new name. In season one viewers observe the foreigner's cute mistakes in Russian and her incredible diligence in studying the new native language. By the end of season one, she speaks native Russian. Her conversion to Orthodoxy is interlaced with the story of French spies trying to poison the future *tsaritsa*. While western medicine does not help, since the doctors are also the poisoners—a story familiar to any Soviet/Russian viewer from the fabricated Doctors' Plot of 1953—a good prayer by an Orthodox priest and Catherine's neophyte's passion for Orthodoxy overcome the chemical machinations of the enlightened French.

The series works hard to represent this future empress as a person who possesses not only inner strength and devotion but also personal, almost supernatural, magnetism through which she attracts men who further her political agenda. She also does not hesitate to replace one favorite with another when it becomes expedient. Another way in which her charisma manifests itself is via her eternal youth. Over the course of three seasons and more than three decades of Catherine's life (from 1744 to 1782) she does not age in the least (Figs. 1 and 2). Meanwhile, her men age, die, lose an eye (Grigory Potemkin) or even lose their mind (Grigory Orlov)—a clear indication of their human nature and her divine one.[11]

[11] The theme of the eternal youth of the ruler aligns Akopov's project with Gerasimov's saga about the youth of Peter and manifests the anxiety of the aging power commissioning the series. In contrast, *The Crown* marks every major period in Elizabeth's life by casting a different actress representing her maturation and aging.

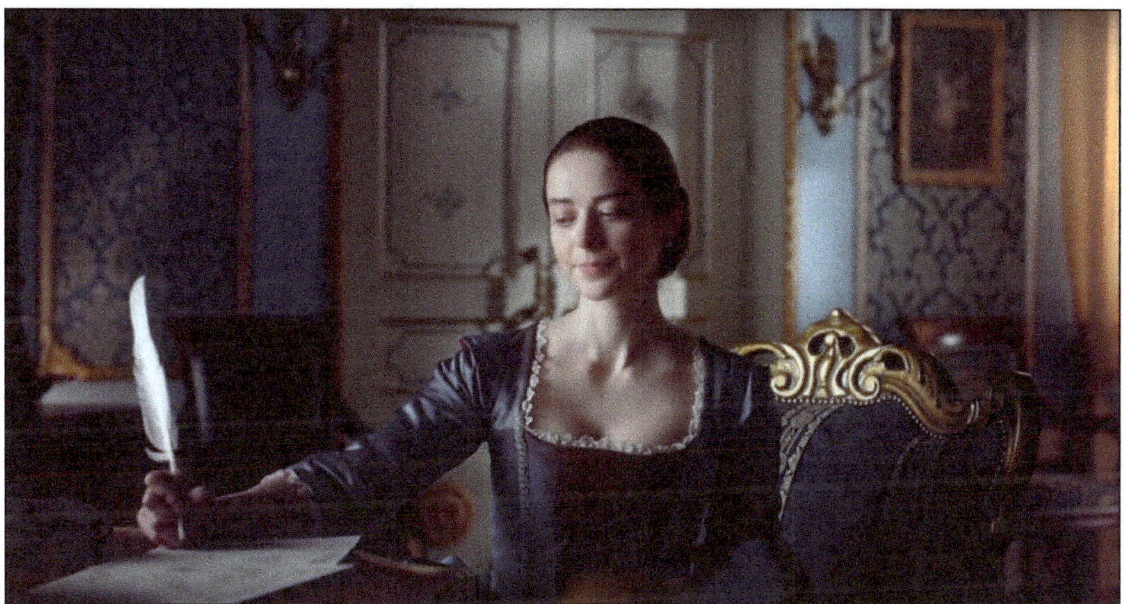

Fig. 1. Catherine in her teens upon her arrival to Russia (season one).

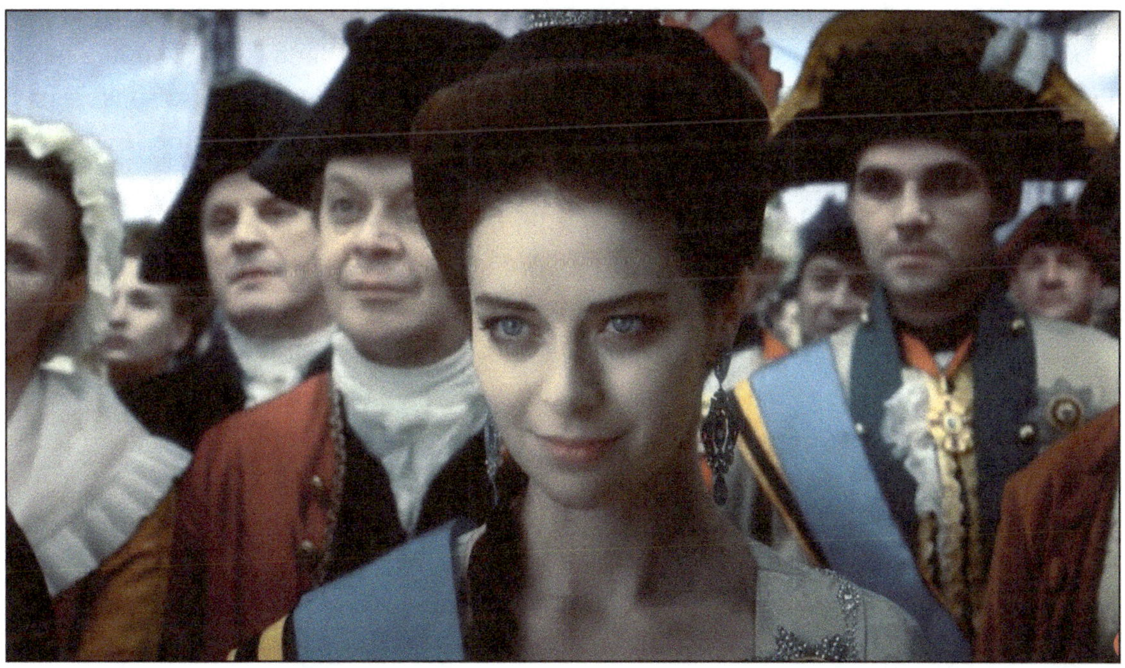

Fig. 2. Catherine at age fifty-three at the unveiling of the monument to Peter the Great in 1782 (season two).

Meanwhile, while relying on her unquestionable charisma, Catherine starts building her traditional legitimacy. Once she claims herself as Russian, she works hard at establishing her spiritual connection to the founder of the empire, Peter the First. In the series, she does so by constantly appearing with his portrait in the background (visual markers), speaking about his policies, and eventually erecting the famous Bronze Horseman, inscribed *Petro Primo Catharina Secunda,* the numerals clearly indicating a continuity of rulers. One form of social authority which is absent from Channel Russia's series is the rational-legal authority of Catherine's rule. It is especially striking when one compares the Russia Channel's series with Helen Mirren's HBO mini-series *Catherine the Great.* In the latter Catherine's first major appearance as Empress is her speech to the Russian nobility about the need to abolish slavery, which will not only improve the condition of Russian peasants but will benefit the ruling class and the overall economy of the empire. This is the rational argument of a public politician who, in this case, relies on the idea of popular support. In contrast, in *Catherine* discussions about the evils of serfdom and any similar issues that concern the policies of the Russian Empire are conducted among the members of the inner circle, which typically includes only two members of Catherine's court, her foreign minister and her head of secret police. For example, in season two of *Catherine,* the empress discovers the terrifying abuses of landowner Dar'ia Saltykova who tortured, maimed, and killed dozens of her serfs. Catherine's first impulse is to try her in a court of law and prosecute those who covered up her crimes. However, her two advisors object to the public nature of such an investigation, claiming that this is far from a unique case and that the exposure of landowners' crimes will ignite opposition to Catherine's rule. Instead of a legal solution and transparent process the three agree on a special operation: imprisoning Saltykova and purging the ranks of officials who cover up for her. While all three are rational beings who are aware of the right way to proceed, they choose a Byzantine and secretive way of handling the crime. Notably, the historical Saltykova faced legal consequences, which included her public display as a criminal in Moscow. The series, however, favors the active measures approach to handling corruption.

In *Catherine,* charismatic authority is portrayed via three distinct types of settings and accompanying camerawork: the palace shot from above, places of incarceration and torture, and awesome palace interiors. All three are designed to provide the viewer with privileged access to the workings of imperial power. All three infuse the settings of historical palaces with the fantasy of being privy to the travails of imperial governance. In fact, viewers get access to the three levels of the imperial universe: the heavenly/aerial realm, the hellish domain, and the purgatory of day-to-day court operation. The heavenly realm is constructed via drone shots of Catherine the Great's palace and gardens, as well as tracking shots of the embankments of the Winter Palace and other spectacular vistas of the imperial capital (Fig. 3).

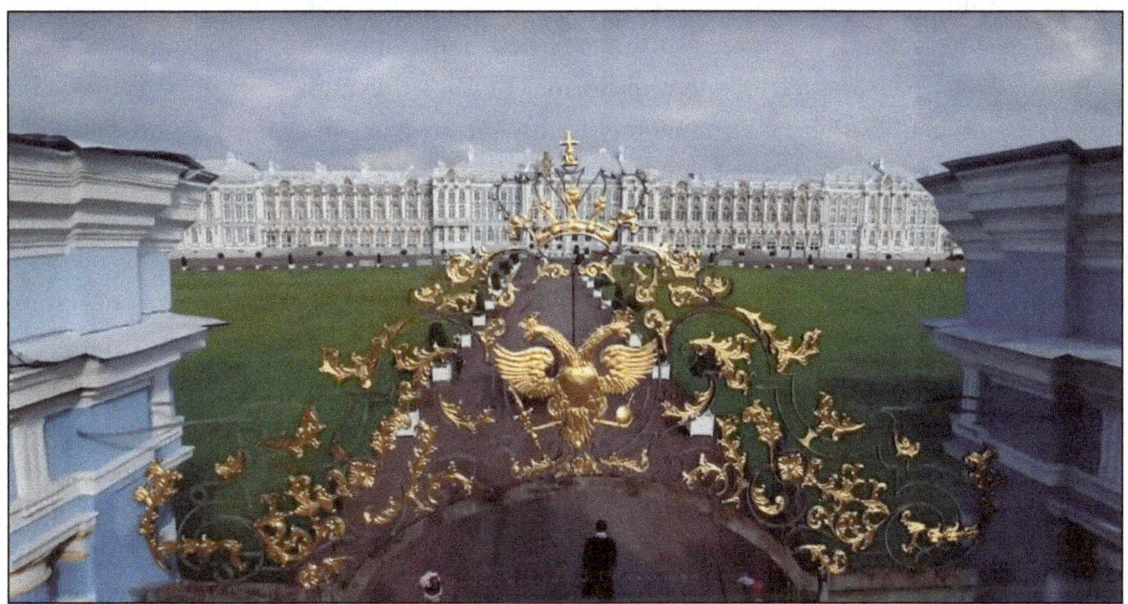

Fig. 3. Drone technology for imperial glory.

The drone shots create a superhuman view of imperial power that is bigger than any one mortal, even Catherine herself.

We are also transported to the dungeons of the Peter and Paul Fortress, the Shlisselburg Fortress, and monasteries in Northern Russia where characters of royal descent, who potentially can compete with the Empress for the throne, are imprisoned. The suffering, darkness, and despair of Dantean proportions create an effect of sublime terror and provide a striking backdrop to the gold decorating Catherine's palaces. Prisoners spend decade after decade locked away in cells with no hope of release. As a reminder of Catherine's awesome power, the series' authors have us accompany the Empress on her periodic visits to her royal prisoners. During one such trip, to Kholmogory, Catherine gives an important lesson to Prince Pavel, the heir to the throne. When he notes that it is unfair and cruel to keep innocent people locked up for decades, she notes that he should stop thinking like an ordinary human being and start assuming responsibility for the well-being of the entire empire. Executing state violence is clearly an awesome burden that the empress must carry by virtue of her charismatic status—she is chosen by higher powers to be the sovereign.

Finally, sandwiched between the divine and the demonic levels of Catherine's universe of power is her palace, wrapped around her bedroom where high politics is discussed, negotiated, and performed. The extended format of *Catherine* allows an unprecedented and detailed depiction of Catherine's engagement with her favorites over the three decades of her reign. While the series pays homage to the popular legend about Catherine's insatiable sexual appetites, it also depicts her romantic relationships as matters of politics rather than just *affaires du coeur.* The series constantly reinforces the idea that the viewer is witnessing something they can never completely understand because they do not belong to the ruler's chosen inner circle. Many of the bedroom scenes use servants as focalizers who eavesdrop and stand guard by closed doors—firmly establishing the identification of viewers with those mere mortals, rather than the aristocrats within. We, the viewers, simply cannot handle the epic cruelty or magnitude of sexual drive when high politics mixes with bodily fluids. Thus, *Catherine* works as a perfect dual-purpose commodity: an exotic series that completely fulfills the expectations of global audiences, as well as a product for domestic distribution explaining authoritarian policies of necessary violence to its viewers.

As in many period dramas, murders play a central role in the narrative. In *Catherine* they come in two flavors. When people without any legitimate claim to power commit murders, these acts of violence are represented as crimes that need to be punished. Such are, for example, numerous acts of brutality by Emel'ian Pugachev, a pretender to the Russian throne. These acts of violence are juxtaposed to the many tortures and murders performed in the name of the empire and its unity. When Sheshkovsky, the head of the Secret Police, suspects treason at Catherine's court, all measures are justified for the sake of the empire's security. TV viewers have to enjoy/endure prolonged scenes of torture in the dungeons of the Peter and Paul Fortress. Moreover, it does not matter what one's position is in the social hierarchy; both aristocrats and commoners are whipped, skinned, and impaled. So heavy is the sacred burden of state service that, from time to time, Sheshkovsky takes a break from torture and prays to an icon, which is conveniently located but a few steps away in the same torture chamber. The role of the icon is somewhat ambiguous: is it there because the torturer asks for forgiveness for his cruelty or does he simply ask for heavenly approval to administer state-sanctioned violence? After all, in this tradition, all power, including the right to violence on behalf of the state, comes from God.

While *Catherine* extended the joys of torture for three seasons, *The Great* had to get its message across fast and dirty. *The Great's* Peter not only expresses disdain for his spousal responsibilities but also scorns Russia's security services, thereby embracing liberal ideas that jeopardize the very existence of the empire. When Peter assumes the crown, he proposes making all religions in the empire equal, thus depriving Russia of its unique identity. Imperiling the empire's integrity even further, he abolishes the Secret Chancery, the empire's secret police, as well as the use of torture as an investigative tool (episode 10, 31:45). In both television series the feared agency is presented as the key institution holding the empire together. The head of the Chancery under Empress Elizabeth, Count Alexander Shuvalov, remarks to Peter that, in his experience, not a single Russian ruler was able to run the empire without the secret police (episode 10, 27:30). Peter's attempt to challenge the powerful Chancery backfires: when the army rebels against him, he cannot count on secret police support. Not surprisingly, the Chancery outlives the naïve reformer.

While both television channels produced their series according to the global blueprints for big-budget period spectacles, they also took into consideration specific national aspects of large scale productions. As Norris tells us, in the aught years Konstantin Ernst and Nikita Mikhalkov articulated the conventions of Russian big-budget film and television productions: namely, spectacular melodrama as a patriotic journey into Russia's imperial—whether hereditary or socialist—past.[12] Both Russia Channel's *Catherine* and Channel One's *The Great* reproduced the masterplot of the patriotic blockbuster augmented with a Cinderella story (a poor German princess arrives in the imperial capital) in order to combine romance with patriotic service to the big family of the Russian Empire.

And where could the invisible working of the ideological occult occur in these two biopic productions if not in the bedroom? Both Akopov, the producer of *Catherine,* and Dishdishian, the producer of *The Great,* chose this key location to combine the international format of sex and violence with a Russia-specific fantasy journey into the imperial past. Both shows depict making love in the imperial palace as important government service—an act of procreation for the sake of the continuity of the imperial lineage. It is painfully clear who plans to help the

12 Norris, *Blockbuster History,* 17.

empire and who, like Peter the Third, is not interested in Catherine and the empire's future. In *The Great* the filmmaker delivers his message in an effective way via cross-cutting. While the future empress earns her right to be the ruler by delivering Russian babies (three in all), Peter the Third engages in recreational sex with his mistress Elizaveta Vorontsova. Catherine's long and difficult labor is juxtaposed to Peter's leisure. It goes without saying that no babies are born from Peter's illegitimate liaison with Vorontsova. It is noteworthy that not only Catherine's maids but even the imperial officer Count Zalessky help and guard Catherine during one of the birth scenes.

Akopov's series also links Catherine's reproductive work for the state with the broader struggle for heteronormativity. That is why Catherine's sexual foil Peter the Third admires the Prussian king Frederick II (whose sexual preferences are invoked in the series) more than his wife or any other woman. When he finally gets somewhat interested in Vorontsova, he dresses her in a Prussian military uniform and spends time with her in military exercises. Channel Russia depicts Peter the Third as a person confused about his sexuality, rather than a follower of the Prussian monarch's sexual preferences. More important than Peter's sexual confusion, however, is his propensity for liberal western ideas, apparently inapplicable to Russia. Peter's aunt, Empress Elizabeth, reinforces the message of what is and is not appropriate in Russia. Speaking from a position of staunch heterosexuality, Elizabeth jokingly notes that the three female empresses of France, Russia, and Austria should start a war to get rid of the Prussian bugger (*muzhelozhets*).

Transnational Story Telling

While Russian television series about rulers of royal descent convey familiar ideologies about the charismatic nature of state power and the importance of the secret police as the major institution for national security, one can easily notice important differences between these new historical series and their Soviet-era predecessors. First of all, contemporary government-controlled channels boast high production values for the television series, a self-promotional gesture that non-commercial Soviet Central Television would not even have dared to contemplate.[13] Second, what distinguishes television productions about Catherine the Great

13 For example, Channel One planned to return with a second season of *The Great* in 2020. It boasted the largest

from their Soviet-era tsar-focused TV series and films is their concern with sex and violence as spectacle. These series are produced by filmmakers who exist in the global media market, not behind the Iron Curtain.[14] They have seen and are fully aware of international conventions for period-set historical melodramas—a fantasy of excess. Moreover, television representations of Catherine the Great's reign relegate the specificity of the national past to the background and instead favor a fantasy world adhering to the conventions of costume melodrama, be it a historical world in the style of *The Borgias* (2007–2010) or *The Tudors* (2011–2013) or the utter fantasy of the Targaryen dynasty from *Game of Thrones*.

Rather than emphasizing the historical uniqueness and authenticity of the period, television series about Catherine the Great populate the tourist attractions of St. Petersburg with dehistoricized male and female characters with magnificent contemporary bodies. They commit violent acts and engage in spectacular romantic adventures. Erotic and violent spectacles set in eighteenth-century interiors use some location shooting of famous Petersburg area palaces and cathedrals. For the most part, however, the authentic imperial heritage yields to CGI-designed animation sequences that showcase the technological capabilities of Russian television in producing world-class high-tech commodities. In a similar manner, the characters of the series showcase the advancements of modern healthcare and nutrition. Several critics noted that Marina Aleksandrova, the star of *Catherine*, has a physique that better fits contemporary perceptions of the ideal female body than eighteenth-century standards.[15] In both shows modern dental work and toned bodies coexist with period costumes, feeding

budget in the history of Russian TV series—300 million rubles ("'Velikaia—vtoroi sezon," Serialy, https://www.kp.ru/putevoditel/serialy/ekaterina-velikaya-2-sezon/). As of June 2021, the second season has not been released.

14 Of course the current political agenda makes its way into the narrative. For example, one of the earliest scenes of *Catherine* season one, set in Crimea, is the slaughter of peaceful Russian merchants by the French-backed Crimean Tatars. Before dying one of the merchants proclaims, "The Russian flag will fly over the Black Sea." This episode is a not so subtle invocation of the popular 2014 meme *Krymnash* targeting jingoistic Russian viewers and pleasing government executives supervising the production. However, the overall narrative agenda of *Catherine* is storytelling for global audiences. In this respect, such episodes are anachronistic exceptions, harking back to late Stalinist cinema, rather than the rule.

15 Elena Smirnova, "*Velikaia* vs. *Ekaterina:* Iuliia Snigir' ili Marina Aleksandrova?," Vokrug.tv, November 5, 2015, https://www.vokrug.tv/article/show/velikaya_vs_ekaterina_yuliya_snigir_ili_marina_aleksandrova_50251/.

fetishistic interest in details of female clothing, such as side hoops.[16] In fact, voyeuristic pleasures frequently border on sheer erotic display. For example, *The Great* dedicates a long scene to the young empress hopping around her bedroom inside hoops without any skirts on them or any narrative motivation, apart from pleasing the male gaze.

In their drive to make a spectacle, the filmmakers let characters slide into pure anachronism. Media scholar Irina Petrovskaia laments the uses of modern Russian idiom in both recent biographical productions about the empress. She notes that the most ludicrous aspect of a series about Catherine is the speech of the main characters. While nobody expects television heroes to speak eighteenth-century Russian, it is somewhat ridiculous to hear Russian aristocrats speak the gangster slang of present day mobsters. Petrovskaia's interlocutor, Kseniia Larina, radio host of Ekho Moskvy, quotes Count Aleksei Orlov of the Channel One production plotting to murder Peter the Third: "K chemu eti glupye voprosy. Da zavalim ego i delo s kontsom" ("Why these stupid questions? Let's whack him and that's that").[17] In another radio show, Petrovskaia notes that in the Russia Channel's *Catherine*, the Empress greets her subjects with "Privet!" ("Hi!"). In the spirit of Mikhail Zoshchenko's characters' semi-literate discourse, Empress Elizabeth struggles to recollect the King of France's exact title: "Etot, Liudovik, pod nomerom 15" ("This one, Louis, under number fifteen").[18] Finally, in the Channel One biopic series about the Empress, the premier scientist of Russia Mikhail Lomonosov arrives at a ball and, when Catherine notes that she remembers him not liking noisy parties, responds with a line from a classical gangster saga: "There are offers one can't refuse." (Admittedly, one can also read such an obvious reference to a Hollywood classic as a knowing wink at viewers, both domestic and international.)

16 Modernizing the world of historical drama is of course a global trend. As the Costume Designer for Hulu's *The Great* (2020) Emma Fryer admits, she was partly inspired by a recent Dior retrospective and fashion from the 1950s when she created costumes for the show. See Rebecca Ford, "Inside HBO and Hulu's Very Different Takes on Catherine the Great and Her 'Super Complicated Relationships,'" Hollywood Reporter, June 29, 2020, https://www.hollywoodreporter.com/lists/inside-hbo-hulus-very-takes-catherine-great-her-super-complicated-relationships-1300760.

17 Kseniia Larina and Irina Petrovskaia, "Chelovek iz televizora," Ekho Moskvy, November 7, 2015, http://echo.msk.ru/programs/persontv/1653660-echo/.

18 Idem, "Chelovek iz televizora," Ekho Moskvy, November 29, 2014, http://echo.msk.ru/programs/persontv/1445692-echo/.

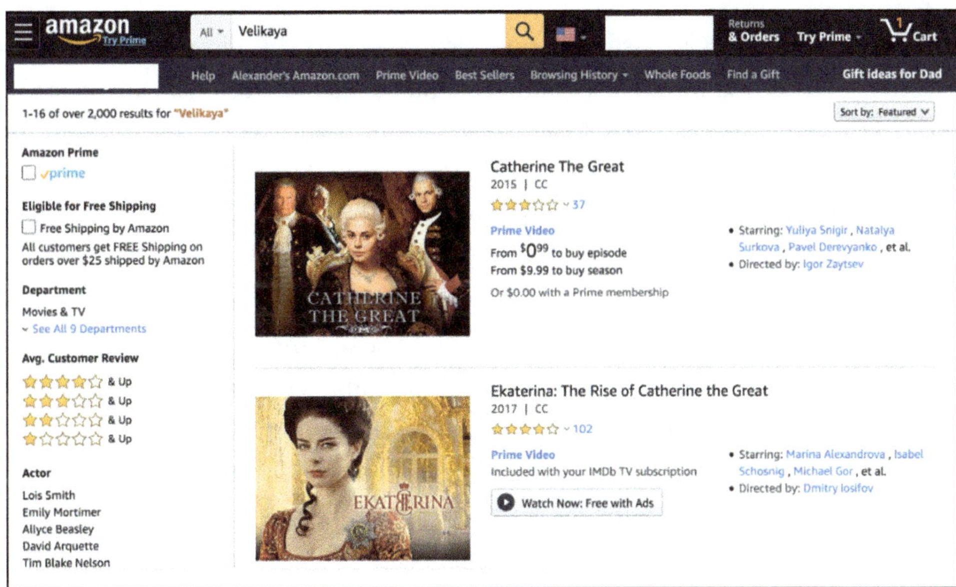

Fig. 4. Two Russian Catherines compete for viewers' attention on Amazon Prime.

While Ekho Moskvy journalists find shocking the jarring contrast between the characters' discussion of the transition of power in the period's terms ("regent," "empress," "heir") and the following scene, in which the Orlov brothers switch to present-day mob discourse, we can easily find a similar break in period verisimilitude in *The Tudors*. In one scene, the characters speak in Latin and in the next scene, frustrated by the Pope's refusal to give a divorce, the king switches to the modern idiom: "I want you to force his fucking holiness into submission, if necessary by telling him that if he does not grant me my fucking annulment then England will withdraw its submission to Rome."[19] This mixing of modern colloquialisms, mafia slang, and modern male and female bodies with details of the past (costumes, buildings, and interiors of the era) in fact becomes the draw of the two Russian shows and makes them part of transnational historical television productions that combine picturesque period settings with dehistoricized characters. Not surprisingly, the global viewer can find both *The Great* and several seasons of *Catherine* on Amazon Prime (Fig. 4).

19 Basil Glynn, "The Conquests of Henry VIII: Masculinity, Sex, and the National Past in *The Tudors*," in *Television, Sex, and Society: Analyzing Contemporary Representations*, ed. Beth Johnson, James Aston, and Basil Glynn (New York: Bloomsbury, 2012), 163.

The conclusion of *Catherine*'s season one also caters to the viewer familiar with global cinema. It is inspired by the famous sequence of the baptism of Michael Corleone's newborn nephew from Francis Ford Coppola's *Godfather*. If Coppola juxtaposes Catholic baptism to the bloody slaughter of Michael's competitors for power in New York's criminal underworld, the production team of *Catherine* juxtaposes invocations of the Bible and beautiful music that Peter the III plays on his violin to the necessary brutality of murdering all possible competitors for the Russian throne. One key difference between Coppola's treatment of Michael's rise to power and Catherine's in the Russia Channel's series is the profound ambivalence about the nature of Michael's power in the Hollywood classic and *Catherine*'s insistence on state-sponsored violence as the indispensable condition for successful imperial rule. Catherine's multiple murders are portrayed as justified by the goal of ensuring the stability of the empire. Notably and in total compliance with the logic of patriarchal order in this final stretch on her way to absolute power, Catherine switches to male costume, the uniform of one of the imperial regiments that brought her to power.

The fashion for depicting Russia's leaders as charismatic continues on transnational streaming channels. While the epic/melodramatic tradition dominates, with numerous series about the royal dynasties and their autocratic leaders, the conventions have become somewhat stale in the twenty-first century and have been parodied in recent film and television productions, such as Armando Ianucci's *The Death of Stalin* (2017), Yorgos Lanthimos and Tony McNamara's *The Favorite* (2018), and Tony McNamara's recent *The Great* (2020) produced for Hulu. These shows openly privilege artistic sensibility above historical authenticity, a problematic category in the first place. Moreover, these films and series follow the serio-comic tradition, carnivalizing not only the rulers themselves but also the exalted attitude to the myth, always malleable and manipulated to fit the agenda of the day, be it commercial or slightly disguised government propaganda. Most importantly, these productions challenge the seriousness and sentimental fantasies that feed the representations of charismatic rulers. Instead they offer a refreshing breath of irony and satire. In the first episode of Hulu's *The Great,* Peter the Third takes Catherine to meet his mother whose mummified body is on display icon-style in the palace, not unlike the relics of a holy person. "She was a goddess, extraordinary, powerful, no one like her," says the devoted son while introducing his fiancée to his mother's adorned corpse. To Catherine's credit, she doesn't blink an eye, curtsies, says that the mother is pretty, and proceeds to behave as an aspiring wife in the presence of the omnipotent boy's mother. While the reference to *Psycho* animates the entire encounter, the scene never slides into a crude parody of Russian monarchy or Catherine's historical persona. What it does, however, is efficiently undermine the aura of charismatic power which we as viewers are tricked to buy into in traditional costume dramas. This, perhaps, is what is lacking in so well-executed and high-budget period dramas about Russia's most enlightened and long-ruling empress.

Bibliography

Condee, Nancy. *The Imperial Trace: Recent Russian Cinema.* Cambridge, UK: Cambridge University Press, 2009.

Fathallah, Judith May. *Fanfiction and the Author.* Amsterdam: Amsterdam University Press, 2017.

Ford, Elizabeth, and Deborah C. Mitchell. *Royal Portraits in Hollywood: Filming the Lives of Queens.* Lexington: University Press of Kentucky, 2009.

Ford, Rebecca. "Inside HBO and Hulu's Very Different Takes on Catherine the Great and Her 'Super Complicated Relationships.'" Hollywood Reporter, June 29, 2020. https://www.hollywoodreporter.com/lists/inside-hbo-hulus-very-takes-catherine-great-her-super-complicated-relationships-1300760.

Glynn, Basil. "The Conquests of Henry the VIII: Masculinity, Sex, and the National Past in *The Tudors.*" In *Television, Sex, and Society: Analyzing Contemporary Representations,* edited by Beth Johnson, James Aston, and Basil Glynn, 157–174. New York: Bloomsbury, 2012.

Larina, Kseniia, and Irina Petrovskaia. "Chelovek iz televizora." Ekho Moskvy, November 29, 2014. http://echo.msk.ru/programs/persontv/1445692-echo/.

Larina, Kseniia, and Irina Petrovskaia. "Chelovek iz televizora." Ekho Moskvy, November 7, 2015. http://echo.msk.ru/programs/persontv/1653660-echo/.

Norris, Stephen. *Blockbuster History in the New Russia: Movies, Memory, and Patriotism.* Bloomington: Indiana University Press, 2012.

Smirnova, Elena. "*Velikaia* vs. *Ekaterina:* Iuliia Snigir' ili Marina Aleksandrova?" Vokrug.tv, November 5, 2015. http://www.vokrug.tv/article/show/velikaya_vs_ekaterina_yuliya_snigir_ili_marina_aleksandrova_50251/.

Sturken, Marita. "Reenactment, Fantasy, and the Paranoia of History: Oliver Stone's Docudramas." *History and Theory* 36, no. 4 (December 1997): 64–79.

Between Pornography and Nostalgia: Valery Todorovsky's *The Thaw* (*Ottepel'*)

Lilya Kaganovsky

Valery Todorovsky's 2013 TV series *The Thaw* (*Ottepel'*) borrows its looks, its inspiration, and its misanthropic protagonist from Matthew Weiner's American breakthrough television series, *Mad Men* (AMC, 2007–2015), as well as following in the wake of Todorovsky's own 2008 film, *Hipsters* (*Stiliagi*), that gave us a glimpse into the brief but colorful non-conformist culture of the Soviet 1950s. Set in 1961, *The Thaw* takes as its subject and operative metaphor the Soviet Union's central filmmaking studio, Mosfil'm, and the lives of its inhabitants: directors, script writers, cinematographers, actors, administrators, costume designers, makeup artists, and the like. A backstage melodrama, *The Thaw* foregrounds the process by which Soviet films were made (or not made), putting a cameraman—Viktor Khrustalev—at the center of the action. The choice of profession speaks to the overarching metaphor of "seeing" that lies at the heart of this series. While Todorovsky readily admits that he was inspired to make the series by his father's career at Mosfil'm, he chose to make his protagonist not a film director, but rather, a cinematographer. (His father, Petr Todorovsky, had been both.) A bystander to the events unfolding around him—including, as it turns out, to World War II—Khrustalev watches rather than acts, beginning with the opening sequence of the first episode in which one of Khrustalev's paramours, hoping to provoke him, goes outside for a smoke, totally naked. But clearly, this act of exhibitionism elicits mostly his professional rather than personal interest: Khrustalev remains at the window, the man behind the glass, a distanced observer of the events that unfold before his dispassionate and mediated gaze (Fig. 1).

This opening sequence also makes clear the kind of television series *The Thaw* is trying to be. *Quality television* as it came to be defined by American television critics, meant not only high production values, good writing, and obsessive attention to period detail and mise-en-scène, but also—in direct opposition to American broadcast television with its strict obscenity rules—for

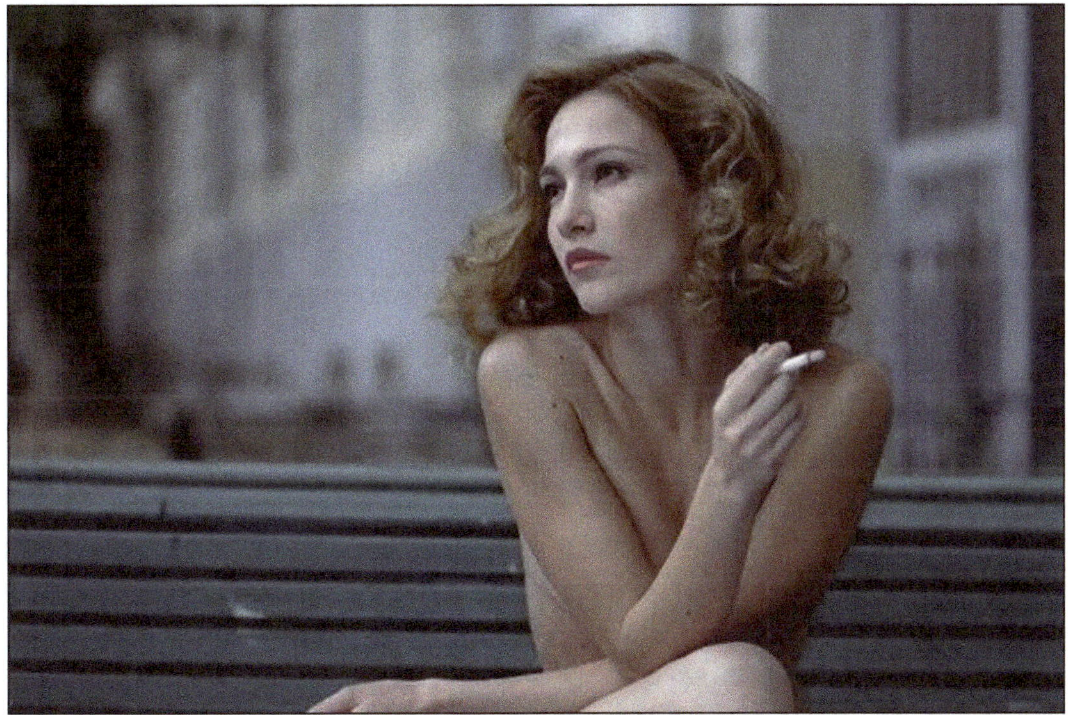

Fig. 1. Natura (Larisa/Evgeniia Brik).

its use of nudity, language, and violence.[1] By opening the first episode with an image of a naked woman smoking on a park bench, *The Thaw* signals its participation in this larger framework of what contemporary television serials can and cannot show, insisting from the start on its "quality" credentials on the global television market. By including, from the very start, both nudity and sexual content, *The Thaw* rejects the myth of "no sex in the USSR"—whether on

1 "Quality television," a term denoting the kind of writerly cable drama, entered the scene with HBO's now classic series *The Sopranos*, the show Matthew Weiner helped to produce in the years before launching his own series, *Mad Men*. The term can serve as a bridge between film and TV, since it is used as code for television that is supposedly "filmlike," as Lynne Joyrich suggests. See Lynne Joyrich, "Media Madness: Multiple Identity (Dis) Orders in *Mad Men*," in *Mad Men, Mad World: Sex, Politics, Style and the 1960s*, ed. Lauren M. E. Goodlad, Lilya Kaganovsky, and Robert A. Rushing (Durham: Duke University Press, 2013), 213–237. Swearing, smoking, and drinking are part of this as well, as the negative press around *The Thaw* was quick to point out. See, for example, the interview with Mark Zakharov in *Komsomol'skaia pravda*, December 7, 2013: "Esli aktery v kadre kuriat po-chernomu, znachit, rezhisseru nechego skazat'," https://www.kp.ru/daily/26169.7/3055754/.

television, in cinema, or in reality.[2] Moreover, it provides a native answer to international TV shows, including *Mad Men*, which are now easily accessible to Russian audiences. As a result, *The Thaw* is a combination of recognizable nostalgic Soviet tropes, but with a contemporary post-Soviet audience in mind. In episode 4, the old guard who make up the creative council at Mosfil'm (*khudozhestvennyi sovet*) make fun of a young director who wants to film a nude scene in all its details: "obnazhennuiu naturu, vo vsekh podrobnostiakh." In episode 5, Todorovsky includes a fairly prolonged full-body shot of our main star, Mar'iana, in the buff, and in all the "details." This way, *The Thaw* gets to both evoke and reject the constraints put on Soviet cinema and television by official Soviet morality—as TV critic Andrei Arkhangel'sky has put it, to provide a kind of "upgrade" to Soviet films of the 1960s, such as *July Rain* (*Iiul'skii dozhd'*, dir. Marlen Khutsiev, 1967) or *Once More About Love* (*Eshche raz pro liubov'*, dir. Georgii Natanson, 1968), that includes erotic content. For Arkhangel'sky, this is symptomatic of our current moment, and our (mistaken) sense that the only freedom Soviet directors lacked was the "freedom to film nude scenes."[3]

But while Todorovsky is very much aware of what can and cannot be shown on Russian television, the series' relationship to the past is more complex, and—most vitally—more self-aware than this criticism allows.[4] The opening credit sequence includes a shot of Todorovsky himself in the director's chair, and he appears briefly in episode 3 in the role of the *mudak* ("asshole") film director at Mosfil'm.[5] The message is clear: not only should we be reminded of the fact that *The Thaw* is artifice and not reality (or even its nostalgic representation), but that its "realism" is an effect created by careful attention to props, costumes, hairstyles, and other objects of design that produce the illusion of authenticity. Even the central conceit of the series—the young director Egor Miachin's attempt to make an updated version of the Stalinist musical, complete with contemporary costumes, on-location shooting, hand-held cameras, and

2 "V 'Ottepeli' Todorovskogo seks est'!," Piter.tv, December 5, 2013, https://web.archive.org/web/20131208111602/http://piter.tv/event/Ottepel_na_Pervom_kanale/.

3 Andrei Arkhangel'skii, "Khrustalev, mashinku!," *Ogonek* 48 (December 9, 2013): 40, https://www.kommersant.ru/doc/2358217

4 Valerii Todorovskii, "Kurit' v kadre mozhno? Pit' mozhno? Golykh zhenshchin mozhno?," 1tv.ru, December 5, 2013, https://www.1tv.ru/shows/vecherniy-urgant/vypuski/vecherniy-urgant-247-vypusk-05-12-2013.

5 Besides nudity and sexual content, strong language is one of the other ways Todorovsky pushes the envelope of what is acceptable for contemporary Russian television.

non-professional actors—in other words, his attempt at *sincerity* in the cinema, is framed within the larger discourse of its impossibility. *The Thaw* understands very well, even if Egor does not, that filmmaking is a series of compromises and untruths; it is a put-on, a make-believe. As Regina Markovna, the second director on *The Girl and the Brigadier* (*Devushka i brigadir*), puts it, "This is our genre: a bit over the top" ("U nas zhanr takoi: chut'-chut' s pereborom").[6]

Set in the 1960s and filled with the fashions, cars, dachas, and other "authentic" objects of that era (recalling both reality and its cinematic representations), referencing Todorovsky's own childhood, the series at the same time is constantly aware of its own fundamentally post-modern, post-Soviet nature. On the one hand, a discourse of *sincerity*—that key word of the Soviet Thaw—runs through the diegesis, mostly focusing on the young director Egor Miachin's love for Mar'iana, and his attempt to turn a trite Stalinist musical comedy into something that reflects the values of the Thaw. On the other hand, this series, like other retro-nostalgia productions really does function as a kind of "upgrade" of the 1960s for the contemporary viewer: included are not only sex scenes, but open political commentary on the Soviet state; while the bright "Technicolor" palette and retro fashions remind us that we are not looking at Soviet sixties' cinema, but at its postmodern reincarnation.[7] Indeed, *The Thaw* is very aware of

6 Many of the characters in *The Thaw* are based on real-world prototypes: Egor Miachin's desire to update the Stalinist musical should remind us of El'dar Riazanov's 1956 *Carnival Night* (*Karnaval'naia noch'*), including Liudmila Gurchenko's initial failure to get the part because the cameraman incorrectly arranged the lighting and put her in the wrong costume. The casting of an unknown actress in a leading role, and the title of the musical comedy also points us to Riazanov's next film, *A Girl Without an Address* (*Devushka bez adresu*, 1957); and back to Gurchenko, whose next role was in *A Girl with a Guitar* (*Devushka s gitaroi*, dir. Aleskandr Faintsimmer, 1958) and who was briefly married to a novice director, Vasily Ordynsky. On Gurchenko, see Rimgaila Salys, "Liudmila Gurchenko: Stardom in the Late Soviet Era," in *Women in Soviet Film: The Thaw and Post-Thaw Periods*, ed. Marina Rojavin and Tim Harte (New York: Routledge, 2018), 28–48. On Ryazanov, see Michele Leigh, "A Laughing Matter: El'dar Riazanov and the Subversion of Soviet Gender in Russian Comedy," in *Women in Soviet Film*, 112–133.

7 Since *The Thaw* premiered on Russian television in 2013, there have followed a number of shows set in the 1950s and the 60s. (This happened in the United States following *Mad Men* also, but without success.) The most striking thing about them is their unapologetic recycling not only of actors and sets, but of objects and characters. *Black Market* (*Fartsa*, dir. Egor Baranov, March 30, 2015) opens with Evgenii Tsyganov—the actor who plays Viktor Khrustalev—trying to escape from the police. *The Optimists* (*Optimisty*, dir. Aleksei Popogrebsky, April 24, 2017) concludes by having one of the diplomats sell his red Moskvich to "some cameraman at Mosfil'm." On contemporary Russian TV series set during the Thaw (of which there have been over a dozen since 2010), see Mark Lipovetskii and Tat'iana Mikhailova, "Bol'she, chem nostalgiia (Pozdnii sotsializm v teleserialakh 2010-kh godov)," *NLO* 169 (3/2021): 127-147.

precisely its place in the larger televisual marketplace, aware of its own origins as both original (based on Petr Todorovsky's life at Mosfil'm) and copy (*Mad Men*), and of its appeal as a means of reimagining the Soviet past in the present moment. In this way, the series straddles the fine line between post-Soviet nostalgia and its rejection that has dominated Russian film and television of the new millennium.

Between Nostalgia and Pornography

From its inception, as Svetlana Boym has suggested, Soviet ideology was radically anti-nostalgic, with "nostalgia" a dangerous atavism of bourgeois decadence that had no place in the new world.[8] Even before the Bolshevik Revolution, nostalgia was perceived as a European disease, not applicable to Russia. The nations that "came of age late" (Russia and America, particularly), wished to distinguish themselves from the aging Europe, and developed their identity on an antinostalgic premise: "Our memories go no further back than yesterday; we are as it were strangers to ourselves," wrote Petr Chaadaev in the first half of the nineteenth century.[9]

If Soviet culture officially rejected nostalgia, post-Soviet culture embraced it; and one of the ironies of the post-Soviet period has been its insistent and largely indiscriminate nostalgia for *everything* that came before—from Imperial Russian culture to the late Soviet period, and even, most recently, for the chaotic 1990s.[10] And while cinema of the immediate post-Soviet period was largely focused on unearthing and reconstructing the sins of the past, Putin-era cinema has been dominated by rosier representations of the Soviet period. This trend began with Karen Shakhnazarov's 2009 *Vanished Empire*, shot in the "golden light" of the 1970s, that reimagined the crash of communism as the crash of something "very personal, innocent, and full of hope"—a largely unreflexive nostalgia for the lost Soviet past.[11]

8 Svetlana Boym, *The Future of Nostalgia* (New York: Basic Books, 2001), 59.

9 Ibid., 17.

10 For example, Gosha Rubchinsky's 2018 S/S collection, inspired by soccer and Russian rave aesthetics of the nineties.

11 As I have suggested elsewhere, Shakhnazarov's film is an exercise in reading Aleksei Yurchak's *Everything Was Forever, Until It Was No More* (Princeton: Princeton University Press, 2005), 8–9.

Most recently, the 1960s in particular have reemerged as the "golden age" of Soviet socialism, and it seems not incidental that the big Thaw exhibition put on by the contemporary wing of the Tretiakov Gallery in 2017, ostensibly to mark the one-hundred-year anniversary of the Russian Revolution, celebrated not the avant-garde twenties, but the 1960s. As the catalogue authors note,

> It's not an accident that this relatively short period of time, which lasted about fifteen years, has been called an "era." The saturation of time with some of the most important historical events produced a sense of fullness. The weakening of state control and the democratization of methods for handling culture significantly revitalized creative processes. The Thaw style was formed—an original version of Soviet modernism of the 1960s—stimulated in many ways by scientific achievements in the fields of space and nuclear energy. The cosmos and the atom—the largest and smallest of quantities—determined the range of "universalist" thinking of the sixties' generation, looking to the future.[12]

Because it was inspired by *Mad Men*—which itself tapped into a deep and unexplored nostalgia for the American mid-century with its modernist style, fashionable clothes, and outmoded race and gender roles—Todorovsky's *The Thaw* led the way in this nostalgic return to the Soviet sixties. Yet, unlike Shakhnazarov's *Vanished Empire*, *The Thaw* was not interested in recreating the feelings of the "personal, innocent, hopeful, or sincere." Indeed, the series is about the impossibility of true love, of genuine emotions, of real friendship, of acts either of bravery or dissidence. When Khrustalev takes his daughter to see Egor's diploma film, the understated beauty of actual Soviet sixties' cinema and its garish Technicolor reproduction in *The Thaw* is put into stark contrast. Todorovsky's serial is in every way the opposite of 60s' Soviet art house films which we will never get to see: in *The Thaw*, we catch only the closing shots of Miachin's diploma film (rain, black-and-white imagery, allegory of hope/youth lost); in *Black Market*, the characters walk out of a screening of Mikhail Romm's *Nine Days of One Year*, offended by the preceding newsreel. Egor is "Romm's student," and his diploma film is a send up of every young filmmaker of the Thaw; as Nadia Krivitskaia (speaking for the Soviet masses) says, it is the kind of picture where "ambience" and "mood" and "dust" take priority over genuine entertainment.

12 See the Tretiakov Gallery website, https://www.tretyakovgallery.ru/exhibitions/ottepel/.

The Thaw, instead, is a very pretty simulacrum, where everything and everyone is "beautiful."[13] Everything about the film's mise-en-scène—the attention to period detail, the overly saturated colors that in no way resemble Soviet reality or stylish black-and-white Soviet new wave cinema—appears in a stark light, as if illuminated by the Klieg light we see at the end of the credit sequence.[14] Like Egor's attempt to make a more "realistic" Soviet musical comedy, which is both made fun of and encouraged, *The Thaw* moves between a desire for authenticity and an awareness of its own artificiality. The focus on period details is excessive, the clothes overly fashionable, the Soviet objects of everyday life do not fade into the background but remain insistently "present," as if we are looking at a Mosfil'm studio lot and all its props—as in fact, we are.

It is precisely this exhibitionist quality that places this series somewhere between nostalgia and "pornography"—the genre that is supposed to "show everything," to hide nothing, to register "all" with an objective camera, and offer it to our view. In pornography, as Slavoj Žižek has argued, "the gaze qua object falls onto the subject-spectator."[15] The events unfolding before us speak to us directly from the screen. We do not need to wonder if they have been staged for us—we know that they have precisely *us* in mind, are there to elicit *our* enjoyment. This is precisely what makes pornography "perverse": not what is being shown on the screen, but the fact that it knows we are looking. The gaze qua object (that is to say, the object that looks back at us, that sees us seeing, that knows about our pleasures and desires), *this* gaze constitutes pornography's perversion. In nostalgia, on the other hand, instead of the object-gaze turned ruthlessly toward us (and forcing us to "see everything"), we have a gaze that is looking away, toward some distant and removed past, a past that is coded as its own hermetically sealed and private world that *does not* require our direct participation. The viewer of nostalgia is safely voyeuristic, invisible to the characters on screen, unseen but all seeing, able to follow their

13 Sergei Efimov, "Valerii Todorovskii: 'Ia reshil, chto v "Ottepeli" vse zhenshchiny budut krasivymi,'" *Komsomol'skaia pravda,* December 2, 2013, http://www.kp.ru/daily/26166.5/3053484/.

14 Klieg lights burned carbon arcs, which gave out an intense burst of light. In the early days of their use actors were alleged to have gone blind. So Khrustalev walking into the Klieg light at the end of the credit sequence is a similar act of suicide as Don Draper falling out of window of his New York skyscraper in the credit sequence to *Mad Men.*

15 Slavoj Žižek, *Looking Awry: An Introduction to Jacques Lacan through Popular Culture* (Cambridge, MA: The MIT Press, 1991), 111.

every move, watch their every action. In nostalgic retro films "the logic of the gaze qua object appears as such": the real object of fascination is not the displayed scene, but "the gaze of the naïve 'other' absorbed, enchanted by it."[16]

Indeed, this is precisely what is staged for us in the opening sequence, when Khrustalev's "all-knowing" gaze is replaced by the gaze of the naïve other, "absorbed" and "enchanted" by the spectacle that has been staged for him. From a shot of Khrustalev gazing dispassionately out of his window, we cut to a young man walking home in the early hours of the morning, and it is *his* astonished gaze that we follow and that gives us the full 180-degree view of the naked Larisa smoking on the bench. This way, the series gets to have it both ways: it maintains the distance between the cynical viewer (of pornography) and the naïve viewer (of nostalgia), suturing us in the space between them.

Between the Look and the Gaze

But there is still another way that *The Thaw* constructs the "look" and the "gaze," that both reinforces and troubles gender binaries of seeing and being seen. By opening the first episode with a woman appearing naked for the male gaze (Khrustalev's, the young man's, ours), *The Thaw* joins the long list of Western representations of the female nude. As John Berger observed in his book *Ways of Seeing* (1972):

> In the average European oil painting of the nude, the principal protagonist is never painted. He is the spectator in front of the picture and he is presumed to be a man. Everything is addressed to him. Everything must appear to be the result of his being there. It is for him that the figures have assumed their nudity. But he, by definition, is a stranger with his clothes still on.[17]

Addressing the gendered nature of spectatorship, this passage anticipates by a few years Laura Mulvey's pronouncement in 1975 on the male gaze in classic Hollywood cinema.[18] The structure of the invisible male spectator for whom the female nude obligingly exhibits herself

16 Ibid., 114.

17 John Berger, *Ways of Seeing* (New York: Penguin, 1972), 54.

18 Laura Mulvey, "Visual Pleasure and Narrative Cinema," *Screen* 16, no. 3 (1975): 6–18.

has haunted the discourse of representation, opening up questions concerning the construction of gender, the limits of identification, and the uses of pleasure (whether voyeuristic, scopophilic, fetishistic, or other). For Mulvey, the position of the cinematic spectator was gendered male in relation to the "feminized" visual image. The woman herself, when she appeared on the screen, displayed the quality of what Mulvey called "to-be-looked-at-ness": she was made up, dressed, and photographed in such a way as to put herself on visual display, to exhibit herself to our gaze. Indeed, cinema itself has often been referred to as the meeting of the "voyeur" and the "exhibitionist." No matter what their sex, gender, or sexual orientation, the spectators' pleasure comes from sneaking a peak into the private world of the characters, while everything about the moviegoing experience is meant to heighten the feeling of the spectator-as-Peeping-Tom. We can look, but we cannot be seen; we are "outside" in the dark, while they are inside with all the lights turned on.

Since the publication of these two seminal works, the notion of the "male gaze" has been problematized, examined, deconstructed, and updated, even by Mulvey herself.[19] In this instance, however, I would like to suggest the direction pointed to by Kaja Silverman in her 1986 essay, "Fragments of a Fashionable Discourse," in which she opposes the "automatic equation of spectacular display with female subjectivity," by looking more closely at the history of Western fashion. To undo the easy equation of woman with spectacle, Silverman suggests that the history of fashion—and in particular, as that history is rendered in both cinematic and literary texts—offers us a "more complex circuit of visual exchange than might at first appear."[20] In place of the passive observer, the "stranger with his clothes still on," Silverman traces the history of the male fascination with female dress, a fascination which, she argues, is always inflected in some way by identification. I cannot help but wonder, she writes, "for whom he is really shopping when Humbert Humbert spends a whole afternoon buying dresses with

19 Many studies have followed Berger's and Mulvey's seminal works, including Mulvey's own "Some Afterthoughts on 'Visual Pleasure and Narrative Cinema,'" *Framework* 15–17 (1981): 12–15. See also Linda Williams's introduction to her *Viewing Positions: Ways of Seeing Film* (New Brunswick: Rutgers University Press, 1995), 1–20. Moreover, cinematic spectatorship is different from the televisual, where the proximity of the viewer to the screen, the television's location inside the home, and the fact that it offers what is classified as "popular culture" together gender the television viewer as female rather than male. See Lynne Joyrich, "Epistemology of the Console," *Critical Inquiry* 27, no. 3 (2001): 439–467; and her *Re-viewing Reception: Television, Gender, and Postmodern Culture* (Bloomington: Indiana University Press, 1996).

20 Kaja Silverman, "Fragments of a Fashionable Discourse," in *Studies in Entertainment*, ed. Tania Modleski (Bloomington: Indiana University Press, 1986): 139–152, here: 139.

'check weaves, bright cottons, frills, puffedout short sleeves, soft pleats, snugfitting bodices and generously full skirts' for Lolita—or when Marcel decides after prolonged deliberation to order not one, but four priceless Fortuny gowns for Albertine."[21]

For Silverman, the male subject is as dependent upon the gaze of the Other as is the female subject, and "as solicitous of it"—in other words, that he is as fundamentally exhibitionist as she is. The cinematic structure of the look and the gaze identified by Mulvey, therefore, should not be understood as the complete aphanisis of male specularity, but merely as its disavowal: "In mainstream fashion, as in dominant cinema, this disavowal is most frequently effected by identifying male subjectivity with a network of looks, including those of the designer, the photographer, the admirer, and the 'connoisseur.'" Specifically, for Silverman, the paradox upon which such an identification turns accumulates around the figure of the fashion photographer (in such films as Antonioni's *Blow Up* or Berry Gordy's *Mahogany*) whose relationship to exhibitionism can only be negotiated through spectacle. It requires the male subject to see himself (and thus to be seen) as "the one who looks at women."[22]

This is remarkably true for *The Thaw* that, from the very beginning, stages the presence of the male gaze as a series of disavowals of male specularity. In place of the fashion photographer, *The Thaw* gives us a cameraman who is always looking at the women around him through an imaginary lens, and a "disinterested"costume designer, who dresses them. Indeed, by splitting the role into two, *The Thaw* performs a series of distancing operations meant to ensure the proper functioning of heterosexuality, which comes under threat of emasculation from the elite, anti-authoritarian, and bohemian world of cinematic "make-believe," where everyone, from the bit players to the gaffers is caught up in specular identification. Indeed, costuming—and women's clothes, specifically—plays a major role in the series, both inside and outside the diegesis. As Vladimir Kuptsov, the costume designer for *The Thaw* explained, the goal was not to make the costumes necessarily authentic to the epoch, but to make them "beautiful." This includes the numerous actresses who appear in the background of the Mosfil'm lot, and even the Soviet citizens on the Moscow metro. (We might compare these fashionable extras to the actual Soviet men and women standing next to the Dior models during their trip to Moscow, as

21 Ibid., 141–142.

22 Ibid., 143.

captured by the photographers of *Life* magazine in 1959.)[23] For the film's style, Todorovsky was less interested in "documentalism" or in what actual people actually wore: "Real life might have been poorer, greyer, simpler. But in the series, everything had to first of all be beautiful."[24] This desire to exaggerate the beauty of the times extended to the extreme attention to detail, which included a search for vintage sixties dresses to be copied, and to authentic foundation garments to shape the figure. As Kuptsov notes, their biggest luck was in finding the right kind of underwear for the actresses, the corsets, girdles, bras, and panties that would create the hourglass figure. The undergarments proved so effective that the actresses "happily" wore them even when they were not visible, in order to maintain the proper feminine silhouette.[25]

This attention to clothes outside the show is likewise thematized within the show by making a costume designer one of the key characters—Aleksandr (Sancha) Pichugin, Mar'iana's brother, Egor's friend, and Liusia's love interest. Sancha designs the stylish costumes for the production of *The Girl and the Brigadier*, updating the Stalinist tractor musical to reflect postwar French fashions. But off the set, he also plays a key role in dressing the other characters in the film, from his sister Mar'iana to Liusia Polynina, the camerawoman whose narrative arc focuses on her transformation from gender-ambiguous tomboy to something resembling traditional heteronormative femininity. Indeed, the attention to clothes as markers of sexual difference on the show goes a long way toward constructing and reinforcing gender norms that might otherwise have been troubled by the presence of a gay man, a masculine woman, and the bohemian morality of the 1960s.

Between Soviet Fashion and Dior's "New Look"

We are first introduced to our leading lady, Mar'iana Pichugina, in the tailor shop where her brother works, when Egor comes to borrow a jacket for his interview with the director of Mosfil'm. Mar'iana steps out of the dressing room wearing one of the full-skirted Dior-style

23 "Christian Dior v Moskve. 1959 god," Fishki.net, December 21, 2011, https://fishki.net/40155-christian-dior-v-moskve-1959-god-30-foto.html

24 "Kino kak zhizn': moda 60-kh godov v seriale 'Ottepel',"' Wday.ru, December 5, 2013, https://www.wday.ru/moda-shopping/style/kino-kak-jizn-moda-60-h-godov-v-seriale-ottepel/.

25 Ibid.

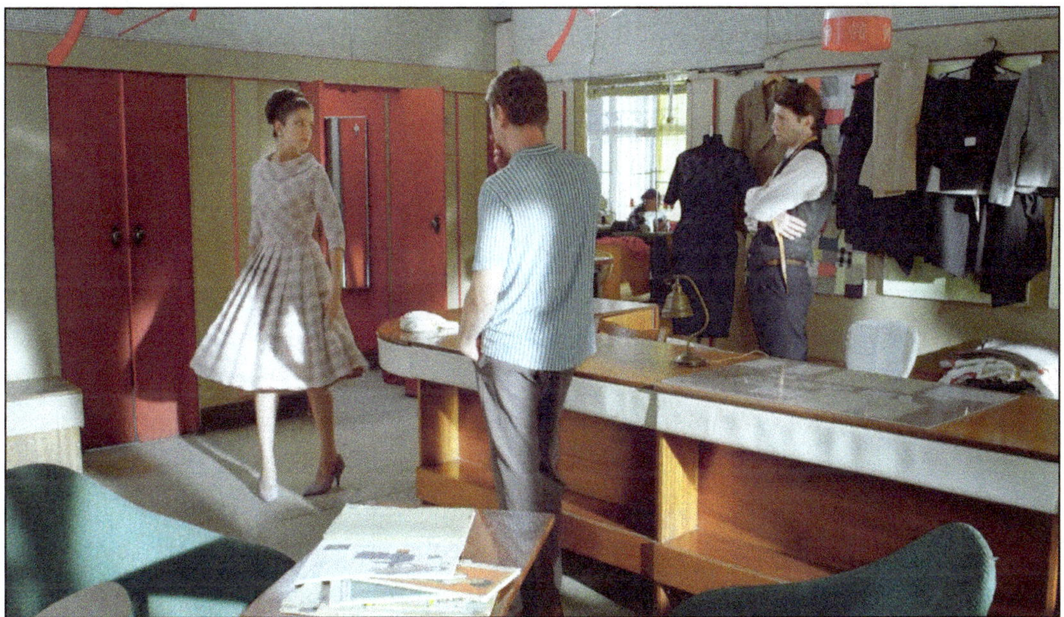

Fig. 2. Dior's "New Look"
(Mar'iana Pichugina/Anna Chipovskaia, Egor Miachin/Aleksandr Iatsenko, Sancha Pichugin/Evgeny Volotsky).

dresses Sancha has made for her, and it is here that Egor falls in love with her based entirely on her appearance, created and shaped by her brother and Dior's New Look. Repeatedly referenced in the series, Christian Dior's reputation as one of the most important couturiers of the twentieth century was launched in 1947 with his very first collection, which featured rounded shoulders, a cinched waist, and a very full skirt. Introduced just two years after the end of World War II, Dior's New Look celebrated ultra-femininity and opulence in women's fashion after years of military and civilian uniforms, sartorial restrictions and shortages. In place of the "soldier girl with a boxer's build," Dior offered the "woman-flower": a feminine silhouette that included a prominent bust, flat stomach, and rounded hips.[26] Immediately dubbed the "New Look" by *Harper's Bazaar* editor in chief Carmel Snow, the hourglass figure and its extravagant demand for fabric created a scandal—but also met with the instant, dazzling success that made it the emblem of the decade. Mar'iana's preferred dress style is

26 *Les années 50. La mode en France, 1947–1957*, exhibition catalogue, Paris Musées, https://www.palaisgalliera.paris.fr/en/exhibitions/50s.

based on the dresses that first exemplified the "New Look" in all its salient elements: sloped shoulder, raised bustline, narrowed waist, and a monumental volume of skirt falling away from a padded hipline. It is unquestionably *young* and unquestionably *feminine*: it is meant to signal to the viewer Mar'iana's (sexual) innocence and inexperience (Fig. 2).[27]

As N. B. Lebina and Larissa Zakharova both demonstrate, while the New Look was popularized in Europe at the end of the 1940s, in the Soviet Union, it began to dominate women's fashion in the second half of the 1950s despite the fact that the New Look was fundamentally bourgeois, and more closely resembled Stalinist preference for the monumental in high fashion than going along with the democratic tendencies of the 1960s.[28] The summer 1957 issue of *Rabotnitsa* (*The Worker*), for example, included a pattern for the underskirt that would produce the desired voluminous effect. By the early 1960s, *Rabotnitsa* followed the directions set by the Ministry of Light Industry in promoting a simplified and more elegant look for the Soviet citizen, whose wardrobe choices should be driven by coherence and elegance in color and style: "When choosing a fabric for a new dress, keep in mind the color of your shoes and purse. It is a plus, of course, if their color matches everything."[29] Indeed, we see this moment reflected in *The Thaw* during a show at the Moscow House of Fashion (Moskovskii dom modelei), in which tailored grey suits for women are promoted as elements of "good taste"; as well as in a conversation between Sancha and Ruslan about the difference between "fashionable" and "elegant."

Because mass production was not available, patterns and cutting-and-sewing guides were offered for every single wardrobe item (including underwear), which meant that women who knew how to sew could get by without factory-made clothing. But this also contributed to

27 By contrast, Inga Khrustaleva—Khrustalev's ex-wife and the co-star of *The Girl and the Brigadier*—favors the pencil skirt and blouse combo. Her tailored look is meant to mark her as an older actress who stands out from the crowd of twentysomethings in their flowing dresses, but also as someone whose sexuality is more adult and whose relationship to femininity is more mature.

28 N. B. Lebina, "Konets epokhi bol'shogo stilia: Antistalinskie tendentsii v mode 1960-kh godov," in *Ottepel'*, exhibition catalogue (Moscow: Gosudarstvennaia Tret'iakovskaia galereia, 2017), 177–191; Larissa Zakharova, "Soviet Fashion in the 1950s–1960s: Regimentation, Western Influences, and Consumption Strategies," in *The Thaw Soviet Society and Culture during the 1950s and 1960s*, ed. Denis Kozlov and Eleonory Gilburd (Toronto: University of Toronto Press, 2013), 402–435. On socialist fashion, see also Djurdja Bartlett, *Fashion East: The Spectre that Haunted Socialism* (Cambridge, MA: The MIT Press, 2010).

29 Lebina, "Konets epokhi bol'shogo stilia," 179–180; Zakharova, "Soviet Fashion in the 1950s–1960s," 403.

the retrenchment of gender norms in the 1950s and the 60s, when women were once again saddled with domestic chores, which were now declared not burdensome, but "pleasant." As Zakharova points out, this new gender orientation was also apparent in new norms of appearance: "For a woman to wear pants in an urban setting was considered the height of *mauvais ton* and poor taste, whereas luxurious skirts à la the Dior 'New Look' gained a firm foothold in Soviet fashion, promoted as a choice for young women for more formal occasions."[30]

We might note, however, that Mar'iana's ultra-feminine Dior look reflects not only the gender codes of the 1960s, but also *The Thaw*'s gender and sexual politics. While the costumes Sancha designs for the production of *The Girl and the Brigadier* are meant to subvert the expectations of the Stalinist musical comedy (as Egor also tries to do with his casting choices, his preference for on-location shooting, and his obsessive attention to detail), the costumes worn by the characters in *The Thaw* do the exact opposite: they reinforce gender norms and expectations—both period and contemporary—especially for the female characters. As signaled by their clothes, gender roles appear to be completely normative here, while all gender-ambiguous characters—including Sancha, the first "sympathetic" gay character in post-Soviet television, and Liusia, the female cinematographer who walks, talks, and smokes like a man—must pay the price for their non-conformity. In *The Thaw*, men are allowed to defy authority, even the state, but women are not allowed to defy gender expectations that remain as rigid as the corsets by which their bodies are shaped. Exaggerated female silhouettes keep the female characters firmly on the side of specularity, while allowing the male characters to retain their fantasy as "subjects who look at women."

Between Men

Indeed, the gender roles for women appear so strict that one begins to wonder if something else here is actually at stake. The insistence on universal female beauty and the inclusion of a gay character whose transgression is severely punished reinforces a heteronormativity that would otherwise be put into play. To begin with, the role of "actor" is itself suspect, as Liusia immediately observes to Sancha: "It's just that being an actor is not exactly (*ne sovsem*)

30 Zakharova, "Soviet Fashion in the 1950s–1960s," 418–419.

a male profession," she tells him, before recalling that being a cinematographer is not exactly a "female" one. This comment is reinforced by the fact that the two male leads in the tractor musical, Gennady Budnik and Ruslan, might both be suspected of a non-traditional sexual orientation, based in part on their familiarity with men's fashions. Budnik, the veteran actor who always plays the leading man, immediately recognizes the Dior influence on Sancha's costume design for *The Girl and the Brigadier*, including the use of the patch pockets from an earlier collection. Indeed, he is the only male character in the series whose sexual relations with women are never mentioned. Compare this to the emphasis placed on the sex lives of other male characters: Khrustalev, Egor, Fedia (the veteran Mosfil'm director, whose drinking often lands him in trouble), and even the props master Arkady Somov (who spends twelve episodes going back and forth between his mistress and his wife). Ruslan, the handsome young actor, is also very familiar with French design, calling Sancha "Dior-Khristian-Diorovich."

Ruslan's knowledge of current men's fashion and his desire to try his hand at modeling lead Sancha to mistake his ease with putting himself on display for non-heteronormativity. Ruslan struts his stuff on the runway at Dom modelei, confident in his display of masculinity as spectacle, unaware that he is crossing some kind of invisible line from "the one who looks at women," to the one being looked at. This might partially explain his surprise and violence when Sancha tries to kiss him: by putting himself on display as the *one to be looked at* Ruslan has opened himself (and the series) up to homosexual desire, which must be immediately eliminated. We might compare this scene of unwanted sexual contact to Liusia suddenly kissing Sancha, a moment of equal misunderstanding, but one that is played for laughs.

Indeed, the problem of the homosocial slipping into the homosexual is precisely what is at stake here. It is clear, for instance, that Mar'iana—while beautiful and charming and talented in her own right—mostly serves the purpose of facilitating relations "between men" as Eve Sedgwick would put it.[31] As I have argued elsewhere, and as *The Thaw* repeatedly confirms, Soviet culture's fear of *heterosexual* relations drives it precisely in the direction it least suspects it wants to go: in the first episode, Vitia Khrustalev and Kostia Parshin willingly abandon two ready and willing actresses in favor of a three-day all-male drinking binge; Khrustalev easily

31 As Eve Sedgwick has argued, the erotic triangle primarily serves the purpose of working out desire between men. See her *Between Men: English Literature and Male Homosocial Desire* (New York: Columbia University Press, 1985), and *Epistemology of the Closet* (Berkeley: University of California Press, 1990).

leaves the love-sick Mar'iana in his apartment to spend the night drinking beer with Egor instead, and gives up Mar'iana to Egor in order to ensure that their film gets made. Even the jacket Egor borrows from Sancha—no longer to meet with the Mosfil'm director but to date his sister—turns out to belong to Rudolf Nureyev, whose recent defection Egor is at pains to understand.[32] Sancha's brief explanation for Nureyev's flight—"don't you understand what kind of country we live in?"—might be heard simply as political commentary on the Soviet state; but given the contemporary viewer's knowledge of Nureyev's sexual orientation, it is also a way of introducing a homosexual subtext that is not just a hint at Sancha's own desires, but at the larger structures at work in the series. "Mar'iana" is there to prevent you from realizing that the jacket you borrow to court the beautiful but unattainable girl once belonged to a famous gay ballet dancer and is now being offered to you by your closeted best friend.

Sancha's role as costume designer and "gay best friend" is one of the means *The Thaw* finds for deflecting our gaze from male-as-spectacle (something that *Mad Men*, on the contrary, courts by making Don Draper a constant object of our visual pleasure). In comparison with the gruff Khrustalev, the goofy Egor, or the "ideally bald" Fedia, Sancha is well put together and traditionally handsome, a feature commented on by numerous women in the series. Liusia is struck by his looks from the beginning, believing initially that he must be an actor; and the entire costume department of Mosfil'm comes to a standstill when Sancha is first introduced there. By conveniently marking Sancha as the target of the female gaze and by making him into an object of desire (and then, possibly, repulsion), *The Thaw* gets around the problem of male specularity: we can safely identify with Khrustalev, Egor, even Fedia as heteronormative male subjects, as the ones "who look at women," rather than as the ones being looked at. The threat of homosexual desire and male specularity opened up by the narrative is safely contained within the diegesis.

32 Nureyev defected from the Soviet Union to the West in 1961, while on tour in Paris. This was the first defection of a Soviet artist during the Cold War, and it created an international sensation.

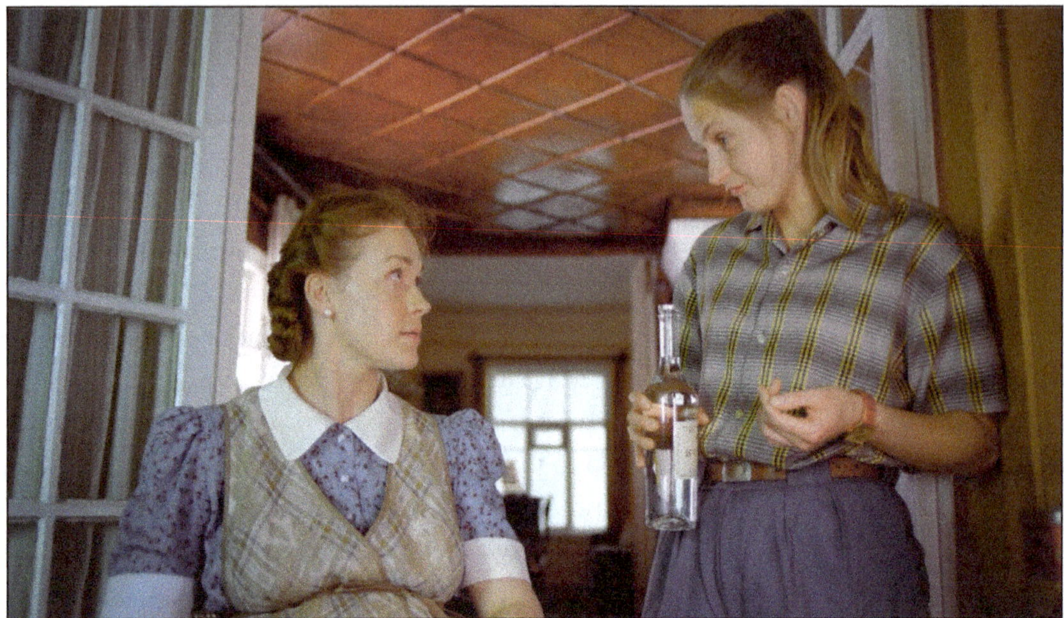

Fig. 3. Alternative femininities (Nadia/Svetlana Kolpakova and Liusia/Iana Sekste).

Neither Masculine nor Feminine

There are of course two notable exceptions in this series to the rule that "all women must be beautiful": the camerawoman Liusia Polynina and Fedia's conservative wife, Nadia, whose role throughout the series is to be the outsider, the normative Soviet viewer for whom cinema is made (Fig. 3). Their stories both trouble and reinforce *The Thaw*'s gender norms. Ostensibly based on the real Thaw-era cinematographer Margarita Pilikhina,[33] initially dressed in slacks and a button down shirt, chain smoking cigarettes and barking orders, Liusia spends most of the series learning to be a "woman": her narrative arc involves a series of makeovers that transform her from a tomboy into some semblance of femininity. But even after the makeovers, her appearance takes the form of a "female masquerade," and always seems "unnatural" when compared to the easy embodiments of femininity of the two leading actresses of *The Girl and*

33 While visually there is absolutely no relation between the two, she is often mentioned as the clear prototype for the character. See, for example, "Abrod," Livejournal.com, January 9, 2015, https://abrod.livejournal.com/684885.html.

the Brigadier, Mar'iana Pichugina and Inga Khrustaleva.[34] While Liusia starts out the series comfortably garbed in men's clothes, with hair pulled back into a messy pony-tail, in the final episode, she is dressed in a stylish red silk evening dress, hair pulled up into a beehive, face made up to resemble the actresses around her. Her transformation is initiated by her effort to make herself visible to Sancha *as a woman*: in other words, to make herself into a spectacle for the male gaze and thereby awaken his sexual desire. When her attempt to kiss Sancha leads to rejection, she sums it up as follows: "As a woman, I am nothing; as a camera operator, I am crap." The relationship between femininity and profession is not incidental: earlier, she had refused to tell Sancha how much the handheld camera weighed, so he would not think she was "an elephant."

Indeed, Liusia's profession of cinematographer is part of her masculinity, part of what makes her not exactly ("ne sovsem") a woman. The profession of cameraman has been consistently described as the most *male* of all of the jobs in the cinema, and cinematography has traditionally been a "boys' club." The job requires a fair amount of physical strength, particularly in the early days of cinema, when cameramen carted around both unwieldy camera equipment and film stock on their own bodies. It also requires (or can require) agility and a certain kind of masculine bravado. As Philip Cavendish has noted, Soviet camera operators famously achieved feats of bravery fighting off wild bears, hanging off the prows of ships, climbing to great heights or descending to great depths with little to no physical support. For the early Soviets, the camera became an emblem of "quasi-fetishized modernity" and the camera operator specializing in newsreel material, in particular in the context of military conflict, acquired iconic status "by virtue of his courage, athleticism, daring and ingenuity."[35] The Soviet film press was full of images of cameramen in positions of potential danger, if not mortal peril: Dziga Vertov and Mikhail Kaufman ascending a steep staircase high above the port of Novorossiisk, Petr Novitsky wearing a gas mask, Anatoly Golovnia "risking life and limb" to secure close-ups of ice-floes floating down a freezing river for *Mat'*; Andrei Moskvin's bruising footage of a roller-

34 Mary Ann Doane, "Film and Masquerade: Theorizing the Female Spectator," *Screen* 23, nos. 3–4 (1982): 74–88.

35 Philip Cavendish, *The Men with a Movie Camera: The Poetics of Visual Style in Soviet Avant-Garde Cinema of the 1920s* (Oxford: Berghahn Books, 2013), 18–20.

coaster ride in *Chertovo koleso*; his colleague, Evgeny Mikhailov, filming on horseback with a camera strapped to his chest for the circus sequence in *SVD*.[36]

Anecdotes from the early Soviet period are full of these and other legendary exploits that have entered cinematic lore and inform representations of cameramen in film and television, including *The Thaw*. In the very first episode, Khrustalev agrees to shoot an oncoming train from below—as Kaufman had done for Vertov in *Man with a Movie Camera*—for nothing more than a crate of cognac. Later in the episode, we watch as Khrustalev calmly lowers himself and his camera into a pit dug in the middle of a train track to get the head-on shot of the train coming toward the camera, while Regina Markovna repeats the phrase, "I'm going to be arrested" ("menia posadiat"). This performance of cool masculinity is in direct contrast to Regina Markovna's fretting, each accentuating their gendered expectations. This is why Liusia's role as "not quite" a woman creates a problem that the show must resolve. Liusia is "in between": her profession masculinizes her and devalues her as a woman, but without giving her access to male privilege. Throughout the series, she plays the supporting role, from chopping vegetables, to couple's counseling, to assistant cameraman; and while she initially has the job of DP on the production of *The Girl and the Brigadier*, it is immediately taken away from her and handed to Khrustalev, her male colleague. Explaining the need for the change, the lead actor Budnik sums up Liusia's shortcomings as follows: "First of all, she's a broad. Can't yell at her properly, can't tell her to go to hell" ("Vo-pervykh, baba. Ni garknut' tolkom, ni na khren poslat'"). Secondly, she is a "weak cinematographer." In the initial screen tests for *The Girl and the Brigadier*, Liusia arranges the lights incorrectly, causing a shadow to fall across the actress's face and losing her the role—a mistake Khrustalev notices, but does not correct. Liusia's placement on the other side of the camera disturbs the normative distribution between "the look and the gaze" typical of patriarchal cinema. Her initial position as "the one who looks" must be reversed: she must become the object, not the subject of the gaze.

Interestingly, Liusia's masculine garb, tomboyish manners, and her professional and erotic disappointments differ substantially from her ostensible prototype, the stylish and successful cinematographer Margarita Pilikhina, and speak instead to our contemporary ideas of what the life of a female cinematographer *must have been like* in 1961, rather than what it actually

36 Ibid., 20.

was.[37] As director Marlen Khutsiev noted in his afterword to Pilikhina's memoirs, "We are used to thinking of cinematography as a difficult, male profession. . . . But *without losing her femininity*, Margarita Pilikhina had all the qualifications necessary for work in this profession, where she has earned the right to one of its most lauded places."[38] In *The Thaw*, to counter the gender confusion produced by the very possibility of a female camera operator, Liusia's arc is about her humiliation and feminization. When we first see her in the Mosfil'm cafeteria, she's as masculine as they come: she chain smokes, barks commands, makes fun of actresses, confidently shakes hands with all the men, wears slacks (as opposed to literally every other woman in the series who only wear dresses and skirts), and even "manspreads" when she sits. First, she is demoted from her role as DP on the set of *The Girl and the Brigadier* to second/ assistant cameraman. Then she falls in love with Sancha, and, in order to make herself visible to him as a "woman," asks the makeup ladies for a makeover. When she makes the first pass at Sancha, she has the requisite feminine up hairdo and proper makeup, but is still wearing her masculine clothes and behaving in a "masculine" way, a combination destined for failure.

To make herself visible as a woman, Liusia must not only dress but also act the part. When Sancha offers to make her an evening gown, the measuring scene is reminiscent of two similar scenes in Thaw cinema: Nadezhda Petrukhina being measured for her conservative suit in the opening sequence of *Wings* (in which we hear that she is a "standard size 48"), and Klavdia Vavilova being measured for a dress in Askol'dov's *The Commissar* (1967). In each case, clothes make the "man." They are a sign of a certain kind of gender confusion that takes place when women take on men's roles in society (in this case, as pilot and commissar; in Liusia's case, as camera operator), with their costumes underscoring the degree to which identity is literally "put on" and can be taken off. Liusia's second attempt at performing femininity comes when she tries to rescue Sancha from jail by pretending to be his common-law wife. For this she dons the red silk dress Sancha had made for her, puts on garish makeup, curls her hair, and

37 Luisia's role in *The Thaw* reflects many of the real-world conditions of being a woman in a "man's" job, but not Pilikhina's own experience. See her memoirs, Margarita Pilikhina, *Ia—kinooperator* (Moscow: Biuro propagandy sovetskogo kinoiskusstva, 1977). For interviews with contemporary female cinematographers, see Alexis Krasilovsky, *Women Behind the Camera: Conversations with Camerawomen* (London: Praeger, 1997); and Harriet Margolis, Alexis Krasilovsky, and Julia Stein, *Shooting Women: Behind the Camera, Around the World* (London: Intellect Press, 2015).

38 Marlen Khutsiev's afterword to Margarita Pilikhina, *Ia—kinooperator*, emphasis added.

indulges in some hysterical tears for the benefit of the police inspectors—but this camp version of femininity fails to convince her audience and leads, once more, to failure.

In the last episode, we see Liusia at Mar'iana and Egor's wedding wearing elegant makeup, an updo, and her red dress, no longer ironically or as a costume but finally as belonging to her. Liusia has finally been transfigured (quite literally, by means of a corset) into a recognizable version of femininity, both for Sancha and for the viewer. It is not clear in the end if her exchange of glances with Sancha is meant to signify a compromise relationship, which will save them both from the suspicion that each remains "not quite" gender compliant.

Between Pornography and Nostalgia

In contrast, on the two occasions Fedia's wife Nadia is removed from her prim Soviet high-neckline dresses, the result is practically pornographic: the first time, it causes her to flirt uncontrollably with a guitar player, the second time, she puts on a Sophia Loren dress that is so "feminine," she is never allowed to wear it again. In general, Nadia is not allowed to leave the confines of the dacha: there her identity is circumscribed by domestic bliss of baby, *salat oliv'e*, *syrniki*, and *tort napoleon*. Best friends with Liusia, Nadia is the opposite of the fashionable actresses of Mosfil'm. As Fedia says in a moment of bitterness, there are only two kinds of women, "the mother and the whore" ("zhenshchina-mat' i zhenshchina-bliad'"), and her role as the first of these is accentuated by her frumpy clothes, her cooking, her medical degree, her conservative artistic and political views, and her isolation at the dacha. The first time we see Nadia, she is nine months pregnant, chopping potatoes and pickles for salad. The next time, she is caring for her newborn baby with one hand, while arranging the pillows for her ailing husband with the other.[39]

Which is why it comes as a particular shock when, for a brief moment, Nadia transforms into an Italian film star by means of a dress Fedia brings back from Rome. Changing out of her housedress, corseted and coiffed, Nadia appears from behind the door looking very much like a Soviet version of Sophia Loren, but disturbingly, campily so. Like Liusia at the police station,

39 Nadia's role is to embody the opposite of "Westernized" urban femininity, to concern herself with keeping house and raising children. In direct contrast, Khrustalev's ex-wife Inga lives in a communal apartment, cannot cook, and blames breastfeeding her daughter for her lack of good roles.

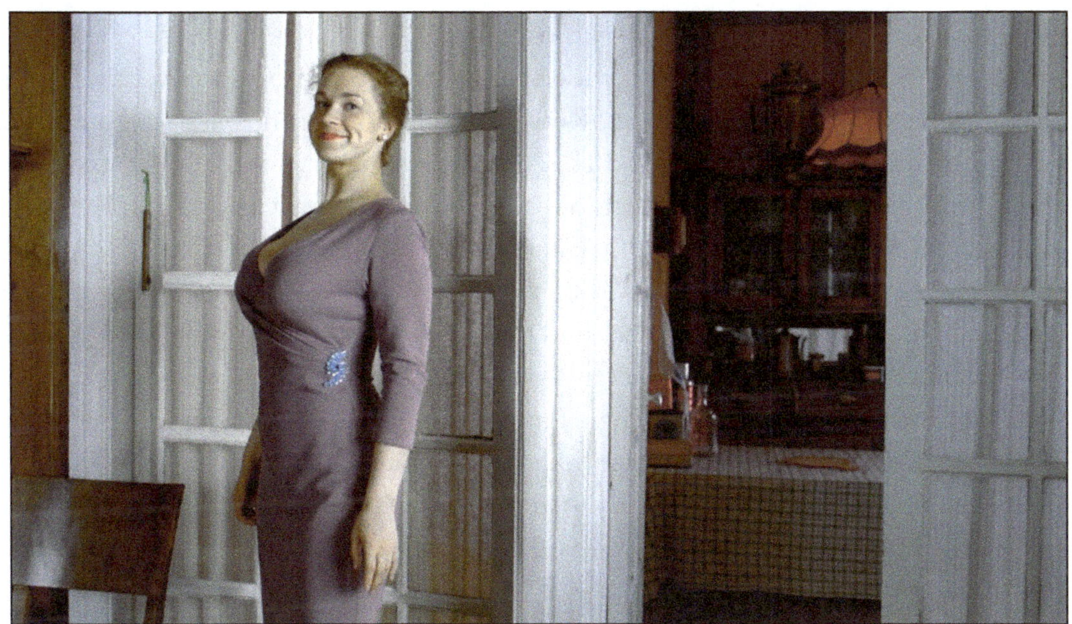

Fig. 4. A Soviet Sophia Loren (Nadia/Svetlana Kolpakova).

Nadia has crossed the line into specularity and has produced an "excess of femininity" that troubles the stable binaries by which she has been defined (Fig. 4). Nadia's transformation reveals the degree to which Fedia's binary construction is of course nothing but an illusion: the real difference between *zhenshchina-mat'* and *zhenshchina-bliad'* is, simply, costuming, while "the woman as such" does not exist.[40] This means that all the binary distinctions on which the series has depended—masculine and feminine, gay and straight, Soviet and Other—are imaginary, and the nostalgic project of visualizing a world in which such categories were "untroubled" is itself destined to failure.[41]

At the core of Todorovsky's *The Thaw* lies an acknowledgement that this nostalgic performance is precisely that: a show put on for our enjoyment that never troubles to hide

40 As Jacques Lacan suggests, "~~The~~ woman does not exist": the barred article means there is no such thing as the predicate that would accompany all women, the feminine "universal." See Jacques Lacan, *Seminar XX* (New York: W. W. Norton & Co., 1998), 7, fn. 28.

41 On the "queer art of failure," see José E. Muñoz, *Cruising Utopia: The There and Then of Queer Utopia* (New York: NYU Press, 2009); and Jack [Judith] Halberstam, *The Queer Art of Failure* (Durham: Duke University Press, 2011).

its own artifice. Channeling—clearly on purpose—not Soviet sixties' arthouse cinema with its stark black-and-white cinematography, wide screens, and forced perspectives, but the AMC *Mad Men* (itself a series meant to both showcase and question our nostalgia for an earlier era when a three-martini lunch, smoking, and shagging your secretary was not only acceptable but expected), *The Thaw* both invites and resists our attempts at unreflexive nostalgia. The striptease that opens the first episode is precisely that: a stripping down to the buff in order to tease the viewer into believing that it will show "everything," all the while insisting on a mediated and distanced gaze. The show moves back and forth between "pornography" and "nostalgia," between exhibitionism and voyeurism, between revealing everything and coyly looking away. At the very end, *The Thaw* stages a nostalgia for its own make-believe by producing a series of "memories" for the viewer: as Khrustalev watches Mar'iana walking away from him, we see flashbacks of memorable moments from all twelve episodes—including the very moment we had just witnessed—but now, like the opening credits, desaturated to a greyscale black-and-white color palette.

We have come full circle, and the real object of fascination now is not the displayed scene, but "the gaze of the naïve 'other' absorbed, enchanted by it": *The Thaw*'s unreflexive nostalgia for itself.

Bibliography

Arkhangel'skii, Andrei. "Khrustalev, mashinku!" *Ogonek* 48 (December 9, 2013): 40. https://www.kommersant.ru/doc/2358217.

Bartlett, Djurdja. *Fashion East: The Spectre that Haunted Socialism*. Cambridge, MA: The MIT Press, 2010.

Berger, John. *Ways of Seeing*. New York: Penguin, 1972.

Boym, Svetlana. *The Future of Nostalgia*. New York: Basic Books, 2001.

Butler, Judith. *Gender Trouble: Feminism and the Subversion of Identity*. New York: Routledge, 1990.

Cavendish, Philip. *The Men with a Movie Camera: The Poetics of Visual Style in Soviet Avant-Garde Cinema of the 1920s*. Oxford: Berghahn Books, 2013.

"Christian Dior v Moskve. 1959 god." Fishki.net, December 21, 2011. https://fishki.net/40155-christian-dior-v-moskve-1959-god-30-foto.html.

Doane, Mary Ann. "Film and Masquerade: Theorizing the Female Spectator." *Screen* 23, nos. 3–4 (1982): 74–88.

Efimov, Sergei. "Valerii Todorovskii: 'Ia reshil, chto v "Ottepeli" vse zhenshchiny budut krasivymi."' *Komsomol'skaia pravda*, December 2, 2013. http://www.kp.ru/daily/26166.5/3053484/.

Goodlad, Lauren M. E., Lilya Kaganovsky, and Robert A. Rushing, eds. *Mad Men, Mad World: Sex, Politics, Style and the 1960s*. Durham: Duke University Press, 2013.

Halberstam, Jack [Judith]. *The Queer Art of Failure*. Durham: Duke University Press, 2011.

Joyrich, Lynne. "Epistemology of the Console." *Critical Inquiry* 27, no. 3 (2001): 439–467.

———. *Re-viewing Reception: Television, Gender, and Postmodern Culture.* Bloomington: Indiana University Press, 1996.

"Kino kak zhizn': moda 60-kh godov v seriale 'Ottepel'.'" Wday.ru, December 5, 2013. https://www.wday.ru/moda-shopping/style/kino-kak-jizn-moda-60-h-godov-v-seriale-ottepel/.

Krasilovsky, Alexis. *Women Behind the Camera: Conversations with Camerawomen*. London: Praeger, 1997.

"Kurit' v kadre mozhno? Pit' mozhno? Golykh zhenshchin mozhno?" 1tv.ru, December 5, 2013. https://www.1tv.ru/shows/vecherniy-urgant/vypuski/vecherniy-urgant-247-vypusk-05-12-2013.

Lacan, Jacques. *Seminar XX*. New York: W. W. Norton & Co., 1998.

Lebina, N. B. "Konets epokhi bol'shogo stilia: Antistalinskie tendentsii v mode 1960-kh godov." *Ottepel'*, 177–191. Exhibition catalogue. Moscow: Gosudarstvennaia Tret'iakovskaia galereia, 2017.

Les années 50. La mode en France, 1947–1957. Exhibition catalogue. Paris Musées. https://www.palaisgalliera.paris.fr/en/exhibitions/50s.

Lipovetskii, Mark and Mikhailova, Tat'iana, "Bol'she, chem nostalgiia (Pozdnii sotsializm v teleserialakh 2010-kh godov)," *NLO* 169 (3/2021): 127-147.

Margolis, Harriet, Alexis Krasilovsky, and Julia Stein. *Shooting Women: Behind the Camera, Around the World*. London: Intellect Press, 2015.

Mulvey, Laura. "Visual Pleasure and Narrative Cinema." *Screen* 16, no. 3 (1975): 6–18.

———. "Some Afterthoughts on 'Visual Pleasure and Narrative Cinema.'" *Framework* 15–17 (1981): 12–15.

Muñoz, José E. *Cruising Utopia: The There and Then of Queer Utopia*. New York: NYU Press, 2009.

Pilikhina, Margarita. *Ia—kinooperator*. Moscow: Biuro propagandy sovetskogo kinoiskusstva, 1977.

Rojavin, Marina, and Tim Harte, eds. *Women in Soviet Film: The Thaw and Post-Thaw Periods*, New York: Routledge, 2018.

Sedgwick, Eve. *Between Men: English Literature and Male Homosocial Desire*. New York: Columbia University Press, 1985.

———. *Epistemology of the Closet*. Berkeley: University of California Press, 1990.

Silverman, Kaja. "Fragments of a Fashionable Discourse." In *Studies in Entertainment*, edited by Tania Modleski, 139–152. Bloomington: Indiana University Press, 1986.

"V 'Ottepeli' Todorovskogo seks est'!" Piter.tv, December 5, 2013. http://piter.tv/event/Ottepel_na_Pervom_kanale/.

Williams, Linda, ed. *Viewing Positions: Ways of Seeing Film*. New Brunswick: Rutgers University Press, 1995.

Yurchak, Alexei. *Everything Was Forever, Until It Was No More: The Last Soviet Generation*. Princeton: Princeton University Press, 2005.

Zakharov, Mark. "Esli aktery v kadre kuriat po-chernomu, znachit, rezhisseru nechego skazat'." *Komsomol'skaia pravda*, December 7, 2013. https://www.kp.ru/daily/26169.7/3055754/.

Zakharova, Larissa. "Soviet Fashion in the 1950s-1960s: Regimentation, Western Influences, and Consumption Strategies." In *The Thaw Soviet Society and Culture during the 1950s and 1960s*, edited by Denis Kozlov and Eleonory Gilburd, 402–435. Toronto: University of Toronto Press, 2013.

Žižek, Slavoj. *Looking Awry: An Introduction to Jacques Lacan through Popular Culture*. Cambridge, MA: The MIT Press, 1991.

The State of Affairs: Screwing Family Values in Putin's Russia

Tatiana Mikhailova

In August 2014 the government of the Russian Federation approved the *Program of a State Family Policy in the Russian Federation for the Period up to 2025* ("Kontseptsiia gosudarstvennoi semeinoi politiki v Rossiiskoi Federatsii na period do 2025 goda"). Conceived and implemented by Elena Mizulina, one of most notable conservatives in contemporary Russia and the Head of the Russian State Duma's Committee for Family, Women, and Children, the *Program* views family as "the fundamental basis of Russian society"[1] and maintains the preservation of traditional family values as one of the main tasks of the state.

In fact, this program formalizes a recent policy of control over family life in compliance with Russia's newly found conservative values and goals. Part three of the *Program*, "Goals, Principles, Tasks, and Priority Directions of the State Family Policy," includes a detailed roadmap of the steps necessary for its realization. Some of them concern the representation of traditional family values in mass media:

> Conducting targeted propaganda in various mass media sources to support traditional values in marriage and the family, morality and virtue; conducting an informational campaign to heighten the social prestige of a family-oriented lifestyle, of having multiple children, and of building multi-generational families through the creation of special television and radio programs, talk shows, newspaper and magazine articles, and other informational projects popularizing traditional family values and facilitating the formation of positive views on marriage, parenthood, and honoring the older generation and the home.[2]

One year after the *Program* was ratified, two popular TV channels, TNT and Domashny (Home Channel), cheered their viewers with a most unorthodox TV series. TNT released *The Affairs* (*Izmeny*) whose protagonist is a woman who, in the course of a single season of the

1 "Kontseptsiia gosudarstvennoi semeinoi politiki v Rossiiskoi Federatsii na period do 2025 goda," *Rossiiskaia gazeta,* August 29, 2014, https://rg.ru/2014/08/29/semya-site-dok.html.

2 Ibid.

series, has affairs with three different men while still married. In *Double Solid Line* (*Dvoinaia sploshnaia*), Domashny introduced a woman simultaneously and happily married to two husbands, residents of two neighboring cities. Both series feature a woman who transgresses the borders of social convention at the center of the narrative. These two series tangibly demonstrate the distance between Russian neoconservative aspirations and the imaginary of contemporary Russian culture which, in turn, reveals its true, rather than imposed values.

My focus will be on *The Affairs* as an aesthetically accomplished and complex work, which deserves close reading not only because it undermines the state-sponsored promotion of conservative family values, but also raises open-ended questions about the actual state of family values in post-Soviet Russia, as well as the new conceptualization of women and their sexual freedom and freedom generally. At the heart of the series' narrative are its protagonist's several simultaneous extramarital affairs. *The Affairs*, however, avoids moralizing and presents adultery as the norm rather than an anomaly in contemporary Russian family life, unlike many other Russian films about female infidelity, such as Valery Todorovsky's *The Lover* (*Liubovnik*, 2002), Andrei Zviagintsev's *The Banishment* (*Izgnanie*, 2007) and *Leviathan* (*Leviafan*, 2014), or Kirill Serebrennikov's *The Affair* (*Izmena*, 2012).

The Affairs became a favorite topic in online forum discussions, and viewers of all genders and ages hotly debated the amorous escapades of the series' protagonist, Asia, as played by Elena Liadova.[3] One year later, in 2016, *The Affairs* was showered with accolades from TEFI, the Russian Television Academy, during its annual awards ceremony. Liadova received the award for Best Actress, while Best Director went to Vadim Perelman, the Canadian-American film director of *The Affairs*, famous for his directorial and screenplay debut, *The House of Sand and Fog* (2003), which brought him three Oscar nominations. Igor Mishin, Aleksei Ageev, and Valery Fedorovich were also rewarded as Best Producers. The Association of Film and Television Producers also added to the list of *The Affairs*' trophies by giving its Best Series award to the entire project and the Best Screenplay award to Daria Gratsevich, the then thirty-one-year-old writer who conceived the series' storyline in 2007.[4]

3 In *Leviathan* Liadova also plays the unfaithful wife of the protagonist.

4 "Dar'ia Gratsevich ob 'Izmenakh': 'Ia by ne khotela prodolzhat' serial,'" Teleserial.com, http://www.teleserial.com/story/25838-serial-izmeni-2015-istoriya-zhenskih-izmen-na-tnt/

The Affairs does not only offer a gallery of female characters, each with her own relationship to sexuality. As if following Michel Foucault, the series also employs sexuality as the key suggesting a system of power relations that does not directly stem from economic forms of control and domination, since "the deployment of sexuality is linked to the economy through numerous and subtle relays, the main of which, however, is the body—the body that produces and consumes."[5] This alternative economy naturally comes into conflict with the system of traditional and economy-based social bonds and obligations. *The Affairs* narrows this system down to the representation of the family as a metaphor for the entire societal structure. The series is unique in its unsentimental approach to the crisis of so-called family values and the family as an institution in contemporary Russia.

Dar'ia Gratsevich claims that "marriage in Russia is something that occurs behind closed doors,"[6] and in her opinion, it is not common to discuss problems associated with family life publicly. Her script creates an alternative family narrative juxtaposing it to the one suggested by the state. No family is lucky in *The Affairs,* and each gender suffers in its own way, despite the apparent triumph of patriarchal values. In this essay I will discuss four case studies, three of them focused on female characters, the grown-up daughters (Asia and Dasha) and Dasha's mother, and one on the overall representation of men in the series. I will attempt to reveal the logic of power relations that *The Affairs* embodies, albeit not entirely consistently, but nevertheless very tangibly and persuasively.

Affairs in *The Affairs*

Although I understand the risks of reading art through the lens of sociology, certain data elucidate the tacit assumptions of *The Affairs.* In Iuliia Sokolova's research on modern families' marital affairs, three reasons for promiscuity are identified as primary for women aged thirty to forty (Asia's cohort): a) an overall feeling of dissatisfaction with the marriage; b) lack of attention from the marriage partner; and c) lack of love towards the partner. It is worth mentioning that

5 Michel Foucault, *The History of Sexuality,* vol. 1: *An Introduction,* trans. Robert Hurley (New York: Vintage Books, 1990), 106–107.

6 Nastia Poletaeva, "Pochemu rossiiskie serialy o zhenskikh izmenakh popali v tochku," *Wonder,* November 10, 2015, http://www.wonderzine.com/wonderzine/life/life/215829-cheating-equally.

none of the women respondents, whose answers form the basis of Sokolova's research, cited the last two reasons from the list of options circulated by the study: the monotony of family life or a desire of a one-night stand. These two reasons were cited only by the men participating in the study.[7]

These three reasons fit Asia's marriage quite well, although she continues to cling to her lifeless husband. Why is this? Is she paralyzed by the idea of violating the sacrament of marriage? Or because a divorce will stigmatize her as a wife incapable of making her marriage work? Or because this man is no different from the others and thus there is no point in changing him for another? This might explain why Asia is so terrified of her lover's proposal to marry her. Nothing will change in her life and status; she will simply move from one disappointment to another, so why bother.

Almost all the characters in this series have doubles: Dasha is an apparent alter ego for Asia, a girlfriend from their teen years, newly reconnecting after fourteen years and one car accident. At first glance, the two families are completely different. Unlike Asia and her husband Kirill (Kirill Käro), Dasha (Glafira Tarkhanova) and her husband Iura (Evgeny Stychkin) are rich and live a life of excess and privilege; their house typifies modern domestic luxury. Unlike Asia and Kirill, they are trying hard to conceive, they communicate, but loudly, abusively, and emotionally, constantly fight and passionately copulate, and yet, like Asia and Kirill, they are anything but happy. The opening scenes of the second episode perfectly illustrate Tolstoy's much abused observation on unhappy families from *Anna Karenina*. Both couples are lying in bed, both having difficulties in getting the flame going. Asia and Dasha are unhappy with their men's inability to perform their marital duty; the men are anxious, frustrated, and angry. The reasons for the men's impotence are different, but somehow it is apparent that their difficulty is psychological, not physical. Huge mirrors in both bedrooms serve as showcase windows for the viewers who peep at the (in)action in the characters' bed. This voyeurism creates the overwhelming effect of sharing the fears and phobias associated with marital sex.

The enormous beds that occupy the center of both couples' bedrooms serve as nuclei of their family life. The bed in *The Affairs* is more than just an object: it is a visual commentary and an argument for or against family life. The dust bunnies we see under this bed through Asia's

7 Iu. A. Sokolova, "Gendernye osobennosti prichin supruzheskikh izmen v sovremennykh sem'iakh," *Uchenye zapiski Rossiiskogo gosudarstvennogo sotsial'nogo universiteta* 7 (2012): 151.

eyes at the moment when she is trying to find a lost ring, tell a sad story of negligence and routine. At the same time, the bed becomes a minefield, when Asia's husband finds there a map left by her young lover Slava (Viacheslav Chepurchenko). If Asia and Kirill's bed is not working for them, Kirill's brother Anton feels right at home there with a casual girlfriend, when he gets a chance. Dasha is trying so hard to conceive that lovemaking becomes a joyless enterprise for her and Iura, who is obliged to have sex with Dasha when she ovulates. Rather than pleasure, the marital bed signifies hard sexual labor or danger. Sex for the married couples is fun only when it is performed outside of the conjugal bed. The places used for sex in the show include a car, a table, a bathtub, a window, but almost never a bed, because this is where married couples fight and hate each other.

Daughter 1: Asia

The Affairs draws on cultural representations of Don Juan, a figure well embedded in the Russian cultural imagination and extending from Pushkin's *The Stone Guest* (*Kamennyi gost'*, 1830), to Aleksandr Blok's, Nikolai Gumilev's, Marina Tsvetaeva's, and Valerii Briusov's poetic interpretations, to Vladimir Vysotsky as Pushkin's Don Juan in Mikhail Shveitser's *Little Tragedies* (*Malen'kie tragedii*, 1979); from Andrei Mironov in the popular TV musical *The Straw Hat* (*Solomennaia shliapka*, dir. Leonid Kvinikhidze, 1974) to Liudmila Ulitskaia's characters—Alik from *The Funeral Party* (*Veselye pokhorony*, 1997) and Shurik from *Sincerely Yours Shurik* (*Iskrenne vash Shurik*, 2003). In all these examples, Don Juan manifests the power of passion that disregards and almost heroically defeats hypocritical societal norms. In each of his incarnations, Don Juan restates the question of personal freedom and its limits (or boundlessness) in confrontation with others' freedoms, as well as the moral or religious norms of a given society. However, he also epitomizes patriarchal power, which allows men transgressions unthinkable for women.[8] The Russian cultural tradition does not offer many examples of female Don Juans, but the culture of Russian modernism presents as ambivalent the Don Juanism of such

8 See Svetlana Mikhienko, *Evoliutsiia obraza Don Zhuana v russkoi literature XIX–XX vekov,* dissertatsiia na soiskanie uchenoi stepeni kandidata filologicheskikh nauk, Piatigorsk State University, 2001, http://www.dissercat.com/content/evolyutsiya-obraza-don-zhuana-v-russkoi-literature-xix-xx-vekov; Veselovskaia, Nadezhda, *Don Zhuan russkoi klassicheskoi literatury.* Dissertatsiia na soiskanie uchenoi stepeni kandidata filologicheskikh nauk, Literaturnyi Institut, 2000.

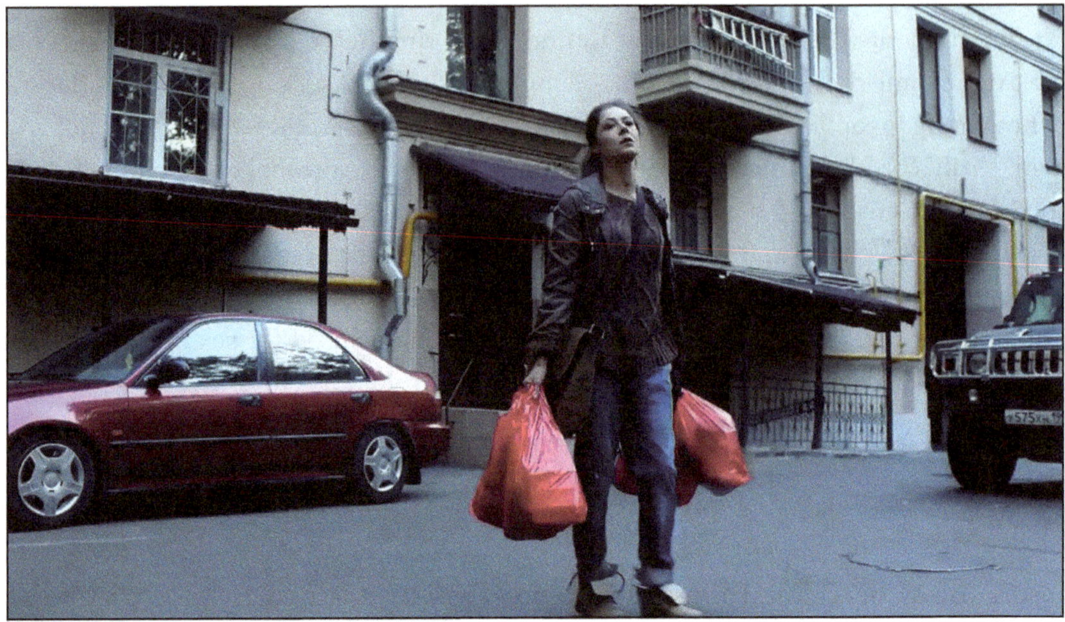

Fig. 1. Elena Liadova as Asia: "We wanted to show an ordinary woman, not gorgeous, but perfectly mundane."

prominent figures as Marina Tsvetaeva, Larisa Reisner, or Lilia Brik. However, it would be no exaggeration to claim that Asia is the first highly sympathetic representation of a female Don Juan in Russian popular culture.

Asia is sexually involved with four men (her husband included), and her close encounters with them provide a detailed examination of a broad slice of Russian society. Aside from her husband Kirill, Asia is involved with her ex-boss, the entrepreneur Vadim; with the police officer Nikita, Asia's emergency contact and magic wand; and with Slava, her enthusiastic young pursuer, the son of the local big shot. These men constantly circle in Asia's orbit, providing new twists to the plot. Even the men who are not immediately relevant to Asia's life are either subjugated to her or recognize her power. Her husband's younger brother Anton (Artem Markarian) considers her his friend and confidante, and her girlfriend's husband Iura sees in Asia the greatest threat to his family life.

Liadova portrays her character as someone with unresolved traumas and thus psychologically scarred and twisted, yet her Asia is razor-sharp, sarcastic, and self-assured, at least on the surface. She is recognizable as a thirty-something urban woman with an average, even meager income (Fig. 1). Liadova says of her character: "We wanted to show an ordinary woman, not gorgeous, but perfectly mundane."[9] Asia dresses casually, and even her boss and lover Vadim describes her looks as those of "a jobless single mother." She drives an old Honda and does not use much makeup; she is not afraid to curse and her voice is a bit raspy, probably because she is a chain smoker. At times she speaks with a nagging, childish tone, especially when she talks to men, playing the role of a spoiled little girl. She lacks the looks of a femme fatale, and yet men fall for her. Moreover, they are eager to offer her marriage: Vadim proposes to her, choosing the promiscuous Asia over his devoted girlfriend, who has been waiting for him to marry her for ten years. Her other lover, Nikita (Denis Shvedov), also likes having her stay at his home; even Slava, the youngest of her lovers, is so obsessed with her (or rather possessed by her) that he seriously considers marriage.

Despite all her suitors, Asia stays married to Kirill, a man who hardly represents the epitome of virility and success. They are childless, perhaps intentionally so on Asia's part. The viewer will not detect in her any desire to have children throughout the sixteen episodes. She is also parentless, and this fact makes her something of an orphan, thereby preventing her from locating the social milieu to which she belongs. The absence of her parents from the narrative limits speculation regarding the social factors that might have shaped her. In this respect, Asia's life sharply contrasts with her girlfriend Dasha's, whose mother is omnipresent in her life.

The only hint as to Asia's background appears in episode thirteen in which Asia, still an innocent and pure teenager, is lying in a hammock reading Emile Zola's *The Ladies' Paradise* (*Au Bonheur des Dames*, 1883). Curiously, this book tells the story of Denise Baudu, a good girl with meager means but ample pride, who gets Octave Mouret, a wealthy man, to marry her. Robert Viti sees her as a warrior and challenger of men in the battle over control of temporal reality: "Denise Baudu, the avenger of women, is above all else a temporal avenger. By refusing his sexual advances . . . she not only deprives Mouret of another conquest, but ultimately tames him of his womanizing by making of him a confirmed one-woman man."[10] The scene may hint at Asia's self-realization based on a reversal of traditional gender models. Indeed,

9 "Obychnuiu zhenshchinu khoteli pokazat': ne laksheri, a samuiu bytovuiu" ("Elena Liadova: 'My zatronuli v "Izmenakh" temu lichnoi svobody,'" Vokrug.tv, September 18, 2015, http://www.vokrug.tv/article/show/elena_lyadova_my_zatronuli_v_izmenah_temu_lichnoi_svobody_49548/).

10 Robert M. Viti, "'A Woman's Time, a Lady's Place': *Nana* and *Au Bonheur des Dames*," *Symposium* (Winter 1990): 297.

the story of Asia's infidelities will not be so shocking if one looks at it through the monocle of nineteenth-century French literature when the "one woman and three men" plot was quite popular.[11]

A married woman with a permanent home and job, Asia is, at the same time, homeless and constantly on the run, perfectly fitting the description of the classical Don Juan:

> Don Juan is characterized as the one who, by definition, is always in motion, never stops. . . . Don Juan is the one who does not stay—both in the spatial sense of remaining in one place, staying at home, inhabiting a place, and in the temporal sense of lasting, enduring, staying the course. . . . Don Juan is a true traveler in the sense that he leaves for leaving's sake: he is the leavetaker who never deviates from his fate, the voyager who, advancing all the while, goes forward only to meet what is following and pursuing him.[12]

Asia's mobility is emphasized through her familiarity with her Honda and the ease with which she commands the vehicle is juxtaposed to Dasha's lack of control over her car (and life). Asia's paradoxical homelessness is firmly inscribed in the visual chronotope of the series. Although she graduated from the famous Stroganovka (Moscow State Stroganov Academy of Industrial and Applied Arts) and is a professional interior decorator, the apartment where she and Kirill reside looks shabby and ill-kept. The wallpaper is dark and unappealing; the chipped paint on the doors looks like it has been through domestic disputes involving breaking and entering. The furniture, both in the bedroom and kitchen, is a depressing relic from the 1980s; their mobile phones and Kirill's computer serve as the only markers of the twenty-first century. Asia is not confined to her apartment and does not have "a room of her own." Above all, her drab apartment testifies to her unhappiness and stagnant life. Nevertheless, after frolicking with her paramours, Asia always returns home to spend the night.

Her boss and lover, Vadim, does not hold Asia in high regard as a professional. When her husband Kirill comes to question Vadim in an attempt to unearth the story of Asia's affair, he sees that Vadim's apartment looks like a dry replica of the office of a lower-rank provincial

11 R. I. Galeeva, "Siuzhet 'Odna zhenshchina i troe muzhchin' do G. Flobera i u G. Flobera ('Gospozha Bovari')," *Uchenye zapiski Kazanskogo gosudarstvennogo universiteta* 151, no. 3 (2009): 111.

12 Shoshana Felman, *The Scandal of the Speaking Body: Don Juan with J. I. Austin, or Seduction in Two Languages* (Stanford: Stanford University Press, 1983), 29–30.

boss. He immediately recognizes Asia's joyless touch in this remodeling. When Vadim confides to him that she is a mediocre designer ("Kak dizainer ona tak sebe"), he implies that he values Asia for her other talents. At the same time, there is the apartment that Asia decorated for her lover, the police officer Nikita—so stylish and artfully decorated that it is hard to believe that she was responsible. Creative, modern, and strikingly expensive, the apartment does not resemble one that could belong to a lowly patrol officer. Asia has the key to this flat in case she needs to recuperate after her failures and disappointments with other men. Nikita's apartment indicates where her true love and feelings lie—not at home with Kirill, not in Vadim's apartment, but here, at Nikita's. Unlike Asia, her interior designs do not lie, allowing a glimpse into her inner world.

Daughter 2: Dasha

A demure beauty who looks like a remake of Botticelli's Venus, Dasha suffers from acute housewife disorder and is eager to escape her boredom through an amorous adventure of any kind, despite having no experience in the matter. She is eager to learn from Asia. To understand every aspect of the taboo craft of infidelity she tirelessly interrogates Asia on all the possible pros and cons of adultery. When Dasha first comes onscreen in the scene at the divorce court lobby, she is wearing a short dress reminiscent of a Soviet high school uniform: the style recalls the white aprons required of girls for special occasions and school celebrations (Fig. 2). This metaphor of Dasha as a pupil reemerges in her conversations with Asia (her mentor) and her mother (her tyrant). Asia pontificates to Dasha on her rules for transgression: one shall never allow the lover to come to her home; one shall know everything about her lover/s and control him/them entirely; one shall always sleep at home; and the first and most profound rule of all, in Asia's own words: "Do not try to persuade yourself that you are not a piece of shit" ("Ne nado pytat'sia ubedit' sebia v tom, chto ty ne govno").

In the course of the series, all these rules and regulations fail. This happens because they are supposed to provide comfortable controls for adultery, thereby making it safe. However, if adultery stands for transgressive freedom, then it inevitably destroys all such protective shields—entering a danger zone where anything becomes possible. If adultery is about freedom, then it cannot be safe. If it is safe, then it is senseless. It is a paradox that the series' writers articulate convincingly.

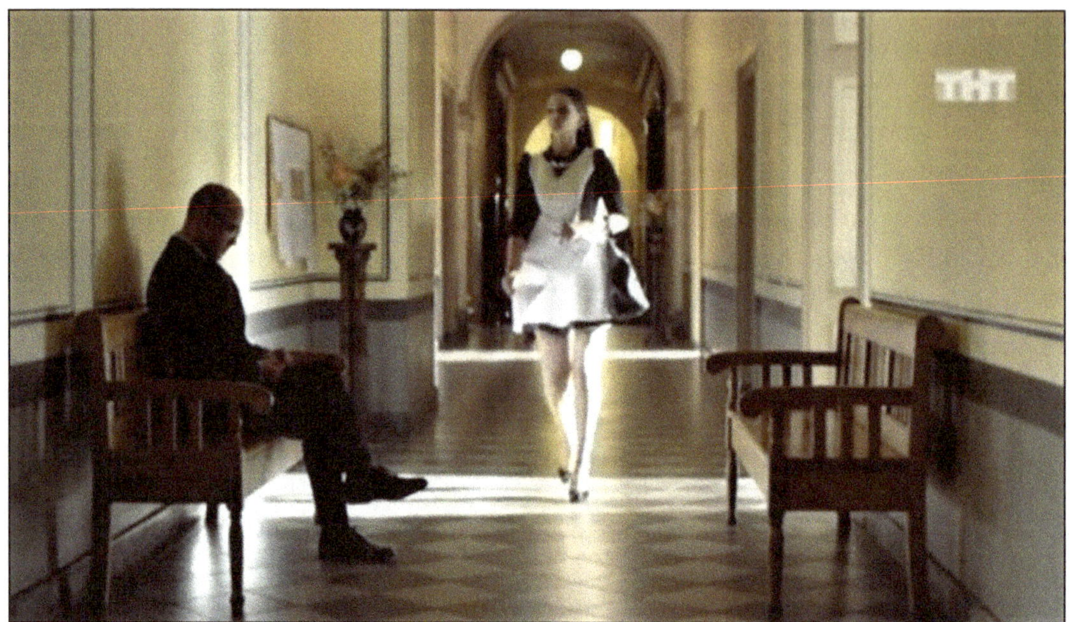

Fig. 2. Glafira Tarkhanova as Dasha dressed as a schoolgirl for the divorce hearing.

Dasha only partially fits the procrustean stereotype of the New Russian spouse as a childless wealthy woman, high on hormones, with the heap of Chanel bags in her closet, holding her husband in high regard (at least as the source of her wealth). Her story is one of longing for sexual and social liberation on her own terms, not following her husband's orders. Dasha is not a good wife by any means. She constantly breaches the boundaries of permissible behavior, acting like a spoiled brat. She assaults her husband Iura not only verbally, but also physically.

She is constantly fighting with Iura, and some viewers and even critics see this as an indicator of mental instability.[13] But Dasha *intentionally* performs the stereotypical patriarchal image of the "hysterical woman." Her irrational, unpredictable behavior is specifically, prejudicially gendered and therefore permissible for women, within the logic of patriarchy. Her performances of hysteria are physical, frightening, and abusively violent. She even

13 See viewers' blogs at the following websites: https://www.kinopoisk.ru/film/839356/;_http://irecommend.ru/content/v-zamuzhnem-omute-lyubovniki-vodyatsya-serial-izmeny-na-tnt-otkryvaet-novye-grani-lyubovnykh.

kicks Iura in the groin, the locus for producing her unborn but highly desired children. She bites his finger in a manner unambiguously suggestive of castration. She breaks his glasses, symbolically blinding him. Her well-groomed hair at times looks unruly and wild, recalling Philippa Rappoport's observation that uncovered hair signifies feminine sexuality and the power of the *rusalki*, the untamed spirits who escape patriarchal constraints and employ their wiles to murder men by drowning.[14]

The Daughters' Scripts

Dasha's quest to commit adultery, the greatest transgression against the patriarchal family, raises the same question as Asia's many transgressions: why does she need a lover? To have yet another cherry on the cake of her luxurious life? Or to punish her husband for failing to see her unhappiness?

As much as one would like to believe that Asia and Dasha are just figments of Gratsevich's imagination; and that even if such women exist, they are exceptions to the rule, sociologists Anna Temkina and Elena Zdravomyslova confirm otherwise. In their article "Sexual Scripts and Identity of Middle-Class Russian Women," they use the concept of sexual script as key to their analysis.[15] The researchers identify the sexual scripts of three generations of Russian women: "the Soviet silent generation," "the late Soviet generation of personalization," and "the post-Soviet generation of articulation."[16] Both in their early thirties, Dasha and Asia were barely six years old when perestroika began, thus personifying the social changes of the last twenty-five years. Too young to reap the fruits of the sexual revolution that took place in the nineties, they matured during the 2000s, so that they resonate with two of the scripts described by Temkina and Zdravomyslova.

14 Philippa Rappoport, "If It Dries Out, It's No Good: Women, Hair and Rusalki Beliefs," *SEEFA Journal* 4, no. 1 (1999): 55–63.

15 Erving Goffman defines scripts as structures that determine the practices of agents and frame individual narratives of experience. See Erving Goffman, "Frame Analysis of Gender," from "The Arrangement between the Sexes," in *The Goffman Reader*, ed. C. Lemert and A. Branaman (New Jersey: Wiley-Blackwell, 1997), 201–208.

16 Anna Temkina and Elena Zdravomyslova, "The Sexual Scripts and Identity of Middle-Class Russian Women," *Sexuality and Culture* 19 (2015): 304.

The script of the "post-Soviet generation of articulation" has two distinct narratives: the hedonistic and the instrumental. The hedonistic narrative frames the purpose of sexuality through pleasure and enjoyment.

> Sexual experiences are described as an autonomous sphere of life, clearly distinct from love, marriage, and reproduction. Sexual desire is understood as a natural drive and sphere of self- realization. The central category in this narrative is sexual pleasure. . . . Sexual interactions are described as a "game," in which partners have to follow certain rules. Women identify themselves as taking an initiative, being active and responsible in sexual relationships.[17]

This script describes Asia perfectly. In the very last episode, when Dasha tries to question her motives for being unfaithful to Kirill, Asia refuses to see her affairs as a way of getting back at him, and claims that she just *loves sex*. This hedonistic approach and openness to sexual experiences, unconstrained by the boundaries of propriety and marital status, constitute the essence of Asia's freedom that fulfills her needs more than any actual man can, no matter how hard he tries. This is why the happy resolution offered by Gratsevich at the end of the first season, when Asia starts anew with Nikita, and his expensive motorcycle carries them away into a perfect future, seems extremely problematic.

At first glance, Dasha fits the instrumental script quite well, since it "commodifies sexuality so that sexual attractiveness is seen as a resource and a sexual act is perceived as a service to be paid for."[18] This creates an identity in which "the gender polarization is reproduced and even reinforced. . . . Women expect from men material support in return for sex and household services. . . . In this version of identity construction women believe that sexual attractiveness is the core of their femininity."[19] With her impeccable dresses, shoes, pricey bags, nails, and a curly mass of hair, Dasha looks like an art object. Her life is filled with visits to the dentist, gynecologist, gym, and a shopping mall—endless acts of upkeep to maintain her sexual value. Yet Dasha has nothing of her own since everything belongs to Iura. Even her mother knows it, when she says to Iura: "You know that nothing belongs to Dasha here, even her toothbrush is

17 Ibid., 308.

18 Ibid., 309.

19 Ibid., 314.

yours," and he agrees with her. One scene in the last episode is especially telling: when Dasha comes home to collect what she thinks is hers—her car—she has to submit to Iura sexually in order to get it. Only after the sex does he allow her to take the car: "Sure, it's yours!" Dasha is jealous of Asia despite the latter's destitute economic status because Asia enjoys sexual freedom, while Dasha does not. Yet, if the story of Asia does not promise any stable resolution for her current "state of affairs"—the first season's happy ending looks like a parody—Dasha's story is different. Dasha is learning and evolving, while Asia is not. The very experience of separation from Iura allows Dasha to question her choices and options in life. She does not jump at the opportunity for extramarital intercourse when it is bluntly offered to her by Kirill or his colleague Gleb (Pavel Maikov). She asks forgiveness from Asia for her teen adventure with Kirill and her unrequited affair with Nikita. She severs the umbilical cord connecting her to her mother and her rigid patriarchal values. Finally, she choses the uncertain freedom of camaraderie or even a surrogate family with Olia, the former prostitute and currently Dasha's personal driver (who is also in love with her), over the safety and luxury of her normative marriage.

The sole power that women in the show wield over men is the power of sex, and when they lose this power as they age, they have to turn to the patriarchal power associated with the position of wife and mother. The men imagine women as those who do not have their own money and cannot resolve their problems without calling for men's help. Thus, Dasha's choice to move in with Olia is highly unorthodox. Her escape plan does not depend on any man, and her association with another woman can be mistaken for a lesbian relationship. Olia is smart, quiet, and very effective in helping Dasha regain her vision and strength. She hates all the kinds of denigrating power associated with men, and her desire to help Dasha is construed by Dasha's mother and by her husband as sexual longing. Molly Haskell suggests that "as lesbianism becomes a more serious threat to the male ego and to heterosexual hegemony, it will probably be shown less rather than more often; it may already have lost its comfortable place as a male turn-on."[20] Dasha's choice provides a sharp contrast to the one that the authors have Asia pursue in the season finale – a bourgeois entanglement with a corrupt cop complete with a motorcycle and a too-nice apartment.

20 Molly Haskell, *From Reverence to Rape: The Treatment of Women in the Movies* (New York: University of Chicago Press, 1973), 355.

The Mother: Galina Sergeevna

The center of the family crisis depicted in *The Affairs* lies in the conflict between the parents' traditional values and the rebellious behavior of their children. This conflict is hidden behind the main narrative that consists of the protagonist's affairs. The parents in this series have all been shaped during the late Soviet period and supposedly represent traits associated with the Soviet heritage. However, their actions represent an outdated, rigid patriarchal logic, which can easily serve as an explanation for contemporary Russia's lost path to modernization.

Galina Sergeevna, Dasha's mother (Ol'ga Khokhlova), who resembles an aging Barbie on steroids, is as close to the image of a professional wife as one could be: neatly groomed and coiffed, in tight sexy suits, she is always ready to cook and serve meals, even when she is just visiting her daughter's home. Despite her aptitude as a capable house manager, her husband, Dasha's father, who is allegedly away on a two-year business trip, has clearly abandoned her. Thus, from the perspective that she herself represents, Galina Sergeevna has failed miserably in her role as a wife, as has nearly every other married woman from the older generation in the series. Her doubles and sisters in misfortune are Anna, Slava's mother (Iulia Iablonskaya), and Galia, the wife of Gleb. Anna prefers to live with her eyes closed and her heart broken, silently suffering from her husband's affairs. Galia, as we learn, is driving Gleb crazy with her nagging and complaints, but she, nevertheless, fries pies at home, while her husband is trying unsuccessfully to get Dasha into bed. These women accept the status quo in their relationships with their men and stoically suffer in invisible battles with their husbands' young concubines.

The existential surrender of the older women characters in *The Affairs* highlights, first and foremost, not only the question of freedom but also of power. Indeed, the women of *The Affairs* are stuck in the most degrading traditional roles, and if some of them can reject the passive-aggressive power of the family martyr (Slava's mother), others can gain another kind of power by transgressing the boundaries of their marriage through adultery. Tellingly, Asia fits into the symbolic role of Galina Sergeevna's daughter much better than Dasha. Despite her position as Dasha's mentor and therefore challenger to the mother's power (Galina Sergeevna calls her a "deviant" and a "rabid dog"), she ascribes to the same old-fashioned rules and observations on family life as Galina, especially regarding affairs. For example, both of them give Dasha similar advice on how to detect whether Iura is having an affair. Asia says: "When he comes home, check him out, sniff his shirt for perfume, see whether it is wrinkled or not, whether he took it off for the night, check his pockets for restaurant checks or bar matches." Galina Sergeevna suggests an almost identical course of sleuthing, sniffing, and checking shirt freshness, idealizing totalitarian control over private life as normative. This similarity between Asia and Dasha's mother in the discourse of snooping recalls the paranoid wives depicted in post-Soviet literature and film, for example, Liudmila Petrushevskaia's *The Time: Night* (*Vremia noch'*, 1992). It also vividly displays the continuity—rather than gap—between post-Soviet and late Soviet sexual mores. What is lamented as a horrid moral decline, in fact, continues the unspoken but broadly accepted norms of sexual misconduct in the 1960s–70s, a period that some label as a hidden sexual revolution in the USSR.[21]

If the position of a childless wife allows some freedom to maneuver, mothers are locked in their family cells forever. The only loci of power that are available to them lie in their ability to control the lives of their daughters, but never their husbands'. Dasha's mother serves as a chilling example of this new domesticity and new maternal devotion, so favored by the conservatives. Her life is that of a bird chirping instruction inside a gilded cage; luxurious as it is, it lacks any sense and purpose without total control over Dasha and her marriage. She embodies the patriarchal ideal with threatening perfection. She is a devoted mother, she found Iura for Dasha and married them. She has her own key to their house, she counsels Iura on how he should act after his alleged affair, and tries to bring Dasha back to her senses when she runs away from Iura. At the same time, she refuses to shelter Dasha on the premise that Dasha has her own home, blackmails her into returning to Iura, and is concerned by Olia and Dasha's tender friendship because she sees it as a threat to heteronormative family life.

However, Galina Sergeevna's character also reveals the real vulnerability of the patriarchal discourse in contemporary Russian society. Women like Galina appear disrespected by their children and their husbands and lack control over property. Thus, their position is redundant even in comparison with previous centuries, when, according to Christine Worobec, elderly women had several loci of informal power: "Control over the bearing and nurturing of children,

21 See Igor S. Kon, "Sexuality and Politics in Russia (1700–2000)," in *Sexual Cultures in Europe. National Histories*, ed. F. X. Eder, L.A. Hall and G. Hekma (Manchester: Manchester University Press, 1999), 197–218; idem, *The Sexual Revolution in Russia. From the Age of the Czars to Today* (New York: The Free Press, 1995); O. A. Bocharova, "Seksual'naia svoboda: slova i dela," *Chelovek* 5 (1994): 98–107.

influence over their offsprings' marriage alliances, economic responsibilities, and the honor accorded women in the patriarchal system. . . ."[22]

Discursively, Galina Sergeevna better fits the nineteenth-century model of the mother than the twenty-first-century one. Karolina Pavlova, whose novel *The Double Life* (*Dvoinaia zhizn'*, 1848) exposed the logic of the patriarchy as it is channeled and internalized by women, provides a compelling example of this type of mother:

> They rely totally on their maternal efforts. They are extremely persistent with their daughters. In place of the spirit they give them the letter, in place of live feeling a dead rule, in place of holy truth a preposterous lie. And they often manage through these clever, precautionary machinations to steer their daughters safely to what is called "a good match." Then their goal is attained. Then they leave her, confused, powerless, ignorant and uncomprehending, to God's will; and afterwards they sit down tranquilly to dinner and lie down to sleep. And this is the very same daughter whom at the age of six they could not bring themselves to leave alone in her room, lest she fall off the chair. But that was a matter of bodily injuries (blood is quite visible, physical pain is frightening), not of the obscure, mute pain of the spirit.[23]

This resurrection of pre-revolutionary patterns in gender behavior may be interpreted as congruent with the state's new approach to family values (recall Mizulina's *Program*), but it appears both archaic and ineffective. Thus, we can interpret Dasha's rebellion and her acceptance of Olia's help and friendship as targeting her mother and her marital law rather than her husband. Dasha's choice foregrounds female camaraderie and support, free of the constraints of practicality and conventional wisdom as an alternative to the failing patriarchal model epitomized by Galina Sergeevna.

22 Christine Worobec, "Accommodation and Resistance," in *Russia's Women: Accommodation, Resistance, Transformation*, ed. Barbara Evans Clements, Barbara Alpern Engel, and Christine Worobec (Berkeley: University of California Press, 1991), 20.

23 Karolina Pavlova, *The Double Life*, transl. Barbara Heldt (Benicia, CA: Barbary Coast Books, 1986), 87-88. Pavlova's novel is virtually unknown to Russian readers, but Gratsevich, an alumna of the Russian State University for the Humanities (RGGU) Philology Department (*filfak*), could have read it.

Powerful versus Powerless?

In a patriarchal society, power is institutionalized by men, belongs to men, and is intended to keep women in a subjugated position, while the status of women indicates the level of democratic freedom in the society, which also, of course, concerns men no less than women. *The Affairs* offers several models of male authority—or the lack thereof. Some of the male characters in *The Affairs* are morbidly funny, others almost tragic, but all display a dramatic gap between the patriarchal self-image and its actual performance.

All the male characters in *The Affairs* fall into two clearly distinct groups—those associated with power and those dissociated from it. The first group encompasses Oleg Ivanovich, a wealthy businessman with possible political connections; his son and heir Slava, who falls tragically in love with Asia; Nikita Mikhalkov, the corrupt but loveable cop and Asia's lover, as well as Iura, another wealthy businessman and Dasha's husband. The other group—Kirill, Asia's husband; Anton, his brother; Gleb, his friend and colleague; Vadim, Asia's boss and lover—are all deprived of real power. However, the series' authors reveal more similarities between these two groups than one would expect.

For example, *The Affairs* dispels the expectation that those who possess either economic or political power automatically dominate in sexual relations. The four male characters from the "power group" enact different and rather contradictory scenarios. Oleg Ivanovich (Aleksandr Kliukvin), Slava's father, appears as the epitome of accomplished power and control over his own and others' lives. He is bulky and imposing and speaks in a soft yet threatening manner. He wears expensive suits, flashes an expensive watch and a Vertu phone. Personal chauffeurs drive him about, and his fleet of cars contains only luxury brands. He represents an alpha male or patriarch in the series, the man with the highest position in the social structure, the true embodiment of hegemonic masculinity. He manages an oil and gas company with unlimited access to monetary and administrative resources. He has his own security team and can have people harassed, beaten, or kidnapped; he is capable of ruining someone's business; he owns five apartments in Moscow and can afford to renovate all of them at the same time. His office is lavishly decorated with luxurious leather furniture, and his secretary and his head of security are at his disposal at all times. His mistress, who is predictably also his secretary, indicates his status as a man in good economic and sexual standing.

However, Oleg Ivanovich's power is seriously undermined when his son falls in love with the wrong woman—with Asia. In fact, love is perceived as a liability by Oleg Ivanovich, as an Achilles heel, since a married woman like Asia once almost destroyed him. Paradoxically, Oleg Ivanovich's veneration of his love story exactly fits the romantic script as described by Temkina and Zdravomyslova: "Extramarital sexual relationships based on love (as opposed to casual and promiscuous relationships) were normalized ideologically, and were seen as morally justifiable. In the late Soviet period, the romantic cultural script became the major discourse justifying sexual relations, even when they occurred out of wedlock."[24]

In the sphere of personal relationships, love, and sexual desire social norms and hierarchies lose their grip, so here Oleg Ivanovich's power fades away. When Oleg Ivanovich's silent and obedient wife tells him that she prays for his death because she is so tired of living with him, he loses the ground under his feet. The scene in which Asia undresses in his office and offers her body to him in order to save her husband from Oleg's henchman is even more telling. Oleg Ivanovich refuses to accept Asia's challenge, to risk engaging her sexuality, thus acknowledging her parity with him—if not superiority over him.

Oleg Ivanovich's son, Slava, possesses the privileges of his father's social standing, yet is victimized both by his father's economic power and Asia's sexuality. He is spoiled by the lavish lifestyle, which made him unable to take "no" for an answer. He is used to conquest, and unable to adjust when Asia, the Don Juan, unsentimentally seduces him just to add another trophy to her collection. Love can significantly reduce one's power, and for Oleg Ivanovich, who survived a similar romantic catastrophe, this means the weakening of his son's social standing. Slava's rebellion against his father's power provokes a chain of demonstrative acts, stripping him of his status: he throws away the keys of his luxury car, he disappears from his apartment, and refuses to answer the phone. Certainly, this rebellion has clear economic limits: Slava continues using his father's name and credit card when he checks into the Metropol' hotel, so he is not yet ready to sleep on the street for the sake of free love. The same can be said of Dasha, who still uses her husband's credit card to check into a hotel after her flight from Iura. For Asia, Slava receives one beating after another: first he is beaten by his father, then by Vadim, and finally he is hit by Asia's car. His experience of sexual education can be described as a series of violent blows, both literal and figurative, challenging his inborn sense of superiority.

Iura, Dasha's husband, represents the most comedic version of the powerless man of power. Dasha is constantly screaming at him that he infuriates her ("Iura, ty menia besish'!"). What

24 Temkina and Zdravomyslova, "Sexual Scripts," 306.

is so infuriating about Iura? Evgeny Stychkin makes his character very sincere and appealing. His Iura is not a bad person, he is just one of "them," a man with social power and means. He sincerely believes that Dasha has everything that she needs to be happy because he has bought or given it to her already. He does not see her dissatisfaction with being his possession, another luxury commodity in his successful business life. This is why Iura loses his cool when he imagines Dasha with another man: he is losing something he considered his property and his alone. As Raewyn Connell explains in *Gender and Power*: "Men are empowered in gender relations, but in specific ways which produce their own limits. For instance, in a patriarchal gender order emphasizing monogamous marriage there is serious tension between men about issues of adultery; a structure that defines women as a kind of property makes men liable in reprisals for theft."[25] Despite his wealth and economic power, Iura appears to be limited in his authority over the sexual and emotional aspects of relationships. He is constantly bossed by the women around him: his secretary ignores his orders to wash the window in his office, his mother-in-law coaches him on how to control his wife, his wife beats him, and her driver Olia is blackmailing him after his failed attempt to sleep with her. When Dasha and Iura meet at the restaurant with Asia and Kirill, Iura confesses that he dreams of owning a small and comfortable hotel. Probably this dream signifies Iura's desire to escape the chilling comfort of his elegant house, decorated, among other things, by a life-size statue-table of a polar bear, hinting at the Arctic climate of this family nest. However, Iura bitterly complains, all the hotel business is already taken and there is no way to get into it.

Only Nikita, the highly idealized and charmingly cynical cop who owns a stylish car and motorcycle, appears as the man with whom Asia will choose to stay in the series' finale. Nikita saves Asia from several difficult situations, and while he imposes no rules, his apartment—the interior of which is designed with taste and skill by Asia herself—is the only place where she feels comfortable. However, his program for Asia's future is outlined in episode fourteen: "I need normal life. I need a woman in my apartment. Dinner, certainty. . . . I will come home today and open the wardrobe. Your clothes should be there. You will feed me dinner, then we will make love, and only after that, only afterward you will tell me what happened to you"—a rather suffocating regime for a free spirit like Asia. The final scene, when Nikita and Asia are riding off into the future, attempts to suggest a happy ending, but in fact, it represents one of

25 R. W. Connell, *Gender and Power* (Stanford: Stanford University Press, 1987), 108.

the weakest points in the series, offering the most patriarchal resolution to the plot. The free woman has found her authoritative hero and is ready to give up her freedom for him. The fact that Nikita represents state power and legal authority, that his last name is "Mikhalkov"—eponymous with that of the famous director best known for his proximity to Putin—and that he is as corrupt as a cop can be (his apartment and vehicles cannot conceivably be afforded on his meager salary as a public servant), makes this coda even less romantic.

In the group of economically and politically powerless characters, the orthodontist Gleb, the unfortunate seeker of Dasha's sexual favors, occupies the comedic pole (similar to the role of Iura in the former group). With Pavel Maikov's hilarious performance, Gleb appears as the most miserable representative of manhood in the series. He is obsessed with extramarital affairs because his wife Galia torments him with her complaining. Maikov makes Gleb believable, although this character borders on a caricature of a contemporary man. He is immature, stupid, and yet blatantly optimistic in his endeavors. His childishness is framed through many visual and aural hints: the ringtone of his telephone is an annoying children's song; his doctor's mask makes him look more like a character from a cartoon than a man, and even while sobering up from a hangover, he grabs a toy to soothe his aching head. When the guards sent by Slava's father put Asia's apartment under surveillance in order to apprehend Kirill, Gleb finds shelter in the children's playground. Gleb is an exemplar of a failed and disastrous manhood; he is practically a clueless child himself, incapable of acting like an adult human being.

Asia's husband Kirill and her lover Vadim represent men's powerlessness in dramatic if not tragic colors. Kirill is an ordinary ear, eye, and throat doctor, who looks and sounds like one himself in need of an otolaryngologist. It is difficult to feel empathy for this man since, from the very beginning of the series, he appears to be a lousy husband in every possible sense. He is not performing in the marital bed. Asia, in fact, recommends that he see a specialist. He is not much of a communicator either, constantly playing an escapist computer game, which seems to be his priority in life. At the same time, he is not possessive and hardly limits Asia's freedom; tellingly, he never asks Asia where she has been when she comes home late. Yet this quality is represented as a sign of his weakness and indifference towards Asia rather than his acceptance of her freedom. People close to him and bystanders alike see Kirill as a loser and weakling (*tiutia*). He can only regain his masculinity when he gets a gun. Only then is he capable of having sex with Asia, although the encounter looks more like rape. At the same time, he does not use the gun even against his rival, Vadim, although the gun serves to mediate Kirill's talk with him.

Violence as a means of communication in the sexual sphere plays an even greater role for Vadim, the owner of a small business without any hope of expansion. Nevertheless, he gives his business away in an attempt to flee the outcome of his brutal beating of Slava. He offers a parodic manifestation of Oleg Ivanovich or Iura's power complexes since he sees Asia as his trophy, mistakenly identifying his feeling of ownership with love. The scene in which he angrily tries to rape her to reestablish his power over her is one of the most graphic and violent in *The Affairs*. As Asia and Vadim are fighting, both become covered in red paint, so the whole episode resembles bloody carnage. The violent desire to control is congruent with the desire to kill and in the last episode, when Asia is taken hostage by Vadim, the expectation that he will kill her is already well established.

Anton (Artem Markarian), the youngest of the male characters, represents an important alternative to *all* of them, in a parallel to Olia's transgressive path. Lucky in his heteronormative relationships, he nevertheless exposes himself to insults and violence when he declares his love to Slava, Asia's young lover and his classmate. "One does not need to be a homosexual to love a woman," says Olia, and Asia repeats the same words to Anton after he kisses Slava, declaring his love for him. Anton and Olia are two of the most trustworthy characters in *The Affairs*, because they rebel against the dogmatic constraints of heternormativity, and the lies and cruelty it requires. Anton's rejection of straightforward sex after Slava propositions him during a moment of despair in the chic setting of the Metropol' hotel suggests his resistance to any attempts to mix economic power with sexual relations. Much like Asia, Anton wants to preserve this sphere for his free self-realization rather than a demonstration of his subjugation to the beloved.

Despite their apparent differences, men from both groups mirror more than contrast each other's actions. They form pairs as each other's doubles: Iura and Gleb, Oleg Ivanovich and Vadim, Nikita and Kirill, Slava and Anton. Furthermore, there are obvious parallels between the male and female characters. Thus, the powerful Oleg Ivanovich parallels the powerless yet ambitious Galina Sergeevna; Asia instructs Slava as she does Dasha, when she gives him "Asia's rules" of sexual (mis)conduct; and Anton, in his exploration of alternative models of sexuality, resonates with Olia. Moreover, all of the series' characters, male and female alike, contribute to our understanding of Asia since each of them offers either an affinity or a contrast to her attitude to sexuality. Asia possesses Gleb and Slava's sexual rapaciousness but rejects Dasha's, Iura's, and Galina Sergeevna's commodification of sexuality; and until the finale, she does not want to sacrifice her freedom to relationships, as do Oleg Ivanovich, Olia, or Anton.

Notably, most of the series' characters relate to each other through violent acts both physical and psychological: Iura hits Kirill twice, Dasha hits Iura and Olia, Kirill hits his brother Anton, Asia hits Slava, Vadim beats Slava and tries to rape Asia, Slava's father beats him, at the same time Slava threatens Asia's lifestyle by breaching the boundaries of her domestic order, and so on and on. At first, Nikita appears to be an exception, but in fact it was he who teaches Asia how to hit pedestrians with her car without killing them and humiliates Dasha when she is willing to begin an affair with him, using her as bait to get back at Asia. Although a gun appears in *The Affairs,* despite Chekhov's dictum, it never fires. However, the gun is a false signifier for violence here, while much more subtle and ordinary things—lacy panties, a ring, a road map, a balcony, a car—transmit violence much more effectively. Even such an innocent thing as house paint literally turns into blood-like substance during the scene of Asia's wrestling with Iura.

Asia is no exception to this rule: she intentionally hits Slava with her car, causing him minor injuries, cuts, and bruises. It is chilling that she feels no remorse or compassion towards him. Instead she threatens to kill him the next time for sure, if he does not stop pursuing her. She could have killed Slava—as she proves by hitting him with her car—while defending her right to be free. Unfortunately, this fight for freedom carries a hefty price tag because the freedom to fornicate appears to be intimately connected with the freedom to kill. This is why Vadim, who almost beats the boy to death in his jealous rage, simply finishes something that Asia has started, and Slava's blood is on both their hands.

In *The Affairs* the men are objectified as much as women. They are seen either as sexual predators, constantly trying to get into the panties of all passing women, or as tough defenders, coming to rescue their damsels in distress. Dasha suspects Iura of sexual misdemeanors and insists that she has the right to control him: "I will get to/into you anywhere: in your phone, your wallet, your ass, if I think you've been unfaithful to me." ("Ia zalezu k tebe kuda ugodno: v telefon, v koshelek, v zhopu—esli budu dumat', chto ty mne izmenil.") Dasha calls her husband an animal, a swine, and a lowlife, as casually as if the words were affectionate nicknames ("Iura, skotina, svin'ia, uzhinai odin, svoloch'!") Asia offhandedly denigrates her lover Nikita

("Nikita is a good guy. I trained him well. He has a stamp from the best dog breeders"),[26] the only man who truly supports and understands her, by giving him as a "coupon" to Dasha. This coupon allows Dasha to use him for sex, prompting a dialogue between Dasha and Olia in which Dasha describes Nikita as a "thing." "—I do not understand how it is possible to give something as a gift and then take it back.—He is not a thing. He is a THING. For Asia, all men are things. She told me this many times."

The prevalence of violence in a series about love and sexuality is symptomatic. It reveals the failure of mutually respectful negotiations between partners and rivals in sex and suggests the desire to subjugate the other's freedom by any means possible as the preferred method of "lovemaking." This logic is unambiguous in all of the characters' thoughts and deeds, a bitter commentary to the spectacular failure of democratic reforms in Russia, and the consistent reemergence of authoritarian and patriarchal models despite their inability to facilitate contemporary subjectivities and their relationships (as embodied in the aforementioned redundancy of Galina Sergeevna).

Notably, even the series' authors hardly avoided this logic. In one of her interviews Gratsevich revealed that she had to argue with the film's director and producers (all men) that Asia should stay alive in the series' finale when she is kidnapped by Vadim. For them, it was obvious that she had to die, which can be interpreted as a desire to punish the protagonist for her *excessive* freedom, for her transgressions that are supposedly incompatible with a good life and a happy ending: a typical way of disciplining an unruly female character.

The parallel belittling of men and women alike, of both those men possessing power and those deprived of it, brings up the political question of the powerlessness that appears to be *evenly* distributed in contemporary Russian society. The constraint of a glass ceiling is familiar to everyone in *The Affairs*, women and men alike. They all are confined within their respective social cells that delimit their range of possibilities and ambitions. That is why Asia insists that at her level there cannot be any grand drama: "I have a small life: an apartment, a husband-otolaryngologist, some loans. People are not getting killed in this kind of life." However, the desire to have an uncontrolled sexual life outside of the marital bed suddenly turns out to be the most threatening factor for the social status quo. Vadim Perelman insists that "all the messages in the film are directed against adultery, because infidelities mean evil and pain.

26 In Russia, purebred dogs used to be identified by a brand on the ear.

They ruin families and the person him/herself. . . . We are not propagandizing adultery and we do not say that it is right." [27] The careful moralizing of this statement is misleading. In fact, the series methodically demonstrates how its characters, men and the women alike, are unable to find happiness and fulfillment either in their family life or outside of their marital beds. As a result, they turn against each other in violent and threatening ways. In other words, sexuality and sex in *The Affairs* breed horizontal violence ("evil and pain") since they manifest *social* frustrations, the rage against the impossibility of significantly changing their lives.

The philosopher Oksana Timofeeva maintains that the "political situation in Russia is such that it creates an elevated erotic pressure."[28] Such a situation is not new for Russian culture: One may recall the hidden sexual revolution of the Stagnation era. The transformation of erotic adventures into an investigation of freedom, its limits and its price, is political indeed.[29] The series not only portrays the desire of married people to exercise sexual freedom outside marriage and not only reveals the sad consequences of these transgressions, but offers a sober analysis of contemporary Russian society, which leaves its subjects with only one freedom—the freedom to copulate.

27 Natalya Vasilieva, "'Izmeny' nado smotret', chtoby potom ne bylo muchitel'no stydno," *Izvestiia*, June 30, 2016, https://iz.ru/news/620081.

28 Iuliia Galkina, "Filosofy Artemii Magun i Oksana Timofeeva—o giperseksual'nosti rossiian," *Village*, September 21, 2016, http://www.the-village.ru/village/people/city-news/245611-sex-philosophy.

29 See Nikolai Chernyshevsky's "The Russian Man at a Rendezvous" (1858), a political analysis of Turgenev's novella *Asya*. The fact that *The Affairs*' protagonist bears the same name as Turgenev's character is hardly a coincidence.

Bibliography

Bocharova, O. A. "Seksual'naia svoboda: Slova i dela." *Chelovek* 5 (1994): 98-107.

Connell, R. W. *Gender and Power.* Stanford: Stanford University Press, 1987.

"Dar'ia Gratsevich ob 'Izmenakh': 'Ia by ne khotela prodolzhat' serial.'" Teleserial.com. http://www.teleserial.com/story/25838-serial-izmeni-2015-istoriya-zhenskih-izmen-na-tnt/.

"Elena Liadova: 'My zatronuli v "Izmenakh" temu lichnoi svobody.'" Vokrug.tv, September 18, 2015. http://www.vokrug.tv/article/show/elena_lyadova_my_zatronuli_v_izmenah_temu_lichnoi_svobody_49548/.

Felman, Shoshana. *The Scandal of the Speaking Body: Don Juan with J. I. Austin, or Seduction in Two Languages.* Stanford: Stanford University Press, 1983.

Foucault, Michel. *The History of Sexuality.* Vol. 1: *An Introduction*, translated by Robert Hurley. New York: Vintage Books, 1990.

Galeeva, R. I. "Siuzhet 'Odna zhenshchina i troe muzhchin' do G. Flobera i u G. Flobera ('Gospozha Bovari')." *Uchenye zapiski Kazanskogo gosudarstvennogo universiteta* 151, no. 3 (2009): 111–118.

Galkina, Iuliia. "Filosofy Artemii Magun i Oksana Timofeeva—o giperseksual'nosti rossiian." *Village,* September 21, 2016. http://www.the-village.ru/village/people/city-news/245611-sex-philosophy.

Goffman, Erving. "Frame Analysis of Gender." From *The Arrangement between the Sexes.* In *The Goffman Reader*, edited by C. Lemert and A. Branaman, 201–208. New Jersey: Wiley Blackwell, 1997.

Haskell, Molly. *From Reverence to Rape: The Treatment of Women in the Movies.* New York: University of Chicago Press, 1973.

"Kontseptsiia gosudarstvennoi semeinoi politiki v Rossiiskoi Federatsii na period do 2025 goda." *Rossiiskaia gazeta,* August 29, 2014. https://rg.ru/2014/08/29/semya-site-dok.html.

Kon, Igor S. "Sexuality and Politics in Russia (1700–2000)." In *Sexual Cultures in Europe. National Histories,* edited by F. X. Eder, L. A. Hall and G. Hekma, 197–218. Manchester: Manchester University Press, 1999.

Kon, Igor S. *The Sexual Revolution in Russia. From the Age of the Czars to Today.* New York: The Free Press, 1995.

Mikhienko, Svetlana. *Evoliutsiia obraza Don Zhuana v russkoi literature XIX–XX vekov.* Dissertatsiia na soiskanie uchenoi stepeni kandidata filologicheskikh nauk. Piatigorsk State University, 2001. http://www.dissercat.com/content/evolyutsiya-obraza-don-zhuana-v-russkoi-literature-xix-xx-vekov.

Pavlova, Karolina. *The Double Life.* Translated by Barbara Heldt. Benicia, CA: Barbary Coast Books, 1986.

Poletaeva, Nastia. "Pochemu rossiiskie serialy o zhenskikh izmenakh popali v tochku." *Wonder,* November 10, 2015. http://www.wonderzine.com/wonderzine/life/life/215829-cheating-equally.

Rappoport, Philippa. "If It Dries Out, It's No Good: Women, Hair and Rusalki Beliefs." *SEEFA Journal* 4, no. 1 (1999): 55–63.

Sokolova, Iu. A. "Gendernye osobennosti prichin supruzheskikh izmen v sovremennykh sem'iakh," *Uchenye zapiski Rossiiskogo gosudarstvennogo sotsial'nogo universiteta* 7 (2012): 148–154.

Temkina, Anna, and Elena Zdravomyslova. "The Sexual Scripts and Identity of Middle-Class Russian Women." *Sexuality and Culture* 19 (2015): 297–320.

Vasilieva, Natalya. "'Izmeny' nado smotret', chtoby potom ne bylo muchitel'no stydno." *Izvestiia*, June 30, 2016, https://iz.ru/news/620081.

Veselovskaia, Nadezhda. *Don Zhuan russkoi klassicheskoi literatury.* Dissertatsiia na soiskanie uchenoi stepeni kandidata filologicheskikh nauk, Literaturnyi Institut, 2000.

Viti, Robert M. "'A Woman's Time, a Lady's Place': *Nana* and *Au Bonheur des Dames.*" *Symposium* (Winter 1990): 291–301.

Worobec, Christine. "Accommodation and Resistance." In *Russia's Women: Accommodation, Resistance, Transformation*, edited by Barbara Evans Clements, Barbara Alpern Engel, and Christine Worobec, 17–28. Berkeley: University of California Press, 1991.

Glocalizing Neo-Noir: Iury Bykov's *The Method* and *Sleepers*

Elena Prokhorova, Alexander Prokhorov, and Rimgaila Salys

Russian television series production began in the late 1990s with crime shows such as *Cops: Streets of Broken Lights* (*Menty: Ulitsy razbitykh fonarei*, season one, 1998) and *Gangster Petersburg* (*Banditsky Peterburg*, 2000). These series identified market reforms with the rise of organized crime and privatized violence. Both take place in St. Petersburg—the gateway of Russia's westernization. In the 2000s, the focus of crime shows shifted to a reflection about the 1990s as the recent history, and to a greater interest in the Soviet past. As critic Andrei Arkhangel'sky points out, crime series revived the Soviet fashion for the glorification of security services. Three shows set up the important trends of the decade: police procedural *Kamenskaia* (dir. Iury Moroz, 2000), gangster saga *Brigada* (dir. Aleksei Sidorov, 2002), and *Liquidation* (*Likvidatsiia*, dir. Sergei Ursuliak, 2007), a melodrama about a violent but glorious Soviet past. The latter influenced numerous crime shows set in the glamorized USSR.[1] Most importantly, to represent this romanticized criminal underworld, one needs to know little history but numerous narrative and culture gimmicks: the motive of competition between the NKVD and the local police, blurred boundaries between the police and the criminal underworld, and a generous dose of Soviet popular songs and criminal jargon, much of it shared by post-Soviet viewers.

Ironically, the filmmaker who pioneered gangster film and noir atmosphere in Russian cinema was an art house director and maverick figure in the post-Soviet cultural scene—Aleksei Balabanov. In *Brother* (*Brat*, 1997), he not only visualized the dystopian mise-en-scène of the Russian neo-noir, but also gave birth and ideology to its protagonist. Arguably, Balabanov was more of a trickster filmmaker.[2] He, however, inspired scores of cinematic and television

1 *Odnazhdy v Rostove* (*Once Upon a Time in Rostov*, 2012), *Leningrad-46* (2014), *Fartsa* (2015), *Krasnaia koroleva* (*The Red Queen*, 2015), *Chernoe more* (*Black Sea*, 2020), and numerous others.

2 Mariia Kuvshinova, Liubov' Arkus, and Konstantin Shavlovskii, *Balabanov* (St. Petersburg: Seans, 2013), 242. For a discussion of the trickster character in Soviet and post-Soviet cinema, see Mark Lipovetsky, "Neither Here, nor There. The Trickster in the Cinema of Perestroika and the Early 1990s," in *Ruptures and Continuities in Soviet/Russian Cinema. Styles, Characters and Genres before and after the Collapse of the USSR*, ed. Birgit Beumers and Eugénie Zvonkine (London and New York: Routledge, 2018), 108–125.

productions about violent masculinity in crisis. We propose that if Balabanov's legacy can be detected in contemporary television, it is above all evident in the crime dramas of Iury Bykov. Bykov's socially minded films, such as *Major* (*Maior*, 2013), *Fool* (*Durak*, 2014), *Factory* (*Zavod*, 2018), have been received as brutal, violent, and almost too blunt in their treatment of social issues and as representations of Russia's heartland devastated by failed market reforms.[3]

Recently Bykov reinvented himself as a successful commercial director in the high-budget television productions *The Method* (*Metod*, 2015) and *Sleepers* (*Spiashchie*, 2017), both of which premiered on Channel One. These two series are trendmakers in the Russian crime television market and a contribution to the global neo-noir genre. David Desser argues that global neo-noir encompasses crime films set in global cities for global markets.[4] The uniqueness of neo-noir is its transnational circulation. In the case of Russia, the lifting of Soviet censorship and the arrival of the market economy coincided with the rise of neo-noir in the United States and beyond. The collapse of value systems, not to mention the astounding crime rate that accompanied the transition to a market economy, attuned the Russian public and cultural producers to the sensibilities of the global neo-noir.

The neo-noir protagonist resides in a morally ambiguous universe, of which he is an extension. As Denis Saltykov notes in his discussion of privatized violence in Russian cinema of the 1990s and 2000s, Russian filmmakers responded to the global trend with narratives of disoriented males trying to cope with violent and dystopian realities, in which all moral and legal certainties are suspended.[5] In the 2010s, neo-noir aesthetics merged with quality television, resulting in shows that were marketable for global distribution via Netflix, Amazon Prime, and other streaming platforms with global outreach. In this article we examine Bykov's two neo-noir television series as antipodes of each other, especially in the way they deal with ghosts of the Soviet past. We contend that in *The Method* Bykov not only demonstrates his mastery of neo-noir conventions but also successfully translates post-utopian realities of contemporary

3 Mark Lipovetsky, "Iurii Bykov: *The Fool* (*Durak*, 2014)," *KinoKultura* 47 (2015), http://www.kinokultura.com/2015/47r-durak.shtml.

4 David Desser, "Global Noir: Genre Film in the Age of Transnationalism," in *Film Genre Reader*, ed. Barry Keith Grant (Austin: University of Texas Press, 2003), vol. 3, 517.

5 Denis Saltykov, "Privatized Violence in the New Russian Cinema," in *Cinemasaurus: Russian Film in Contemporary Context*, ed. Nancy Condee, Alexander Prokhorov, and Elena Prokhorova (Boston: Academic Studies Press, 2020), 119.

Russia into global neo-noir vernacular. *Sleepers*, on the other hand, while quite successful in exploiting the striking mise-en-scène and narrative turns, tries to combine those features with Soviet-era conventions of a film about government agents fighting foreign spies aided by a fifth column inside of Russia. In this article we focus primarily on *The Method,* which we argue is a more complex and sophisticated text than *Sleepers* with its wooden, Soviet-style FSB hero and blatant propaganda message.

Russian TV Noir: Rodion's "Method"

The Method follows a team of two investigators, Rodion Meglin (Konstantin Khabensky) and his intern Esenia Steklova (Paulina Andreeva), who track and execute serial killers. Most of the series is set in Russia's heartland. Each episode/criminal case is framed by a scene with two internal affairs officers, one played by Bykov himself, questioning Esenia after something extraordinary happened to Meglin. Only by the end of season one do viewers learn why the investigators were interrogating Esenia: Meglin is dead after having succumbed to his mysterious disease and convincing Esenia to mercy-kill him. Thus the security services need a new "terminator" to do Meglin's job. It takes fifteen episodes to learn about Meglin's demise, each of which sees the evildoer stopped in one way or another. Still, this gloomy and hopeless mise-en-scène is matched with a disorienting sense of how the social structure of contemporary Russia operates and doubt over whether it is possible to run it without constant recourse to violence.

One of the defining features of the neo-noir narrative is the mystery of the protagonist's past, causes of his/her behavior, and, consequently, a certain looseness of the narrative.[6] *The Method* is structured both as a vertical television series, in which each new episode presents a new case and a new mystery, and a horizontal one, with certain narrative lines continuing from one episode to the next. The two major lines are the mystery of Esenia's mother's murder and the nature of Meglin's method—the reason he is the way he is. The continuing suspense is in stark contrast with the straightforward resolution of every episode. Meglin cracks each case,

6 Jerold J. Abrams, "Space, Time, and Subjectivity in Neo-Noir Cinema," in *Philosophy of Neo-Noir,* ed. Mark Conard (Lexington: University of Kentucky Press, 2007), 7–8.

and by the episode's end the perpetrator is usually not only apprehended but also spectacularly executed or allowed to take his own life.

The mysteries of the two main characters are, perhaps, what makes them dark and the series truly noirish. Even after we learn the details of the two protagonists' origins, we get neither a sense of resolution or redemption, nor even a complete clarity about characters' true nature. Can you really know somebody else's psychosis? We learn that Meglin shot Esenia's mother who, however, was not an innocent victim but a violent schizophrenic who had herself killed a person. Moreover, her execution was ordered by Esenia's father, Andrei. In this hellish labyrinth it is impossible to separate victims from perpetrators. Esenia seems to be an exception. Nevertheless, she has already demonstrated a taste for violence herself. After she gouges out a serial killer's eyes, ostensibly in self-defense, Meglin asks her how she felt about it and she admits that deep inside she enjoyed every moment.

Like Meglin, Esenia becomes a regular at Dr. Bergich's psychiatric clinic, usually on an assignment. But there are many scenes in which she simply observes the inmates as part of her natural habitat, even before she learns about her mother's illness and the hereditary nature of the disease. It is not surprising that "the method" that Esenia craves to learn from Meglin has nothing to do with rationality and logic. Instead, Meglin's insights coincide with his epiphanic fits, which resemble epileptic seizures. At those moments of revelation, the detective can feel or see the crime in progress and identify the perpetrator.

The series is structured as a classical fatalistic noir melodrama in which all events are in flashback and nothing can be changed. The two officers who interrogate Esenia obviously see her potential as an independent contractor with a license to kill and a standing appointment with a psychiatrist. To clarify things to the best of her ability, Esenia mixes her answers with frequent sips from Meglin's flask. The prop portends both her inheriting Meglin's job as well as his mental illness and unhealthy addictions. Nothing can be changed in the past nor, apparently, in the future. Esenia inherits not only Meglin's job but also his mental volatility and propensity for self-destruction.

But the series has a much more obvious double of Meglin in Aleksei Anofriev (also known as the Shooter), his classmate from the Soviet-era police training school. Released from jail by Esenia's father in order to contain Meglin's unorthodox methods of cleansing society from criminals and to separate Meglin and Esenia, he appears in the concluding three episodes. The two have unfinished business: their rivalry that began during their training. They are equally skilled, psychotic, and violent; but Meglin serves with the police, whereas the Shooter chose the dark side. Both characters are played by leading Russian male stars, Khabensky and Aleksei Serebriakov. The Shooter's agenda is to bring Meglin to his side, to convince him that people are already spiritually dead and that killing their biological shells only satisfies the natural drive they share. Both characters have dark secrets, including the truth about Esenia's mother. The Shooter goes on a killing spree, which he stages as a macabre series of rituals. First, he kills three people, then nine, and then forty, parodying traditional rituals of mourning. Being a talented and creative mass murderer, he plans to extend the ritual into 365 murders in one day, but is stopped by Meglin and Esenia before carrying out the massacre.

The Method is set on the outskirts of Moscow and in Russia's heartland where most of the crimes take place. The trope of neo-noir homelessness is central to the representations of Russia's heartland. In fact, the sense of homelessness in *The Method* is both metaphorical and physical. The main settings of the episodes are Russian towns such as Lipetsk, Serpukhov, Troitsk, Vladimir, and Nizhny Novgorod, all within a one-day drive from Moscow. Neither domestic warmth nor traditional Russian values reside in those towns. Instead, domestic spaces serve as sites of trauma in the past or brutal murders in the present. To add insult to injury, Bykov settles his detectives in abominable provincial hotels where Meglin's uncouth, provocative behavior is a perfect match to the grotesque settings of half-destroyed rooms with decrepit beds and dirty linen. In the best tradition of cinema of despair and cynicism, we see those hotels primarily at night. Ironically, they carry optimistic Soviet-era names, such as "Sunrise," whose clash with the gloomy setting can be read as black humor (Fig. 1).

The chronotope of the road is another important motif of noir homelessness in *The Method*.[7] Each episode portrays the detectives traveling in Meglin's old car towards a crime site and a new devastating experience.[8] Meglin's own domicile too is located next to a highway interchange, which provides incessant background humming, undermining any attempt to establish a domestic atmosphere. Notably, this converted industrial space does not belong to

7 In his fixation on homelessness Bykov is a true heir of Balabanov's cinema starting with Balabanov's first feature *Happy Days* (1991). For further discussion see Nancy Condee, *The Imperial Trace: Recent Russian Cinema* (New York: Oxford University Press, 2009), 221–225. She calls his first work "a film about the impossibility of shelter."

8 Meglin drives a blue Mercedes, model E class W123 from the 1970s. The color and model matches one of the cars of Vladimir Vysotsky, the cult singer and actor of the late socialist era.

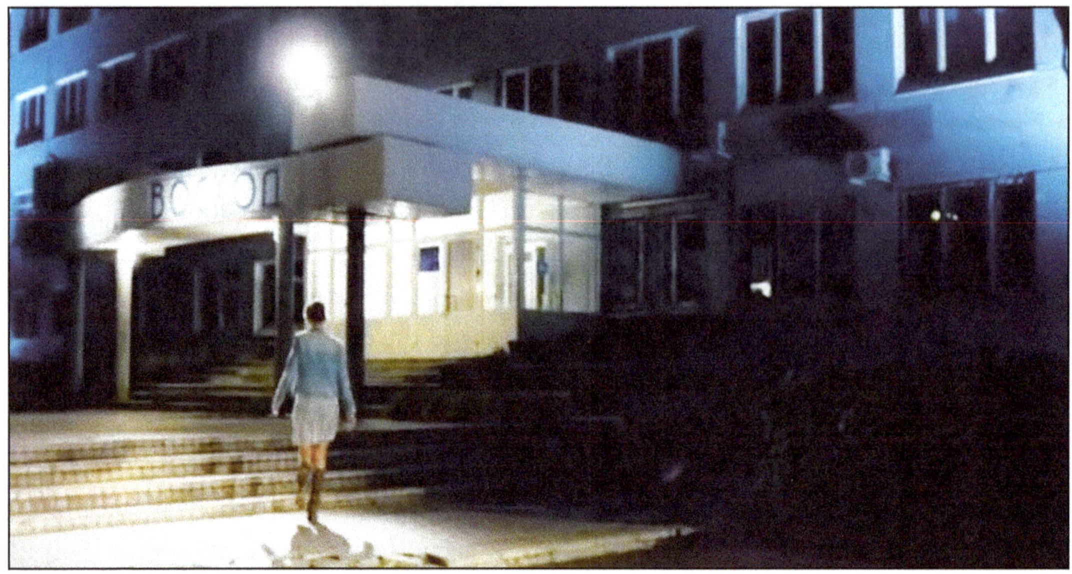

Fig. 1. Hotel *Sunrise* as noir setting.

Meglin; rather he was settled in it by his police mentors or handlers. Like this halfway house itself, Meglin's stay there depends on his utility to the police. When we learn how he came to live there, the sense of transitory existence is only confirmed.[9] In place of a hearth Meglin uses half of a discarded fuel barrel. He also has house plants: dozens of tiny cacti, each representing a serial killer apprehended and, we assume, executed by Meglin.

Similarly, Esenia tells Meglin that her sense of home disappeared with her mother's death. What used to be domestic space turned into its empty shell. About her father's house she says: "That's how I would think: 'Ok, I am going to the building [instead of a home].'" Esenia, who is clearly attracted to Meglin, tries to make his loft her home and fails miserably. Her first attempt at cleaning his mess provokes Meglin's rage. Later, after she moves in, she puts her amulet with an image of St. George above the bed, asking the saint to look over the two of them. This happens, however, very close to the season finale, in which not only is Meglin killed but this loft is revealed to be the very site of Esenia's mother's murder, committed by the very

9 Linda Ivanits notes that in Russian folk belief crossroads were haunted by unclean forces and that suicides were usually buried at the crossroads. See Linda Ivanits, *Russian Folk Belief* (Armonk: M. E. Sharpe, Inc., 1992), 40, 120.

same Meglin. Apparently, in the logic of neo-noir, home is where your heart is (repeatedly) broken.

Finally, when the characters are overwhelmed and hurt, they find refuge in a symbolic location, which stands at the center of most episodes both in the present and in flashbacks—the insane asylum headed by Dr. Bergich. After Meglin loses his family and later his identity (on paper he is executed for the crimes he commits and his identity is erased), this is the only place where he can be himself and learn who he is. Dr. Bergich explains to Meglin that, because of his childhood trauma, he acquired the "gift" of sensing psychopaths—because he became one himself. This is also the place where Meglin coins the term "ours" (*nashi*) referring to the mentally disturbed, potential serial killers. The location of this asylum is left for viewers to guess. One thing is clear: this is the halfway house for some of the luckier "ours."

Apart from Meglin's elusive method, "ours" is yet another key word of the series. Meglin frequently observes about various criminals, suspects, or mental patients: "He is ours, one of us" ("On nash"). Which community he refers to is ambiguous. Clearly, these are disturbed individuals, like Meglin himself, who are capable of or have committed violent crimes. "Ours" also refers to individuals who can sense others like them. Curiously, many of these people are somehow connected to each other and are known by name to the four key players in the story: Meglin, his arch-nemesis—the Shooter, the police, and Dr. Bergich, the head of the psychiatric hospital. One key moment in the past when all four come together is when Meglin is recruited to the special forces. In the training camp he meets the Shooter, who is also a trainee there, and begins seeing his psychiatrist while being supervised by Grigor'ev, his police handler and mentor. Thus, the "ours" constitute a loose community of volatile individuals barely contained and manipulated by two surveillance bodies: the police force and the mental institution.[10]

It is, of course, not insignificant that "ours" is a concept inherited from Soviet-speak, where it referred to the ideological community of Soviet people. Its reversal in the series undermines the stability of this signifier and points to the roots of this idea in a pre-modern, like-minded

10 The power of these institutions and bodies of knowledge to discipline and dehumanize is ever present in Bykov's series and evokes Michel Foucault's notion of "medical gaze" and the panopticon surveillance of prison institutions. See Foucault's *The Birth of the Clinic: An Archeology of Medical Perception* (New York: Vintage, 1993); and his *Discipline and Punish: The Birth of the Prison* (New York: Vintage, 1995). The only Soviet-era director who consistently linked the two institutions as ubiquitous power structures that discipline the character's body and mind was Leonid Gaidai. See, for example, Alexander Prokhorov, "Diamond Arm," in *Russian Cinema Reader*, ed. Rimgaila Salys, vol. 2 (Boston: Academic Studies Press, 2013), 114–125.

or like-crazy community. In its subversive potential, an important antecedent of Bykov's use of the concept of "ours" is Sergei Dovlatov's story collection *Ours: A Russian Family Album.* It has a hybrid structure similar to the Bykov TV series, namely, each chapter focuses on one member of the main narrator's extended family. Together they are the "ours." The absurdist, somewhat surreal and humorous tone of the book is a counterpart of the gothic and at times darkly humorous tone of Bykov's noir series. Of course Dovlatov, not unlike Bykov, does not entirely bracket the Soviet connotations of the word "ours" because he ends his book with a paradoxical observation about the birth of his American son: "My son was born on December 23, 1981 in New York. He is an American, a citizen of the United States. His name is—just imagine—Mr. Nicholas Dowley. This is what my family and our motherland have ultimately accomplished."[11] Meglin plays with his sliding signifier "ours" in a similar manner and does not allow us to pin down its exact meaning or the borders of the community.

The chronotope of Bykov's *The Method* would be incomplete without its iconography of power. It begins as a run-of-the-mill series about the glorious security services—an image that is almost immediately deflated when a maniac kills at the graduation party of the law school and the only person capable of identifying the murderer is a person in civilian clothes with a doubtful reputation—Meglin. This is the image of the police that the series will highlight. They are marginal to Meglin's investigations, and incapable of apprehending or even understanding the crimes. Their only purpose seemingly is to contain Meglin's investigative zeal. The sense of the authorities, simultaneously awesome and impotent, is effectively channeled through the portraits of Putin displayed in public offices, lurking behind civil servants failing at fulfilling their duties.

The portrait of the Russian president as an authority is an image with ambiguous status in the narrative. In some episodes Putin is almost a character. For example, in episode four, his portrait appears in the office of the head of city government who is in love with the serial killer Tolik. As she rages against Meglin's insinuation about Tolik's involvement in the disappearance of children and paces around her office, Putin constantly remains behind her (Fig. 2). But while the presence of the president's portrait in the mise-en-scène is obviously intentional, at the same

11 "23 dekabria 1981 goda v N'iu Iorke rodilsia moi synok. On amerikanets, grazhdanin Soedinennykh Shtatov. Zovut ego—predstav'te sebe—mister Nikolas Douli. Eto to, k chemu prishla moia sem'ia i nasha rodina" (Sergei Dovlatov, "Nashi," in his *Sobranie sochinenii*, vol. 2 [St. Petersburg: Azbuka, 1999], 380).

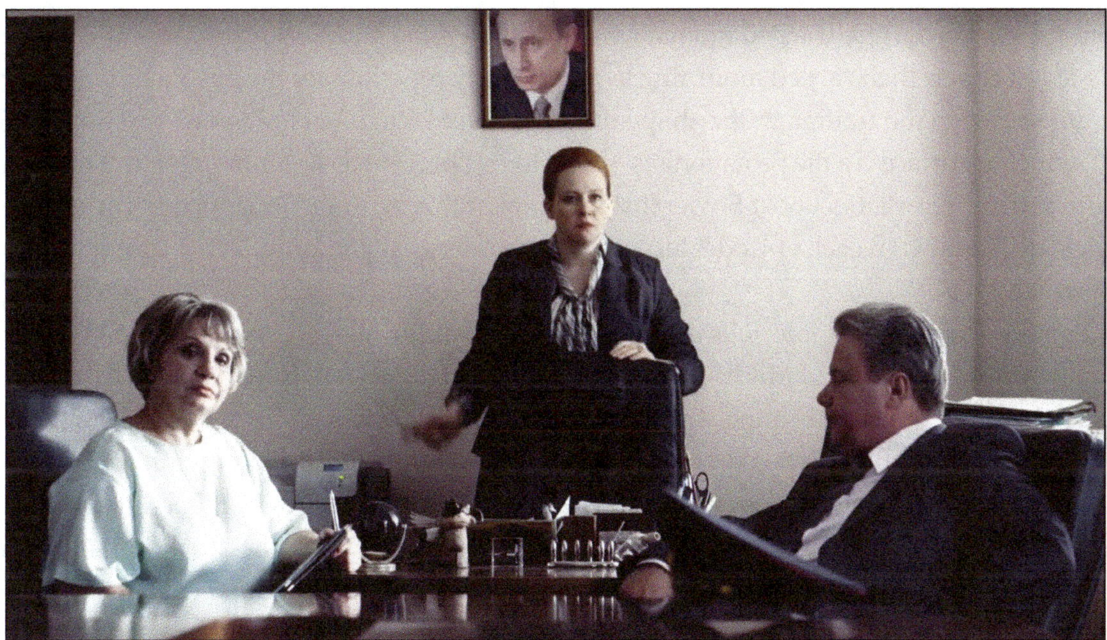

Fig. 2. Vertical of Power.

time its meaning is not quite legible. One thing is clear: Putin "supervises" the administration which is blind and impotent in dealing with true evil. The portrait thus adds to the macabre atmosphere of dystopian neo-noir narrative.

What are the cases that Meglin and his partner investigate? Who are these "ours," what do they do and why? All cases have one thing in common: the origins of serial killers' deviant behavior can be traced back to their childhoods in late Soviet society. This is also the time when Meglin's parents were murdered and when Esenia's mother was diagnosed with her mental illness. It is important that this time of troubles in the lives of the characters is the historical period that Putin-era media depict as the Golden Age of prosperity and social stability. Bykov's series, in contrast, suggests that the late Soviet era was a time of social crisis, the traumas of which have not been addressed. They have remained repressed and have continued to resurface long after that country ceased to exist. In *Warped Mourning*, Alexander Etkind argues that a normal mourning process accepts the reality of the loss. In Russia, where no public discussion of the socialist past took place, no Soviet-era perpetrators were punished, and no true debate about the past occurred, warped mourning replaced healing and distancing from the trauma.[12] *The Method* enacts this warped mourning as an uncanny repetition of the past, where the horror narratives revive the trauma in the shape of unprocessed fragments of Soviet mythology. The past, which resurfaces in the protagonists' (detectives') present, is a common feature of the neo-noir narrative. The distinct post-Soviet instantiation of this neo-noir series is that the gruesome crimes investigated in each episode derive from unprocessed and unreflected traumatic Soviet experience.

Episode four, for example, tells the story of an upstanding citizen, Anatolii (Tolik) Golovko, from the provincial town of Mikhailovsk. He works with teenagers from troubled families and divides his time between beating their abusive alcoholic fathers and leading hiking trips for their sons and daughters. The name of the club, Romantik, the dilapidated former Soviet-era community center where it is located, and the general look of the town immediately indicate that nothing has changed here since 1991. Both Tolik and his town are stuck in late socialist times. While the camping trips could be construed as modern day scouting routines, Tolik's rhetoric evokes Soviet slogans, preparing the kids for the military effort, sacrifice, and the collectivist cause. City administration hails Tolik as a hero, while explaining away the recurring disappearance of children as a statistically insignificant matter. When Meglin and Esenia begin to investigate the cases of missing children, they meet resistance from both the local police and the city administration.

With an egalitarian performance of a song by club members sitting around a bonfire, we are taken on a trip back in time. Behind this Soviet-style utopia, however, lurks a nightmare. The "paternal" Tolik brings individual boys into the woods, dresses them in young pioneer outfits (white top, black bottom) and asks them to endure a hanging test in preparation for the ultimate sacrifice (*podvig*), which, in his words, will be remembered and admired by exemplary Soviet heroes: pilots, submariners, and polar explorers. The trusting boys submit to their mentor who takes pictures of them suffocating in a noose. Tellingly, it is not clear through whose consciousness we see the ritualistically staged crimes. Is it Tolik's perception or Meglin's or even Esenia's? After all, it is her answers to the investigators that frame each episode. The ritual displays all the familiar ingredients of the young pioneer-hero mythology but without the

12 See Alexander Etkind, *Warped Mourning: Stories of the Undead in the Land of the Unburied* (Stanford: Stanford University Press, 2013), 16–19.

noble ideological cause, which used to justify violent images in Soviet propaganda.[13] Instead, we witness an infinite repetition of the uncanny sexual fantasies of a serial killer who alone provides narrative coherence to the recurring murders. The makers of *The Method* thus suggest that Soviet-era state-sponsored violence and sacred martyrdom have outlived communist ideology and continue to breed mayhem in post-Soviet culture.

While episode four deals with the consequences of Soviet-era discourses of violence, episode six opens with a scene from the year 1971 at the site of trauma itself: the elementary school no. 71. The theme of the lesson is the martyrdom of Zoia Kosmodem'ianskaia.[14] The teacher brings the images of Zoia's disfigured and violated body to her elementary school class and insists on every child imprinting in their memory the images of the martyr. One of the iconic images is Zoia hanging from the gallows with the sign saying "Partisan" on her chest. Several decades later the town is shaken by the discoveries of young women's bodies hanging from trees, with the same placard on their chests. Before the killer displays his prey, he incapacitates the women with truth serum. Obviously, this impressionable man, whose identity we learn at the episode's end, chose to be the perpetrator and not the martyr in this violent fantasy scenario.

In his treatment of violence, Bykov follows in the footsteps of the patriarch of neo-noir, Quentin Tarantino. Violence is abundant in his films and carries no redeeming value or metaphysical message. It is a commodity among others in the global market. At best, it is part of the post-utopian urbanscape. The graphic and repeated violence of crimes is matched by equally violent and bloody retribution without any promise of redemption. In one of the early episodes Meglin uses Esenia as bait to catch a serial killer who turns out to be a cop. Instead of bringing order to the provincial town, the scene of the murderer's apprehension is as terrifying

13 The narrative of heroic children and adolescents who fought the Nazis during the Great Patriotic War was an indispensable component of Soviet patriotic education. These heroes were the subjects of multiple quasi-hagiographic books, films, and posters that often recounted the martyrdom of a young hero in great detail. See, for example, Lev Kassil' and Maks Polianovsky's *Street of the Younger Son* (*Ulitsa mladshego syna*, 1949).

14 Zoia Kosmodem'ianskaia is a resistance fighter whose torture and execution by the Germans became part of the Soviet canon of war heroes after Petr Lidov's article published in *Pravda*. Lev Arnshtam's 1944 film *Zoia* made Kosmodem'ianskaia a household name. Since Putin's first term the story was brought back as part of the concerted effort to use World War II mythology to legitimize the current political order. In 2020 Leonid Pliaskin and Maksim Brius directed a new cinematic story of Zoia's martyrdom.

and chaotic as the murders themselves. First, Meglin waits quite some time while the murderer is strangling Esenia; then, finally, Meglin stabs the murderer in the neck, while explaining to him that he will never have his female soccer team of corpses because he managed to kill only ten women. Meanwhile, the eleventh potential member of the maniac's "dream team" gasps for air, blue in the face. Finally, Meglin extracts his knife from the murderer's wound, blood gushes out and befouls the entire streetcar where the dénouement takes place. Meglin then throws the murderer out of the tram to bleed out at a streetcar stop. No stability or social order is restored in the mise-en-scène. Instead, the viewers are left with the image of the red streetcar, evoking the bloodbath motif of the scene.

In his interview to Iury Dud', Bykov notes that his approach to his art house films differs from the way he works for television. While in both cases his authorial style includes extreme violence, he avoids graphic scenes in his films. For example, he notes that in *Major* not a single drop of blood appears on screen; all violence is relegated to off-screen space. In contrast, *The Method* relies on spectacular violence, such as Esenia's stabbing a serial killer in both eyes with a sharp pencil, blood gushing from the ocular cavities. Not only does she incapacitate the killer, but she does it by neutralizing the male gaze. And the spectacle does not end there. When Meglin brings the killer to the hospital for the survivor to identify him, blood still flows from the killer's eyes. As he stumbles down the hall, he leaves bloody smears on the hospital walls. Violence becomes an attraction that adds commodity value to the series.

Each episode of *The Method* begins with Meglin's solemnly intoned epigraph implying that the series has vaguely literary-philosophical ambitions. Besides drawing on global neo-noir, *The Method* engages the local context, the Russian cultural tradition, as it gradually emerges that its literary subtext is Dostoevsky's *Crime and Punishment* (1866), whose gritty, gloomy Petersburg slums, the locus of violent crime, is the most famous nineteenth-century example of Russian novelistic noir. *Crime and Punishment* serves as a touchstone for several fraught issues in the TV series: reason versus intuition and feeling, criminal mental illness and, most importantly, the differing justifications for murder.

Before his crime, Raskol'nikov struggles with contemporary economic theories, such as David Ricardo's laissez-faire doctrine and Jeremy Bentham's Utilitarianism, which posit scientific laws explaining the functioning of society. The sight of a girl on the street who has been made drunk and raped elicits in Raskol'nikov reflections on the statistics for prostitution: "They say that's just how it ought to be. Every year, they say, a certain percentage has to go . . .

somewhere . . . to the devil, it must be, so as to freshen up the rest and not interfere with them."[15] On the way to commit the murder, he becomes absorbed in a reasoned plan for tall fountains that would freshen the air in public gardens.[16] In effect, Raskol'nikov lives in a world of theories while avoiding contact with the concrete, quotidian aspects of life. His ideological foil, Porfiry Petrovich, achieves his ends by intuition, observation, as well as reasoned inference.

Esenia's admirer, Sasha, attempts to solve the murder of their classmate Ania (episode one) by theorizing and diagramming aspects of the case on a bulletin board, all without going out on the street to search for clues. In contrast, Meglin works through observation, intuition, and, of course, his ability to experience the murderers' pathologies, but without disdaining deductive reasoning. In training Esenia he asks her: "What do you see? Not with your eyes, with your gut. Use your gut. What do you feel? Answer me a simple question: why did you kill her?" (13).[17] In the final episode of the series he introduces Esenia to Vitaly, an eidetic with a photographic memory,[18] who holds the detective's entire archive in his head. Meglin explains that he does not understand or trust computers, and instead prefers people.

In *Crime and Punishment* characters who murder, notably Raskol'nikov and Svidrigailov, experience serious mental disturbance. In his article "On Crime" Raskol'nikov writes "that the act of carrying out a crime is always accompanied by illness."[19] He himself is feverish, delirious, and mentally unstable before and after the murder. Dr. Zossimov suspects that Raskol'nikov may be mad and his mother is frightened by the look in his eyes: "There was something in them fixed, even as if mad."[20] Svidrigailov hallucinates, believing that he is visited by the ghosts of his dead wife and his serf Fil'ka, whom he apparently drove to suicide.[21] In Siberia Raskol'nikov's feverish delirium produces a dream about men driven mad by trichinae, although they believe

15 Fyodor Dostoevsky, *Crime and Punishment*, trans. Richard Pevear and Larissa Volokhonsky (New York: Vintage, 1993), 51, 555.

16 Ibid., 73.

17 Episodes are indicated by number in parenthesis.

18 Neither phenomenon has a scientific basis.

19 Dostoevsky, *Crime and Punishment*, 258

20 Ibid., 190, 197.

21 Ibid., 286–288.

themselves to be in possession of the truth, with unshakeable beliefs and moral convictions, not unlike the violent madmen of *The Method.*[22]

Both Meglin and most of the murderers appear to suffer from some form of psychosis. After questioning Meglin regarding his symptoms, Dr. Bergich diagnoses him as suffering from paraphrenia, now classified as a later stage of schizophrenia, and insists on a hospital stay (14).[23] Nevertheless, Meglin cuts short his treatment, instead choosing to continue his pursuit of the mass murderer, Anofriev, because "you alone are saving the world from the approaching darkness,"—Bergich's ironic comment on his psychosis. Both Meglin and Anofriev manifest symptoms of paraphrenia: hallucinations, insomnia, delusions of grandeur, and the belief in a special mission, but with minimal deterioration of intellect and personality.

Raskol'nikov argues two justifications for his crime, both of which function as a subtext for *The Method*. Initially he reasons that the murder of the pawnbroker, a useless parasite on society, will benefit others in need of assistance: "Kill her and take her money, so that afterwards with its help you can devote yourself to the service of all mankind. . . . One death for hundreds of lives—it's simple arithmetic!"[24]

In *The Method* Meglin is a skilled detective who also dispenses vigilante justice. Although charged with solving difficult murder cases, he usually kills the criminally insane in order to protect the innocent from further bloodshed. He breaks the law, but over the years law enforcement officers have unofficially approved of his actions. Grigor'ev, the senior police official who recruits Meglin approximately in 1988, during perestroika, explains: "It's a complicated time right now. All kinds of scum have crawled out of the corners, but we can't do anything—it's the law. Our hands are tied. Sometimes we have to choose between the law and justice. And this is where you come in" (11). He hands Meglin his first case, that of a pedophile, along with a knife. As Raskol'nikov argues, murder for the sake of justice and benefit to society is not a crime. Of course, law enforcement officials, most notably Esenia's father, Andrei Steklov, repeatedly break the law, often in their own self-interest.

22 Ibid., 547.

23 "Parafreniia (Parafrennyi sindrom)," Rosa Clinic, https://rosa.clinic/psikhiatriya/parafreniya-parafrennyy-sindrom/; "Priznaki parafrenii," Psihomed, https://psihomed.com/parafreniya/.

24 Dostoevsky, *Crime and Punishment,* 65. In this passage Raskol'nikov overhears a student voicing his own argument.

Raskol'nikov's second (genuine) motive for murdering the pawnbroker resonates even more deeply in *The Method* because it pertains to most major characters in the series. He argues for two types of humanity: a lower category that serves only to reproduce its own kind and a higher tier with the "talent of speaking a *new word* in their environment. . . . Those of the second category all transgress the law, are destroyers or inclined to destroy, depending on their abilities. . . . Most of these benefactors and founders of mankind were especially terrible blood-shedders."[25] Among the historical figures he names, Raskol'nikov singles out Napoleon Bonaparte who "makes a slaughterhouse of Paris, *forgets* an army in Egypt, *expends* half a million men in a Moscow campaign . . . and when he dies they set up monuments to him—and thus *everything* is permitted."[26] Raskol'nikov thinks of the courage to kill in cold blood as stepping over a boundary: "I was in a hurry to step over . . . but I didn't step over, I stayed on this side . . . All I managed to do was kill."[27] Unlike the great men of history, he is tormented after the murder by fear and the humiliation of confessing to what he did not consider to be a crime.

In *The Method* the opera singer Ptakha notes that "the law is for the poor" (12). Anofriev despises ordinary humanity whom he sees as already spiritually dead: "People are pathetic, contemptible pieces of meat. They sleep, reproduce, and watch TV" (15). In the luxurious apartment of Zhenia, a general's son and classmate of Esenia, the camera pans across busts of great men who dared to murder: Julius Caesar, Ivan the Terrible, and Stalin. Zhenia, who openly despises the masses who watch lowbrow TV shows like *Pole chudes* (*Field of Miracles*), is framed with a bust of Napoleon. In this first episode Esenia seems to be incongruously framed with Stalin, but we later learn that she also dares to kill without regret and even with pleasure, as she tells Meglin: "It's like sex, only cooler" ("Kak seks, tol'ko kruche," 9).

The Method is plotted around two groupings: the "you won't catch me" ("Ty menia ne poimaesh'") killer and his disciples, and Meglin's dark double, Anofriev. But for all these characters, the motives driving their actions form a continuum: daring to step over the limit, murder as identity formation, killers as prophets, obsession with power, and a recognition of Meglin as one of their own. The epigraph to episode fifteen concerns Anofriev, but applies

25 Ibid., 260.

26 Ibid., 274.

27 Ibid., 274.

equally to Meglin who speaks the words: "Do you think I'm a monster? I'm the same kind of person as you. I simply dared." Fedia, the neo-Nazi vigilante, asserts: "I did what others want to, but can't" (7). Nikita, the school shooter, explains that he has lived in fear all his life, but has overcome it after murdering—the only way "to find myself" (11). At this point Meglin remembers his own fear when forced by the murderer to finish off his mother, which he overcame years later by killing the perpetrator. Even Kolia, the likeable arsonist, tells Meglin, "I am myself, don't change me. I'm like you" (14). The epigraph to episode seven echoes Raskol'nikov's musings about Napoleon: "The lawbreakers are first called criminals. Then—psychos. And finally prophets," and Anofriev believes he will only be understood by future generations. Both Anofriev and the "you won't catch me" mastermind (an orderly in Bergich's hospital who "enlightens" the inmates and arranges the murders they commit) relish their controlling power during the cat-and-mouse games they play with Meglin. Finally, Anofriev draws the connection between his own admitted pleasure in killing and the detective's summary executions of criminals: "Meglin enjoys his right to murder" (15).

The insistent "be yourself" rhetoric of the killers is the outcome of the traumas, fears, and humiliations experienced during the late Soviet era when the individual personality was suppressed and distorted by the collective but has returned as compensatory mental illness in the post-Soviet present. In a society of fluctuating and blurred values, Meglin, Esenia, the "you won't catch me" killer, his disciples, and Anofriev are all "ours" because they step across the boundary to kill successfully, with pleasure, and without pangs of conscience, like Raskol'nikov's great men. In this way, *The Method* recasts the moral and social issues raised by Dostoevsky for the twenty-first century.

While catering to viewers' appetite for violence, *The Method,* arguably, does important cultural work that Alexander Etkind describes as proper mourning and distancing from the ghosts of a traumatic past. Many tragic stories in the past and their criminal consequences in the present are confronted, talked about, mourned, and their ghosts buried. In the case of the Shooter, it happens literally: the serial killer trained in a Soviet-era special forces camp is put to rest forever. As viewers, we are forced to look the evil in the eye and move beyond the traumas of the past. Bykov's next project, *Sleepers,* approaches remembering in a very different way and does quite different cultural work. Instead of burying the ghosts of the past, the series reawakens narratives and characters that reignite phobias and paranoias of the Soviet era and hails the FSB as heroes of the new Cold War.

Imitation Noir: Colonel Rodionov's Method

Two years after *The Method*, Channel One and Fedor Bondarchuk's Art Pictures Group hired Bykov to produce a different kind of series. In the guise of a noir spy thriller the director awakened the long dead ghost of a Soviet genre—the cinematic KGB hagiography. This genre matured in the 1960s and 1970s and glorified the heroic work of KGB officers, above all the counter-intelligence units' ability to uncover foreign agents and their accomplices, often dissident intellectuals.[28] A common ideological trick in Soviet films about the KGB was justifying political terror by the necessity of exposing spies during times of national emergency, such as the Great Patriotic War. In the Putin era, the genre was revived. Most TV series, however, were set during World War II when SMERSH was catching endless Nazi spies. These action thrillers went for the most part unnoticed by critics. *Sleepers*, meanwhile, raised many eyebrows because it was set in present-day Moscow, where the FSB was conducting mass searches and arrests. Russian viewers, who remembered how in Soviet times the release of KGB-sponsored films coincided with secret police operations, were rather alarmed by a TV series set in the present, advocating torture as valuable in finding terrorists, and pointing to oppositional journalists and politicians as a fifth column.

Sleepers employ some conventions of the global neo-noir genre to disguise the familiar narrative celebrating Russia's security services. For example, Bykov uses low-key lighting and unusual camera angles to create a threatening and disorienting image of the new-old Cold War enemy. The filmmakers employ German expressionist scene composition and a palette drained of color to represent underhanded deals in CIA headquarters. Another setting where low-key lighting is consistently used is the Herzen coffee shop where Russian oppositional bloggers and politicians mingle with CIA recruiters. Finally, *Sleepers* juxtaposes cell phones emitting pernicious messages from American puppet masters to the landline, which the FSB high officials use to fight domestic and international terrorism. In fact, the instant messages awakening the dormant CIA assassins arrive via evil and global mobile lines.

28 Among the most notable examples are Veniamin Dorman's cycle of films about Mikhail Tul'ev (*The Secret Agent's Blunder* [*Oshibka rezidenta*, 1968], *The Secret Agent's Destiny* [*Sud'ba rezidenta*, 1970]), television series such as Sergei Kolosov's *Operation Trust* (*Operatsiia Trest*, 1967), Tat'iana Lioznova's *Seventeen Moments of Spring* (*Semnadtsat' mgnovenii vesny*, 1973), and innumerable others.

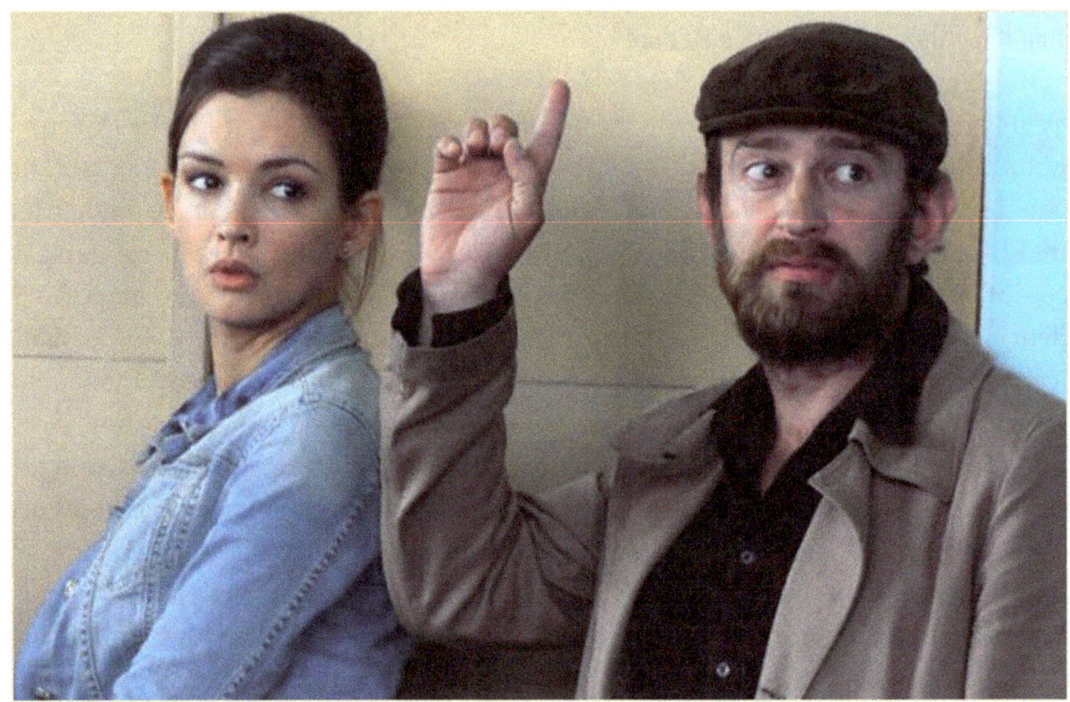

Fig. 3. Meglin . . .

According to the series, "Sleepers"' is a program devised by the CIA, originating in the 1990s when Russia naively opened up its borders to Western influences and put the ghost of the Cold War to rest. The eponymous sleepers are Russians who were recruited by American intelligence to be "awakened" when a need for US national security arises to undermine the now prosperous and stable Putin-era Russia. The series begins with a spectacular sequence of the massacre at the Russian embassy in Libya. Although initially it seems that the attackers are local warlords, it soon emerges that the CIA misled them in order to poison relations between Russians and friendly locals. Even more importantly, in the chaos the CIA steals the paperwork for a Sino-Russian contract to develop Libyan oil fields. From this massacre emerges our superhero—FSB colonel Andrei Rodionov (Igor' Petrenko),[29] the chief security officer at

29 As is clear from the previous discussion, Meglin's first name, Rodion, evokes the iconic Russian literary hero, while Rodionov is a last name that implies an entire nation of Rodions, and conflates the state and the nation. If you serve your state, it is an automatic license to kill.

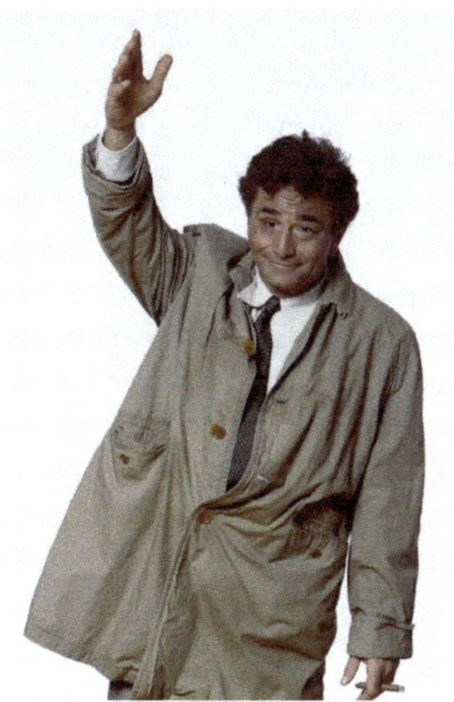

Fig. 4. . . . and his role model.

the embassy, who tries to protect a little girl from a grenade paid for with CIA dollars. He is tall, good-looking, and single, but most importantly, loyal to his FSB brotherhood. Rodionov even left the love of his life back in Moscow when he was deployed abroad fifteen years ago and she hesitated to join him. She did not wait for him and paid for it dearly with an unhappy marriage. In 2018 the actor Igor' Petrenko, who himself has been loyal to the corporation, received the FSB Prize "for the talented and objective representation of the institution of state security."[30]

In short, Colonel Rodionov is everything that Rodion Meglin is not. Meglin is a loner who defies institutional identity by his behavior and even his costume. In fact, he developed his own style, which points to a distinctly non-Soviet model— Lieutenant Columbo, a police investigator who serves on the LAPD force but always appears in shabby civilian clothes. Meglin's raincoat, with its sandy color and distinct unkemptness, is explicitly modeled on Columbo's sartorial choices, hinting at a tense relationship with all hierarchies and institutional structures (Figs. 3 and 4).

In contrast, the world of *Sleepers* is punctuated by the portraits of Feliks Dzerzhinsky and Iury Andropov tenderly looking at the modern-day heirs of the CheKa and KGB. Ensconced in the blue and steel gray colors of their situation room, they are a formidable force—a corporation rather than a synergy between distinct individuals.

The noir lack of clarity and the protagonist's inability to tell friend from foe is only skin deep in the *Sleepers.* When Rodionov returns to the global capitalist Moscow, with its dangerous coffee houses, pretentious art shows, and treacherous corporate culture, he initially does not quite know how to navigate this world. He fails to see what happens right under his nose,

30 The FSB Prize in Literature and Arts has a telling history: it was established in 1978 as the KGB Prize and was awarded annually until 1988. It was revived in 2006 under Putin as the FSB Prize.

which leaves him one step behind the spies. For those who are familiar with noir conventions, this makes for the most interesting part of *Sleepers*, with spectacular murders, dark streets, and the most unexpected villains. For example, the most effective assassin in the series is a woman. Unfortunately, this noir fog must dissipate to fulfill the series neo-socialist realist promise to separate "us" from "them" once and for all.

If in *The Method* the investigation is conducted via Meglin's borderline experience between reason and insanity, in *Sleepers* the investigation is driven by preset assumptions and ideological certainties. In *The Method* we have to listen and learn in order to understand the characters' identities. The characters evolve; even Meglin begins to hope that he may be cured. In *Sleepers*, Colonel Rodionov at the beginning is equal to Colonel Rodionov at the end, and both of them are merely a function of the corporation they serve. Instead of trying to learn who the characters are, viewers need only to learn the positions of play pieces on the neo-Cold War chessboard. If the character works at the US embassy in Moscow or is mentioned in the dialogue by an embassy employee, most likely he plays for the enemy team. If the positive characters are limited to Russian security services officers (notably all male), then people who talk about freedom of the press, use western laptops and iPhones, and hang out in coffee shops are default suspects. If someone doubts that the Starbucks-style coffee shop is a nest of American spies, the mise-en-scène has a useful prop on the wall next to the Russian traitor—the Star-Spangled Banner. In this binary world, journalists and bloggers are at best useful idiots. Ultimately, at the core of Rodionov's method is what Condee identifies as "the principle of exceptional compliance—obeying urgent orders, trusting the emergency crew, preserving the hierarchy"[31] in the fight against external and internal enemies.

If homelessness is both the human experience and the chronotope of *The Method*, *Sleepers* from the very outset channels the sense of home inherited from Soviet statist ideology. Rodionov returns to Russia where a border guard tells him "Welcome home!" and immediately arrives at the Lubianka FSB Headquarters, where he shaves and cleans himself up. The FSB corporation is obviously his true home, isomorphic to his motherland. He and his colleagues even have a term of endearment for this real home—*kontora* (the bureau). After putting on a fresh suit, he goes to report to the FSB chief. Home is thus defined as an ideologically marked public space.

31 Nancy Condee, "Cold Snap (Part II): Russian Film after Leviathan," Jordan Center for the Advanced Study of Russia, July 2015, http://jordanrussiacenter.org/news/cold-snap-part-ii-russian-film-leviathan/#.Xqh3hJp7mjQ.

Many reviewers noted that the homosocial paradise of FSB officers' brotherhood harks back to Soviet-era productions, such as *TASS is Authorized to Announce* (*TASS upolnomochen zaiavit'*, 1984), made under the direct supervision of Iury Andropov's *kontora*.[32] In these productions, the major eye candies are all male Soviet film stars: Viacheslav Tikhonov, Iury Solomin, and Ivar Kalnynsh, all playing KGB operatives.[33] None of them has a private home. Home is their KGB offices. *Sleepers*, however, is a post-Soviet television series, which has to appeal not only to secret police officers but also to the broader and more spoiled audience of post-Soviet Channel One. Hence Colonel Rodionov gets an apartment and a minimal, ideologically useful, private life. His apartment is quite austere: his kitchen cabinets lack doors or much in them, and he sleeps on the couch, reliving in his dreams battle episodes from his missions. Obviously, he will not sleep well until he uncovers the web of conspiracies and identifies the mastermind behind the crimes on the night streets of Moscow.

Coincidentally, the CIA spymaster, Ivan ("Ethan"), whose identity Rodionov learns near the end of the series, is also Rodionov's romantic rival. Ivan is a liberal journalist who lives in a palatial suburban house, in stark contrast to Rodionov's ascetic abode. Despite the sunlit designer space of Ivan's house, it hides not only dark political conspiracies but also a dysfunctional family life. Ivan is married to Rodionov's former girlfriend who never stopped loving her FSB colonel. Ivan's son is a teenager whose father is not available when he gets in trouble at school or with the police. So when the son needs help, it is Rodionov who assumes responsibility and serves as the paternal figure.

The makers of *Sleepers* also use melodramatic conventions to obfuscate the statist binarisms of the series. Melodrama is central to the noir world, which features individuals caught in the whirlwind of modernity, committing irreparable mistakes, assuming unfamiliar identities (weak males or strong females), and suffering the consequences of their actions. In short, neo-noir is about individual agency, however misguided it might be. The Soviet-style KGB

32 Oleg Kashin, "Kino pro 'Naval'nogo.' Serial *Spiashchie*—ekranizatsiia strakhov i illiuzii Kremlia," Republic, October 11, 2017, https://republic.ru/posts/86928.

33 Tikhonov stars as a super-agent and KGB general in *Seventeen Moments of Spring* and *TASS is Authorized to Announce* respectively. Solomin plays CheKa and KGB agents in *The Adjutant of His Excellency* (*Ad''iutant ego prevoskhoditel'stva*) and *TASS is Authorized to Announce* respectively. Notably, in 2020, he received the star of the Hero of Labor of the Russian Federation from Vladimir Putin himself. Ivar Kalnynsh plays chief security officer of the Soviet embassy in *TASS is Authorized to Announce.*

propaganda television series, *The Sleepers*, uses both the conventions of the noir film and those of family melodrama as a disguise. The story about the love triangle—Rodionov, Kira, and Ivan—is instrumentalized to foreground the importance of service to the state. While *Sleepers* includes a personal story to appeal to a more diverse audience, the triangle's primary function is to personalize the ideological conflict. In an almost Stalinist logic, the divide between "us" and "them" cuts right through the triangle. In the best traditions of World War II Soviet poetry, the "wait for me" trope becomes central for *Sleepers.* While Colonel Rodionov served his motherland on heroic missions abroad, Kira married his friend who betrayed the motherland and keeps on cheating on Kira. Ivan and Kira's son Artem is a troubled teenager because of the constant duplicity and hypocrisy he witnesses.

Melodrama, in fact, disguises the ideological reforging of the confused and guilty woman. Rodionov gradually opens her eyes to Ivan's true nature: from adultery to high treason. In episode five, right in the middle of season one, Kira and Ivan have a fateful conversation regarding how they feel about each other. They begin with clarifying their ideological standing, in particular their thoughts about Russia and patriotism. When Ivan proposes to Kira to move to the United States where he has a job offer—no less than *The New York Times*—and says that living in Russia is unbearable, Kira is ready to end the relationship. She steadfastly asserts that for her leaving Russia is unthinkable. Only then does the atmospheric music kick in, and the characters remember that their argument is personal and they are husband and wife. Kira tells Ivan that she does not love him and probably never did. This is the perfect merger of the ideological and the personal: the only reason *Sleepers* spends so much time on the love story is because the love triangle is not about who is a better man but who is a spy and who is a noble secret police officer. The CIA agent Ivan/Ethan is so evil and itching to hurt Colonel Rodionov (and, most importantly, the FSB) that he does not hesitate to sacrifice the woman that he supposedly loves by implicating her in a terrorist act. This statist agenda masquerading as melodrama is a well-tried ghost narrative, honed to perfection by Soviet filmmakers.[34]

34 The premier practitioners of the simulation melodrama promoting statist ideology in late Soviet cinema include Sergei Gerasimov, Iuly Raizman, and Stanislav Rostotsky. For a detailed discussion see Alexander Prokhorov and Elena Prokhorova, *Film and Television Genres of the Late Soviet Era* (New York: Bloomsbury, 2017), 188.

Being a maverick art cinema filmmaker, Bykov likes to make quasi-cameo appearances in his television series. In *The Method,* he plays the role of an investigator who debriefs Esenia in the framing narrative and who is genuinely curious about Meglin's method and the serial killer psychology. In *Sleepers* Bykov chose the arguably symbolic role of a person trapped in an impossible situation between two camps: he plays a suicide bomber with a death wish who tries to exit the narrative even at the expense of his own life. Not surprisingly, after the release of *Sleepers* Bykov publicly disavowed his creation and declared that he was leaving cinema as a profession: "I betrayed the entire progressive generation that tried to change something in this country."[35] Judging by Bykov's interviews, while he is passionate about the hardships of life in Russia's heartland, political activism leaves him indifferent. Perhaps this explains why, while making *Sleepers,* Bykov was under the impression that he was making nothing more than a big-budget commercial spy thriller.

Meanwhile, *Sleepers* caused a scandal because it hit too close to home in a society still weary of mass political terror as recent history. A number of characters in *Sleepers* are unambiguous cyphers for the iconic figures of Russian political life, some recently assassinated, such as Anna Politkovskaia (portrayed in caricature as Vera Tyrshitskaia). Critics claim that the prototype for the opposition politician Petr Asmolov is Aleksei Naval'ny, although one can also argue that, because Asmolov is assassinated in *Sleepers,* the prototype might have been the recently assassinated opposition politician Boris Nemtsov. *Sleepers* also takes a shot at the former US ambassador to Russia Michael McFaul who, according to Putin's propaganda machine, arrived in Moscow to conspire with the opposition and stir up a revolution against the current authorities.[36]

While *Sleepers* is an obvious propaganda vehicle, both TV series belong to the growing number of Russian-made big-budget quality television products for global distribution.

35 "Rezhisser Iurii Bykov: 'Ia predal vse progressivnoe pokolenie,'" BBCNews, October 13, 2017, https://www.bbc.com/russian/news-41611017. See also Tom Balmforth, "Russian Director Vows to Quit Cinema after 'Hysteria' over TV Spy Thriller," Radio Free Europe, Radio Liberty, October 17, 2017, https://www.rferl.org/a/russia-director-vows-to-quit-cinema-after-tv-spy- thriller/28800376.html. In 2016 Bykov tried his hand at another big-budget state-funded flick—a space exploration biopic about Soviet cosmonaut Aleksei Leonov, *The Age of Pioneers* (*Vremia pervykh*). After filming two thirds of the film he was fired from the project. It is unclear whether he could not stomach the narrative of Soviet nostalgia or the producers felt that he was not a good fit (Dud', interview with Bykov).

36 See "Spetsialist po demokratii," Lenta.ru, January 18, 2012, https://lenta.ru/articles/2012/01/18/mcfaul/.

Premieres on Channel One are no doubt prestigious, if scandalous, but secondary to a more lasting existence on streaming services domestically and internationally. Both projects were successful in this regard. *The Method* was purchased by Netflix, while *Sleepers* is sold on Amazon Prime Video.[37] The long-expected season two of *The Method* finally materialized in 2020, while *Sleepers* released a second season soon after the first one. But this is a different matter altogether. Bykov refused to participate in season two, which was directed by Sergei Arlanov and filmed within one month, as part of the media campaign supporting the 2018 presidential elections in Russia.

Bibliography

Abrams, Jerold J. "Space, Time, and Subjectivity in Neo-Noir Cinema." In *Philosophy of Neo-Noir*, edited by Mark Conard, 7–20. Lexington: University of Kentucky Press, 2007.

Arkhangel'sky, Andrei. "Rodnee nekuda: O chem govoriat i progovarivaiutsia rossiiskie serialy." Colta, April 15, 2015. https://www.colta.ru/articles/media/7020-rodnee-nekuda.

Balmforth, Tom. "Russian Director Vows to Quit Cinema after 'Hysteria' over TV Spy Thriller." Radio Free Europe, Radio Liberty, October 17, 2017. https://www.rferl.org/a/russia-director-vows-to-quit-cinema-after-tv-spy- thriller/28800376.html.

Condee, Nancy. "Cold Snap (Part II): Russian Film after Leviathan." Jordan Center for the Advanced Study of Russia, July 2015. http://jordanrussiacenter.org/news/cold-snap-part-ii-russian-film-leviathan/#.Xqh3hJp7mjQ.

———. *The Imperial Trace: Recent Russian Cinema.* New York: Oxford University Press, 2009.

Desser, David. "Global Noir: Genre Film in the Age of Transnationalism." In *Film Genre Reader*, edited by Barry Keith Grant, vol. 3, 517–536. Austin: University of Texas Press, 2003.

Dostoevsky, Fyodor. *Crime and Punishment*. Translated by Richard Pevear and Larissa Volokhonsky. New York: Vintage, 1993.

Dovlatov, Sergei. "Nashi." In his *Sobranie sochinenii*, vol. 2. St. Petersburg: Azbuka, 1999.

Dud', Iurii. "Yuri Bykov -- o 'Metode,' Khabenskom i BadComedian." YouTube video, June 20, 2017. https://www.youtube.com/watch?v=fWNgXYCnbG0.

[37] In 2018 Netflix released a ten-episode crime drama, *Seven Seconds*, based on Bykov's film,*The Major*. The series received several prestigious awards and nominations, including The Black Reel Awards and the Golden Globe.

Etkind, Alexander. *Warped Mourning: Stories of the Undead in the Land of the Unburied.* Stanford: Stanford University Press, 2013.

Foucault, Michel. *Discipline and Punish: The Birth of the Prison.* New York: Vintage, 1995.

———. *The Birth of the Clinic: An Archeology of Medical Perception*. New York: Vintage, 1993.

Ivanits, Linda. *Russian Folk Belief.* Armonk: M. E. Sharpe, Inc., 1992.

Kashin, Oleg. "Kino pro 'Naval'nogo.' Serial *Spiashchie*—ekranizatsiia strakhov i illiuzii Kremlia." Republic, October 11, 2017. https://republic.ru/posts/86928.

Kuvshinova, Mariia, Liubov' Arkus, and Konstantin Shavlovskii. *Balabanov.* St. Petersburg: Seans, 2013.

Lidov, Petr. "Tania." *Pravda,* January 27, 1942.

Lipovetsky, Mark. "Neither Here, nor There. The Trickster in the Cinema of Perestroika and the Early 1990s." In *Ruptures and Continuities in Soviet/Russian Cinema. Styles, Characters and Genres before and after the Collapse of the USSR*, edited by Birgit Beumers and Eugénie Zvonkine, 108–125. London and New York: Routledge, 2018.

———. "Iurii Bykov: *The Fool* (*Durak,* 2014)." *KinoKultura* 47 (2015). http://www.kinokultura.com/2015/47r-durak.shtml.

———. *The Charms of the Cynical Reason: The Trickster's Transformations in Soviet and Post-Soviet Culture.* Boston: Academic Studies Press, 2011.

Prokhorov, Alexander, and Elena Prokhorova. *Film and Television Genres of the Late Soviet Era.* New York: Bloomsbury, 2017.

Prokhorov, Alexander. "Diamond Arm." In *Russian Cinema Reader,* edited by Rimgaila Salys, vol. 2, 114–125. Boston: Academic Studies Press, 2013.

"Rezhisser Iurii Bykov: 'Ia predal vse progressivnoe pokolenie.'" BBCNews, October 13, 2017. https://www.bbc.com/russian/news-41611017.

Saltykov, Denis. "Privatized Violence in the New Russian Cinema." In *Cinemasaurus: Russian Film in Contemporary Context,* edited by Nancy Condee, Alexander Prokhorov, and Elena Prokhorova, 117–133. Boston: Academic Studies Press, 2020.

"Spetsialist po demokratii." Lenta.ru, January 18, 2012. https://lenta.ru/articles/2012/01/18/mcfaul/.

Queer Families: Gender, Sexuality, and the Neoliberal State on Russian Television

Vlad Strukov

Introduction: Theorizing Queer Presences

In the literature, phrases such as "Putin's Russia" and "Putin's hybrid regime" are often used to connote a particular political structure of the modern state and associated values, including traditional nuclear family, patriarchy, and heternormativity.[1] These constructs are often grouped together and labelled as "traditional values." However, despite being a frequently used term, its meaning remains obscure. In this chapter, by using the recent television series *Ol'ga* (2016–2018, TNT network, totalling fifty-six episodes) as a case study, I enquire about what actually constitutes "traditional values" in the Russian context and specifically investigate the role of independent cultural producers in advancing a broad set of views on gender and sexuality. To frame my questions, I use the theoretical notion "queer," meaning a purposeful opposition to hegemonic discourses about sexuality. Originally used derogatively to connote sexual behavior of "emasculated" men,[2] in recent research the term "queer" has been used to account for a broad range of cultural phenomena aimed at challenging repressive approaches to sexuality.[3] It has been noted that "queer theorists in humanities champion the fluid, flux, disruptive, transgressive, interpretivist, and local knowledges."[4]

1 See for example, Dale Roy Herspring, *Putin's Russia. Past Imperfect, Future Uncertain* (Washington D.C.: Carnegie Endowment, 2003).

2 Natalie Oswin, "Critical Geographies and Uses of Sexuality: Deconstructing Queer Space," *Progress in Human Geography* 32, no. 1 (2008): 89–103.

3 Amin Ghaziani and Matt Brim, eds., *Imagining Queer Methods* (New York: New York University Press, 2019).

4 Ibid., 4.

In this regard, "queerness" and "queer culture" are considered as strategies differing from those advocated by the LGBT movement.[5] For many, LGBT is a political phenomenon of the twentieth century, whereas queerness is an expression of a differing sexuality, connoting fluidity, experimentation, and non-normativity, whichever the norm. For example, some queer activists consider the LGBT agenda as normative and therefore in need of contestation through queer practice.[6] Moreover, queerness challenges identity politics, including those of gender and sexuality according to which people have predetermined social and sexual roles.[7] Some even "opine that a 'cultural politics,' as a form of common sense revolves around the naturalness of the market, primacy of the competitive individual, and the superiority of the private over the public."[8] Thus, queer practices challenge identity politics by decoupling sexual preferences from sexual "identities," meaning that to be queer is always to negate a (perception of) "identity," especially in the context of neoliberal ideology.

In Russia, the situation is complex due to the variety of cultural traditions governing gender and sexuality across the constitutive units of the Federation, and also the government's introducing anti-LGBT legislation while allowing—and even encouraging—queer practices. Indeed, Russian Section 28[9] speaks of "non-traditional sexuality" and makes no explicit references to LGBT communities per se, permitting ambiguity and indeterminacy in terms of

5 See, for example, Emma Russel, *Queer Histories and the Politics of Policing* (London: Routledge, 2019).

6 Manon Tremblay, *Queering Representation: LGBTQ People and Electoral Politics in Canada* (Vancouver: University of British Columbia Press, 2019).

7 Malay Mandal, "Neo-Liberalism, Cinema and Trajectories of South Asian Queer Visibility," Paper presented at YSI Asia Convening, Hanoi, August 12–14, 2019.

8 Ibid., 1.

9 Indeed, in 2013 the Russian Duma passed a law that prohibits promotion of "non-traditional sexuality" to minors in state-funded and public institutions such as schools. (The title of the law reads as follows: "For the Purpose of Protecting Children from Information Advocating for a Denial of Traditional Family Values.") The law was modelled on Margaret Thatcher's 1986 law, in use in the United Kingdom until 2003, and commonly known as Section 28. It was repealed by the Labour government and its withdrawal paved the way for British sexual equality legislation such as civil partnership law in 2004. The negative effects of Russian Section 28 on LGBT communities have been examined by sociologists. (See, for example, Alexander Kondakov's "The Influence of the 'Gay Propaganda' Law on Violence against LGBTIQ People in Russia.") Western journalists and activists have expressed their grave concerns about the law, making a connection to the Russian government's illiberal policies more generally. However, the examination of the impact of the legislation on other discourses remains limited, making it possible to enquire about other forms of differing in the Russian context.

sexuality, discourse and acceptable forms of behavior. On the one hand, the law effectively imposes a regime of homophobia, transphobia, and other-phobia through the construction of an entity—not an identity—which is "not to be spoken about." On the other hand, the law acknowledges an existence of agency and symbolic capital, which is differing, and must be taken into account. To paraphrase Heidegger, the law points at "an inarticulable presence" or at something, which is different, but indivisible.[10] Hence I argue that the law invites interactions, interpretations, and interventions from politicians, activists, and cultural producers in order to ascertain realms of invisibility and ambiguity. As a result, while imposing restrictive sexual regimes, the Russian government has paved the way for queer practices to emerge whereby queerness takes the form of "inarticulable presence." These presences emerge in a variety of contexts and realms of cultural production such as popular music.[11] In this chapter I investigate how Russian media, particularly popular comedy television, have responded to the introduction of Russian Section 28 and construction of the "inarticulable presence."

My specific purpose is to examine representations of family in the context of the neoliberal state and global media exchange. What undergirds my discussion is an understanding that neoliberal reforms such as privatization of resources, de-nationalization of social institutions, and intolerance to underperforming economic units were introduced in the Russian Federation from the West at a time when repressive sexual regimes were in place in the West.[12] The emergence of contemporary Russian media coincided with the circulation of these values on international media networks such as the BBC and CNN, thus entering Russian mainstream discourse. As a result, thanks to shows such as *Friends*, illiberal approaches to non-heteronormative sexuality were adopted alongside neoliberal conceptions of economy, politics and society, including those of family. Using *Ol'ga* as my case study, I reveal below how Russian television engages with these conceptions critically, including through constructions of queer forms of family such as a "friemily" (friend + family = friemily, or a social group consisting of close friends with a family level of intimacy but not structured as a traditional bourgeois family). To reiterate, I do so through the lens of queer sexuality, not (non-)traditional sexuality. The latter imposes

10 Jacques Derrida, *Of Grammatology* (Baltimore: John Hopkins Unversity Press, 2016), 36.

11 Maria Engstrom, "From Sexual Revolution to 'Sexual Sovereignty': Queer-Art Exhibitions in Post-Soviet Russia," Paper presented at ASEEES Convention, Chicago, November 9–12, 2017.

12 See, for example, Thatcher's Section 28 and the US "Don't ask, don't tell" rule.

a binary, normative structure on the phenomenon, its representations, and analysis. By contrast, as I pointed out above, queerness allows a consideration of "something being different and indivisible" in all its complexity and variety.

I do not seek cases that portray a "(non-)traditional" family such as one consisting of two male parents and a child. These representations affirm binary, heteronormative forms of family, while permitting divergences such as sexual orientation of the participating partners. Instead, I seek cases that interrogate the very notion of family in the framework of queer practices, challenging all kinds of normativity. I employ both diachronic and synchronic segments of engagement, namely, I analyze reinterpretations of the Soviet legacy and reassessments of contemporary hegemonic narratives. The Soviet experience undergirds contemporary constructions of identity, whether through affirmation or rejection of Soviet models. The hegemonic narrative encompasses Hollywood productions insofar they dominate the Russian media market, including the formation of popular ideologies. I do not mean to suggest that Hollywood is responsible for the formation of the conservative agenda, but rather that, as an ideology, it functions as a denominator and regulator of trends, including values concerning family and identity politics.[13]

The television series *Ol'ga* tells the story of Ol'ga (Iana Troianova), an unmarried woman in her mid-thirties who lives in Moscow with her alcoholic father Iury (Vasily Kortukov) and two children, Ania (Kseniia Surkova) and Timofei (Mukhamed Abu-Rizik). The children have two different fathers, a Russian crook who now lives in Thailand, and an Azerbaijani businessman who has returned to his other family in Baku. Ol'ga has a younger sister Elena (Alina Alekseeva) who, to afford a car and her own apartment, lives off wealthy men. The rest of the family—eventually, all four generations—occupy a poorly decorated Soviet-era apartment in Chertanovo,[14] a traditionally working-class area of Moscow. Ol'ga, who is very independent and strong-willed, works in a beauty salon and spends all her time fulfilling her professional and familial obligations. She soon meets Grisha (Maksim Kostromykin), a young man who begins chasing her. The gender aspect is central to the series insofar as Grisha is younger than

13 On Hollywood homophobia, see, for example, David Greven, *Manhood in Hollywood from Bush to Bush* (Austin: University of Texas Press, 2010).

14 Chertanovo is the setting of Fedor Bondarchuk's sci-fi blockbuster *Attraction* (*Pritiazhenie*, 2017), thus establishing the neighborhood as a trend mark for Russian suburbs.

Ol'ga. In a country where the ratio of men and women is skewed and where men, including the political establishment, often have liaisons with women three times younger, *Ol'ga*'s narrative predisposition reads as a critique of patriarchal norms.

Television drama and especially the genres of laughter have a checkered history in the Russian context.[15] Until recently in many countries, comedy had a low cultural status that has hindered its academic study.[16] Humor had an ambivalent position in communist states and its production was strictly controlled.[17] Although some comedy shows were permitted, comedy never developed into a mainstay of Soviet television. However, entertainment programs such as KVN[18] and films made for TV by El'dar Riazanov offered a satirical investigation of late socialist society. They also supplied representations of non-normative sexualities and queer sexualities through, for example, the use of drag and critical explorations of masculinity.[19] Nowadays they are fondly remembered by older generations and have recently been remade for the new era.[20] In these cinematic offerings, both the Soviet past and the neoliberal Russian present are a source of jokes, advancing a reconciliatory agenda: rather than rejecting the past, the viewer is encouraged to understand and embrace it. This is a departure from the 1990s agenda when Soviet notions and institutions were categorically dismissed. Equally, KVN was

15 The nuances of the relationship between the genre of sitcom and comedy are outside the scope of this essay.

16 To date, the most innovative theory of humor as a form of resistance was developed by Mikhail Bakhtin during the totalitarian years of the USSR. First published in 1965 during the Thaw; his writing became available world-wide in the 1990s. See Glen Creeber, *The Television Genre Book* (London: Bloomsbury, 2015), 89.

17 See, for example, Seth Graham, *Resonant Dissonance: The Russian Joke in Cultural Context* (Evanston: Northwestern University Press, 2009) and John Etty, *Graphic Satire in the Soviet Union: Krokodil's Political Cartoons* (Jackson: University Press of Mississippi, 2019).

18 KVN is a Soviet era talent show focusing on humor and satirical sketches. It was revived in the Russian Federation and remains one of the most popular original programs on Russian television. For a discussion of the programme, see Alexander Prokhorov and Elena Prokhorova, *Film and Television Genres of the Late Soviet Era* (New York: Bloomsbury, 2017).

19 Ibid.

20 For example, in 2007 Timur Bekmambetov released an interpretation of *The Irony of Fate* (*Ironia sud'by, ili S legkim parom,* 1975) and in 2010 Sergei Ivanov directed a new version of Leonid Gaidai's *The Diamond Arm* (*Brilliantovaia ruka,* 1969).

brought into the orbit of pro-government lobbies and think tanks that use the show to test public attitudes to societal concerns.[21]

In the 1990s, with the liberalization of media markets, networks—especially cable television—started showing Western sitcoms, often with poor translation into Russian. Linguistic errors were an additional source of humor to viewers in the 1990s. The extremely popular *My Fair Nanny* (*Moia prekrasnaia niania*, aired on STS in 2004–2009) was an adaptation of the American *The Nanny*, which originally ran in the 1990s.[22] The first original Russian sitcom, *Daddy's Daughters* (*Papiny dochki*), aired in 2007,[23] after a few years of experimentation with international formats. While Russian shows were being developed, screenings of current Western shows—with dubbed translations—became common on television and on the internet, including torrents and other illegal channels of content distribution. *Ol'ga* represents a new era in the development of Russian sitcoms due to its emphasis on domestic production and articulation of local, grassroots-level concerns, including queerness.

In the discussion below I use the term "queer" to account for various transpositions of family, applying it in relation to space, networks, and exchange. I analyze how *Ol'ga* registers transformations in those units of meaning vis-à-vis the hegemonic discourse. I argue that these transformations signal ambiguity and indeterminacy and therefore cannot be categorized in binary terms such as progressive and conservative, pro- or anti-Kremlin, pro- or anti-LGBT. In other words, they are queer insofar as they elide those categorizations and appoint complex subjectivities through purposeful contestation. In this context, comedy functions not as a release safety valve,[24] or a mode of resistance,[25] but a space in which these subjectivities

21 Christine Evans, "The 'Soviet Way of Life' as a Way of Feeling," *Cahiers du Monde Russe* 56, nos. 2–3 (2015): 543–569.

22 2004–2009, STS, 173 episodes, produced by Aleksandr Akopov, Aleksandr Rodniansky, and Konstantin Naumochkin. For a discussion of this series, see Stephen Hutchings and Natalia Rulyova, *Television and Culture in Putin's Russia: Remote Control* (London: Routledge, 2009), 29.

23 Broadcast by STS, the series ran from 2007–2013, with 410 episodes, produced by Viacheslav Murugov, Aleksandr Rodniansky, and Konstantin Kikichev. There was apparently an unsuccessful attempt to produce an original sitcom in the mid-1990s.

24 Graeme Dunphy and Rainer Emig, *Hybrid Humour: Comedy in Transcultural Perspectives* (Amsterdam: Rodopi, 2010).

25 Mikhail Bakhtin, *Rabelais and His World* (Bloomington: Indiana University Press, 1984).

emerge and evolve. In *Ol'ga* queerness transpires in language, forms of solidarity, and representations of social determinators such as class. The analysis of *Ol'ga* reveals a complex system of values, which so far has not been registered and analyzed in research on contemporary Russian media, sexuality, and cultural practice.

Friemily: *Ol'ga* and New Forms of Solidarity

Ol'ga is a modern version of the Bildungsroman, which originally denoted a novel dealing with one person's—predominantly a man's—formative years or spiritual education.[26] Indeed, in the first decade of the twenty-first century Russian filmmakers exploited the theme of a person's maturation by staging dramas of cinepaternity.[27] *Ol'ga* abandons the masculine (father-son) narrative in favor of the feminine (mother-daughter) dynamic, thus queering the precepts of Bildungsroman and its cinematic iterations of the 2000s. *Ol'ga* traces the evolution of the main character, including her emotional maturation and her relationship with other characters. The series presents three female duos: (a) Ol'ga and Ania (mother-daughter), (2) Ol'ga and Elena (two sisters, Fig. 1), and (3) Ania and Elena (a niece and an aunt), cumulatively challenging the roles ascribed in patriarchal societies to female relatives.

These duos form units of meaning that are queer insofar as, while they consist of two elements, they are not binary, such as "a man versus a woman" or "a parent versus a child." In fact, in *Ol'ga* even the maternal and parental roles are fluid insofar as, depending on the context, they are assumed by one character in relation to the other two in spite of their gender. As a result, these roles are not hegemonic, but rather shared, horizontal, and therefore queer. For example, Ol'ga's father has fulfilled a maternal role: in episode three it is revealed that Ol'ga's mother had abandoned the daughters when they were still little girls and Iury became responsible for the raising of the children, a somewhat exceptional situation for a family in the 1980s, the peak of Thatcher and Reagan politics in the West when neoliberalism with its conservative stance on sexuality and family was employed as an ideology. Those events are

26 See for example, Franco Moretti, *The Way of the World: The Bildungsroman in European Culture* (London: Verso, 2000).

27 Helena Goscilo and Yana Hashamova, eds., *Cinepaternity: Fathers and Sons in Soviet and Post-Soviet Film* (Bloomington: Indiana University Press, 2010).

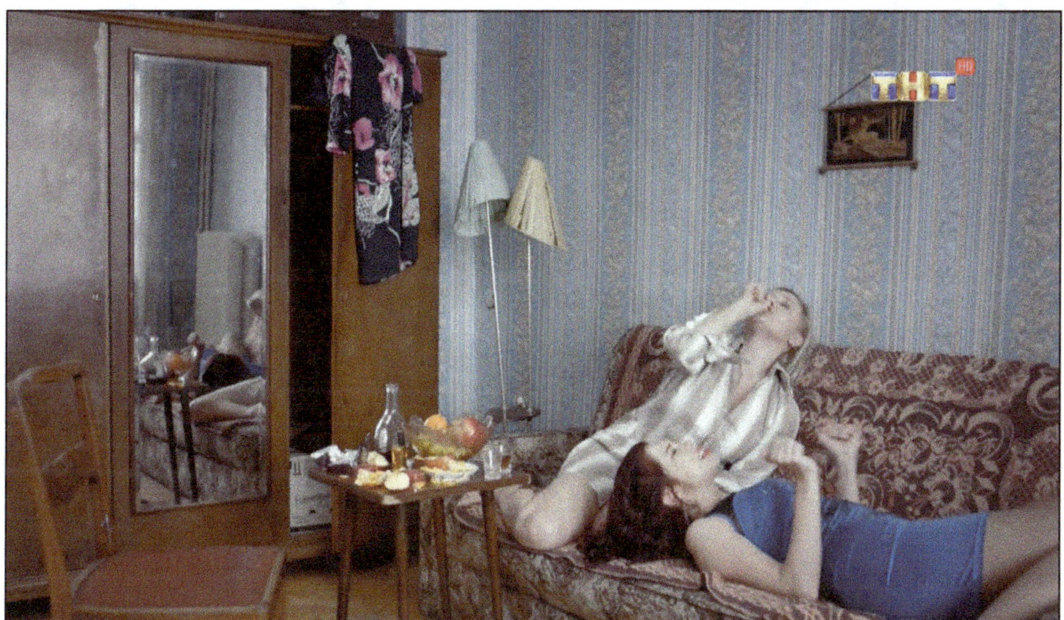

Fig. 1. Ol'ga and Elena relaxing in Ol'ga's apartment filled with Soviet-era furniture and elements of décor. Those are contrasted with the sisters' contemporary clothes, placing emphasis on the body as a cultural arena that has been "modernized."

not portrayed in the series but are evoked a few times inviting a queer reading of the Soviet past, namely, that a non-nuclear patriarchal family is not an invention of recent times but is a time-honored socio-cultural phenomenon. In this paradigm, Ol'ga's family is non-binary, yet it is not a (non-)traditional family either (Fig. 2)

The notion of a queer family extends beyond the unit of Ol'ga's children and sister. Living together and supporting each other (as illustrated by the character of Chicha, a man with a speech defect played by a little person, Timofei Zaitsev), the characters form a community that has the features of a family and a friends' union at the same time—a friemily.[28] It encompasses members on the basis of solidarity, not nuclear familial relations; it is fluid but stable, unlike a traditional family, which is fixed discursively, but unstable pragmatically. *Ol'ga*'s friemily is reminiscent of the late socialist friemilies or systems of mutual support, otherwise known as

28 A comparison with the US series *Friends*, which remains one of the most popular television productions in Russia, is outside the scope of this chapter.

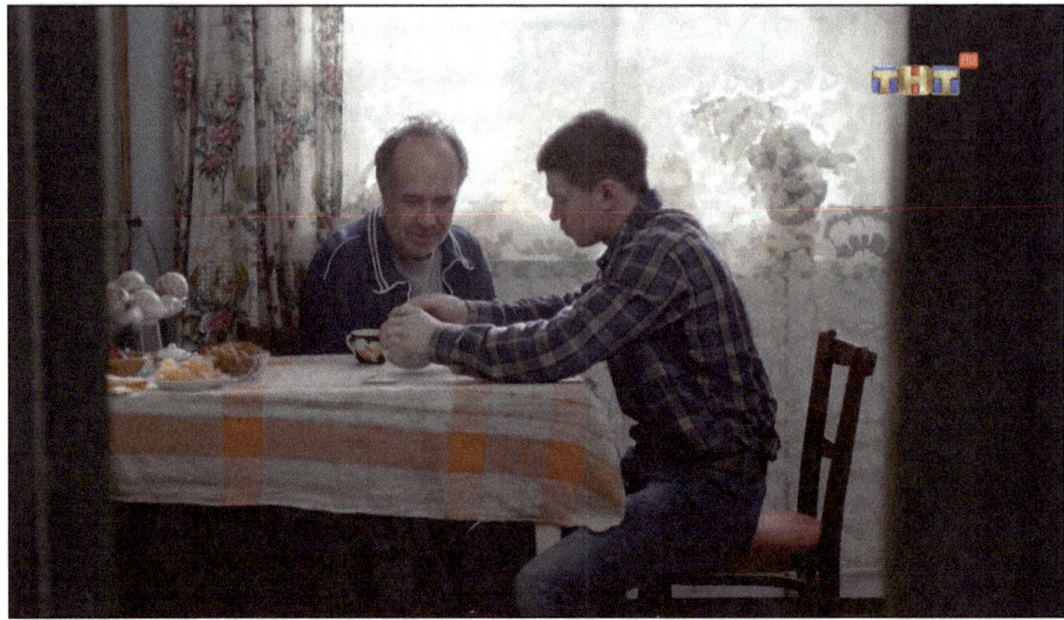

Fig. 2. Grisha confiding in Iury, his "father-in-law." The kitchen as the setting for a secret chat is typical to Russia. The mise-en-scène (especially the fruit, the tablecloth, the flowered and lace curtains) effeminizes Iury, questioning the distribution of roles in a traditional heteronormative family.

"informal networks," facilitating economic survival and personal fulfilment.[29] Alexei Yurchak has shown that in the USSR informal networks were a means to construct a parallel society, simultaneously feeding on and opposing the communist regime.[30] In *Ol'ga*, these networks exist within and contest the neoliberal regime of Putin's Russia. However, unlike during the Soviet era, they are visible, empowered, and in charge of their own choices. More importantly for my discussion, they are predicated on explicit expressions of sexuality, unlike the suppressed "politeness" of the non-conformists' circles of the Soviet era.[31]

Ol'ga's family is typical of contemporary Russia, but is anything but traditional. Indeed, children are brought up by single parents, women have multiple sexual partners and get

29 See Alena V. Ledeneva, *Russia's Economy of Favours: Blat, Networking and Informal Exchange* (Cambridge: Cambridge University Press, 1998).

30 Alexey Yurchak, *Everything Was Forever, Until It Was No More* (Princeton: Princeton University Press, 2006).

31 Ibid., 44.

pregnant outside marriage, and the family patriarch is shown to be a completely dysfunctional figure (Iury's alcoholism) and has to be replaced with a matriarch (Ol'ga), struggling to maintain her authority in the face of multiple challenges. Family life is not organized around a particular space (it is never clear who is living in Ol'ga's apartment and who is visiting or in the process of moving in and out) or a ritual or ceremony (they never have meals together or celebrate family occasions). Family hierarchy is constantly under attack with children challenging Ol'ga socially, economically, and also linguistically. Instead, the characters form circumstantial solidarities, which are more like connections among friends than familial bonds. Thus, *Ol'ga* presents Russians in a new social setting, which queries the discourse about the traditional nuclear family advocated by Russian authorities and propagated at film festivals such as *Russia's Family* (*Sem'ia Rossii*), supported by the Russian Orthodox Church, and in productions such as Andrei Popov's feature *Dreams of Happiness* (*Beskonechnye mechty o schast'e*, 2012). Indeed, in comparison with families presented in these productions, Ol'ga's family is deliberately queer in its dysfunctionality.

In *Ol'ga* humor is employed not to judge a dysfunctional family, but to construct solidarities among the characters and viewers. These solidarities are circumstantial and fluid and not predicated on traditional forms of belonging such as age, gender, or ethnicity. For example, in episode two, Elena decides against having breast enhancement surgery. She is inspired by her nephew Timofei and his school friend whom she previously helped overcome adolescent anxiety over the size of their penises. From the perspective of neoliberal ideology, her decision is conservative as she rejects the "freedom" to modify her body in order to express her individuality.[32] However, in actual terms, her decision is progressive as she chooses to celebrate her actual body and selfhood, having recognized social pressures regulating contemporary perceptions of beauty. For my argument, though, it is important that her decision was prompted by an earlier conversation with other individuals who are different from her in age, gender, and even ethnicity. (Both boys have mixed ethnic backgrounds.)

To summate, an analysis of the television series shows that in contemporary Russia solidarities are built within and beyond social categories such as age, gender and ethnicity, so

32 An early critique of this type of neoliberal ideology was provided by the French artist Orlan through her work on plastic surgery and body modifications. See, for example, Simon Donger and Simon Shepherd, eds., *Orlan: A Hybrid Body of Artworks* (London: Routledge, 2010).

long as they are perceived to be part of the private realm of an individual, namely, their family and friends. In the following section I consider the categories of space, class, and sexuality in order to apprehend how solidarities perform vis-à-vis competitive frameworks. I am also concerned with how *Ol'ga* responds to normative and transgressive notions of class available both from Russian and international television contexts.

Suburbia: *Ol'ga* and the Neoliberal State

Ol'ga is one of those series in which the action takes places in multiple locations, with the main character's apartment being one of the principal settings. *Ol'ga*'s dynamism is rooted in the rapid change among locations; in spite of these alterations, the series is focused on a domestic space in Russian suburbia. As a socio-cultural phenomenon, suburbia is a relatively new development in the Russian Federation. The majority of Soviet cities were (re)designed in the post-World War II period. Areas that had been bombed by the Germans were filled in with new housing, and new factories and research facilities were built for the workers. These new areas were incorporated into cities, creating a confusing pattern of urban life whereby social housing was mixed in with industrial facilities. Overall, in terms of layout and social life, Soviet cities were oriented towards the great cities of continental Europe such as Berlin, Paris, and Vienna. In the USSR, the difference was maintained between cities and the countryside, with the former being a desirable place to live for many. The suburban sprawl of London or Los Angeles was considered to be a Western phenomenon due to its predication on consumerism as the key factor in terms of organization of urban life.

Only in the brief period of the late 1970s–early 1980s do we see a reimagining of industrial outskirts as spaces of consumption. For example, the second part of Vladimir Men'shov's 1980 Oscar-winning *Moscow does not Believe in Tears* (*Moskva slezam ne verit*), begins when the main character named Katerina (Vera Alentova) wakes up in an apartment filled with consumer goods and appliances. Katerina, who is now a manager at a textile factory, drives a car to work, a symbol of her social status and financial independence. This initial period of socio-cultural reassignment of suburbs was put on hold in the 1990s when the Russian economy dipped following the dissolution of the USSR and introduction of neoliberal economic reforms. Indeed, *Moscow does not Believe in Tears* portrayed suburbs as spaces of modernity and affluence, underpinned by the Soviet industrial base. A decade later, after the collapse of Soviet industry, these same areas became the most deprived.

In the 1990s, while in actuality Russian citizens were getting used to the harsh realities of the rapid economic decline, in terms of entertainment, they were preoccupied with the seductive life of American suburbia: *Santa Barbara* premiered in Russia in January 1992, and ran until April 2002 (2,040 episodes), proving to be one of the most popular shows on Russian television.[33] Lacking an understanding of US race and class politics, Russian viewers revelled in *Santa Barbara*, a series about two rival families from a wealthy California suburb. The show provided Russians with neoliberal models of family life, individual expression and, most importantly, conspicuous consumption. The ideals of the suburban lifestyles portrayed in *Santa Barbara* were eventually realized in the homes of the superrich in the Moscow suburb of Rublevka, a topic of many popular films and items of television drama and fiction such as Oksana Robski's novels. Indeed, the first ten years of Putin's leadership have been labelled "the glamour decade"[34] due to the focus on consuming and emulating Western styles, especially in the realm of fashion, cars, and domestic interior design. However, "the cult of conspicuous consumption and the celebration of the economic success on television and in popular media have hardly masked the hardships of Russia's non-privileged citizens."[35]

A number of elements in *Ol'ga*'s storyline permit parallels with *Moscow does not Believe in Tears*.[36] The comparison reveals a lot about the country's transition from the late-Soviet industrial economy to the contemporary Russian post-industrial economic order. For example, unlike Katerina from the Soviet film, all characters of *Ol'ga* work in the service sector, not at factories or other industrial outlets, which is characteristic of the neoliberal regime. Ol'ga works in a beauty salon; Iury is a football coach; and Grisha drives a funeral van. Ol'ga's children,

33 For a recollection of the series and life in Russia in the 1990s, see Mikhail Iossel, "The 1980s American Soap Opera that Explains how Russia Feels about Everything: A Look at the Peculiar Obsession with 'Santa Barbara' in the Post-Soviet Experience," *Foreign Policy* (July/August 2017), https://foreignpolicy.com/2017/07/24/american-soap-opera-explains-how-russia-feels-about-everything-santa-barbara-trump-putin/.

34 Helena Goscilo and Vlad Strukov, eds., *Celebrity and Glamour in Contemporary Russia: Shocking Chic* (London: Routledge, 2010).

35 Ibid., 1.

36 For example, the similarities in the name of the man the central character falls in love with, her strained relationship with the daughter, and so on.

including her future son-in-law Andrei (Sergei Romanovich), turn to social media to make a living. For example, Ania gets involved in internet prostitution: she makes money by stripping in front of a webcam. Andrei is constantly scheming with his friends to make money: at one point he is trying to open a shop, later in the series he gets involved in transportation of illegal produce. Much of this activity is semi-legal and/or off the books: the suburb appears to be a hybrid, queer space where the new economics of the neoliberal era thrives.

Unlike in the television series of the 2000s such as *Gangster Petersburg*,[37] the suburbs are not criminalized. Rather than being portrayed as a space controlled by mafia with a few incursions from the state aimed at imposing order, in *Ol'ga* the suburbs are portrayed as a space where—in the absence of the state—real debates take place about education, health care, and the rule of law. They are coded as storylines involving the main characters. For example, Ania's attempts to make money online point to the problems with the education reform (does the school equip young women with skills to secure employment that is not based on sexual exploitation?) and the media and technology reform (what should the state do to protect minors from online abuse?). Ultimately, it is a debate about what, in the neoliberal system, constitutes work, how it should be regulated, and who—if anyone—is responsible for citizens during the transition to new economic regimes. Consequently, the suburbs are depicted neither as areas of prosperity or decline but rather as spaces of economic experimentation.

Yes, members of Ol'ga's family are a little crazy and are themselves responsible for their own miseries, but ultimately, according to the series, the new capitalist Russia provides them with few opportunities and maintains severe inequalities. The state is inefficient because it neither protects its citizens nor provides for them. Yet the series sets the characters free, meaning that, unlike in the USSR, they are free to express their individualities and care for themselves and their families. This is a powerful articulation of a specifically Western concept of freedom, one advanced in Anglophone popular culture.[38] Indeed, when Ania gets pregnant, no one suggests she should seek support from the state, like social housing. That would be expected in socialist countries such as Denmark and Finland.[39] Instead, Ania draws plans that

37 *Banditskii Petersburg* (2000–2007), NTV, created by Vladimir Bortko and others.

38 Jason Dittmer, *Popular Culture, Geopolitics and Identity* (Lanham: Rowman & Littlefield Publishers, 2010).

39 Johanna Lammi-Taskula et al., *Parental Leave, Childcare and Gender Equality in the Nordic Countries* (Copenhagen: Nordic Council of Ministers, 2011).

include only the members of her family, thus ascribing to the Western neoliberal framework of individual freedom, the representations of which are available in Hollywood blockbusters and mainstream television.

To confirm, this is a reversal of values that were propagated during the Soviet era and were still widespread in the 1990s and 2000s, thus signalling a victory of neoliberalism. To be fair, the series simultaneously celebrates and critiques neoliberalism. On the one hand, it shows how the characters are free to express their individualities, that is, "to be free". On the other, it shows how they are trapped within this neoliberal economy of "freedom": generation after generation, they replicate contexts and concerns without ever resolving them. This is symbolized by the space of the suburbs, which the characters never leave. In fact, in the opening episode, Ol'ga gets ready to go on holiday to Turkey. Many viewers would read this as a reference to her plans for sexual exploits in Turkey, not just an opportunity to relax. While at work, she starts daydreaming about the upcoming holiday, reliving the lifestyle offered by commercial advertising. Her dream—and her desire—are interrupted by an unhappy customer, which signifies the impossibility of escape from the neoliberal world.

The episode emphasizes the gap between neoliberal fantasy (a holiday in Turkey) and reality (the hardships of everyday life) by using two distinct visual languages—flamboyant visual glamour and textured realism. These two languages reflect different periods in recent Russian history, the 2000s (glamour and consumption) and the 2010s (economic crisis and austerity). One by one, the main characters crash out of deterritorialized neoliberal fantasy in order to embrace the reality of contemporary Russia. After a drinking bout, which is shown through an ironic reference to Hollywood rites of passage comedies, Iury is hospitalized. Having tried to assert his masculinity and cultural identity (a process stylized as rap music videos), Timofei gets into trouble after sexually harassing girls and his teacher in school. Thus, *Ol'ga* contextualizes the complexities of economic transition, memory, and experience. For example, Ol'ga's room is decorated with a giant photograph of a tropical resort. It hangs in place of a textile or synthetic rug that would have been popular under late socialism and mocked by the Russian intelligentsia as a sign of bad taste. Indeed, *Ol'ga* is a testimony to the transformation of the class system in Russia under a neoliberal regime whereby class differences are revealed through the regimes of gender and sexuality.

Sex Away from the City: *Ol'ga* and Class in Contemporary Russia

Ol'ga follows global trends in terms of format, focus, and characterization, including an interest in the issues of sex, sexuality, and class identity. In the series representations and discussions of (female) body, bodily functions, and body problems are unrestrained by Western social conventions. For example, already in the first episode, the series touches upon puberty, safe sex, sexual harassment, teenage sexuality, teenage pregnancy, abortion, sexually transmitted diseases, prostitution, aging, sex among seniors, addiction, and obesity. The discussions are framed verbally and visually; for example, in one scene Elena confides that she is in love with a man while urinating in the bathroom (Fig. 3). The door to the bathroom remains open, making female urination visible, and thus queering the heteronormative regimes of Hollywood where that function is commonly reserved to men.[40] While urinating, she tells her sister and unsuspecting children that she is suffering from a urinary tract infection, which was caused by unprotected sex with another man. As is evident from this account, *Ol'ga*'s storyline is direct and expeditious, keeping the viewer alert at all times.

By placing women at the center of the discussion and by openly engaging with issues of sex and sexuality, *Ol'ga* pays homage to *Sex and the City* (*SATC*, hereafter),[41] a comedy that was extremely popular in the Russian Federation in the 2000s, influencing a whole generation of young women. Just like the protagonists of *SATC*, the female characters in *Ol'ga* negotiate their relations to the city. The conflict in *Ol'ga* and *SATC* revolves around their sexual partners and their experiences of growing up in large metropolises. Each series accounts for different kinds of masculinity as imagined by the contemporary woman. In *Ol'ga* Andrei is an example of unrelenting masculinity: everything is hard and angular about him, he is virile but daft and inexperienced; Iury is inept as a lover, worker or citizen, but he is a brilliant father, having raised two independent women and taking part in the education of the new generation; Grisha is a provider and carer: to impress Ol'ga on their first date he gifts her vegetables (Fig. 4), but he is weak and awkward; and Sergei (Maksim Bramatkin), Elena's boyfriend, is strong and romantic, but is in jail and thus unattainable. If men in *SATC* are no longer sure about what

40 As a visual code of "raw" heteronormative masculinity, urination was used in the recent exhibition at Barbican, "Masculinities. Liberation through Photography" (2020).

41 1998–2004, 94 episodes, HBO, created by Darren Star.

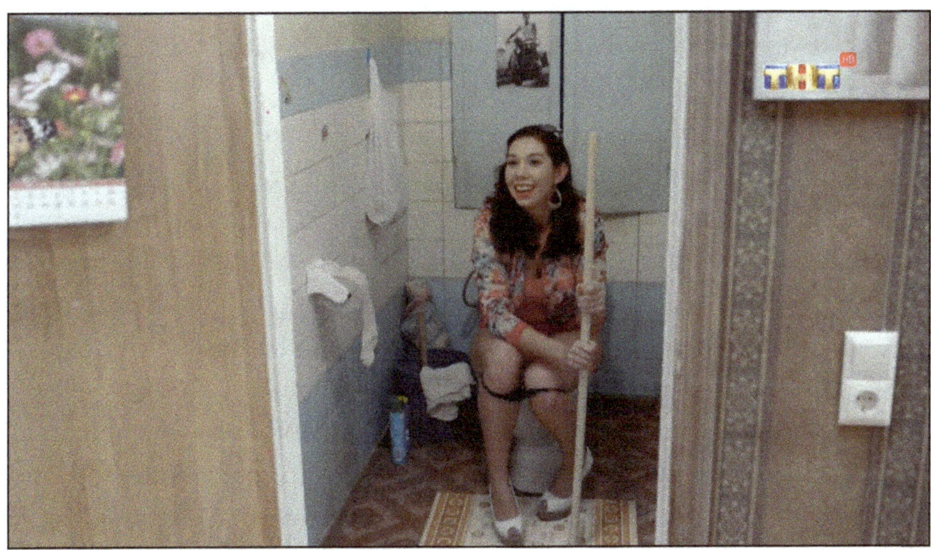

Fig. 3. Elena tells her sister about her sexual exploits. With Ol'ga being out of the frame, the camera turns the viewer into the observer (voyeur) and Elena herself into a fetish (urophilia). In the background, on the bathroom cabinet a male pinup is visible. Its placement inverts the gender dynamic of the family, with sexual desire (dominance) being associated with the "female patriarch."

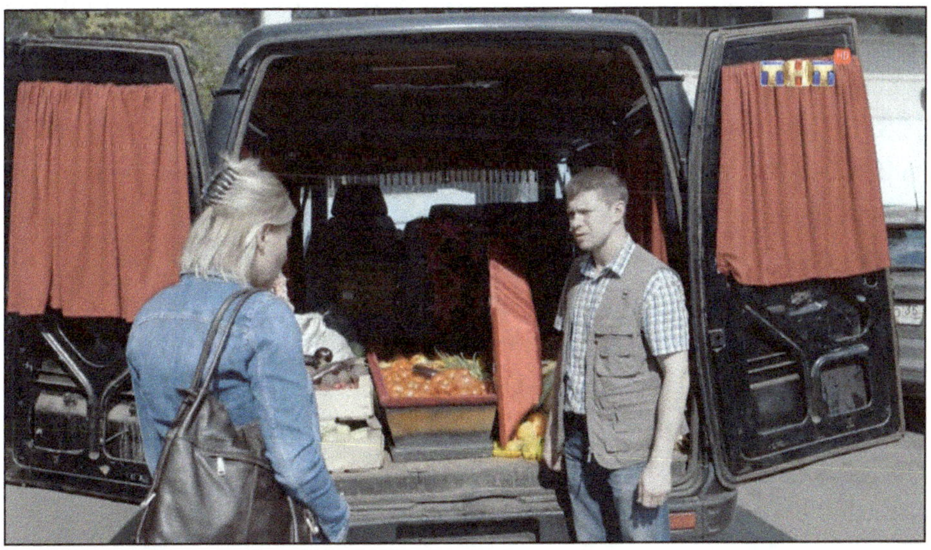

Fig. 4. Grisha brings Ol'ga a gift of home-grown vegetables placed inside a coffin in the funeral vehicle. This type of vehicle is widely used to carry both people and goods. It has become a symbol of post-Soviet entrepreneurship, or what in the West is called "small business" and is believed to be the backbone of the economy.

is expected of them in private and public spheres, men in *Ol'ga* continue to perform their stereotypical roles without realizing that they are irrelevant.

The comparison with the US series also reveals some major differences. The first is that *SATC* centers on women from one age group. (Samantha [Kim Cattrall] is a bit older than the other women but still belongs to the same generation.) In *Ol'ga* the age spectrum is much broader, with Ania and Grisha's grandmother[42] occupying the two ends of the spectrum. Indeed, the four women represent four decades of recent history—Soviet (grandmother), the 1990s (Ol'ga), 2000s (Elena), and 2010s (Ania)—each embodying a particular system of beliefs, styles, and fashions ("reserved," "make-do," "glamour," and "post-glamour," respectively). Thus, *Ol'ga* reads as an examination of femininity across generations, not within a singular social group. This is important for the Russian context insofar as social and inter-generational transformations have been extreme, with huge gaps opening between members of different generations, much greater than those in the West. *Ol'ga* emphasizes—and at times exaggerates—these differences, for example, when stylizing—and stereotyping—the grandmother (Chanel-inspired blazers) and Elena (Gucci-esque miniskirts and tight, revealing tops).

The second difference is that *SATC* tells the story of the women and of New York in equal measure. The viewer gets tips about fashion, trendy restaurants, changes in urban structure, new gallery openings, and so on. As I outlined above, *Ol'ga* depicts Moscow suburbs, not its fashionable center, never commenting on the shopping malls and cultural institutions inside the Garden Ring, Moscow's central thoroughfare separating the metropolitan core from its peripheries. If New York is the fifth character in *SATC*, in *Ol'ga* Moscow remains insignificant. In fact, the events could take place anywhere in the Russian Federation.[43] In that sense, *Ol'ga* does not supply aspirational lifestyles—this model of television had been exhausted in the 2000s just when the popularity of *SATC* started to fade away—but rather speaks to "middle Russia" where schools and hospitals, not new boutiques, matter to citizens. In equal measure, *SATC* presents women who appear to have specific goals—to be independent, successful, and attractive—which they have to negotiate and compromise on if they wish to maintain

42 A role played by Roza Khairulina whose outstanding talent had only recently been discovered.

43 From the psychoanalytical perspective, Moscow has always been imagined as a feminine entity and thus, in Russian culture, it is desired by men, not women. For further discussion, see Katerina Clark, *Moscow, the Fourth Rome. Stalinism, Cosmopolitanism and the Evolution of Soviet Culture, 1931–1941* (Cambridge: Harvard University Press, 2011).

a relationship with men (read: men redefine their goals). By contrast, *Ol'ga* presents women who are not so sure about their goals—it seems like their only objective is to make sure their family gets by—but who develop their goals as a result of their encounters with men (read: men inspire women to have goals). This leads me to the final difference: the representation of class.

In both series, class identity is revealed through sexual practice. This is important not only in the national but also comparative, international context. For example, *SATC* portrays professional women who have the means to explore their sexual fantasies and desires. They talk about getting married but delay doing so for professional and some would say hedonistic reasons. In *Ol'ga,* women lack professional training (see my analysis of the new suburban economics above) and they already have a family or are pregnant. In this regard, *Ol'ga* stereotypes the working-class woman just as *Ugly Betty*, *Little Britain*, and other productions did a decade ago. However, unlike these Western series, *Ol'ga* does not place blame on women, thus presenting an entirely different vision of the human condition. *SATC* rehearses a traditional notion of romantic love as quest so that the main character (Carrie Bradshaw) is fragile and always in need of rescue.[44] By contrast, in *Ol'ga* the woman is the rescuer: she is strong—even perhaps a little too strong—and her "quest" is about surviving in the harsh reality of neoliberal capitalism. If Carrie succeeds—she buys her own apartment and then buys it back from her ex—Ol'ga is on the verge of losing everything to a scammer who is, as the viewer learns, an even more ruthless woman.

Unlike *SATC,* in *Ol'ga* the camera is invasive, breaking the boundaries of private and public lives and documenting contemporaneity in what appears to be an unstaged, documentary manner. Its aesthetic consists of extreme close-ups, shots revealing the (naked) human body, and so on. The other source of energy is the characters' language and body language. In *SATC*, Carrie's anxieties were partly caused by her inability to find the most refined and accurate vocabulary to express her feelings. In *Ol'ga,* the language is spontaneous, raw, and casual, just like the sex that the women pursue. It is, indeed, queer insofar as it challenges the norm.[45] The

44 Michael Mario Albrecht, *Masculinity in Contemporary Quality Television* (London: Routledge, 2016), 12.

45 The implication of language trickery in the context of the law banning profanities in stage and screen are outside the scope of this chapter.

series celebrates the diversity of the Russian language, with all its accents, registers, and verbal trickery. Ol'ga speaks with a strong regional accent,[46] which may be understood by some as a sign of a lower-class upbringing. She often uses colorful expressions that have recently entered the mainstream.[47] She can be rude and aggressive; she spares no one when she needs to make a point; and yet she remains full of charm and is known for her kindness and fairness. As a new matriarch, she represents the moral law in a situation when the law of the state—the figure of the patriarch—is ineffective.

Conclusions

The contextual assessment of the series reveals that in a number of ways *Ol'ga* is path-breaking, if not revolutionary. First of all, it depicts a new kind of Russia, the Russia of suburbs—the areas in-between—where a new kind of economy is being forged. It is not the economy of technological modernity promoted by the Russian government, especially during Medvedev's presidency, but the economy of symbols[48] whereby subjects are responsible for the production of wealth in their communities. The series characters reclaim and reposition their environments, in this case suburbs, ascribing to them new value. They operate in largely unregulated realms, building new associations and developing their own networks. New forms of circumstantial solidarity—including the friemily—are employed in place of links associated with the traditional nuclear family. As a result, *Ol'ga* allows for greater gender fluidity insofar as characters take on roles and responsibilities not typically assigned in Russia to their gender. Also, *Ol'ga* documents new attitudes to sexuality, especially female sexuality, stopping short of engaging directly with the issues of homosexuality and transgenderism.

46 The accent is particular to working-class people from the Urals region. Troianova is also from that area, and so in her on screen performances she often uses the same accent.

47 "I thought my life was difficult, but it turns out other people's life is complete Hiroshit" ("Ia dumala u menia problemy, a tut u liudei voobshche Khirosima").

48 In the introduction to *Russian Culture in the Age of Globalization*, I defined the economy of symbols as "an attempt to evaluate the economic value of cultural artefacts, on the one hand, and to assign meaning to economic activities, on the other." See Vlad Strukov and Sarah Hudspith, eds., *Russian Culture in the Age of Globalization* (London: Routledge, 2018), 7.

Secondly, while celebrating new individualities and attitudes to the self, one's body and life, *Ol'ga* supplies a critique of the Russian version of neoliberal capitalism. Indeed, *Ol'ga* shows that there has been a change of attitudes to a number of societal concerns such as prostitution, which is now considered to be sex work. Yet, *Ol'ga* reflects on the exploitative aspects of these developments: not only does it acknowledge the existence of sex workers in the Russian Federation, the series emphasizes that they are not protected by the state or professional unions. Similarly, in spite of female characters having a more liberal view on sex and sexuality, they find themselves in situations in which patriarchy remains a hegemonic force. Overall, the makers of *Ol'ga* are interested in exploring what life should be like when the state withdraws in actual terms while promoting greater controls discursively. Stylistically, these contradictions, or rather nuances, of contemporary Russian life are conveyed through a creative use of the Russian language, references to global popular culture such as *Friends* and *Sex and the City*, and genre hybridization—dramedy.

Thirdly, *Ol'ga* presents a new kind of reality and new forms of revealing the truth. To paraphrase Alain Badiou,[49] the series maintains that "reality" is grounded in a void or a system of multiplicities, not in an ideology of "normality" prescribed by the state, embodied in the notion of family, or determined by other social institutions. *Ol'ga* is about events, but not about some sort of happenings, but rather about ruptures in the appearance of normality, thus compelling the viewer to inquire about the nature of that reality. In advancing a new kind of agency—independent, critical and engaged, not predetermined by class, gender, and ethnicity—*Ol'ga* stages a new kind of politics in the Russian Federation. *Ol'ga*'s project is not about building a political movement or advocating a regime change, but about querying and queering the regime and striving for a new truth. This new regime of truth points to a redistribution of political, economic, and cultural capital whereby new agency necessitates new forms of culture, drama, and television. While it is a form of localized content, *Ol'ga* addresses global concerns such as new labor markets, modes of being, and new solidarities. Furthermore, due to its focus on women, it celebrates a new kind of "gendered television."

"Gendered television" speaks to the concerns and from the perspective of women. The series was filmed by two male directors, Aleksei Nuzhnyi and Igor' Voloshin, but in the

49 Alain Badiou, *Being and Event*, trans. Oliver Feltham (London: Continuum, 2007).

post-feminist manner.[50] Here, it is not their gender but directorial disposition that acquires prominence. *Ol'ga*'s concerns are similar to those of fourth wave feminism insofar as the focus is on justice for women and opposition to sexual harassment and violence against women.[51] As a proposition to be examined in future research, I wish to suggest that, in the Russian context, feminist and anti-feminist (or anti-genderist) modes coexist, creating possibilities for queer subjectivities.

50 In fact, Voloshin is responsible for a few arthouse films that explore the fluidity of gender identities. For example, his 2008 *Nirvana* is a film about two young women who form a bond so strong that they start sharing a man who eventually betrays them. The duality of the women's identities and individualities is emphasized in extraordinary costumes and makeup, which stand for their inner subjectivities, not prescribed identities. For an in-depth discussion of the film, see Vlad Strukov, *Contemporary Russian Cinema* (Edinburgh: Edinburgh University Press, 2016), 129.

51 See Kira Cochrane, *All the Rebel Women: The Rise of the Fourth Wave of Feminism* (London: Guardian Books, 2013).

Bibliography

Albrecht, Michael Mario. *Masculinity in Contemporary Quality Television*. London: Routledge, 2016.

Badiou, Alain. *Being and Event*. Translated by Oliver Feltham. London: Continuum, 2007.

Bakhtin, Mikhail. *Rabelais and His World*. Translated by Hélène Iswolsky. Bloomington: Indiana University Press, 1984.

Clark, Katerina. *Moscow, the Fourth Rome. Stalinism, Cosmopolitanism and the Evolution of Soviet Culture, 1931–1941.* Cambridge: Harvard University Press, 2011.

Cochrane, Kira. *All the Rebel Women: The Rise of the Fourth Wave of Feminism.* London: Guardian Books, 2013.

Creeber, Glen. *The Television Genre Book*. London: Bloomsbury, 2015.

Derrida, Jacques. *Of Grammatology*. Translated by Gayatri Chakravorty Spivak. Baltimore: John Hopkins University Press, 2016.

Dittmer, Jason. *Popular Culture, Geopolitics and Identity*. Lanham: Rowman & Littlefield Publishers, 2010.

Donger, Simon, and Simon Shepherd, eds. *Orlan: A Hybrid Body of Artworks*. London: Routledge, 2010.

Dunphy, Graeme, and Rainer Emig, eds. *Hybrid Humour: Comedy in Transcultural Perspectives*. Amsterdam: Rodopi, 2010.

Engstrom, Maria. "From Sexual Revolution to 'Sexual Sovereignty': Queer-Art Exhibitions in Post-Soviet Russia." Paper presented at ASEEES Convention, Chicago, November 9–12, 2017. https://www.academia.edu/35193972/From_Sexual_Revolution_to_Sexual_Sovereignty_Queer-Art_Exhibitions_in_Post-_Soviet_Russia.

Etty, John. *Graphic Satire in the Soviet Union: Krokodil's Political Cartoons.* Jackson: University Press of Mississippi, 2019.

Evans, Christine. "The 'Soviet Way of Life' as a Way of Feeling." *Cahiers du Monde Russe* 56, nos. 2–3 (2015): 543–569. https://journals.openedition.org/monderusse/8201.

Ghaziani, Amin, and Matt Brim, eds. *Imagining Queer Methods*. New York: New York University Press, 2019.

Goscilo, Helena, and Yana Hashamova, eds. *Cinepaternity: Fathers and Sons in Soviet and Post-Soviet Film*. Bloomington: Indiana University Press, 2010.

Goscilo, Helena, and Vlad Strukov, eds. *Celebrity and Glamour in Contemporary Russia: Shocking Chic*. London: Routledge, 2010.

Graham, Seth. *Resonant Dissonance: The Russian Joke in Cultural Context.* Evanston, Northwestern University Press, 2009.

Greven, David. *Manhood in Hollywood from Bush to Bush*. Austin: University of Texas Press, 2010.

Herspring, Dale Roy. *Putin's Russia. Past Imperfect, Future Uncertain*. Washington D.C.: Carnegie Endowment, 2003.

Hutchings, Stephen, and Natalia Rulyova. *Television and Culture in Putin's Russia: Remote Control*. London: Routledge, 2009.

Iossel, Mikhail. "The 1980s American Soap Opera that Explains how Russia Feels about Everything: A Look at the Peculiar Obsession with 'Santa Barbara' in the Post-Soviet Experience." *Foreign Policy* (July–August 2017). https://foreignpolicy.com/2017/07/24/american-soap-opera-explains-how-russia-feels-about-everything-santa-barbara-trump-putin/.

Kaylan, Melik. "Kremlin Values: Putin's Strategic Conservatism." *World Affairs* 177, no. 1 (2014): 9–17. https://www.jstor.org/stable/43555061?seq=1.

Kondakov, Alexander. "The Influence of the 'Gay Propaganda' Law on Violence against LGBTIQ People in Russia: Evidence from Criminal Court Rulings." *European Journal of Criminology* (2019). https://journals.sagepub.com/doi/abs/10.1177/1477370819887511.

Lammi-Taskula, Johanna, et al. *Parental Leave, Childcare and Gender Equality in the Nordic Countries*. Copenhagen: Nordic Council of Ministers, 2011.

Ledeneva, Alena V. *Russia's Economy of Favours: Blat, Networking and Informal Exchange*, Cambridge: Cambridge University Press, 1998.

Mandal, Malay. "Neo-Liberalism, Cinema and Trajectories of South Asian Queer Visibility." Paper presented at YSI Asia Convening, Hanoi, August 12–14, 2019. https://repository.vnu.edu.vn/handle/VNU_123/70932.

"Masculinities. Liberation through Photography." Exhibition, Barbican, 2020. https://www.barbican.org.uk/whats-on/2020/event/masculinities-liberation-through-photography.

Moretti, Franco. *The Way of the World: The Bildungsroman in European Culture*. London: Verso, 2000.

Novitskaya, Alexandra. "Patriotism, Sentiment, and Male Hysteria. Putin's Masculinity Politics and the Persecution of Non-Heterosexual Russians." *Norma. International Journal for Masculinity Studies* 12, nos. 3–4 (2017): 302–318. https://www.tandfonline.com/doi/abs/10.1080/18902138.2017.1312957?forwardService=showFullText&tokenAccess=TE39ZfnyscfHsiaHfEtT&tokenDomain=eprints&doi=10.1080%2F18902138.2017.1312957&doi=10.1080%2F18902138.2017.1312957&journalCode=rnor20.

Oswin, Natalie. "Critical Geographies and Uses of Sexuality: Deconstructing Queer Space." *Progress in Human Geography* 32, no. 1 (2008): 89–103. https://journals.sagepub.com/doi/10.1177/0309132507085213.

Petro, Nicolai N. "How the West Lost Russia: Explaining the Conservative Turn in Russian Foreign Policy." *Russian Politics* 3, no. 3 (2018): 305–332. https://digitalcommons.uri.edu/cgi/viewcontent.cgi?article=1023&context=psc_facpubs.

Prokhorov, Alexander, and Elena Prokhorova. *Film and Television Genres of the Late Soviet Era*. New York: Bloomsbury, 2017.

Russel, Emma. *Queer Histories and the Politics of Policing*. London: Routledge, 2019.

Strukov, Vlad. *Contemporary Russian Cinema*. Edinburgh: Edinburgh University Press, 2016.

Strukov, Vlad, and Sarah Hudspith, eds. *Russian Culture in the Age of Globalization*. London: Routledge, 2018.

Tremblay, Manon. *Queering Representation: LGBTQ People and Electoral Politics in Canada*. Vancouver: University of British Columbia Press, 2019.

Troianova, Iana. "'Ia nikomu ne khochu podrazhat'": Interview with Iana Troianova." By Natal'ia Prokhorova. *OK*, July 27, 2012. http://www.ok-magazine.ru/stars/interview/6094-yana-troyanova.

Yurchak, Alexey. *Everything Was Forever, Until It Was No More*. Princeton: Princeton University Press, 2006.

The Web Series *Bitches* (*Stervochki*) and Post-Legacy Television in Russia

Saara Ratilainen

> White roses, white roses—unprotected thorns.
> What did snow and frost do to them, the ice of blue shop windows?
> People decorate their party with you, just for a few days.
> Then they leave you to die at the white, cold window.
>
> —*Iurii Shatunov, "Laskovyi mai," 1989*

Introduction

This chapter discusses contemporary Russian post-legacy television, that is, television productions created for the internet-era audience. Post-legacy television is characterized by interactive media technologies, collaborative production models, multi-platform distribution across different online content providers, decentralized and transnational audiences, and a DIY aesthetic.[1] My analysis will focus particularly on youth and teen drama series produced for online distribution and consumption, which invite the audiences to adopt the identity of "prosumers," simultaneous producers and consumers of media content.[2] Internet television, especially web series created outside big production companies, remains a marginal area of media and cultural studies, especially in the Russian and post-Soviet context. However, there has been a powerful convergence between traditional media and different online services, as well as increasing competition over viewers' attention between industry-driven broadcast television and video content produced by amateur and independent filmmakers available online, free of charge.[3]

1 On the relationship between legacy and post-legacy television, see Aymar Jean Christian, "The Web as Television Reimagined? Online Networks and the Pursuit of Legacy Media," *Journal of Communication Inquiry* 36, no. 4 (2012): 340–356.

2 On "prosumption," see George Ritzer and Nathan Jurgenson, "Production, Consumption, Prosumption: The Nature of Capitalism in the Age of the Digital 'Prosumer,'" *Journal of Consumer Culture* 10, no. 1 (2010): 13–36.

3 See Henry Jenkins, *Convergence Culture: Where Old and New Media Collide* (New York: New York University Press, 2006).

Characteristic of networked media systems, web series are an interactive and participatory genre often defined through crowdfunding, bottom-up production structure and a devoted fan community. According to Aymar Jean Christian, web series "suggest the maturation of online video from one-off amateur content to more rigorous . . . production."[4] As a storytelling genre, web series are located between old and new media. Following a continuous storyline and developing over an accumulating number of seasons, their sequential structure is familiar from traditional network television series. At the same time, web series offer an important venue of cultural production for authors, like women and those belonging to ethnic and sexual minorities, who remain marginalized in commercial and state television.[5] This chapter discusses in particular how Russian teenagers and young internet users, also marginalized in broadcast television, define their role with relation to the conventions of popular television series genres and how they position themselves against the well-known cultural and gender stereotypes used in post-Soviet society to explain societal and economic changes.

Overall, the current corpus of web series is extremely diverse and comprises productions by both professional and non-professional filmmakers in a vast number of different genres. In this chapter, my aim is, first, to give an overview of the development of web series on the Russian-speaking internet (also known as the Runet), with some comparison to the international context. Second, I will analyze how especially low- or zero-budget, non-professional productions and fan participation around them characterize current televisual culture, especially as it relates to young internet audiences in Russia today.

My analysis is mainly based on a close reading of one of the most successful Russian amateur produced web series, the criminal drama *Bitches* (*Stervochki*) launched in 2011.[6] My primary research material comprises forty episodes of the series produced between 2011 and

4 Aymar Jean Christian, "Fandom as Industrial Response: Producing Identity in an Independent Web Series," *Transformative Works and Cultures* 8, no. 1 (2011), https://journal.transformativeworks.org/index.php/twc/article/view/250/237.

5 Idem, *Open TV: Innovation Beyond Hollywood and the Rise of Web Television* (New York: New York University Press, 2018).

6 I have presented a shorter version of my analysis of *Bitches* and its fan community in Saara Ratilainen, "Popular and Independent? Russian Youth Videos in the Age of Globalization," in *Russian Culture in the Age of Globalization*, ed. Vlad Strukov and Sarah Hudspith (London: Routledge, 2018). An earlier analysis of *Bitches* has also appeared in Finnish in Essi Katila and Saara Ratilainen, "Internet ja venäläinen amatööritelevisio," *Idäntutkimus* 23, no. 1 (2016): 53–69.

2015 and posted on YouTube as individual video clips approximately once a week during each season. I will also analyze the fan profile of *Bitches* on VKontakte, the most popular social media site among Russian-speaking internet users. I focus particularly on the ways in which *Bitches* performs and cultivates new interpretations of women's roles and agency as criminals in post-Soviet society that are far from typical within the traditionally hyper-masculinized genre of Russian post-Soviet crime fiction. These interpretations encompass criminal women's experiences and expectations of such societal institutions as marriage and family, set against the realities of modern-day Russia. In the case of *Bitches,* a multi-season crime fiction that develops around a mob of female gangsters succeeded in engaging thousands of internet users in a fan culture. This, I argue, demonstrates that horizontal digital networks can be culturally subversive and consequently deserve closer examination in studies of Russian television series. In other words, my chapter aims to demonstrate that web series are an increasingly significant facet of contemporary Russian television culture. A closer scrutiny of this particular genre will also allow us to detect some of the most important ways in which digital intermediaries and platforms have increased their role in distribution of televisual content and technologically changed the production and reception of televisual serial fiction in Russia.

My discussion draws on a number of contemporary television scholars in arguing that the emergence of internet and digital communication technologies have brought television into a new context of horizontal communication networks, individualized media consumption, and globalized media infrastructures.[7] In this context, digital video sharing platforms, such as YouTube, and social media sites, such as Facebook and VKontakte, have become equally important channels for distribution of television content as traditional television networks (that is, national broadcast services, cable, and satellite television).[8] Networked media have also changed the way media users in general and television viewers in particular are currently conceptualized as active participants and potential editors and creators of new content, which is quite different from the traditional "mass audience" approach to television consumption.[9]

7 For example, see Jan Teurlings and Marjike de Valck, introduction to *After the Break: Television Theory Today,* ed. Jan Teurlings and Marjike de Valck (Amsterdam: Amsterdam University Press, 2015), 8.

8 Jean Burgess and Joshua Green, *YouTube: Online Video and Participatory Culture* (Cambridge: Polity, 2009).

9 Large circulation press and broadcast media as a central part of modern industrialized societies engendered the concept of the "mass audience," which refers to large heterogeneous groups of people that can be gathered

Since YouTube is one of the most popular websites not only in the world but also among the Russian-speaking internet community, it is nearly impossible to separate online video sharing from traditional broadcast television when analyzing contemporary Russian televisual culture. In other words, YouTube has become an important technological environment for both industry television and user-generated video content. This chapter contributes to the study of Russian television series through a reconsideration of the role of new communication technologies in the development of television fiction and its viewership. It aims to answer the following questions: how do internet technologies and interactive communication tools frame televisual culture in contemporary Russia? In what ways do online series produced by amateur filmmakers reuse and deconstruct the conventions of traditional television? What is the significance of web series as social networks to the changing practices of symbolic production in contemporary Russia?

I will first contextualize my case study with a brief discussion of web series' development in the framework of convergence culture, drawing examples from Russian online television and beyond. I will then move on to analyze the videos constituting the "core text" of *Bitches* (plot and key themes) building on previous scholarship on post-Soviet popular culture and television drama. I will then analyze *Bitches* as online social network and creative community. In this section, I will also delve more deeply into the sub- and countercultural undercurrents of Russian web series, accessible through the digital networks of *Bitches*. In the final section, I will draw conclusions and raise questions for further discussions on the diversifying field of Russian television series. Along the way, I will introduce also some other non-professional, independent, youth-, and fan-driven series as complementary examples in order to place *Bitches* in the broader context of Russian and international internet television and fan culture.

together and easily influenced, manipulated and entertained through media. Mass audience as a concept also implicates reification of high cultural objects for entertainment and assumptions of the mass audience's low cultural tastes. The notion of the mass audience has been challenged with the development of new media technologies that allow for a formation of narrower and more specified audiences, such as cable television and the internet. See, for example, W. Russel Neuman, *The Future of the Mass Audience* (New York: Cambridge University Press, 1991); Philip M. Napoli, "Revisiting 'Mass Communication' and the 'Work' of the Audience in the New Media Environment," *Media, Culture & Society* 32, no. 3 (2010): 505–516. The mass audience approach to popular television drama has been challenged by the Birmingham School Cultural Studies scholars. One of the most seminal works in this line is Ien Ang's study that concentrates on viewers of *Dallas*, popular American soap opera and a 1980s cult series. See Ien Ang, *Watching Dallas: Soap Opera and Melodramatic Imagination* (New York: Methuen, 1985).

Web Series and Convergence Culture

Web series have established themselves as an autonomous genre of televisual culture, which means that they have developed their own narrative conventions, quality standards and production models. At the same time, web series are rooted in convergence culture, which involves exploring the boundaries between traditional broadcast media and new digital technologies, as well as using the potential of new media to bring together and consolidate novel audience groups. In this chapter, I rely on cultural studies scholar Henry Jenkins's ideas of media convergence as not only a technological process but also "a paradigm shift . . . toward the increased interdependence of communication systems . . . and towards ever more complex relations between top-down corporate media and bottom-up participatory culture."[10] According to this view, convergence characterizes the entire process of production and consumption of media content, which reflects the ways we understand and define culture in the age of personal technology and mobile internet.

At the earliest stages of online television, the internet functioned mainly as an extension of network productions, helping professional and commercial producers create a fuller "multimedia experience" through additional materials distributed through corporate websites.[11] The increased prominence of independent and non-professional filmmakers in the field, however, has made online television incredibly diverse and open to experimentation.[12] The current phase of online television is defined by a huge variety of different authors, types of content as well as production models. Different actors from amateur filmmakers and aspiring independents to big television networks and advertising companies come together on "omnibus platforms," through which they can reach potentially global audiences. This also means that large global companies which provide services for sharing and archiving media content, but do not produce their own original content, currently dominate the market of online distribution. This has also increased the role of "digital giants" as cultural gatekeepers.[13] In the case of videos,

10 Jenkins, *Convergence Culture*, 243.

11 It is important to note that previous scholarship has identified different stages, or at least typical patterns in the development of web series from the early 1990s up until today. See Christian, "Online Networks." This scholarship is based mainly on American examples analyzed by American scholars.

12 See Christian, "Producing Identity"; and idem, *Open TV*.

13 The role of digital companies and intermediaries in contemporary cultural production has been discussed in

this is undoubtedly YouTube, whereas other video sharing websites, such as Vimeo and in the Russian case the national platform, Rutube, are used as complementary resources. Web series exist in a number of genres, which have developed through both technological and cultural convergence between different industries (including digital industries, software development, and television production).

An important subgenre of web series, closely connected to early internet technologies and new practices of digital reproduction of images, is animation. One of the best-known post-Soviet animation heroes, Masiania, originates in this development. *Masiania* is an interesting example in the framework of Russian online television due to its longevity and existence through various stages of the evolution of Runet from an avant-garde and elitist communicative space to a mass medium and dominant communication technology.[14] Masiania is a friendly and exuberant cartoon girl from St. Petersburg created by artist and graphic designer Oleg Kuvaev with Macromedia Flash image generator. The primitive style of this animation refers at once to the early digital technology that gave birth to Masiania, but also to the upbeat mood of the series. Masiania has a large oval-shaped head with three individual hairs sticking out on both sides, large round eyes, and just strokes of pen as hands, which makes her look like an ant rather than a human being. Her cultural background is the Russian underground (punk rock) and St. Petersburg city life. *Masiania* appeared in 2001, first in short videos distributed hand-to-hand through emailing lists. Soon, Kuvaev launched the website Mult.ru, which became a portal for a number of new animation series. The first episodes of *Masiania* were less than two-minutes-long "video anecdotes" depicting Masiania's small everyday life incidents, peppered with her absurd humor and trademark laughter (made with the computerized voice

the literature on algorithmic culture. See, for example, Ted Striphas, "Algorithmic Culture," *European Journal of Cultural Studies* 18, nos. 4–5 (2015): 395–412; Blake Hallinan and Ted Striphas, "Recommended for You: The Netflix Prize and the Production of Algorithmic Culture," *New Media and Society* 18, no. 1 (2014): 117–137; Scott Kushner, "The Freelance Translation Machine: Algorithmic Culture and the Invisible Industry," *New Media and Society* 15, no. 8 (2013): 1241–1258; Paul Dourish, "Algorithms and their Others: Algorithmic Culture in Context," *Big Data & Society* 3, no. 2 (2016): 1–11.

14 On the history of the Runet as cultural and communicative space, see Natalya Konradova and Henrike Schmidt, "From the Utopia of Autonomy to a Political Battlefield: Towards a History of the 'Russian Internet,'" in *Digital Russia: Language, Culture and Politics of New Media Communication*, ed. Michael S. Gorham, Ingunn Lunde and Martin Paulsen (London: Routledge, 2014), 34–54.

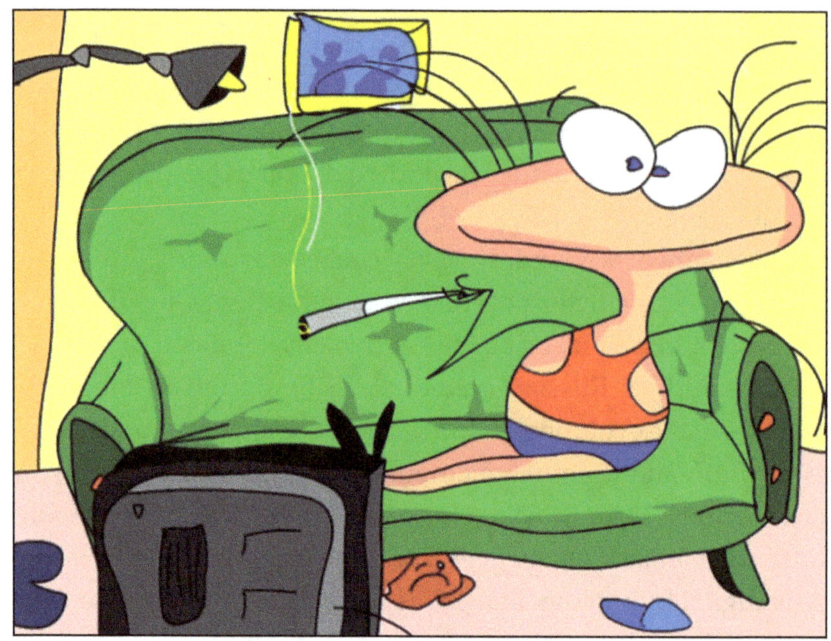

Fig. 1. Masiania enjoying her time in an episode called "Television" ("Televizor") from 2001.

of Kuvaev himself).[15] Gradually, the videos grew longer, introduced additional characters and increasingly complicated plots. Soon the series became hugely popular and started to be shown on state television and reproduced in numerous commercial products, both legally and illegally.[16] This illustrates how *Masiania* transitioned from a very small-scale indie project into a heavily franchised media product and brand name that happened together with the gradual evolution of internet technologies and diversification of digital media. *Masiania*'s popularity peaked in the early 2000s and it has now shrunk to an average-scale web production with a few hundred thousand views for each video, which is on par with the most popular episodes of *Bitches* to be analyzed later in this chapter. Currently, the website Mult.ru works as *Masiania*'s homepage and Kuvaev continues to release new episodes on YouTube with the support of various sponsors (Fig. 1).

15 On Russian video anecdotes, see Vlad Strukov, "Video Anekdot: Auteurs and Voyeurs of Russian Flash Animation," *Animation* 2, no. 2 (2007): 129–151.

16 Birgit Beumers, *Pop, Culture, Russia! Media Arts and Lifestyle* (Santa Barbara: ABC-CLIO 2005), 102–104.

As several scholars point out, digital media have brought user participation, especially fan creativity from the cultural margin into the mainstream of media consumption.[17] In fact, some of the most emblematic independent web series are fan productions, created as a response to famous works of cinematography and popular culture. This is the case, for example, with the American web series *The Real Girls' Guide to Everything Else* (2010), which was one of the early productions to participate in the stream of gay and lesbian web series by American independent filmmakers.[18] The series is, as Christian points out, both a fan and anti-fan take on the legendary HBO series *Sex and the City* (1998–2004) and its two spin-off films (*Sex and the City: The Movie*, 2008; and *Sex and the City 2*, 2010). Similar to the original series, *The Real Girls' Guide* depicts women's friendship, professional quests, and sexual adventures. However, unlike the original series, it also presents lead characters with diverse ethnic backgrounds and sexual identities and is critical of popular culture's stereotypical portrayal of women and femininity. I assert that these globally circulating productions participate in providing the transnational cultural context for the contemporary Russian web series as well. There is, for instance, an emerging group of Russian minority web series that can be seen as relating to the international conventions of LGBTQI web series, such as *Glass* (*Steklo*, 2013), *It's Happening Right Next to You* (*Eto proiskhodit riadom s vami*, 2015) and *Ready or Not* (*Ia idu iskat'*, 2019).[19] In the manner of their American counterparts, these series also adapt to both the online video format as well as the traditional television series through cultural references to better known works and genres of popular culture.

The romantic comedy series *It's Happening Right Next to You*, about the love, friendship, and St. Petersburg nightlife of young lesbian women, in particular, can be seen as contributing directly to the global pool of gay and lesbian web series. All episodes of the series are available dubbed into English. Although *It's Happening Right Next to You* occupies a marginal place, it is indicative of the diversity of global television models available on the Russophone internet today. I will come back to the theme of sexual minorities in Russian online television in the

17 See Jenkins, *Convergence Culture*; Jason Wilson, "Playing with Politics: Political Fans and Twitter Faking in Post-Broadcast Democracy," *Convergence: The International Journal of Research into New Media Technologies* 17, no.4 (2011): 445–461.

18 Christian, "Fandom as Industrial Response."

19 *Glass* and *Ready or Not* were not produced beyond pilot episodes due to lack of funding.

later parts of this chapter since different LGBTQI productions also figure as important nodes of cultural exchange in *Bitches'* online social networks.

In general, all types of fandom, ranging from social media community sites to literary fan fiction to fan-produced spin-off materials and independent productions, has become such an integral component of web series that it cannot be left out of the analysis. In addition, such internet-specific video genres as live-streaming (webcams) and video blogging ("vlogging") have contributed significantly to the development of web series.[20] For example, in *Bitches* the producers often use these forms of online communication to address the fans in additional materials, in which they introduce the set and the actors or send video greetings to their fans. This creates a feeling of direct and personal connection between the producers and viewers of the series. It is also not unusual for popular vloggers to post reviews of interesting new web series (or even single episodes) and thereby increase their online visibility outside the fan community sites. Overall, new media practices have significantly strengthened the idea that "anyone" can become a filmmaker online, which inspires more amateur producers to enter the field.

Another possible source of inspiration for budding filmmakers who use the web and non-professional networks to boost their creative input are popular television productions filmed in unpolished, documentary style, often targeted at young audiences. For example, raw lighting, hand-held camera work and an amateur cast—the trademark qualities of independent film productions and web series—are often used to indicate a certain authenticity and/or provocative content in network television. One such well-known production on Russian television is the youth drama series *School* (*Shkola*) directed by Valeriia Gai Germanika[21] and broadcast on the federal television Channel One (Pervyi kanal) in 2010. It ran for sixty-nine episodes and was set in one of Moscow's public schools.[22] *School* is also an important example of convergence culture

20 Christian, "Fandom as Industrial Response."

21 Gai Germanika (b. 1984) is one of the leading Russian filmmakers of her generation. Before *School* she attained recognition with short documentary films (*Sisters* [*Sestry*], *The Girls* [*Devochki*], and *The Infanta's Birthday* [*Den' rozhdeniia infanty*], 2005) that stood out with their frank and unapologetic portrayal of adolescence in Russia. See Peter Rollberg, *Historical Dictionary of Russian and Soviet Cinema* (Lanham: Rowman & Littlefield, 2016), 748.

22 *School*'s story centers around a group of ninth-graders, the class 9A, their social dynamics and school work, interaction with teachers and families, as well as their experiences of growing up in current-day Moscow. The series includes scenes in which schoolkids drink alcohol, have sex, and behave disrespectfully towards

between network television and internet communication because it was one of the first Russian television series to rely on fan participation when developing the story for further episodes. The production company launched a website with social media features, inviting internet users to share their personal memories and stories about school and then incorporating some of these stories in the script.

The series was completely new to Russian network television and, in my view, this is to some extent due to its close proximity to evolving online culture. I am intentionally drawing parallels between new-generation network television series, such as *School*, and amateur produced web series, such as *Bitches*, in order to emphasize the two-way cultural exchange between old and new forms of filmmaking (network versus online), as well as traditional ways of televisual storytelling and personalized, mobile technology. Furthermore, I would like to think of *School* as being an example of such cutting-edge production on state television that might also have inspired the young creators of *Bitches* to start their own series with such a rigorous approach to the television series format as a means of storytelling and outlet for creativity regardless of the lack of quality equipment and funding.

School's camera work has particularly close resemblance to cellphone video quality. In some scenes, the camera is so incredibly shaky and takes such surprising angles (for instance, extreme close-ups of fragments of people's facial features or blinking computer screens) that it creates an impression that one of the pupils is documenting the class with his or her cell phone, perhaps one of the lower price range brands.[23] We can see the amateur web series *Bitches*, created by a group of school kids with their cell phones, to be a "continuation" of *School*, stemming from its example of cultural exchange between traditional media and online communication, unpolished and technology-driven visual style, as well as its portrayal of Russian teenagers as a significant social and cultural force.

parents and teachers. *School* quickly earned a reputation as being "provocative" and unsuitable for primetime television. *School* was also accused of using the bleak *chernukha* style, familiar from the perestroika era and 1990s cinematography, to convey the everyday realities of contemporary youth to the Russian television audience. *School* evoked a lot of criticism, especially among more conservative viewers. On Russian *chernukha* film see Seth Graham, "Chernukha and Russian Film," *Studies in Slavic Cultures* 1 (2000): 9–27.

23 Gai Germanika is also known to be sympathetic to the Dogma/Dogme 95 school of cinematography, which rejects polished post-production and special effects. See Rollberg, *Historical Dictionary*, 748.

Bitches as Amateur TV: Crime Fiction Meets Popular Images of Post-Soviet Consumer Society

Bitches starts with a scene in which a young woman named Liza (played by Irina Riaposova) dances seductively to the popular song "Tantsui" ("Dance") performed by the early 2000s rock band Zveri. She has obviously chosen her outfit to fit the occasion: high heels, a pink mini skirt, and a light top that flies open in the back. She is performing her dance for an oligarch who watches sitting nonchalantly on a sofa, sipping from his glass of brandy, and smoking a cigarette. The dance ends with a passionate kiss, during which the oligarch's wife, Marina (played by Anastasiia Luzina), storms into the room and the man is caught red-handed, cheating on his wife with another woman. The scene ends with both women slapping the man in the face and leaving the room one after another. Marina throws her wedding ring onto the floor with a dramatic gesture. In the following scene the two women meet up at Marina's car and it turns out the seduction was a set-up: Liza and Marina are a criminal duo, and they specialize in scamming rich men for large sums of money. With Liza's help, Marina is now able to file for divorce and leave her marriage with half of the oligarch's money.

These opening scenes introduce some key "ingredients" that *Bitches* is now famous for and which capture the DIY spirit of the series, as well the power of imagination required from both the creators and viewers of this zero-budget production. The female protagonists, for example, are in favor of luxury consumer goods but this is expressed solely through the enormous quantity of jewelry and makeup worn by the actresses, which obviously compensates for the cheap quality of the actual props. The oligarchs, whose role in the story is to provide the women with their glamorous lifestyle, live in Soviet-style apartments with the ubiquitous carpets hanging on the wall and entrances to muddy courtyards. The story revolves around characters with dark pasts, extensive experience in crime, and layers of secrets, but these characters are played by smooth-chinned teenagers who manage to look adorable even when pointing a gun at someone. Finally, the urban scenery for crime is depicted through repetitive images of lazy afternoon traffic and pedestrians slowly crossing the street in bright daylight. Among these images, it is important to notice that from time to time the camera captures an apartment building with the sign "Sberbank" on the top, signifying Russia's oldest bank and hence the power of money as the leitmotif of *Bitches*.

In addition to being a distinctively amateur production, *Bitches* is also an auteur project and a cult product of the Russian-speaking internet. One online reviewer even calls it the *Citizen*

Kane of contemporary Russian amateur series.[24] *Bitches* was created by Il'ia Vereshchagin who was seventeen years old when he began filming the show in 2010 in the small town Pervoural'sk, located near the provincial center Ekaterinburg in the Ural Mountains. The first episodes were filmed with a mobile phone but the equipment and editing improved significantly over the course of the seasons, the last season being at times close to professional image quality. The producers share all technological details related to the equipment and camera work on the series' VKontakte page as if inviting fans to start filming their own videos. Likewise, all actors in the first seasons are Vereshchagin's friends, family, and schoolmates from Pervoural'sk but in later seasons new actors are recruited through screen-tests. *Bitches* follows the typical web series short video format: each episode is from ten to twenty minutes long, with the exception of season finales, which last closer to a half hour.

Between seasons three and four the *Bitches* crew also produced the feature film *The Secret of Lady X* (*Taina ledi X*), which was released in 2014. The film is based on the same characters as *Bitches*, revealing the background story of the series' main villain, Lola, a cold-blooded criminal boss with a traumatic past. In the style of daytime soap operas, the storyline of *Bitches* is extremely complicated and involves a large number of characters. Flashbacks are a frequently used trick that explains a sudden change in the behavior of a certain character or the appearance of new characters in the story. Each episode ends with a cliffhanger, which almost forces the viewer to click on the next video and bingewatch the entire series.

As a teen-produced sequential web series, distributed exclusively online, *Bitches* has proved to be unusually successful. The most popular episodes have from 250,000 to over half a million views on the series' YouTube channel, with an overall total of 4.2 million views. In addition, the episodes are shared through other YouTube channels and content providers. The YouTube channel of *Bitches* has close to 17,000 subscribers; its fan profile on VKontakte has almost 29,000 followers (as of February 2018). The number of followers on VKontakte is diminishing, most likely due to the delay in the launch of the fifth season, which the fans already expected to see in fall 2016. For each season finale, the fans organized live screenings all over Russia,

24 Il'ia Bozhko, "Zapiski iz podpol'ia. Kak ustroeny liubitel'skie rossiiskie serialy," Disgustingmen.com, September 1, 2015, https://disgustingmen.com/kino/kak-ustroenyi-lyubitelskie-rossiyskie-serialyi/. *Disgusting Men* (*Otvratitel'nye muzhiki*) is an independent lifestyle portal for male audiences. It publishes entertainment news focusing primarily on international film, music, video games, sex, and food. One of the main contents on the website is the podcast *Disgusting Men*.

from St. Petersburg and Moscow to Ekaterinburg and Novosibirsk, as well as in some Ukrainian cities.

The online presence of *Bitches* also includes video commentary by a number of vloggers, discussion threads on several forums and chatrooms (including Kinopoisk.ru), and reviews and articles published in a number of different (more or less established) online outlets, such as the lifestyle magazines *Afisha*, *FurFur*, *Baten'ka da vy transformer*, and the regional newspaper of the Sverdlovsk district *Novaia era*. Fan activities are also acknowledged in these materials. For example, vlogger Andrei Nifedov, the host of the popular YouTube channel "School bloggers, Omsk TV" (Shkolobloggery, Omskoe TV), traveled to St. Petersburg to participate in the live screening of the season three finale of *Bitches*. His video report shows a few dozen youngsters gathered in a nightclub near New Holland in the center of St. Petersburg, after paying an entry fee of 1,000 rubles, to watch the episode on the big screen and to talk with the *Bitches* cast on Skype.

Most online reviews of *Bitches* point out its importance as a cultural text that exposes how Russian youth think about adulthood and conceptualize dreams and hopes of a better life in contemporary society. These ideas are then served up to the viewer in a format borrowed from the hard-boiled criminal series available on post-Soviet television and mixed with widespread cultural stereotypes of the post-Soviet nouveau riche class.[25] Certain gender stereotypes are also important to the worldview of *Bitches*. The original Russian-language title *Stervochki* is the plural diminutive form of Russian *sterva* and denotes a sexy young woman who appears cold and manipulative, but often has a good heart. The *sterva* is seen as the opposite of the traditional, "soft" type of Russian femininity characterized by motherhood and other nurturing qualities such as housekeeping and caretaking. The *sterva* emerged as a widespread female stereotype of popular culture during the 1990s when gender roles and ideals were under powerful renegotiation in all spheres of society due to political, social, and economic change, including the transition to a liberal market economy through the fast-paced privatization of state assets. Popular stereotypes emphasizing the new capitalist values, such as self-promotion and competition, as well as the social roles of consumer, businesswoman, and sexually liberated

25 On representations of newly rich women on post-Soviet television and popular culture see, for example, Saara Ratilainen, "Business for Pleasure: Elite Women in the Russian Popular Media," in *Rethinking Class in Russia*, ed. Suvi Salmenniemi (London: Routledge, 2012), 45–65. Also, the special issue on "New Russians," *The Russian Review* 62 (2003), ed. Helena Goscilo.

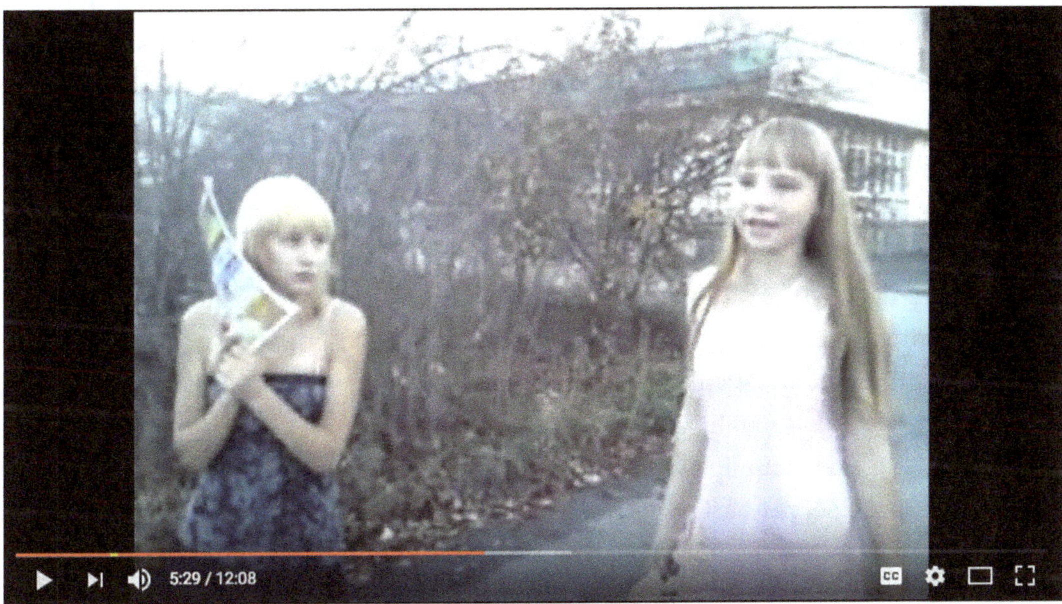

Fig. 2. Marina and Liza in the first episode of Bitches. Marina is hiding from her mother behind a newspaper.

female acquired by post-Soviet women, combined in *stervologiia*, a pseudo-scientific media discourse that was used to explain women's behavior and survival strategies in the "New Russia" (Fig. 2).[26]

Along with the plethora of women's genres portraying glamorous and hedonistic lifestyles and in response to society's demand for educating Russian consumers in matters of style and taste after decades of Soviet consumer austerity, the criminal saga emerged as an important post-Soviet genre to describe the unruly and violent side of economic transition. The archetypal hero of this genre is, of course, the male gangster, a pumped-up and brutal type seeking fast money and social relevance in organized crime.[27] As an embodiment of early post-Soviet "wild"

26 On *stervologiia*, see Suvi Salmenniemi and Maria Adamson, "New Heroines of Labour: Domesticating Post-Feminism and Neo-Liberal Capitalism in Russia," *Sociology* 49, no. 1 (2015): 88–105.

27 For example, see Elena Prokhorova, "Can the Meeting Place be Changed? Crime and Identity Discourse in Russian Television Series of the 1990s," *Slavic Review* 62, no. 3 (2003): 512–524; idem, "Flushing Out the Soviet: Common Places, Global Genres and Modernization in Russian Television Serial Productions," *Russian Journal of Communication* 3, nos. 3–4 (2010): 185–204. On military series, see chapter five in Stephen Hutchings and Natalia Rulyova, *Television and Culture in Putin's Russia: Remote Control* (London: Routledge, 2009), 114–138.

capitalism, the mobster can also be seen as the masculine counterpart to the *sterva*. In *Bitches*, these two post-Soviet cultural tropes of the (female) *sterva* and the (male) mobster are brought together and mixed in unconventional ways compared to mainstream television's treatment of the same archetypes. In *Bitches*, it is *female* gangsters who simultaneously run the mob and are portrayed as gold diggers in relation to rich men. In other words, by placing the female criminal community, loyalty, and sisterhood between the main characters at the center of the narrative, *Bitches* deconstructs the gender representation of the hyper-masculinized genre of hard-boiled criminal fiction and opens up new possibilities for female agency within a symbolic realm important to post-Soviet culture. However in doing so, it still relies on some traditional representations of female sexuality.

The highly sexualized image of woman and polarized gender representation of 1990s popular culture thus serves as the symbolic backdrop to the portrayal of female crime in *Bitches*. The young female criminals use their body and sexuality as their main weapon to access money and wealth accumulated and managed by men. When women in the series are shown as having achieved their goals, they indulge in everyday consumerist pleasures: spend time at the country house with a pool, serve pasta with salmon sauce and cheesecake home-delivered from a restaurant, take baths with rose petals and champagne, and book tourist trips to Turkey, while their oligarch husbands go to work at their flourishing businesses. True love is represented merely as an obstacle to be removed from one's way to material wealth. For example, in the first season Liza falls in love with Stepan, an "ordinary" man she meets in a nightclub. Although Stepan is also madly in love with Liza, she does not give in to the feeling but, instead, drugs him and takes his wallet. Liza explains her behavior to Marina by recounting the popular *sterva* ideology, "we smile at men we're not interested in and we flirt with the ones we don't need at all. To the ones we love, we are the worst bitches."

Although the main female characters in *Bitches* are portrayed as being stripped of all the access to social mobility one expects to find in a modern society (such as education, career development, or societal support), and thus forced to pursue a better life by getting married to rich men, they are still the main agents and driving force of the story. All events evolve through female characters who make plans and carry out smaller and bigger crimes from shoplifting to bank robbery to kidnapping and murder. When things do not go as planned, the women take the trouble to cover their tracks in all imaginable and equally illegal ways. For instance, when Marina's oligarch husband Anton is accidentally killed at the end of a fight, Liza and Marina, without hesitation, wrap him in plastic bags, drive his body to the outskirts of the city, and burn it in the forest by the highway.

Almost all male actors play secondary roles as lovers and husbands, assistants in crime, police officers and private detectives, doctors and car mechanics. Even the most important male character in the series, Marina's true love and local drug lord Leo, stays in the background and is actually physically absent for half the series. The actor who plays Leo leaves the series after the second season, although he keeps appearing in flashback scenes, as well as in the additional materials produced for fans.

Marriages between female criminals and rich oligarchs are thus a manifestation of abusive relations between men and women in a corrupt society. In this context, in the scene in which Marina marries Anton, the city official's uplifting speech about family values sounds like a message from another world with a different moral code. However the deconstruction of normative society and its family ideals does not end with the instrumentalization of the marriage institution. All three main characters, Marina, Liza, and Kira, go through personal struggles to become part of a family, which they nevertheless lose to the vicious cycle of crime, betrayal, and revenge.

Marina's struggle, for example, centers around her role as a daughter. Marina has staged her own death in order to escape from Leo and to protect her family from crime. Marina's mother is heartbroken, unaware of the fact that Marina lives across the street in a shared apartment with Liza. Marina misses her family, but her longing is poisoned by an almost biblical sibling rivalry. Marina's little sister Marta is envious because the mother appears to favor Marina. Marta is also jealous of Marina for her relationship with Leo. In her quest for love and approval, Marta goes so far as to kill a classmate who threatens to spread information on Leo's drug business at school. Marta also gets her way by becoming Leo's lover and companion in crime, and together they begin to blackmail Marina. As if referring to the parable of the Prodigal Son, Marina's return to her mother at the end of season three is one of the emotional high points of the entire series. She is able to reveal herself to her mother only after Marta has died and Leo has disappeared to St. Petersburg.

Liza's personal tragedy is that she cannot be reconciled to her role as potential wife and mother in a traditional nuclear family. Despite her resistance, Liza ends up living with Stepan with the possibility of starting a normal life without crime. However their cohabitation is soon interrupted by Stepan's former girlfriend Vera who has moved to the city from the countryside

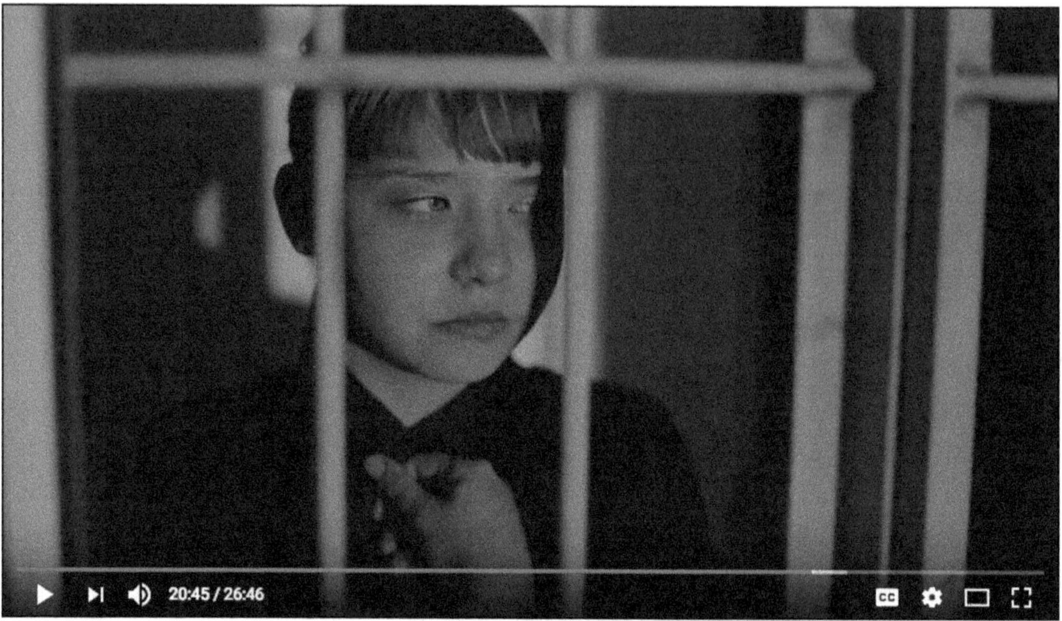

Fig. 3. Film quality of Bitches improved by season four. Liza is behind bars convicted of murder.

to reclaim Stepan as father of her newborn child. In later seasons, Liza falls in love with Vova, a car mechanic. Liza leaves her oligarch husband Vlasov for Vova and they share a moment of familial happiness until Vova is attacked by a serial killer and Liza becomes the main suspect (Fig. 3).

Kira's struggle for personal happiness and her attempt to create a family is one of the main storylines of the fourth season. Kira starts her own tourist agency and lives with her boyfriend Tima who grows increasingly possessive and paranoid towards her. Kira suggests they "take a break from the relationship" and moves to the nouveau riche country house of her client Artem in the woods outside the city. Every day Artem and his family gather together for family dinners with the father always at the head of the table, which creates the illusion of familial closeness made possible by the traditional patriarchal order. Despite the exquisite multi-dish meals, these family gatherings are filled with quarrels and tension between the grown-up daughter, Artem's sister Angelika, and the father's new wife. Soon the viewer learns that this is not the only problem in the family. Artem and Angelika have an incestuous relationship and are both involved in violent crime. Developing her role from girlfriend of a possessive man to both a self-appointed stepdaughter in Artem's family and his romantic interest (potential bride-to-be), Kira's story offers a window into the failure of yet another family model, the wealthy "modern" family, which disintegrates before the viewers' eyes. In its depiction of different family models *Bitches* explores different gradations of social taboo: gender roles are violated, family structures do not look the way they are supposed to, ultimately involving the most ancient social taboo of incest.

Bitches as Social Network and Creative Community

YouTube is a foundational platform of networked digital culture and important to *Bitches*, especially in the way Jean Burgess and Joshua Greene define its significance: "a high-volume website, a broadcast platform, a media archive and a social network."[28] This approach highlights YouTube's role as everyday media and "mediated cultural system."[29] YouTube has an impact on the development of online popular culture through its "disruptive influence on established media business models" and its "double function as both a 'top-down' platform for the distribution of popular culture and a 'bottom-up' platform for vernacular creativity."[30] As part of Google, one of the world's biggest new media companies, YouTube is central to the global digital market, where different service providers compete for advertising revenue. As a result, when assembling lists of recommended videos to be shown on the side of the webpage, YouTube's algorithm prioritizes commercially attractive videos. Consequently, the economy-driven and algorithm-assisted system of cultural consumption on digital platforms favors commercially produced content rather than amateur-produced videos.[31]

Burgess and Greene, however, point out that according to popularity measures other than number of views, independent and amateur productions tend to score higher than commercial content. For example, they seem to generate more social interaction through responses and comment sections and thus contribute more extensively to YouTube's function as social

28 Burgess and Greene, *YouTube*, 5.

29 Ibid., 7.

30 Ibid., 6.

31 Tarleton Gillespie, "The Politics of 'Platforms,'" *New Media and Society* 12, no. 3 (2010): 347–364.

network and platform for participatory culture.[32] Social interaction is also important from the perspective of digital economy in which the users' attention functions as a valuable currency. Serial watching, repetitive viewing of videos, and lengthy discussion threads in the comment section expand the digital footprint of an individual media product, while simultaneously producing different types of user data, which digital companies sell to advertisers and use to develop their services. This means that affective media use characteristic of online fan communities is the cornerstone of the contemporary digital economy and impacts not only YouTube but practically all digital platforms.

YouTube is thus a good example of the hybridity and multi-functionality of digital platforms. In the case of *Bitches*, however, video sharing and social networking take place across multiple platforms. Video sharing and social networking, equally important functions for the success of *Bitches*, are divided mainly between YouTube and VKontakte.[33] Videos are archived and distributed through YouTube, and the fan community comes together on VKontakte, which makes *Bitches* an interesting example of how Russian internet users communicate at the intersection of national and global platforms.[34] Created as the "Russian Facebook," VKontakte obviously provides Russian television fans with a better environment for social networking than YouTube.[35] For example, in the manner of online discussion forums, the discussion board on VKontakte can be divided into separate conversation threads on different topics. This function

32 Burgess and Greene, *YouTube*, 38–47.

33 The producers of *Bitches* have an Instagram profile with just a handful of followers, and a number of comments and images about *Bitches* are shared in Twitter using the Cyrillic hashtag *stervochki*.

34 Comments on the YouTube channel of *Bitches* are disabled, which directs all fan activity, commenting, and interaction to other social media sites, mainly the Russian platform VKontakte. This policy blocks comments from YouTube's community and highlights the role of national, Russian-speaking social media networks, formed mainly through VKontakte, where YouTube videos of the episodes and additional video materials are embedded. This means that in the case of *Bitches* VKontakte has "hijacked" the social networking function of online videos. I have not interviewed the producers about their social media strategies and thus cannot speculate on other possible reasons behind this decision. At the same time, it is important to mention that some YouTube users share episodes of *Bitches* through their personal accounts and some vloggers have posted video reviews of the series. This way, the series, as well as its fan culture, spread horizontally from one user to another on YouTube as well.

35 On VKontakte, see Tine Roesen and Vera Zvereva, "Social Network Sites on the Runet: Exploring Social Communication," in *Digital Russia: The Language, Culture and Politics of New Media Communication*, ed. Michael S. Gorham et al. (London: Routledge, 2014), 76–77.

has been particularly productive when developing the series in collaboration with viewers. After filming the second season, the creators of *Bitches* have devoted specific sections of the discussion board for sharing ideas and suggestions on how to develop the story for upcoming seasons. As a result, the show's fans have produced a significant number of fan fiction stories. Correspondingly, these stories generate ideas for the creators, resulting in an unusual feeling of reciprocity between the production team and the audience, as one of the fans observes:

> The second season . . . guys, do you feel like they really listened to our suggestions? As a result, we are writing the new screenplay for our favorite series together with the director. As we requested, there is more bitchiness [*stervoznost'*], drugs, complicated plots and appalling criminal episodes.

In their comments, the show's fans do not hesitate to put forward their wildest ideas. For example, they often include suggestions for new crimes that the characters should commit in future episodes. These ideas include money laundering, drug trafficking, becoming a revolutionary leader in Libya, and opening a brothel. One of the most intriguing comments (judging by the number of responses by other fans) suggests a new plotline, in which Marta murders her mother, sells all her belongings, and uses the money to buy a new iPhone. Responses to this comment add ideas for various exchangeable details, which could make the crime even more thrilling: will Marta sell her mother's organs too, or just the apartment? What else can she buy with the money? One comment suggests bluntly that, in addition to a new phone, Marta can also buy an iPad. These comments show how users' ideas and creativity accumulate on social media. New stories are created in a dialogue not only with the original text but also, and perhaps more importantly, with other participants in the fan community. Through its social network, *Bitches* expands into a multidimensional reserve of established, alternative and potential stories, relationships and realities, which in one way or another reflect how contemporary Russian youth understands the possibilities and limitations of current society. Maintaining this reserve is as crucial to the success of *Bitches* as the actual YouTube videos.

In addition to crime fantasies, a considerable portion of fan fiction stories based on *Bitches* involves sexual fantasies. In shorter comments fans repetitively request more sex, particularly gay sex, and especially between the female characters. These wishes are met as the amount of sex and nudity scenes increases over the seasons. For example, the fourth season starts with a steamy sex scene between Marina and a new male character, Max. Marina's sexual adventures continue to follow the fans' wishes and in the final episodes of the fourth season, she sleeps with a young woman, Nadia. However, Marina feels confused and wants to continue the relationship "as friends." Even though this storyline about lesbian love does not reach its full potential (in relation to the fan fiction stories), we can read *Bitches'* take on sexuality and sexual norms against what has been written on other fan fiction communities both in the Russian-speaking context and elsewhere. As a number of scholars observe, stories about sex, written in a style that ranges from soft eroticism to "pornography without plot" (PWP) are extremely popular in global fan fiction.[36] Some scholars explain the centrality of sexual fantasies in fan fiction through their ability to provide a creative channel for negotiating body and sexuality issues, as well as gender norms, especially for young women who constitute the majority of fan fiction writers in certain literary communities.[37]

Cultural studies scholar Natalia Samutina, who focuses on the Russian-speaking Harry Potter fan community, argues that Russian fan fiction about homosexual romance and sex has the additional value of challenging the state-supported conservative and homophobic discourses.[38] In the fan fiction community, alternative representations of sexuality are legitimized by appropriating internationally well-known genres, such as *slash* (the pairing of same-sex characters in erotic stories), as well as male pregnancy stories.[39] This type of cultural exchange between global forms and local cultural contexts emphasizes popular culture's ability to bring highly politicized and sensitive issues to the level of personal engagement.

Nevertheless, it is important to note that although fans of *Bitches* continuously fantasize about gay sex on VKontakte, the topic of same-sex love remains somewhat problematic, which can be seen especially in fan-produced stories about men having relationships with other men.

36 Natalia Samutina, "Sex, Love and Family in Harry Potter Fan Fiction," *Studies in Russian, Eurasian and Central-European New Media* 10 (2013): 17–36.

37 Sirpa Leppänen, "Cybergirls in Trouble? Fan Fiction as a Discursive Space for Interrogating Gender and Sexuality," in *Identity Trouble: Critical Discourse and Contested Identities*, ed. Carmen Rosa Caldas-Coulthard and Rick Iedema (New York: Palgrave Macmillan, 2008), 157–179.

38 One of the central tools for state-supported homophobia is the Federal Law against homosexual propaganda passed in June 2013. It bans "propaganda for non-traditional sexual behavior and relationships among minors." This law is also one of the most important legal initiatives marking the conservative turn in Russia.

39 Samutina, "Sex, Love and Family."

In general, these stories are in the minority in comparison with requests to include sex and romance between women. At the same time, they point out the contradictory nature of *Bitches'* discourse of sexuality, located between the limited space of Russian mainstream culture and the uninhibited, subcultural context of global fan fiction. This tension results in stories that represent (male) homosexuality as desirable and romantic but at the same time "unnatural" and "deviant," as the following fan comment from VKontakte demonstrates:

> Why are there no gays in the series? Why can't Leo change his sexual orientation for some time and kiss Stepan and other young men [of the series] a couple of times? And once the girls find out about these deviant [*porochnykh*] gay relationships, they will want to kill and dismember the boys. And there, holding a knife at Leo's and Stepan's throat, the women understand that they love them. Furious sex [*erotika*] and a wedding follow.

Another fan fiction story introduces a fantasy about homosexual romance (again between Leo and Stepan), but it soon turns into the most heteronormative scene about Stepan's and Marta's reunion:

> Leo falls in love with Stepan and they start a romance, however it turns out Stiopa is straight [*natural*] and misses Liza at nights under the covers. Leo leaves for good and Stepan starts to think about Marta seriously. He travels to Crimea . . . and there he finds a group of women sitting on the seaside, washing laundry, among them Marta. When she sees Stepan, Marta quits washing socks and throws herself at him. And only here the story concludes with a happy end!

It is possible that, in addition to contributions from the fan community, the producers of *Bitches* decided to include a lesbian subplot in the series as inspired by a collaboration with the Russian LGBTQI web series *It's Happening Right Next to You*, produced and distributed on YouTube at the same time as the last two seasons of *Bitches*, 2014–2015. Once the fourth season of *Bitches* was released, the producers shared links to all episodes of *It's Happening Right Next to You* on the series' VKontakte profile. Furthermore, Vereshchagin announced that he is going to make the fifth season of *Bitches* in collaboration with the St. Petersburg director Iuliia Fil who is behind *It's Happening Right Next to You* and also several other video productions about the St. Petersburg lesbian community. In response, some followers of *Bitches* shared information about other Russian gay web series available on YouTube.

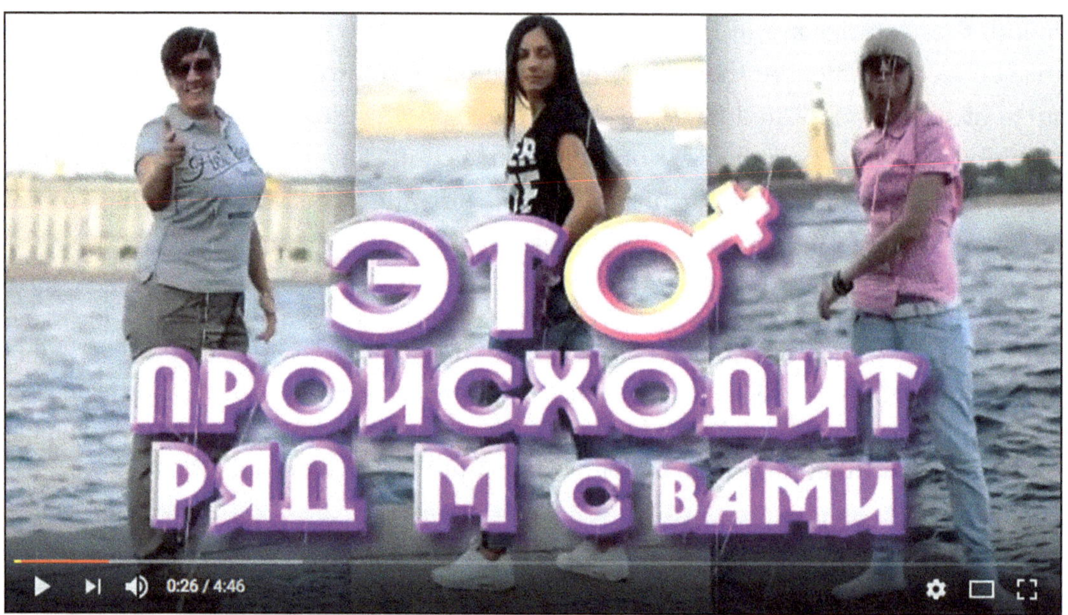

Fig. 4. It's happening right next to you is an independent web series about the Russian LGBTQI community.

This stream of comments on the VKontakte profile of *Bitches* shows that through participating in the wider network of Russian web series, *Bitches* adopts not only subcultural but also counter-cultural representations of sexuality produced within the gay community in different parts of Russia. This type of social networking online provides diverse tools of cultural communication and promotes the exchange of ideas between global televisual genres such as criminal drama and soap opera, as discussed earlier. The development of web series opens up as a space for the "average" Russian youth to support the cultural margins as well as engage in vernacular creativity. An analysis of different facets of the lesbian subplot of *Bitches* on the videos and VKontakte also demonstrates that independent and amateur YouTube series provide a context for social networking in three different senses. First, they enable reciprocity between producers of the series and their audiences. Second, they provide an open platform for fans' literary experimentations on non-normative topics. Third, they connect creative communities coming from different geographical and cultural contexts (Fig 4).

Conclusion

In this chapter I have discussed a new genre of Russian (and global) television, namely the web series. Through this example, I have argued that Russian television is increasingly defined by new media technologies and social media communication. The case of web series shows that popular television in Russia is to an increasing degree distributed through global online platforms instead of traditional (federal/national) networks and created by amateurs and independents instead of production companies within the industry. In order to highlight these developments, I have conducted a close analysis of one of the most successful Russian web series, the teen amateur series *Bitches*.

Fan participation and collective storytelling on online forums, grassroots production and peer to peer distribution are the most important qualities of *Bitches* (and a number of similar productions) that call for the renegotiation of foundational categories of television studies. In this process, the television series is to be seen rather as an online network (instead of "cultural product") in which different forms of creativity intersect, and distinguishing "creators" and "producers" from "consumers" becomes impossible. My analysis of *Bitches* has also relocated one of the most avant-garde user groups of new media—technology-savvy youth—in the framework of cultural traditions, in this case the tradition of post-Soviet televisual storytelling in the genre of crime fiction. The producers of *Bitches* follow the conventions of criminal drama and use it to renegotiate issues of gender, family, and sexuality. Their reappropriation of the genre reflects how Russian teenagers see their roles in future society. It also enables participants in the fan community to reimagine and readjust existing boundaries for cultural hierarchies, social norms, and even taboos.

This chapter has treated contemporary Russian online television as an arena of cultural diversification and celebration of citizen creativity and an important alternative to state-produced television series. While this approach is valuable in offering insights into the grassroots-level and everyday context of Russian television consumption, it might also convey a somewhat idealized image of new participatory cultures and online communities. Though this new model of viewer and creator interaction aligns with liberal thinking and democratic values, it is important not to overemphasize its political meaning.

While detached from traditional formal/state cultural institutions and industries, participants in grassroots communities live as part of existing social hierarchies and systems of oppression. This means that, although participants in the social network of *Bitches* subscribe to the "rules of fandom," they do not necessarily share the same liberal values and worldviews that the series seemingly promotes. Collective storytelling around sensitive topics in the fan forum produces conflicted representations that can appear offensive to some participants in the community, as my analysis of homosexual subplots in *Bitches* demonstrates. Furthermore, some significant identity categories are not even acknowledged as sensitive, productive, or in need of creative collective processing. For example, ethnic othering and outright racist comments repeatedly appear on the forum without further response from the community. It makes one wonder why questions of ethnicity are not discussed through alternative and potential stories and how cultural diversity and tolerance among television audiences should generally be understood.

Bibliography

Ang, Ien. *Watching Dallas: Soap Opera and Melodramatic Imagination*. New York: Methuen, 1985.

Beumers, Birgit. *Pop, Culture, Russia! Media Arts and Lifestyle*. Santa Barbara: ABC-CLIO, 2005.

Bozhko, Il'ia. "Zapiski iz podpol'ia. Kak ustroeny liubitel'skie rossiiskie serialy." Disgustingmen.com, September 1, 2015. https://disgustingmen.com/kino/kak-ustroenyi-lyubitelskie-rossiyskie-serialyi/.

Burgess, Jean, and Joshua Green. *YouTube: Online Video and Participatory Culture*. Cambridge: Polity, 2009.

Christian, Aymar Jean. *Open TV: Innovation Beyond Hollywood and the Rise of Web Television*. New York: New York University Press, 2018.

———. "The Web as Television Reimagined? Online Networks and the Pursuit of Legacy Media." *Journal of Communication Inquiry* 36, no. 4 (2012): 340–356.

———. "Fandom as Industrial Response: Producing Identity in an Independent Web Series." *Transformative Works and Cultures* 8, no. 1 (2011). https://journal.transformativeworks.org/index.php/twc/article/view/250/237.

Dourish, Paul. "Algorithms and Their Others: Algorithmic Culture in Context." *Big Data & Society* 3, no. 2 (2016): 1–11.

Gillespie, Tarleton. "The Politics of 'Platforms.'" *New Media and Society* 12, no. 3 (2010): 347–364.

Graham, Seth. "Chernukha and Russian Film." *Studies in Slavic Cultures* 1 (2000): 9–27.

Hallinan, Blake, and Ted Striphas. "Recommended for You: The Netflix Prize and the Production of Algorithmic Culture." *New Media and Society* 18, no. 1 (2014): 117–137.

Hutchings, Stephen, and Natalia Rulyova. *Television and Culture in Putin's Russia: Remote Control*. London: Routledge, 2009.

Jenkins, Henry. *Convergence Culture: Where Old and New Media Collide*. New York: New York University Press, 2006.

Katila, Essi, and Saara Ratilainen. "Internet ja venäläinen amatööritelevisio." *Idäntutkimus* 23, no. 1 (2016): 53–69.

Kushner, Scott. "The Freelance Translation Machine: Algorithmic Culture and the Invisible Industry." *New Media and Society* 15, no. 8 (2013): 1241–1258.

Konradova, Natalya, and Henrike Schmidt. "From the Utopia of Autonomy to a Political Battlefield: Towards a History of the 'Russian Internet.'" In *Digital Russia: Language, Culture and Politics of New Media Communication*, edited by Michael S. Gorham, Ingunn Lunde, and Martin Paulsen, 34–54. London: Routledge, 2014.

Leppänen, Sirpa. "Cybergirls in Trouble? Fan Fiction as a Discursive Space for Interrogating Gender and Sexuality." In *Identity Trouble: Critical Discourse and Contested Identities*, edited by Carmen Rosa Caldas-Coulthard and Rick Iedema, 157–179. New York: Palgrave Macmillan, 2008.

Napoli, Philip M. "Revisiting 'Mass Communication' and the 'Work' of the Audience in the New Media Environment." *Media, Culture & Society* 32, no. 3 (2010): 505–516.

Neuman, W. Russel. *The Future of the Mass Audience*. New York: Cambridge University Press, 1991.

Prokhorova, Elena. "Can the Meeting Place be Changed? Crime and Identity Discourse in Russian Television Series of the 1990s." *Slavic Review* 62, no. 3 (2003): 512–524.

——— "Flushing Out the Soviet: Common Places, Global Genres and Modernization in Russian Television Serial Productions." *Russian Journal of Communication* 3, nos. 3–4 (2010): 185–204.

Ritzer, George, and Nathan Jurgenson. "Production, Consumption, Prosumption: The Nature of Capitalism in the Age of the Digital 'Prosumer.'" *Journal of Consumer Culture* 10, no. 1 (2010): 13–36.

Ratilainen, Saara. "Business for Pleasure: Elite Women in the Russian Popular Media." In *Rethinking Class in Russia*, edited by Suvi Salmenniemi, 45–65. London: Routledge, 2012.

———. "Popular and Independent? Russian Youth Videos in the Age of Globalization." In *Russian Culture in the Age of Globalization*, edited by Vlad Strukov and Sarah Hudspith, 240–263. London: Routledge, 2018.

Roesen, Tine, and Vera Zvereva. "Social Network Sites on the Runet: Exploring Social Communication." In *Digital Russia: The Language, Culture and Politics of New Media Communication*, edited by Michael S. Gorham, Ingunn Lunde, and Martin Paulsen, 76–77. London: Routledge, 2014.

Rollberg, Peter. *Historical Dictionary of Russian and Soviet Cinema*. Lanham: Rowman & Littlefield, 2016.

Salmenniemi, Suvi, and Maria Adamson. "New Heroines of Labour: Domesticating Post-Feminism and Neo-Liberal Capitalism in Russia." *Sociology* 49, no. 1 (2015): 88–105.

Samutina, Natalia. "Sex, Love and Family in Harry Potter Fan Fiction." *Studies in Russian, Eurasian and Central-European New Media* 10 (2013): 17–36.

Striphas, Ted. "Algorithmic Culture." *European Journal of Cultural Studies* 18, nos. 4–5 (2015): 395–412.

Strukov, Vlad. "Video Anekdot: Auteurs and Voyeurs of Russian Flash Animation." *Animation* 2, no. 2 (2007): 129–151.

Teurlings, Jan, and Marjike de Valck. Introduction to *After the Break: Television Theory Today*, edited by Jan Teurlings and Marjike de Valck, 7–18. Amsterdam: Amsterdam University Press, 2015.

Wilson, Jason. "Playing with Politics: Political Fans and Twitter Faking in Post-Broadcast Democracy." *Convergence: The International Journal of Research into New Media Technologies* 17, no. 4 (2011): 445–461.

INTERVIEWS

Television Producer and Showrunner

Alexander Dulerain

How did you come to work in television?

I was working as an independent director and during the 1998 crisis I earned money through some advertising orders. But when the crisis turned really terrible and it became clear that there were no orders, and I had a baby, I realized that I had to earn money somewhere . . . I got a job right away at the STS channel, which was American, and wasn't very much affected by the crisis. I knew nothing about television and viewed it extremely negatively. I simply didn't watch it. For me, the series explosion hadn't yet happened. I remember that my American boss, Alexis Bruner, told me to watch the wonderful series *Friends*. I watched it and didn't at all understand why she liked it. I watched it in Russian. Then I watched it in English. Since then I've watched each season three times, the first time by myself, and then with each of my children. But when I got into TV, I did commercials, and my main job was marketing. Apparently I had some talent for it. I made a successful career fairly quickly, first at STS, where Roman Petrenko noticed me and later invited me to join TNT, and I followed him there.

I also worked in marketing there and at the same time made my independent films. And then I suddenly fell in love with TV series, and as a result even made a series, *The Bunker or Scientists Underground*—a wonderful series. Vania Vyrypaev wrote the script; I created the plot with him and Serezha Koriagin. I have to admit, it was kind of a weird series. Here's the plot: a bunker underground, God knows where. And there's an experiment being conducted there, but no one knows the purpose of the experiment, except for the leader. They have a doctor, but the doctor fell ill. And everything begins from the fact that they're sent a veterinarian. He himself is in shock: why am I needed here? There are no animals here. Unfortunately, the series didn't get high ratings.

Parallel to this I proposed a Comedy Lab, a laboratory of comedy, to Roman Petrenko. I wanted to produce comedies. Comedy is still my favorite genre. So that's how I became a producer. The first successful project was *Our Russia* (*Nasha Rasha*). Semen Slepakov and

Garik Martirosian wrote it. My main idea as producer was to connect comedy authors with a cinematic approach to production. Maksim Pezhemsky shot the first season of *Our Russia*, Petr Buslov the second. After the *Our Russia* comedy lab I started working mostly on producing.

In general, I think the main thing in the work of a producer for a channel is to make the correct choice of whom to work with. And I've always been incredibly lucky.

We had already understood that long sitcoms could be the engines of growth after the success of the *Married with Children* adaptation, done under the leadership of the then general producer of TNT and my friend Dmitry Trotsky. However, at that time sitcoms were viewed as a low genre for small channels or not for prime time.

But Roman saw a huge potential in this genre. In general, after becoming head of TNT, he took a number of radical steps. I think he was the first head of the TV channel—not a producer, not a broadcaster. With his background as a marketing specialist, Roman applied the laws of marketing to production and programming. And this produced a phenomenal result. For example, he introduced a daily program line of film comedies—we branded it—and for many years afterward TNT showed film comedies every evening. They told Roman, "That's impossible, you won't get that many comedies," but this turned out to be an extremely successful solution.

We put sitcoms into the heart of prime time, at 8 pm, and they also told us that it wasn't done, that it was impossible, they won't last. But it was precisely sitcoms that were one of the main engines that "lifted" TNT from 2.2% of the national viewing audience in 2002 to 13% and the position of leader among all channels by 2013. The secret was in their repetitiveness that seemed almost endless. We probably produced the least number of all series in the market, but we "polished" each title to the maximum—and almost always won in the ratings.

We were incredibly lucky. Three brilliant teams of producers worked and still work with us: Comedy Club Production is Viacheslav Dusmukhamedov, Garik Martirosian, and Semen Slepakov; Good Story Media is Anton Zaitsev, Artem Loginov, and Anton Shchukin; and there's Evgeny Nikishov and Valery Fedorovich's 123 Production. The latter began as producers on the channel, but later formed their own production company and, in addition, they run the TV3 channel. It's this big three that's "responsible" for all the TNT series hits—mainly comedies, but not just those.

They're all very different—each has its own style, its own language—but, in my opinion, they were all united by a desire to make uncompromisingly cool series as well as possible. In my view, no channel in Russia has had so many outstanding exclusive producers. We absolutely dominated the comedy genre. In principle, we were competing with ourselves for the young audience (ages fourteen to forty-four). And, of course, I could only envy myself: working with these teams is pure joy.

Could you talk about your work on the series *The Affairs* (*Izmeny*) and *Ol'ga*?

The main problem with *The Affairs* was finding a director. It had a totally wonderful script by Dasha Gratsevich with an unusual main heroine, and we couldn't find either an actress or a director who could show us screen tests that we found believable. After all, it's a story about very unusual relationships. We got the idea that a foreign director might be able to do it. And our friend, Aleksei Ageev found a foreign director—Vadim Perel'man. Vadim did a test with Elena Liadova and there were no doubts—she was the main heroine and he was the director.

With the series *Ol'ga* it was this way: when Artem Loginov showed me the script, I was full of doubts. The script was wonderful, but TNT is a channel for young people. Here the main heroine is not a girl, but an adult woman with two children. One of the main heroes, her dad, a former soccer player, is an alcoholic. So it was somehow disturbing. But a wonderful script. We shot a pilot. And when we shot the pilot, it became clear that this was an incredible hit. My assistant watched it; she simply cried at the end. She was laughing like crazy throughout, but at the end she cried. It was clear from the pilot that this was a powerful story.

Alexander, could you talk about *House Arrest* (*Domashny arest*), another important and very successful project?

Series are usually collective creations. But in the case of *House Arrest*, even though it had a wonderful director, Petr Buslov, the famous cameraman Kozlov, and incredible acting, even with all that—*House Arrest* is very much the auteur series of my brilliant friend, Semen Slepakov. Semen dealt with all aspects of it in infinite detail—from the script to the opening credits, seeking the exact realization of what he wanted to do. At any rate, that was my impression from observing the production process. The series had an unusual premiere: the TNT Premier streaming service in fact "launched" it, that is, it came out only on the internet. After so many years of work, Semen was very worried that *House Arrest* would have such an experimental start, that it wouldn't be found, wouldn't be seen. But everything worked: *House Arrest* became a huge hit; everyone loved it. The secret, in my opinion, is that *Arrest* became a new encyclopedia of Russian life.

Tell us, who is your audience?

Our audience is youth aged twenty-five to thirty-five. But you understand that youth aged twenty-five to thirty-five doesn't exist as a single, real category. It's just that those in this age group are all active consumers. It's a colossal group. I'd rather say that our audience . . . Do you know the Maslow pyramid? There are basic values: reproduction, survival, love. And there is self-reflection, self-awareness. I don't exactly remember what's in the Maslow pyramid . . . Our audience is about basic values, not reflection. It's content for people who are either young, or young in spirit. I'm fifty years old, but I watch all these series. There are many people and many identities that live in each of us. And our channel is for these young identities in each Russian.

How have streaming platforms changed the TV market?

They are only beginning to change it. The process is just beginning in Russia. For now, everyone is beginning to invest huge amounts of money with childish excitement and inhuman enthusiasm to become their own Netflixes, and thanks to this, the content producers win. On the one hand, this is profitable for the TV channels because we can share the costs of a series with a platform, but at the same time we are slowly but surely sharing the audience. It's clear that sooner or later everyone will leave to watch everything on streaming. How long the flow from vessel A to vessel B will take, no one knows. Some say that it will be done in three years, some say that the flow will take ten years. At the same time, it's clear that not everyone will become a Netflix, and the quantity and variety of types of money being spent on series for streamers will, of course, decrease. But, at the same time, the audience will also increase. That is, those who survive will feel good. It's what we're seeing with Airbnb and Uber, one or two will survive. And further on, the shadow of friendly Netflix, which has so much money that it could buy all of Russian television, hangs over us. They probably spend around that much money on their employee vacations.

What role do series festivals play in the production of series?

Well, they're terribly inspiring for creators. Their role in Russia ends there. But inspiring creators is an important task.

Even Kinotavr now devotes part of its program to the pitching of series.

Unfortunately or fortunately, cinema, especially independent film, is lagging behind. We'll see how it goes. But right now series are slowly but inevitably taking the place of independent film. There are many series; if you were to release them as one piece—you would have a real independent film. That is, ten years ago this would have been an independent film. It would have been shorter, of course. And thank God. Because someone commissions it and you don't need to run around to different people and ask them for money.

Thank you for the interview.

Producer and Studio Executive

Sergei Fiks

Could you talk about yourself and how you began your career in the television industry?

This is how it was: I loved cinema. At that time there was no internet. So my knowledge of cinema came from VHS tapes, which I watched while spending time at the Foreign Literature Library in Moscow, where I was reading *Cahiers du cinema.* In 1992 I started working at the first private film magazine, *Video-ASS* (*Video Agency of the Soviet Union*). For a short time they were licensed to publish the Franco-American magazine *Premiere* and I was chief editor of *Video-Ass Premiere.* Next I worked as a press secretary at the Gemini Film Company, then it was Twentieth Century Fox CIS, now owned by the Disney Corporation. We also distributed films for Warner and Columbia. From there I was hired as an executive in charge of programming international films for domestic release at the NTV-Plus TV channel. Later I joined the NTV channel. When Boris Jordan's management team was dismantled, I moved to The All-Russia State Television and Radio Broadcasting Company (VGTRK). That's my biography. You know my filmography. There were some interesting moments. For example, our film *Vanechka* (2007) had a budget of 1.5 million dollars and was scheduled on Channel Russia for New Year's Eve. If I am not mistaken, they screened it in the same time slot as one of the *Pirates of the Caribbean* movies. The *Pirates'* share of the audience was thirty-three percent, while *Vanechka* got thirty percent. Meanwhile, *Vanechka*'s budget was equivalent to 1.5 shooting days of *Pirates.*

Do channels target different audiences?

Channel One, Russia is considered to be a channel for everyone, a sort of global audience channel. They claim to make projects for everyone because they are the flagship channel of the nation. The de facto audience of Channel Russia is women, sixty-five years of age and older. The NTV Channel reputedly targets male viewers even though, as far as I know, a lot of women watch it too. But by and large it is a channel of male stories, male TV series. Channel STS targets urban viewers, predominantly younger women. In the industry they joke that it's the channel of sunny disposition. Everything is great, just tremendous. Everyone is happy, satisfied, fashionable, successful, progressive. All this has little to do with reality. Channel TNT is known for Comedy Club projects. They do indeed have a lot of great projects. They are allowed to cross some boundaries. Many of their projects are not as simple as they seem at first glance. But there is a limit to what is permissible, of course. The rest of the channels are smaller and they do not change the general picture.

In Soviet times ideological censorship determined programming. What about now? What factors are at play?

Now there are very clear audience preferences. That is to say, women over sixty-five years of age, who watch Channel One, Russia, the Home Channel (Domashny), they don't like certain genres that are alien to them. And it is clear why: those genres weren't around when those viewers were growing up. In Soviet times there was practically no horror or fantasy, for example; and TV series like these only air on specialty channels, such as TV-3. There are also obvious topics that are taboo on prime-time television: nudity, profanity, hate speech. Besides, producers themselves know what is acceptable and what is not. Meanwhile we have series such as *The Method*, which graphically depicts serial killers and their shocking crimes. Shows like this are scheduled after 11:30 pm and somehow get away with it. Such projects have their own audience, which does not watch mainstream Russian TV.

What is the situation with the production of TV series in the CIS?

After 2014 Ukraine banned a lot of [Russian-produced] content, which was a serious blow to producers who often owned the rights to distribute TV series in the CIS countries. And now you have to jump through hoops to sell a series to Ukrainian channels. I know that Ukraine now tries to buy Polish TV series, but they are not really popular with audiences. Kazakhstan and Azerbaijan try to air Indian and Turkish TV series. This often works better. To be honest, I don't really follow these developments. When the Russian TV industry had a lot of money, we could use any shooting location: Vietnam, Israel, Western Europe, naturally, if necessary the United States, Cuba . . . Now, of course, this is very difficult because of the weak ruble.

Which recent TV series caught your attention?

Well, for instance, Start Studios recently made the TV series *Gold Diggers* (*Soderzhanki*) about the Moscow elite, now in its third season. Renowned theater director Konstantin Bogomolov made the first season. The series was broadcast on Russia's Start OTT platform and they sold this show to Amazon Prime. It's a big-budget series with good actors. And they have solid viewership. Recently Bogomolov and Start Studios made the TV series *A Good Man* (*Khoroshii chelovek*, 2020), based on the story of a serial killer from Angarsk. Another VoD Platform, Kinopoisk, owned by Yandex, made the comedy TV series *Project Anna Nikolaevna* (*Proekt Anna Nikolaevna*, 2020). It's a story about a female android who works as a cop. They uploaded police rules and regulations into her and sent her to enforce law and order in a provincial town. I watched this series because my friend Maksim Pezhemsky is the director. It's not only daring for the present time, but also quite funny. They sold this series to the TNT Channel and are quite happy about it. It's definitely a quality job. In short, streaming services brought a whiff of fresh air but, as you understand, the Covid pandemic upset everyone's plans. The future is uncertain.

What remains Soviet in post-Soviet series?

A lot has changed, of course, but the fashion for Soviet-era culture remains strong. Let's consider some TV series broadcast on Channel One or some military-patriotic films. They follow Soviet blueprints embodying a familiar belief system. Even their approach to filmmaking is reminiscent of Soviet times. Of course, they use modern technologies. Also, there are fewer taboos than in Soviet times. For example, you can show a bullet entering a character's skull and, in general, spectacular violence, which was impossible in Soviet cinema. By and large it is still Soviet-style epic cinema. There aren't many such films and series, but people still like them because they are well made by professional filmmakers. For example, director Iury Moroz, who made the first three seasons of the TV detective series *Kamenskaia* (1999–2001), produced the TV series *Gloomy River* (*Ugrium-reka,* 2020). If you remember, in Soviet times there was such a television film made, if I am not mistaken, by Iaropolk Lapshin (1968). Moroz's big-budget remake was filmed on location in Siberia, Belarus, and near Moscow. He hired famous actors, used expensive stage sets, and a lot of horses. This is indeed an epic TV series. I saw a trailer and it looks impressive. It's worth noting that Iury Moroz is a disciple of Sergei Gerasimov. So on the one hand, Moroz embodies the Soviet cinematic tradition; on the other, he is fairly young and understands modern technology and present-day production practices. The synergy of the old and new results in really high-quality production. This is Channel One.

Another Channel One project set in the 1960s' and 1970s' Soviet Union is a detective series produced by Denis Evstigneev, in which actor Andrei Smoliakov plays the policeman Major Ivan Cherkasov. The first season was titled *Mosgaz* (2012). Based on true events, it is the story of Moscow police hunting a serial killer. The director, Andrei Maliukov, is a veteran of Soviet cinema. For example, in the 1970s and the 1980s he made popular action films about Soviet paratroopers. Cherkasov then reappears in several seasons filmed by other directors, including, for example, Iury Moroz. The Cherkasov series evoke well-made police procedurals of the Soviet era: excellent period sets, costumes, props, all of Soviet material culture. Producers invite major stars for these productions. And if the protagonists keep appearing in new seasons, it means that ratings are strong and people watch the show. This show reproduces a thoroughly Soviet value system: good versus bad, "us" versus "them," but it is a twenty-first-century television series. In Soviet times, you couldn't make a story about serial killers or show a graphic bedroom scene.

What is the cost of one episode?

You know, it depends. When a major channel makes a series, an episode can cost one hundred thousand dollars or more. Because if you are filming a big and expensive historical series, when you need famous actors who charge over 300,000 rubles a day, when you need to build an expensive set, when you have a lot of special effects or war scenes, of course you cannot film it for one hundred thousand dollars per episode. So the budget depends on the project and the project depends on how much the channels trust the filmmakers. Because if we take the major showrunners, Sergei Ursuliak or Valery Todorovsky, they cannot make it on the cheap. It's a question of creating the fictional world without which the project wouldn't make any sense.

How are the contemporary Russophone television viewers different from Soviet viewers?

We used to have ideology, which we don't anymore. There used to exist certain values, which now, even if they are proclaimed, are not followed. There used to be a multinational country, which is now fragmented. It is what it is. There are, so to speak, Russophone communities: Russia, Belarus, Ukraine . . . there is a problem with Ukraine now, of course. There are the Baltic countries, there is Central Asia, the Southern Caucasus. And all of them used to watch the same TV channel while now I cannot even imagine something like that. The change is enormous. For example, now there is such a thing as a strict format: forty-four and fifty-two minutes' running time. In Soviet times the filmmaker would end the episode whenever he felt like it.

Besides, the television audience is fragmented. Soviet ideology simply wouldn't allow this. And now not only ideology itself fell apart but the cultural space as well. For example, we used to watch the Polish TV series *Four Tankmen and a Dog* (*Czterej pancerni i pies*, dir. Konrad Nałęcki, 1966). At the heart of the story was a tank crew with a Polish and a Georgian character who were all friends with the Red Army soldiers, something quite unimaginable nowadays. There was also the Polish TV series *More than Life at Stake* (*Stawka większa niż życie*, dir. Andrzej Konic and Janusz Morgenstern, 1967–1968), the Czechoslovak series *Thirty Cases of Major Zeman* (*Třicet případů majora Zemana*, dir. Jiří Sequens, 1975–1980). There were even French mini-series such as *The Gallant Lords of Bois-Doré (Les Beaux Messieurs de Bois-Doré*, dir. Bernard Borderie, 1976). That is, we watched not only Soviet television productions but also European TV series. And now it is hard to imagine mass viewership for such shows. Or, to put it differently, you can find an audience for any show but it will be a niche audience. In Russia there are, for example, people who love anime, TV series about samurais, or sci-fi. But they are not the broad audience of millions of viewers that a major television channel needs. For example, you can watch *The X-Files* on TV-3 and it used to be broadcast on Channel One. But it wasn't popular there because the older generation is not in the habit of watching science fiction, the occult, and such. They don't know it. They don't need it. It doesn't interest them. If we had a Russian *X-Files,* maybe it would get an audience, but this would be an expensive project: CGI, special effects, expensive sets and costumes. If they borrow Western formats, they remake, for example *Everybody Loves Raymond* into *The Voronins,* something that you can adapt more or less. But there are things like *Orange is the New Black* that are impossible to adapt.

And what's the near future of the industry?

Sociology tells us that, for example, five years ago Channel One, Channel Russia, and NTV together had seventy percent of viewers; now they barely get thirty-five percent. That is, people, especially younger audiences, stopped watching broadcast television. They watch shows like *Game of Thrones* (2011–2019). They prefer niche channels, such as hunting and fishing, politics, sport. They choose internet television, VoD, computer games, and if they watch films, they watch them on the internet. This process has been going on for quite a while and most likely it will continue. The thing is, it's very hard to produce something that would bring together the entire family because people have different interests. That's why TV channels and TV audiences will continue to splinter.

Scriptwriter, Executive Producer, and Film Critic

Denis Gorelov

How did your work on Leonid Parfenov's project *The Other Day* (*Namedni*) begin? What exactly did you do there?

In 1996 Parfenov got interested in Soviet history. And, without making it obvious, he began this history from his own birth year. The project was initially called *Russia 61–91*, thirty years, events, people, phenomena without which it is hard to imagine—let alone understand—us. I'll say off the bat that it was a quality idea. By 1960–1962 the Soviet regime had turned into what our generation remembers and knows: late socialism, fairly vegetarian [less repressive], relatively abundant as a result of the newly discovered oil fields in Tiumen', and so forth, a kind of consumer-oriented socialism.

And you joined the project as a scriptwriter, right?

There was a scriptwriting team, three people plus Parfenov, who reviewed the texts and edited them for length. He actually encouraged us to write longer texts so that he could see the full picture, and then he squeezed out a shorter version from the whole. In a lot of things, due to the fact that he really is an expert on Soviet history, I learned many things from him and he learned many things from me. That is, I brought him the topic of the birth of folklore about Rzhevsky from the film character in *Hussar's Ballad* (*Gusarskaia ballada*, dir. El'dar Riazanov, 1962). And vice versa: the story about the German Democratic Republic being the only country that refused to sing in Russian and which, therefore, didn't have its own music star who was popular in the USSR, such as a Czech Karel Gott, a Yugoslav Radmila Karaklajić, or a Polish Anna German. Or perhaps the Soviets advised East Germans not to sing in Russian so as not to frighten Russians with a German accent—bad memories after World War II.

We divided our tasks in the following way: I covered domestic and foreign politics, which automatically made up about one third of the story items. Since I've done this work my entire life, it didn't require any kind of immersion in unfamiliar material. I knew all about the Penkovsky spy scandal and I was well-informed about the Cuban missile crisis, and I was familiar with the details of Kennedy's assassination, including the name of Abraham Zapruder, who caught everything on film. Consequently, this was not too time-consuming. Plus, the cinema of the era, which I knew well, was on me of course. I partially took on political jokes and some stories on literature. Liza Listova was responsible for all cultural history, except for film, more precisely all high culture: ballet (even though she actually did handle television), . . . ballet, literature, the La Scala tour in the USSR, plus theater in all its aspects. By the way, television became increasingly important by the mid-to-late 1960s. 1969 is a watershed year in the history of Soviet television, I would say. In 1969 the first episode of *Well, Just You Wait!* (*Nu pogodi*, dir. Vyacheslav Kotenochkin) was released. The first episode of *Cheburashka* (dir. Roman Kachanov) appeared. And, of course, the same year the first episode of Fedor Khitruk's *Winnie the Pooh* came out. Finally, the first episode of *The Bremen Town Musicians* (*Bremenskie muzykanty*, dir. Inessa Kovalevskaia) was released. Soiuzmul'tfil'm Studio was tasked by the government with generating content for the small screen. Television became a national pastime. Right at this time, during the mid-late 1960s, there appeared the most important television series, those that defined the late socialist mindset. Liza Listova worked on this topic. Another addition to the team was Maksim Sokolov, who covered all topics on material culture: Bologna raincoats, flippy skirts, high heels, iconic Soviet-era foodstuffs, such as Soviet-style Bologna sausage, candies, such as the Alenka chocolate bar, spaceships, and everything else, everything Soviet that you could touch with your hands.

Parfenov outlined our task clearly: we talk only about those things that became events for the entire Soviet population of 300 million, and not for those who lived in downtown Moscow or on Nevsky Prospekt in St. Petersburg. So the film *Liberation* (*Osvobozhdenie,* dir. Iury Ozerov 1970) must be included, a film that the entire country watched, and, most importantly, Stalin's first appearance onscreen since his death in 1953. The films *Brief Encounters* (*Korotkie vstrechi,* dir. Kira Muratova, 1967) and *The Long Farewell* (*Dolgie provody,* dir. Kira Muratova, 1971) will not be included, not because they are bad, but because no one knew about their existence at the time, apart from a few intellectuals. Andrei Tarkovsky himself had to be included because, even having never watched Tarkovsky's films, the Soviet people knew: those Moscow nerds have their famous Tarkovsky. He is highly spiritual and heavily Russian Orthodox, which deserves at least some respect.

Thus, Tarkovsky was bundled with the story of the production and release of *Andrei Rublev* (1966), the triumph of *Ivan's Childhood* (*Ivanovo detstvo*, 1962) at the Venice Film Festival, and *Stalker* (1979) unexpectedly becoming a national cult film.

How long did you work on Parfenov's project?

I worked there for a year. During that time we created twelve episodes. That is, it took us a while to get going and the first episodes were released when we already had around ten ready to go, I don't remember exactly. After all, we released one episode per week and wanted to make sure we had a supply of them ready. It was rough at the beginning. For example, we realized that when Parfenov goes to Cuba for the Bay of Pigs story, he has to record standups for all Cuba-related events relevant to Soviet history for other years. And my job was to rush and write up all the stories about Cuba up to the end of the Soviet Union. After 1991 Cuba stopped being part of Russian popular culture. Two weeks later Parfenov flies to the United States for stories about Nikita Khrushchev and corn, and I had to produce not this but all relevant stories involving the United States, Kennedy's assassination, the détente, and, of course, the space race. And then there was a lot of flying back and forth from Moscow because he could not fly directly from the United States to Cuba.

At the beginning he laid out all the episodes by watching each year's *News of the Day* (*Novosti dnia*). He collected the important events, then we brainstormed to fill in the gaps, and planned from twenty-four to twenty-six stories per year. If we had too many stories for a year, we moved some of them to the next or previous year, if they were not too specific. 1961 was a phenomenally busy year: the Cuban Revolution, Iury Gagarin's flight, Stalin's removal from the Mausoleum and the Twenty-Second Communist Party Congress with the exposure of Stalin's crimes, Khrushchev's corn, the financial reform. And then, of course, *The Amphibian Man* (*Chelovek-amfibiia*, dir. Vladimir Chebotarev and Gennady Kazansky, 1962) comes out, which coincides with the huge boom in moviegoing. The kids of the post-war baby boom were ready for cinema and went to the movies en masse. And suddenly it became clear that the Soviet film industry was not at all prepared. They rushed to admit more students to film schools, expand movie studios, and build more theaters. Half of the movie theaters in Moscow were built during the 1960s. Furthermore, young people's taste was not what was expected by the main actors of the time, the Communist

Party on the one hand and the Soviet intelligentsia on the other. The Soviet intelligentsia got excited by *Nine Days of One Year* (*Deviat' dnei odnogo goda,* dir. Mikhail Romm, 1962) and the Communist Party promoted the film *Everything Remains for the People* (*Vse ostaetsia liudiam,* dir. Georgii Natanson, 1963). But the people went to *The Amphibian Man* where, as I put it, "Soviet creatures from the Black Lagoon participated in class struggle."

Tell us about your work at Amedia film company.

I joined the company at the point when Alexander Akopov was, as I understand it, expanding production. In his first official speech he put it bluntly: "Dear friends, our task is to become the best television production company in the world. The goal of becoming Russia's best television production company, that's not such a serious task, as it is quite achievable; we should instead be shooting for the stars."

What exactly did you work on?

I read and edited scripts. At that time anyone who had time on their hands—parking lot security guards, for example—started writing screenplays. It was a total mess. Furthermore, the central message of all of these texts was how to make more money without doing anything. Half of the scripts were about an inheritance, half dealt with winning the lottery. At that time Mexican telenovelas were extremely popular here. What did Mexican telenovelas and Russian TV series have in common? A huge disparity between the haves and have nots in a very poor country, and always the kind of wealth gained by chance, rather than by merit. What matters is who you know, who you married, who you met by chance. Such melodramatic coincidence defines the telenovela. And it is the central narrative turn in Russian TV series.

What was the secret of Amedia's success?

The first successful project for Amedia was *My Fair Nanny* (2009). That was Akopov's aha moment, as they say. He bought the American *The Nanny*. He decided that our country couldn't handle a Jewish nanny. After 2014, to be frank, our country can't even handle a Ukrainian nanny. But at that moment, it was a huge success and a training ground for Akopov's producers and writers. He said that cautious people had objected that the series was built on three characters, none of whom exist in Russian society: a butler, a superrich music producer, and the third I can't remember. But the phrase, "She was working in a boutique in Biriulevo" quickly became an iconic one-liner, and even snobbish intellectuals accepted the national popularity of the sitcom.

As far as we understand, you think that *The Other Day* is a kind of television for the intelligentsia, while Amedia works with popular narrative models and caters to everyone, right?

Yes, I would say this: Parfenov worked with high-brow themes, hoping that they would be comprehensible to everyone. As someone from the city of Cherepovets, he knows very well what people over there are interested in. He is essentially a bridge, uniting the two Russias. Amedia, on the contrary, wishes to work with a broad national audience, without alienating the intellectual public.

Director and Scriptwriter

Nataliia Meshchaninova

Could you talk about how you began to work on TV series?

It happened pretty much spontaneously because before series I was making documentary films. And in this work I was the camera operator, director, editing director, and sound director. You walk by yourself with a camera and enter the lives of the heroes. Valeriia Gai Germanika called me and said she was getting ready to shoot *School* (*Shkola*, 2010) and that it would have a documentary approach to the actors' lives. Material was collected in different Moscow schools as well. She asked if I wanted to shoot the series with her because there were sixty-nine parts, and it was hard for one person to manage it. I was terribly interested, even though I had no experience working with actors or in feature film generally. It was a challenge for me, of course. And I agreed and stayed with the project. Then I actively worked with the scriptwriting group when the storyline ideas ran out in part twenty. We would meet, we made the storyline more dynamic. It was the kind of experience that resulted in my stepping into the world of feature film. There were difficulties, including production issues, because I had to keep to a tight schedule and shoot a lot of scenes in one day. I had to think very quickly. We shot several scenes in one take. All in all, it was like being at war.

About your documentary work: how did it influence your approach to the material?

It had a very, very strong influence. Because it seems to me that all higher education institutions should first teach documentary film, and only then take a person into feature film because a feature film director must go through the experience of observing life. Moreover, observing not with the eyes, but precisely through the camera. Because you won't see a lot of things with the eyes. Through the camera you look at an object, a hero, much more selectively. And, of course, when I shot a lot of documentary stuff, I was in different situations and environments which you would never find yourself in, if not for film. Then when you're writing a feature film, after this experience you go where you know what a person can and cannot do. Is the hero believable or not? If he looks like this, can he live there then? You come up with a more expanded picture of the world thanks to documentary. Of course, in feature film people also go and research, as we did, for example, in *Arrhythmia* (*Aritmiia*, 2017). We talked endlessly with doctors, I sat with them for a long time. And they only didn't let us go on ambulance calls because it's forbidden by law. The time we spent with the doctors was unforgettable. Documentary principles then help you guide the actor in his performance. You feel if it's false, or not false.

How is television work different from working in film?

It's not. There are simply other laws of dramaturgy there. Pictorially, there are different requirements for a series. In film I think more about inner things, about depth, about the plasticity of the image, about the camera, much more than in a TV series because there's time for this. You have to simplify in a series, you think less about the image. Otherwise you won't get anything done. In Russia you always have to straddle two worlds. On the one hand, the volume [of production] per day is very large; it's not profitable for producers to make overly small series. You must, on the one hand, deal with this volume and, on the other, tell the story in a visually interesting way. So in this sense, things are more difficult in a series. There's no way to stop, cancel the shoot, reshoot a scene if it didn't work out. In feature film this is possible. When we were filming *Core of the World* (*Serdtse mira*, 2018), we waited three days for a sunny day because you can't bathe a dog in freezing weather. And sex on the lakeshore won't happen if the mud is knee-deep. So we could afford to wait. Some of the scenes with the dogs didn't work out, and we reshot them. There's probably more responsibility in feature film compared to TV series.

Could you talk about your work on *An Ordinary Woman* (*Obychnaia zhenshchina*, 2018 and 2020–2021)?

It was very important for me not to ruin anything because I'm absolutely in love with season one, made by Boris Khlebnikov—his heroes, his language. That's probably what helped me a lot with the work. I didn't want to break anything, redo it, as happens, you know, when something doesn't work for you and you want to do something in your own way. What also played a big role here was that Boria and I are close friends, we did several projects together, we have similar tastes and approaches to acting—the same understanding of "good" and "bad." But season two turned out differently anyway. It has more action, stunt scenes, more open emotion, a more exciting storyline, and it has higher stakes for the characters.

What is the role of women in the contemporary Russian television industry?

Well, I have to say that, during the past five years, so many wonderful women have come into both the television and film industries, including as camera operators, thanks to technological improvements. They have declared themselves in a powerful and striking way. We know their names—directors such as Nigina Saifullaeva, Oksana Bychkova, Anna Melikian, Valeriia Gai Germanika, Natal'ia Merkulova, Anna Parmas. A lot of the young ones made their debuts at Kinotavr. Many actresses have begun to make films—Alisa Khazanova, for example, who was immediately successful at festivals and Mariia Shalaeva, whose film is coming out soon. Among the producers is the wonderful Natasha Drozd, who works successfully in co-productions with foreign partners. There's the amazing Katia Filippova. She produced a film that was in Venice—Natasha Merkulova and Aleksei Chupov's *The Man Who Surprised Everyone* (*Chelovek, kotoryi udivil vsekh, 2018*). There's the wonderful producer Iuliia Mishkinene, also Natasha Mokritskaia. The directors of photography Kseniia Sereda, Iuliia Galochkina, Siuzanna Musaeva, Sasha Kulak.

In general, although men, of course, still occupy the main leadership positions in the television industry, as general producers and so on, women are increasingly gaining momentum and strength. We have a platform called Start with the creative producer Irina Sosnovaia. She provides so much energy, launches many projects, and simply brings a huge number of projects to the channel. And she has, of course, succeeded as a producer. There are many women directors and producers. There are no obstacles to this, no gender inequality—at least I don't feel it myself.

How have streaming platforms changed the production and distribution of TV series?

There's a huge jump in development. The main thing that the platforms have done is to allow series to become auteurist, with one's own signature, and allowed series to be experimental. Fortunately, this does not depend on format, ratings, advertising, or prime time. That is, it's a much more independent show. And in this sense, since everyone has thrown a huge amount of money there, right now, to be honest, the demand is much larger than what the industry can satisfy. We don't have enough people who could make series. In competing with each other for the position of majors, the platforms are ready to attract the main talents in the profession. And in this sense the path is much more open for the young than in broadcast TV. There you don't have to go through director's casting; did the head of the channel approve or not approve you. It's enough to bring a strong story that would be interesting and engaging. Right now everyone is just interested in new forms and new themes, statements like *Chicks* (*Chiki*, 2020) and *The Storm* (*Shtorm*, 2019). At the moment, I'm doing a series with Start whose heroine will be a teenage girl.

Then there are sales and co-productions. It has become very profitable to produce not for one channel but to enter a co-production between channels in order then to get into the international market as well. *An Ordinary Woman* is being bought for Finland or Sweden . . . I don't remember exactly. They liked the style and language of the series. We have more limitations even in auteur cinema than on the platforms. They remain the only free entities that are not obliged to report to the state. For example, what relates to, say, obscenities, certain kinds of speech, edgy scenes. You are completely free and there's no such thing as they're being able to refuse you a release permit, and your film ends up in the trashcan, as happened with my first film *The Hope Factory* (*Kombinat Nadezhda*, 2014). It happened due to the vocabulary because the law forbidding obscenities in film came out that year and they didn't give us a release permit. Right now in auteur film you self-censor anyway, you cut certain things because it may not pass the Minkul't [Ministry of Culture] commission. But on streaming platforms—it's "go right ahead." This is not my first project and they tell me, "Don't limit yourself. Don't worry about anything." During the summer I shot a series about a young standup comedian, also a teenager; they fascinate me lately. It has very edgy topics, jokes about religion, obscenity, and everything of that sort. The life of these young kids without any understatement or an attempt to retouch it. And, in general, this doesn't scare anyone, it's cool. I hope this will continue for as long as possible. Of course, one has the feeling that the state will introduce bans here too.

What other Russian series besides *An Ordinary Woman* are being bought abroad?

As far as I know, they've bought the series *To the Lake* (*Epidemiia*, 2019–2020). I think *Gold Diggers* (*Soderzhanki*, 2019–2020), also from Start, was sold to some international platform. The series *Dead Mountain: The Dyatlov Pass Incident* (*Pereval Diatlova*, 2020) will get international distribution. *The Storm* definitely. I don't know how things stand with *Chicks*. In short, there is international interest in Russian series.

In your opinion, what are the most interesting and important genres of TV series?

Maybe it's not even about genres, but in the way the story is told. Series go beyond the borders of traditional genre formats. They tell a genre story, but in more varied ways, with differing languages. Take, for instance, *An Ordinary Woman*, which is generally a comedy with black, scary humor, but at the same time it's a criminal tale, which then turns into a drama. It's that sort of genre mix. But at the same time we understand that we're watching genre film and that this series has some kind of language of its own that doesn't repeat that of any other series. It's simply that a sitcom may have different languages: there may be textual humor, there may be situational humor and so on. Also, a lot of cool authors have appeared there who write paradoxically, and it's funny. There are authors now who can do the unexpected, and it's funny. Thanks to the popularity of standup in Russia, these authors are on TV and their humor is not your typical rah-rah stuff. It's cool, young, and alive. Everyone watches these new comedies with pleasure. Because of the pandemic the "screenlife" genre is popular now. We have a lot of series in this genre.

Which comedy series do you consider successful?

For example, *The Anna Nikolaevna Project* (*Proekt Anna Nikolaevna*, 2020), *House Arrest* (*Domashny arrest*, 2018), *Cursed Days* (*Okaiannye dni*, 2020), *Comfort Zone* (*Zona komforta*, 2020). Be sure to see them.

Thank you so much for the interview.

Producer, Showrunner, and Scriptwriter

Maksim Stishov

Could you please talk about your career path in the film and television industries?

I'm a "career" scriptwriter. I graduated from Gerasimov Institute of Cinematography's film school in 1990 and managed to make my first film just as the Soviet era was coming to an end. I never wanted to work in television, but in the 1990s the existence of the film industry practically came to an end and by some miracle I managed to hold on to the profession, and even managed to work on two very successful and long-lasting series, *Trifles of Life* (*Melochi zhizni*, 1992–1994) and *The Imposters* (*Samozvantsy*, 1998). Both shows had extremely high ratings, which is hard to imagine nowadays, with the increased competition and lots of available content. At the beginning of the 2000s the scope of the television industry started to grow and I decided to try out the American format of showrunner: dual scriptwriter and producer, essentially becoming the first showrunner in Russia. To this day, actually, the situation has barely changed; unfortunately, the showrunner profession in the Russian industry still hasn't caught on. My partners and I created a production company for television shows and completed a fair number of projects over the course of sixteen years—*Balzac Age, or All Men Are Bast . . .* (*Bal'zakovsky vozrast, ili Vse muzhiki svo . . .*, 2004) and The *Lawyer* (*Advokat*, 2004), among others.

How is production organized at Motor Film Studio and what is your relationship to broadcast channels?

The production process in our company is essentially the following: we generate an idea and try to sell it to a channel. Sometimes—although rarely—we produce a product with our own funds or loans. That being said, we are our own company, with our own editing rooms, equipment, casting, and so forth. We only rent the studios. I'm not sure whether this is the best business model nowadays, but as the saying goes, "old habits die hard."

There exist two main models of production companies' work with channels. There is work commissioned by the channel in which the channel has full or partial rights over the final product and the profit margin constitutes the bulk of the producer's honorarium. Or—this typically applies to big companies—screening rights are sold to different channels with full control over the rights and ownership of all the content produced. In this case, the profit margin may be absent or minimal and the producer's bonus comes in the form of royalties from ownership of rights to the content. We do not consider here corruption schemes in which there exists a big profit margin because of the inflated budget, as well as royalties, and everything else under the sun.

Tell us about the TV series production process, starting with an idea and all the steps of its realization. For example, let's talk about *Balzac Age*.

For *Balzac Age* it was like this: I wrote the pilot episode, then kept revising it for a long time with Sergei Shumakov, at the time the producer general of the NTV channel. Then we spent a lot of time on casting and finally shot the pilot episode with the director Dmitry Fiks. The channel liked the pilot and commissioned the first season. Then we shot another two seasons. I refused to write the fourth season, even though the channel wanted us to continue. I had a feeling that we had already done our best work and going forward we would start repeating ourselves, as it happens with the majority of successful shows. To this day my colleagues still rebuke me for this decision, but I don't regret it.

Could you talk about how political changes affected your work?

Alas, the period of political freedom, the 1990s, is now in the distant past. A great deal of things are currently prohibited. Very far from Soviet-style censorship, of course, but very similar processes. This concerns the present day, its politics, and so forth. But there exist other taboos. For example, the 1990s. They say that the viewer doesn't want to watch anything about this time. It is, in fact, possible that these fears are justified. Thankfully, it's still relatively acceptable to make historical series about the 1930s or the 1970s; I really hope that this won't change. Although everything here is in the hands of the authorities. I believe that the regular viewer will watch shows about the October Revolution, and about Joseph Stalin as the great leader, and about benign Leonid Brezhnev, and so forth, with equal enthusiasm.

What do you consider your most successful TV series?

My most successful show is, of course, *Balzac Age*. It's great serendipity when three usually incompatible components come together in one project: the thrill of creativity, success with viewers, and high revenue. I think we've been unbelievably lucky.

How is the Russian TV series different from Soviet and Western ones?

Russian shows are more of a series, while the Soviet shows were more like multi-episode films. Russian series, despite the implicit censorship of the recent years, can afford to say and show much more, especially in historical genres. The genre memory of the Soviet tradition, it goes without saying, is still there. The Soviet mold didn't disappear. If you want success with an audience over forty, make a show in the Soviet format!

The main difference between Russian and Western or Israeli shows is in the ways the programs are arranged in broadcasting and viewer expectations. Vertical blocking, adopted in most developed countries, didn't catch on in Russia. As before, the Soviet style of television programming or running a show every day during the week dominates TV schedules, which turns practically every show—even those that we would consider quality television—into a soap opera. Unfortunately, there is not enough demand for quality content; on the contrary, we're currently seeing opposite trends: the more primitive, the more "successful." Russian producers have to work for the most lowbrow audience, hence the consequences. We follow the "Latin American" approach, not the American-European one, and surely not the Israeli approach, with their ability to create talented content for little money. Recently a few streaming platforms diversified the Russian television market. Some call it a revolution, but I take it with cautious optimism, because the only way to compete with free-of-charge state TV and—even more importantly—with monsters like Netflix, is to provide one hundred percent censorship-free content. When I say "censorship-free," it does not translate to cheap simulacra of wide use of obscene language and sex scenes. Rather, I'm talking about dealing with reality, with the so- called "truth of life," which was deliberately and successfully pushed out of broadcast television. Free media is hard to imagine in the atmosphere of fear that has paralyzed Russian society nowadays . . . But let's hope for the best. I really count on those young and brave, the so-called "unflogged generation" . . .

You worked as both a filmmaker and TV series producer. What's the difference?

A film—if it's a real film, of course—demonstrates quality through production. The rate of production is lower, the budget is bigger, and so forth. Or it could be low budget, as with TV, but the creativity of its authors makes up for this lack of money. This creative zeal is rarely found in TV shows. Until recently, it was possible to film something worthy, explore new themes and aesthetic horizons. Our *White Moor*, for example, was such a creative project. But now this happens increasingly rarely.

CONTRIBUTORS

Alyssa DeBlasio is associate professor in the Department of Russian at Dickinson College, where she also contributes to the Film Studies Program and Philosophy Department. She is the recipient of numerous fellowships and grants for her research on the intersections of Russian film, philosophy, and literature, including awards from the American Council of Learned Societies, the National Endowment for the Humanities, Fulbright-Hays, and the American Philosophical Society. She is the author of two monographs: *The End of Russian Philosophy* (Palgrave, 2014) and *The Filmmaker's Philosopher: Merab Mamardashvili and Russian Cinema* (Edinburgh University Press, 2019), the latter of which appeared in Russian translation in 2020. Together with Mikhail Epstein (Emory University), DeBlasio is co-editor of the online resource *Filosofia: An Encyclopedia of Russian Thought*. She is a member of the Russian Guild of Film Critics and Scholars and is the editor of Brill's book series in Contemporary Russian Philosophy.

Alexander Dulerain is a television producer, film and TV series creator. He holds a science degree from the Moscow Institute of Electronic Technology. In 1995, he graduated from Boris Yukhananov's Studio of Individual Directing with a major in stage and screen directing. In 1996, he completed an internship at the New York Film Academy in the workshop of Adam Stoner. Dulerain participated in the Parallel Cinema movement in the late Soviet and post-Soviet era. He is one of co-creators of the Cine Phantom Club. In 1998, he became a copywriter at the STS channel. In 1999, he was appointed executive producer and STS Channel marketing director. In 2002, he moved to the TNT channel, becoming the deputy general producer and then the channel's general producer (2013–2017). Since 2018 he has been a major showrunner on Russian television, creative producer at TNT channel and chief content officer of Storyworld Entertainment. Dulerain produced the most successful comedy series in new Russian television history, including *Our Russia* (*Nasha Rasha*), *Interns* (*Interny*), *Swell Guys* (*Real'nye patsany*) and *House Arrest* (*Domashny arest*), among others. He also produced *Ol'ga* and *The Affairs* (*Izmeny*).

During his time at TNT, the channel has won forty prizes (including fifteen first prizes) from Promax BDA Promotion, Marketing, and Design Awards in London, Berlin, and Moscow.

Sergey Fiks joined the motion picture industry in 1991, when he got his first job as a reporter, and later senior editor, for the first Russian independent film magazine, a Russian edition of the Franco-American film magazine *Premiere*. In 1993 he became press-secretary for Gemini Film (Russian distributor for Warner Bros. and Columbia-TriStar), as well as the producer of several independent US and European films. In 1996 he became programming director for NTV Plus, the first Russian pay television channel, and later for the NTV channel. Between 2003 and 2016 he worked as adviser to the CEO of the Russia channel and producer at The All-Russia State Television and Radio Broadcasting Company (VGTRK). He has produced more than twenty TV series and films for different TV channels, as well as several feature films. At present, he is an independent producer. He is a member of TEFI (Russian Academy of Television), which awards the Emmies for Russian TV.

Denis Gorelov is currently working with the editors of the forthcoming encyclopedia *Russian Cinema from the Silents to the Present Day* (*Seans*). He is the author of the award winning volume *Rodina slonikov* (Fluid FreeFly, 2018). He was the curator of *Komsomol'skaia pravda*'s series on great Soviet films, for which he also contributed twenty-four books. In addition to co-writing scripts for the television series *The Other Day: Our Era—1961–1991*, he wrote the screenplay for *The Great Vacations of the 1930s*, a chronicle film made for Gosfil'mofond. His articles have appeared in *Moskovsky komsomolets, Segodnia, Russky telegraf, Izvestiia, Russkaia zhizn'*, and other newspapers and journals.

Lilya Kaganovsky is the Richard and Margaret Romano professor of Slavic, Comparative Literature, and Media & Cinema Studies at the University of Illinois, Urbana-Champaign. Her publications include *The Voice of Technology: Soviet Cinema's Transition to Sound, 1928-1935* (Indiana University Press, 2018) and *How the Soviet Man was Unmade* (University of Pittsburgh Press,

2008); the co-edited volumes *Arctic Cinemas and the Documentary Ethos* (Indiana University Press, 2019); *Sound, Speech, Music in Soviet and Post-Soviet Cinema* (Indiana University Press, 2014), and *Mad Men, Mad World: Sex, Politics, Style and the 1960s* (Duke University Press, 2013); as well as numerous articles on Soviet and post-Soviet cinema. She is a member of the editorial board of the journal *Studies in Russian and Soviet Cinema* and the associate editor for Film and Media at *The Russian Review*.

Nataliia Meshchaninova is an award-winning TV and film director and scriptwriter. In 2007 she graduated from the school of documentary cinema Real Time 2, a workshop led by Marina Razbezhkina and Nikolai Izvolov. She co-wrote scripts for Aleksei Fedorchenko's *Anna's War* (*Voina Anny*, 2018), Boris Khlebnikov's *Arrhythmia* (*Aritmiia*, 2017), and the TV series *The Storm* (*Shtorm*, 2019), among others. Her 2018 film *Core of the World* (*Serdtse mira*) won the Grand Prix at the Kinotavr Film Festival in Sochi. In 2020 she directed season two of the TV series *An Ordinary Woman* (*Obyknovennaia zhenshchina*).

Tatiana Mikhailova is lecturer in Russian at Columbia University. Her publications discuss such diverse subjects such as Russian film, political caricature, and the representation of women in post-Soviet culture. She has written on the films of Alexei Fedorchenko and Larisa Shepit'ko, among others. Her articles have appeared in collections such as *Women in Soviet Film: The Thaw and Post-Thaw Periods* (Routledge, 2018); *Transgressive Women in Modern Russian and East European Cultures: From the Bad to the Blasphemous* (Routledge, 2017); *The Contemporary Russian Cinema Reader* (Academic Studies Press, 2019); *Embracing Arms: Cultural Representation of Slavic and Balkan Women in War* (Central European University Press, 2012); *Celebrity and Glamour in Contemporary Russia: Shocking Chic* (Routledge, 2010), as well as in the journals *Studies in Soviet and Russian Cinema; Zeitschrift für Slavische Philologie; Znamia; Neprikosnovennyi zapas*; and *KinoKultura*.

Stephen M. Norris is Walter E. Havighurst professor of Russian History and the director of the Havighurst Center for Russian and Post-Soviet Studies at Miami University (OH). He is the author of two books on Russian cultural history, including *Blockbuster History in the New Russia: Movies, Memory, Patriotism* (Indiana University Press, 2012), and the editor or co-editor of six books, including *Museums of Communism: New Memory Sites in Central and Eastern Europe* (Indiana University Press, 2020) and *The Akunin Project: The Mysteries and Histories of Russia's Bestselling Author* (with Elena Baraban, University of Toronto Press, 2021). He co-edits the Bloomsbury Press series "Russian Shorts," which publishes short insightful books on historical and cultural subjects. His current research project, *Communism's Cartoonist*, is a biography of the Soviet political caricaturist Boris Efimov.

Alexander Prokhorov is professor of Russian and Film Studies at William & Mary. He is co-editor of *Cinemasaurus: Russian Film in Contemporary Context* (with Nancy Condee and Elena Prokhorova, Academic Studies Press, 2020), co-author (with Elena Prokhorova) of *Film and Television Genres of the Late Soviet Era* (Bloomsbury, 2017), and the editor of *Springtime for Soviet Cinema: Re/ viewing the 1960s* (Carnegie Museum of Art, Pittsburgh Film Symposium, 2001). His articles and reviews have been published in *Journal of Film and Video, KinoKultura, Russian Review, Slavic Review, Slavic and East European Journal, Studies in Russian and Soviet Cinema, Art of Cinema* (*Iskusstvo kino*), and *Wiener Slawistischer Almanach*.

Elena Prokhorova is professor of Russian Studies at William & Mary, where she also teaches in the Film & Media Studies program. Her research focuses on identity discourses in late Soviet and post-Soviet television and cinema. She is co-editor of *Cinemasaurus: Russian Film in Contemporary Context* (with Nancy Condee and Alexander Prokhorov, Academic Studies Press, 2020) and co-author (with Alexander Prokhorov) of the monograph *Film and Television Genres of the Late Soviet Era* (Bloomsbury, 2017). Her publications have also appeared in *Slavic Review, Slavic and East European Journal, KinoKultura, Russian Journal of Communication*, and in edited volumes.

Saara Ratilainen, is senior lecturer in Russian Language and Culture at Tampere University, Finland. Her field of expertise covers Russian media and cultural studies, especially contemporary popular culture, digital networks, fan studies, and media and feminism. She has worked on Russian and post-Soviet gender, sexuality, and feminism. She is currently finalizing a research project that focuses on creative productions by online grassroots communities. She coedited the special issues "Culture in Putin's Russia: Institutions, Industries, Policies" (*Cultural Studies*, 2018) and "Women and Tech in the Post-Socialist Context: Intelligence, Creativity, Transgression" (*Studies in Russian, Eurasian, and Central European New Media*, 2018). Her most recent publication is "Norway Reimagined: Popular Geopolitics and the Russophone Fans of Skam" (*Nordicom Review*, 2020).

Rimgaila Salys is professor of Russian Studies emerita at the University of Colorado-Boulder and a specialist in twentieth-century Russian film, literature, and culture. She is the author of *Leonid Pasternak: The Russian Years (1875–1921). A Critical Study and Catalogue*, 2 vols. (Oxford University Press, 1999), *Laughing Matters: The Musical Comedy Films of Grigorii Aleksandrov* (Intellect, 2009 and NLO, 2012), editor of *Yury Olesha. Envy. A Critical Companion* (Northwestern University Press, 1999), *Tightrope Walking: The Memoirs of Josephine Pasternak* (Slavica, 2005), *The Russian Cinema Reader*, 2 vols. (Academic Studies Press, 2013), and *The Contemporary Russian Cinema Reader* (Academic Studies Press, 2019). Recent articles include "Liudmila Gurchenko: Stardom in the Late Soviet Era" and "Grigorii Aleksandrov's *Spring*: The Last Musical Hurrah." "Antiheroes from an Imagined West: *The Very Same Munchhausen* and *The House That Swift Built*" is forthcoming.

Maksim Stishov, the author of the hit series *Balzac Age, or All Men are Bast . . .* (*Bal'zakovsky vozrast, ili Vse muzhiki svo . . .*, 2004–2007), is a prolific screenwriter, producer, short story writer, and one of the first showrunners on Russian television. In 2000 he wrote the script for Egor Konchalovsky's film *The Recluse* (2000). For his work on the TV series *The Lawyer* (2004–2017) Stishov received the medal "For Distinguished Service in the Field of Human Rights" and the F. N. Plevako Gold Medal—the highest distinction awarded by the Russian Federal Chamber of Lawyers.

Vlad Strukov is a London-based multidisciplinary researcher, curator, and cultural practitioner, specializing in art, media, and technology crossovers. He is an associate professor at the University of Leeds (the United Kingdom) and a researcher at Garage Museum of Contemporary Art (Russia), working on global visual cultures. He is currently carrying out a major research project, funded by the Swedish Research Council, on contemporary queer visual culture. He is the author of many research publications, including *Contemporary Russian Cinema: Symbols of a New Era* (Edinburgh University Press, 2016). He makes regular appearances in international media such as Al Jazeera, American Public Radio, the BBC, RBK, and others.

INDEX

www.ingramcontent.com/pod-product-compliance
Lightning Source LLC
LaVergne TN
LVHW081250100826
845148LV00009B/1187
9781644696446